Towards Understanding the Qur'ān

Vol. II

SŪRAHS 4–6

English version of
Tafhīm al-Qur'ān

SAYYID ABUL A'LĀ MAWDŪDĪ

Translated and edited by
Zafar Ishaq Ansari

The Islamic Foundation

Reprinted 1992/1412 A.H. and 1996/1417 A.H.

ISBN 0 86037 188 3 (PB)
ISBN 0 86037 187 5 (HB)

Translated and edited by Zafar Ishaq Ansari

Cover illustration: Rashid Rahman

Published by
The Islamic Foundation,
Markfield Dawah Centre,
Ratby Lane, Markfield,
Leicester LE67 9RN,
United Kingdom

Quran House,
P.O. Box 30611, Nairobi, Kenya

P.M.B. 3193, Kano, Nigeria

British Library Cataloguing in Publication Data

Mawdūdī, Sayyid Abul A'lā
Towards Understanding the Qur'ān
Vol.2, Surahs 4–6
1. Islam. Koran – Critical studies
I. Title II. Anṣārī, Ẓafar Isḥāq
III. Islamic Foundation IV. Tafhīm al-Qur'ān. (English)

297'.1226

ISBN 0-86037-187-5
ISBN 0-86037-188-3 Pbk

Printed and bound by The Cromwell Press Limited, Melksham, Wiltshire

بسم الله الرحمن الرحيم

Contents

TRANSLITERATION TABLE

Consonants. Arabic

initial: unexpressed
medial and final: ء ʾ

		د	d	ض	ḍ	ك	k
ب	b	ذ	dh	ط	ṭ	ل	l
ت	t	ر	r	ظ	ẓ	م	m
ث	th	ز	z	ع	ʿ	ن	n
ج	j	س	s	غ	gh	ه	h
ح	ḥ	ش	sh	ف	f	و	w
خ	kh	ص	ṣ	ق	q	ي	y

Urdu and Persian the same except the following:

پ	p	ڈ	d̲	ژ	z̲
ٹ	t̲				
چ	ch	ڑ	r̲	گ	g

Vowels, diphthongs, etc.

short: ـَـ a; ـِـ i; ـُـ u.

long: ـَا ā ـُو ū ـِي ī ـِيّ īy

diphthongs: ـَوْ aw

ـَيْ ay

Editor's Preface

This is the second volume of *Towards Understanding the Qur'ān* and comprises *Sūrahs* 4–6. It is heart-warming to note that two volumes of the work are seeing the light of day within a span of twelve months. All praise and thanks are for God Who has made this possible.

In this volume we have done our best to retain the features of the previous volume. We have attempted, as in the previous volume, to provide adequate documentation. The documentation of *Ḥadīth* follows, again, the system of A.J. Wensinck in his *Concordance*. The references to *Tafsīr* works in the notes indicate the numbers of the *sūrahs* and verses in question rather than the numbers of the volumes and pages of the *Tafsīr* works cited. All quotations from the Bible have been taken from the *Authorized Version* and the *Revised Standard Edition*. Likewise, Glossary of Terms, Biographical Notes, and Bibliography have been added. There are again two indices – the Subject Index and the General Index.

In the preparation of this volume I have benefited greatly from the editorial suggestions of Mr. M. Holland, Mr. P. Moorman and Miss S. Thackray. Dr. A.R. Kidwai of the Islamic Foundation also looked at the final draft of the work and favoured me with his critical comments. In preparing the Biographical Notes and Glossary of Terms I have received much assistance from Dr. Ahmad Khan and Shagufta Naheed of the Islamic Research Institute, and from my daughter, Sarah. Mr. E.R. Fox assisted me in the technical editing of this and the previous volume.

To these, and to many others who assisted and encouraged me, I record my profound sense of gratitude. May Allah bless them all.

Islamabad,
21 Ṣafar, 1409 A.H.
4 October, 1988

Zafar Ishaq Ansari

N.B. ▶ *refers to the continuation of the paragraph adopted by Mawdūdī in the Urdu translation.*

Sūrah 4

Al-Nisā'

(Madinan Period)

Period of Revelation

This *sūrah* comprises a number of discourses revealed between the later part of 3 A.H. through to the end of 4 A.H., and possibly even the early part of 5 A.H. It is hard to determine precisely which verses belong to which discourse, just as it is difficult to fix the exact period of the revelation of those verses. Several of these verses, however, contain allusions to certain injunctions and events the dates of which can be ascertained with the help of traditions.

On this basis we can broadly divide the *sūrah* into a number of discourses. We know, for example, that the injunctions relating to inheritance and to the protection of the rights of orphans were revealed after the Battle of Uḥud, in which seventy Muslims were martyred. The result of this was that the small town of Madina was faced with the problem of distributing inheritance and safeguarding the rights and interests of the orphans left behind by the martyrs. We can thus infer that verses 1–28 were revealed during this period.

Traditions mention *ṣalāt al-khawf* (Prayer in the state of insecurity) in connection with the Battle of Dhāt al-Riqā' which took place in 4 A.H. So the section which contains directives regarding this Prayer (verses 101 ff.) must have been revealed around this time. Likewise, we know that the expulsion of Banū al-Naḍīr from Madina took place in Rabī' al-Awwal 4 A.H. It is therefore probable that the section which contains the final warning to the Jews: 'O you who have been granted the Book! Do believe in what We have (now) revealed, which confirms the revelation which you already possess. Do this before We alter countenances, turning them backwards . . . ' (*Sūrah al-Nisā'* 4: 47), was revealed shortly before their expulsion. In the same way, the permission to do *tayammum* (symbolic ablution attained through wiping the face and hands with clean earth) in place of ablution was granted on the occasion of the Battle of Banū al-Muṣṭaliq, in 5 A.H. The section which deals with *tayammum* may, therefore, be taken as belonging to this period (see verses 43 ff).

Background and Subject Matter

Let us now survey briefly the situation in order to appreciate more fully the contents of this *sūrah*.

The tasks before the Prophet (peace be on him) at this time may be classified into three broad categories. First, to develop the newly-organized Islamic society which had come into being in and around Madina as a result of the influx of believers, a society which was attempting to give effect to new principles in the moral, social, economic and political spheres of life, and to do away with the old ways and practices of the days of Ignorance (*Jāhilīyah*). Second, to counter the fierce opposition of the polytheists, Jewish tribes and the hypocrites. Third, to spread the message of Islam in the face of hostility from these opposing forces and to win over the minds and hearts of the people. The various discourses revealed by God at this time deal with these different problems.

The Islamic society at this juncture, thus, required additional directives to those which it had received earlier, and which are embodied in *Sūrah al-Baqarah*. In the discourses of this *sūrah*, the Muslims are told in much greater detail how to mould their collective life in accordance with the dictates of Islam. They are told how to organize their family life. Regulations are laid down with respect to marriage, prohibiting union with certain categories of relatives. The pattern of relationships between men and women is enunciated. The rights of orphans are clearly defined. Laws for the distribution of inheritance are promulgated. Directives are issued to ensure that economic activities continue to be based on sound moral principles. Muslims are taught what measures to adopt to solve their family disputes. The foundations of a penal code are laid. The drinking of intoxicants is prohibited. Fresh directives are given to ensure purity of the heart as well as righteousness of conduct. Muslims are clearly told what man's attitude should be towards God and towards His creatures. Instructions are given to establish discipline within the

Islamic body-politic. The moral and religious attitude of the People of the Book is criticized, thus warning the Muslims against following in the footsteps of the religious communities which preceded them. Likewise, the conduct of the hypocrites is criticized, thereby highlighting the requirements of true faith and clearly distinguishing the characteristics of true faith from those of hypocrisy.

The struggle waged by the forces opposed to the Islamic reform movement assumed even more menacing proportions after the Battle of Uḥud. The reverse suffered by the Muslims in that battle had infused a new spirit into the pagan Arab tribes, the neighbouring Jews and also the hypocrites (who were an integral part of the Islamic body-politic). The result was that the Muslims found themselves confronted by dangers from all sides. In such a circumstance God urged the Muslims to meet these dangers bravely. He revealed inspiring passages and gave them instructions how to conduct themselves when faced with armed conflict. In Madina the hypocrites and those of weak faith were disseminating all kinds of rumours so as to demoralize the Muslims. To counteract this, the Muslims were asked to pass on all such rumours to responsible people, who were to prevent their further dissemination unless and until they could be confirmed after proper investigations.

Let us take another case occasioned by these circumstances. The Muslims often had to go on military expeditions, sometimes with and sometimes without the Prophet (peace be on him) and they often travelled by routes where water was unavailable. They were now told that it was permissible for them to resort to *tayammum* (symbolic ablution attained through wiping the face and hands with clean earth) in place of both major and minor washing.* Likewise, permission was granted to shorten Prayers while travelling, and instructions were given on how to perform Prayers when danger was imminent. At that time, some Muslims lived outside the Islamic realm, and were scattered throughout Arabia living in the midst of pagan tribes. At times they were drawn into the orbit of war and thus suffered harm. This had become a matter of great anxiety for the Muslims, and the Islamic community was instructed in how to deal with it. At the same time, Muslims living in the midst of non-Muslim tribes were urged to migrate to Madina, the *Dār al-Islām* (the Domain of Islam).

*Major washing (*ghusl al-janābah*) is necessitated by either sexual intercourse or seminal ejaculation. Minor washing (*wuḍū'*) is a necessary condition for the performance of Prayer and should be revived if it has expired – Ed.

The attitude of one Jewish tribe in particular, Banū al-Naḍīr, had become particularly hostile. Its people blatantly violated the agreements they had concluded with the Muslims, and identified openly with the enemies of Islam by giving them support. They engaged in conspiracies and machinations against the Prophet (peace be on him) and his followers even within the city of Madina. In this *sūrah* their conduct is severely criticized and they are given a final warning in categorical terms. After this warning they were expelled from Madina.

The hypocrites comprised several groups, each of which behaved in a different manner so that it was difficult for the Muslims to decide how to deal with them. In this *sūrah*, the hypocrites are classified into separate categories, and the Muslims are told what treatment should be accorded to each group. They are also told what attitude they should adopt towards the neutral tribes which had entered into agreements with them.

Most important of all, the Muslims are made to realize the necessity of developing blameless moral character. For if they were to triumph in their struggle then this triumph would come about primarily through moral excellence. The Muslims are urged, therefore, to cultivate the highest moral qualities and are reproached severely for any past lapses.

Another aspect of religious duty for the Muslims – preaching their faith and inviting people to share it with them – is also stressed. In addition to elaborating a blueprint for the moral and social reform envisaged by Islam in contradistinction to non-heavenly doctrines (*Jāhilīyah*), the *sūrah* criticizes the erroneous religious concepts and the moral perversion and corruption of the Jews, Christians and polytheists, and invites each of them to embrace Islam.

In the name of Allah, the Merciful, the Compassionate.

(1) O men! Fear your Lord Who created you from a single being and out of it created its mate; and out of the two spread many men and women.[1] Fear Allah in Whose name you plead for rights, and heed the ties of kinship. Surely, Allah is ever watchful over you.

بِسْمِ ٱللَّهِ ٱلرَّحْمَٰنِ ٱلرَّحِيمِ

يَٰٓأَيُّهَا ٱلنَّاسُ ٱتَّقُوا۟ رَبَّكُمُ ٱلَّذِى خَلَقَكُم مِّن
نَّفْسٍ وَٰحِدَةٍ وَخَلَقَ مِنْهَا زَوْجَهَا وَبَثَّ مِنْهُمَا
رِجَالًا كَثِيرًا وَنِسَآءً ۚ وَٱتَّقُوا۟ ٱللَّهَ ٱلَّذِى تَسَآءَلُونَ
بِهِۦ وَٱلْأَرْحَامَ ۚ إِنَّ ٱللَّهَ كَانَ عَلَيْكُمْ رَقِيبًا ﴿١﴾

---

1. What are the mutual rights of human beings, what are the principles on which a sound and stable family life can be established, are questions that are discussed a little further on in this *sūrah*. As an appropriate introduction to the subject, the *sūrah* opens by exhorting the believers to fear God and to avoid courting His displeasure, and by urging them to recognize that all human beings have sprung from the same root and that all of them are, therefore, of one another's flesh and blood.

The expression 'Who created you from a single being (*nafs*)' indicates that the creation of the human species began with the creation of one individual. At another place, the Qur'ān specifies that the one person from whom the human race spread in the world was Adam. (For Adam being the progenitor of mankind see *Towards Understanding the Qur'ān, Sūrah* 2, verses 31 f. and *Sūrah al-A'rāf* 7: 11, etc. – Ed.)

The details how out of that 'being' its mate was created are not known to us. The explanation which is generally given by the commentators of the Qur'ān and which is also found in the Bible is that Eve was created out of a rib of Adam. (The Talmud is even more detailed in that it states that Eve was created out of Adam's thirteenth rib on the left side.) The Qur'ān, however, is silent on the matter and the tradition which is adduced in support of this statement does not mean what it is often thought to be. It is thus better that we leave the matter in the same state of ambiguity in which it was left by God, rather than waste our time trying to determine, in detail, the actual process of the creation of man's mate.*

---

*The author alludes to, but does not quote, the text of the following tradition:

إن المرأة خُلقت من ضلع، وإن أعوج شيء في الضلع أعلاه، فإن ذهبت تقيمه كسرته، وإن استمتعت بها استمتعت
بها وفيها عوج

Muslim, 'Riḍā'ah', 61 and 62; Tirmidhī, 'Ṭalāq', 12; Aḥmad b. Ḥanbal, *Musnad*, vol. 2, pp. 428, 449, 497, 530 and vol. 6, p. 279 – Ed.

(2) Give orphans their property,[2] and do not exchange the bad for the good,[3] and do not eat up their property by mixing it with your own. This surely is a mighty sin.

(3) If you fear that you might not treat the orphans justly, then marry the women that seem good to you: two, or three, or four.[4] ►

وَءَاتُوا۟ ٱلْيَتَٰمَىٰٓ أَمْوَٰلَهُمْ ۖ وَلَا تَتَبَدَّلُوا۟ ٱلْخَبِيثَ
بِٱلطَّيِّبِ ۖ وَلَا تَأْكُلُوٓا۟ أَمْوَٰلَهُمْ إِلَىٰٓ أَمْوَٰلِكُمْ ۚ إِنَّهُۥ
كَانَ حُوبًا كَبِيرًا ﴿٢﴾ وَإِنْ خِفْتُمْ أَلَّا
تُقْسِطُوا۟ فِى ٱلْيَتَٰمَىٰ فَٱنكِحُوا۟ مَا طَابَ لَكُم
مِّنَ ٱلنِّسَآءِ مَثْنَىٰ وَثُلَٰثَ وَرُبَٰعَ ۖ

2. God directs the guardians of the orphans to spend out of the latter's property while they are still minors, and to restore it to them when they attain majority.

3. The order not to exchange the bad for the good has several meanings. On the one hand, it means that one should not replace honest by dishonest living. At the same time, it also means that one should not exchange one's own property which is of little value for the more valuable property of the orphans.

4. Commentators have explained this in the following ways:

(i) There is the view of 'Ā'ishah who says that men tended to marry orphan girls who were under their guardianship out of consideration for either their property, beauty or because they thought they would be able to treat them according to their whims, as they had no one to protect them. After marriage such men sometimes committed excesses against these girls. It is in this context that the Muslims are told that if they fear they will not be able to do justice to the orphan girls, then they should marry other girls whom they like. (This interpretation seems to be supported by verse 127 of this *sūrah*.)

(ii) The second view is that of Ibn 'Abbās and his disciple 'Ikrimah who expressed the opinion that in the *Jāhilīyah* period there was no limit on the number of wives a man could take. The result was that a man sometimes married as many as ten women and, when expenses increased because of a large family, he encroached on the rights either of his orphan nephews or other relatives. It was in this context that God fixed the limit of four wives and instructed the Muslims that they may marry up to four wives providing they possessed the capacity to treat them equitably.

If you fear that you will not be able to treat them justly, then marry (only) one,[5] or marry from among those whom your right hands possess.[6] This will make it more likely that you will avoid injustice.

فَإِنْ خِفْتُمْ أَلَّا تَعْدِلُوا فَوَٰحِدَةً أَوْ مَا مَلَكَتْ
أَيْمَٰنُكُمْ ذَٰلِكَ أَدْنَىٰٓ أَلَّا تَعُولُوا ٣

(iii) Sa'īd b. Jubayr, Qatādah and some other commentators say that while the Arabs of the *Jāhilīyah* period did not approve of subjecting orphans to wrong, they had no concept of justice and equity with regard to women. They married as many women as they wanted and then subjected them to injustice and oppression. It is in this context that people are told that if they fear perpetrating wrongs on orphans they ought to be equally worried about perpetrating them on women. In the first place they should never marry more than four, and of those four, they should marry only as many as they can treat fairly.

Each of the three interpretations is plausible and all three may possibly be correct. Moreover, the verse could also mean that if a person does not find himself able to treat orphans in a fair manner, then he might as well marry the women who are looking after those orphans.

5. Muslim jurists are agreed that according to this verse the maximum number of wives has been fixed at four. This conclusion is also supported by traditions. It is reported that when Ghaylān, the chief of Ṭā'if, embraced Islam he had nine wives. The Prophet (peace be on him) ordered him to keep only four wives and divorce the rest. Another person, Nawfal b. Mu'āwiyah, had five wives. The Prophet (peace be on him) ordered him to divorce one of them. (For the relevant traditions see the comments of Ibn Kathīr and Qurṭubī on this verse – Ed.)

This verse stipulates that marrying more wives than one is permissible on the condition that one treats his wives equitably. A person who avails himself of this permission granted by God to have a plurality of wives, and disregards the condition laid down by God to treat them equitably has not acted in good faith with God. In case there are complaints from wives that they are not being treated equitably, the Islamic state has the right to intervene and redress such grievances.

Some people who have been overwhelmed and overawed by the Christianized outlook of Westerners have tried to prove that the real aim of the Qur'ān was to put an end to polygamy (which, in their opinion, is intrinsically evil). Since it was widely practised at that time, however, Islam confined itself to placing restrictions on it. Such arguments only show the

(4) Give women their bridal-due in good cheer (considering it a duty); but if they willingly remit any part of it, consume it with good pleasure.[7]	وَءَاتُوا۟ ٱلنِّسَآءَ صَدُقَٰتِهِنَّ نِحْلَةً ۚ فَإِن طِبْنَ لَكُمْ عَن شَىْءٍ مِّنْهُ نَفْسًا فَكُلُوهُ هَنِيٓـًٔا مَّرِيٓـًٔا ﴿٤﴾

mental slavery to which these people have succumbed. That polygamy is an evil *per se* is an unacceptable proposition, for under certain conditions it becomes a moral and social necessity. If polygamy is totally prohibited men who cannot remain satisfied with only one wife will look outside the bounds of matrimonial life and create sexual anarchy and corruption. This is likely to cause much greater harm than polygamy to the moral and social order. For this reason the Qur'ān has allowed those who feel the need for it to resort to polygamy. Those who consider it an evil in itself may certainly denounce it in disregard of the Qur'ān and may even argue for its abolition. But they have no right to attribute such a view to the Qur'ān, for it has expressed its permission of polygamy in quite categorical terms. Indeed, there is not the slightest hint in the Qur'ān that could justify the conclusion that it advocates abolition of polygamy. (For further elaboration see my book, *Sunnat kī Ā'inī Ḥaythīyat*, Lahore, 3rd edition, 1975, pp. 307–16.)

6. This expression denotes 'slave-girls', i.e. female captives of war who are distributed by the state among individuals. The purpose of this verse is to tell men that if their financial circumstances do not permit them to support a free woman as their wife then they may marry a slave-girl (see verse 25 below); if they consider it necessary to have more than one wife and it would be difficult for them to treat their free wives equitably they may resort to slave-girls, for here the burden of obligations is lighter by comparison. (For further injunctions regarding slave-girls see n. 44 below.)

7. In the opinion of 'Umar and Shurayḥ, if a woman gives up either the whole or a part of the bridal-due (*mahr*) in favour of her husband and later reclaims it from him then he is bound to pay it. The claim on the woman's part would be tantamount to her unwillingness to remit either the whole or a part of the bridal-due. For further details see the section entitled '*Mahr*' in my book *Ḥuqūq al-Zawjayn*, 16th edition, Lahore, 1976, pp. 31–3 and 119–23.

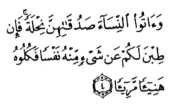

(5) Do not entrust your properties – which Allah has made a means of support for you – to the weak of understanding, but maintain and clothe them out of it, and say to them a kind word of admonition.[8]

(6) Test the orphans until they reach the age of marriage,[9] and then if you find them mature of mind hand over to them their property,[10] and do not eat it up by either spending extravagantly or in haste, fearing that they would grow up (and claim it). If the guardian of the orphan is rich let him abstain entirely (from his ward's property); and if he is poor, let him partake of it in a fair measure.[11] When you hand over their property to them let there be witnesses on their behalf. Allah is sufficient to take account (of your deeds).

وَلَا تُؤْتُوا السُّفَهَاءَ أَمْوَالَكُمُ الَّتِي جَعَلَ اللَّهُ
لَكُمْ قِيَامًا وَارْزُقُوهُمْ فِيهَا وَاكْسُوهُمْ
وَقُولُوا لَهُمْ قَوْلًا مَعْرُوفًا ﴿٥﴾ وَابْتَلُوا الْيَتَامَىٰ
حَتَّىٰ إِذَا بَلَغُوا النِّكَاحَ فَإِنْ آنَسْتُمْ مِنْهُمْ
رُشْدًا فَادْفَعُوا إِلَيْهِمْ أَمْوَالَهُمْ
وَلَا تَأْكُلُوهَا إِسْرَافًا وَبِدَارًا أَنْ يَكْبَرُوا
وَمَنْ كَانَ غَنِيًّا فَلْيَسْتَعْفِفْ وَمَنْ كَانَ
فَقِيرًا فَلْيَأْكُلْ بِالْمَعْرُوفِ فَإِذَا دَفَعْتُمْ
إِلَيْهِمْ أَمْوَالَهُمْ فَأَشْهِدُوا عَلَيْهِمْ وَكَفَىٰ
بِاللَّهِ حَسِيبًا ﴿٦﴾

---

8. This verse covers a very wide spectrum of meaning. It emphasizes to the community of believers that wealth is one of the main supports of human life. It should not be left, therefore, at the mercy of those who are incompetent to handle it properly. By misusing wealth such people might destroy the bases of social and economic life and wreck the moral foundations of human society. The right to private property is not so absolute; if a person is incapable of exercising this right properly and if he might cause grave social harm by wanton expenditure then his right may be forfeited. The necessities of such a person's life should always be provided for. But so far as the exercise of his proprietary rights is concerned, due restrictions should be placed on it in order that the owner is restrained from spending his resources in brazen disregard of the dictates of morality,

collective welfare and economic interests of the community. According to the directive embodied in the verse, anyone who entrusts his property to someone else's care should satisfy himself that the latter is capable of making good use of it. At a higher level, it is incumbent upon an Islamic state to take over the management of the properties of those who either lack totally the capacity for good management or cause social damage by misuse. In such cases the state is responsible for providing these people with their livelihood.

9. When such people approach their majority their mental development should be watched so as to determine to what extent they have become capable of managing their own affairs.

10. Two conditions have been laid down for handing over the charge of their properties to such people. The first of these is the attainment of puberty, and the second is that of mental maturity – i.e. the capacity to manage their affairs in a sound and appropriate manner. There is full agreement among Muslim jurists with regard to the first condition. As for the second condition, Abū Ḥanīfah is of the opinion that if an orphan does not attain mental maturity after he has attained puberty, the guardian of the orphan should wait for a maximum of seven years after which he should hand over the property to its owner regardless of whether he has attained maturity or not. According to Abū Yūsuf, Muḥammad b. al-Ḥasan and Shāfi'ī, maturity is an indispensable pre-condition for the handing over of property. If one were to apply the doctrine of the latter jurists it would probably be more appropriate to refer particular cases to a judge under Islamic law. If the judge is convinced that the person concerned lacks maturity he should make adequate arrangements for the supervision of that person's financial affairs. (For a more complete study of the subject see Jaṣṣāṣ, vol. 2, pp. 59 ff.; Ibn Rushd, *Bidāyat al-Mujtahid*, 2 vols., Cairo, Al-Maktabah al-Tijārīyah al-Kubrá, n.d., vol. 2, pp. 275 ff. – Ed.)

11. The guardian is entitled to remuneration for his service. The amount of this remuneration should be such as is deemed to be fair by neutral and reasonable people. Moreover, the guardian is instructed that he should take a fixed and known amount by way of remuneration, that he should take it openly rather than secretly, and that he should keep an account of it.

(7) Just as there is a share for men in what their parents and kinsfolk leave behind, so there is a share for women in what their parents and kinsfolk leave behind – be it little or much[12] – a share ordained (by Allah).

(8) If other near of kin, orphans and needy are present at the time of division of inheritance give them something of it and speak to them kindly.[13]

(9) And let them fear, those who, if they would themselves leave behind helpless offspring, they would surely have been fearful on their account. Let them, then, fear Allah and make the right statement. (10) Behold, those who wrongfully devour the properties of orphans only fill their bellies with fire. Soon they will burn in the Blazing Flame.[14]

لِّلرِّجَالِ نَصِيبٌ مِّمَّا تَرَكَ ٱلْوَٰلِدَانِ
وَٱلْأَقْرَبُونَ وَلِلنِّسَآءِ نَصِيبٌ مِّمَّا تَرَكَ
ٱلْوَٰلِدَانِ وَٱلْأَقْرَبُونَ مِمَّا قَلَّ مِنْهُ
أَوْ كَثُرَ نَصِيبًا مَّفْرُوضًا ﴿٧﴾ وَإِذَا
حَضَرَ ٱلْقِسْمَةَ أُوْلُواْ ٱلْقُرْبَىٰ وَٱلْيَتَٰمَىٰ
وَٱلْمَسَٰكِينُ فَٱرْزُقُوهُم مِّنْهُ وَقُولُواْ
لَهُمْ قَوْلًا مَّعْرُوفًا ﴿٨﴾ وَلْيَخْشَ
ٱلَّذِينَ لَوْ تَرَكُواْ مِنْ خَلْفِهِمْ ذُرِّيَّةً
ضِعَٰفًا خَافُواْ عَلَيْهِمْ فَلْيَتَّقُواْ ٱللَّهَ
وَلْيَقُولُواْ قَوْلًا سَدِيدًا ﴿٩﴾ إِنَّ ٱلَّذِينَ
يَأْكُلُونَ أَمْوَٰلَ ٱلْيَتَٰمَىٰ ظُلْمًا إِنَّمَا
يَأْكُلُونَ فِي بُطُونِهِمْ نَارًا
وَسَيَصْلَوْنَ سَعِيرًا ﴿١٠﴾

12. This verse embodies five legal injunctions. First, that women as well as men are entitled to inheritance. Second, that inheritance, however meagre it might be, should be distributed; even if the deceased has left a small piece of cloth and he has ten heirs, that piece of cloth should be distributed among them all. This does not exclude, however, the permissibility of one heir purchasing the shares of other heirs with their consent. Third, this verse indicates that the law of inheritance is applicable to all kinds of property – movable and immovable, agricultural, industrial and so on. Fourth, it shows that the right of inheritance comes into force as soon as a person dies leaving property. Fifth, it implies the rule that immediate blood-relatives exclude those that are further removed.

(11) Allah thus commands you concerning your children: the share of the male is like that of two females.[15] If (the heirs of the deceased are) more than two daughters, they shall have two-thirds of the inheritance;[16] and if there is only one daughter, then she shall have half the inheritance. If the deceased has any offspring, each of his parents shall have a sixth of the inheritance;[17] and if the deceased has no child and his parents alone inherit him, then one-third shall go to his mother;[18] and if the deceased has brothers and sisters, then one-sixth shall go to his mother.[19] All these shares are to be given after payment of the bequest he might have made or any debts outstanding against him.[20]

يُوصِيكُمُ ٱللَّهُ فِىٓ أَوْلَٰدِكُمْ ۖ لِلذَّكَرِ
مِثْلُ حَظِّ ٱلْأُنثَيَيْنِ ۚ فَإِن كُنَّ نِسَآءً
فَوْقَ ٱثْنَتَيْنِ فَلَهُنَّ ثُلُثَا مَا تَرَكَ ۖ وَإِن
كَانَتْ وَٰحِدَةً فَلَهَا ٱلنِّصْفُ ۚ
وَلِأَبَوَيْهِ لِكُلِّ وَٰحِدٍ مِّنْهُمَا ٱلسُّدُسُ
مِمَّا تَرَكَ إِن كَانَ لَهُۥ وَلَدٌ ۚ فَإِن لَّمْ يَكُن لَّهُۥ
وَلَدٌ وَوَرِثَهُۥٓ أَبَوَاهُ فَلِأُمِّهِ ٱلثُّلُثُ ۚ فَإِن كَانَ
لَهُۥٓ إِخْوَةٌ فَلِأُمِّهِ ٱلسُّدُسُ ۚ مِنۢ بَعْدِ
وَصِيَّةٍ يُوصِى بِهَآ أَوْ دَيْنٍ ۗ

---

13. This directive is addressed to the heirs of the deceased. They are told not to be niggardly towards their relatives whether they be close or distant. Nor should they be niggardly towards either poor and needy members of the family or towards orphans who are present when the inheritance is distributed. Although they are not legally entitled to any share it is seemly for people to act magnanimously and give them something out of their inheritance, and especially to desist from making hurtful remarks.

14. It is reported in a tradition that after the Battle of Uḥud the wife of Sa'd b. Rabī' brought her two daughters to the Prophet (peace be on him) and said: 'O Messenger of God! These are daughters of Sa'd who was with you in the Battle of Uḥud, where he was martyred. The girls' uncles have seized the whole property and left nothing for them. Who will now marry these girls?' It was after this incident that these verses were

revealed. (See Muḥammad 'Alī al-Ṣābūnī's comments on this verse in his *Ṣafwat al-Tafāsīr* and the sources quoted therein – Ed.)

15. This is the first general rule in connection with inheritance, viz., that the share of the male should be double that of the female. Since Islamic law imposes greater financial obligations on men in respect of family life and relieves women of a number of such obligations, justice demands that a woman's share in inheritance should be less than that of a man.

16. The same applies in the case where there are two daughters. If the deceased leaves only daughters, and if there are two or more daughters then they will receive two-thirds of the inheritance and the remaining one-third will go to the other heirs. But if the deceased has only one son there is a consensus among jurists that in the absence of other heirs he is entitled to all the property and if the deceased has other heirs, he is entitled to the property left after their shares have been distributed.

17. If the deceased leaves issue each of his parents will receive one-sixth of the inheritance irrespective of whether the issue consists either only of daughters, only of sons, of both sons and daughters, of just one son or just one daughter. The remaining two-thirds will be distributed among the rest of the heirs.

18. If there are no other heirs than the parents, the remaining two-thirds will go to the share of the father; otherwise the two-thirds will be distributed between the father and other heirs.

19. In the case where the deceased also has brothers and sisters the share of the mother will be one-sixth rather than one-third. In this case the sixth that was deducted from the share of the mother will be added to that of the father, for in this circumstance the father's obligations are heavier. It should be noted that if the parents of the deceased are alive, the brothers and sisters will not be entitled to any share in the inheritance.

20. The mention of bequest precedes the mention of debt, for although not everyone need be encumbered with debt it is necessary that everyone should make a bequest. (However, other Mufassirūn (exegetes) regard making a bequest as a discretionary act – Ed.) As for legalities, there is consensus among Muslims that the payment of debts takes precedence over the payment of bequests, i.e. if the deceased owes a debt and also leaves a bequest, the debt will first be paid out of the inheritance, and only then will his bequest be fulfilled.

We have already stated in connection with bequest (see *Towards Understanding the Qur'ān*, vol. I, *Sūrah* 2, n. 182) that a man has the right to bequeath up to a maximum of one-third of his inheritance. The principle laid down in regard to bequest is that a man can allot a portion of his inheritance either to a relative who is not legally entitled to any prescribed share in the inheritance or to others whom he considers deserving of help, e.g. either an orphaned grandson or grand-daughter, the widow of a son

You do not know which of them, your parents or your children, are more beneficial to you. But these portions have been determined by Allah, for He indeed knows all, is cognizant of all beneficent considerations.[21]

(12) And to you belongs half of whatever has been left behind by your wives if they die childless; but if they have any children then to you belongs a fourth of what they have left behind, after payment of the bequest they might have made or any debts outstanding against them. And to them belongs a fourth of what you leave behind, if you die childless; and if you have any child then to them belongs one-eighth of what you have left behind,[22] after the payment of the bequest you might have made or any debts outstanding against you.

ءَابَآؤُكُمْ وَأَبْنَآؤُكُمْ لَا تَدْرُونَ أَيُّهُمْ
أَقْرَبُ لَكُمْ نَفْعًا فَرِيضَةً مِّنَ ٱللَّهِ
إِنَّ ٱللَّهَ كَانَ عَلِيمًا حَكِيمًا ﴿١١﴾
۞ وَلَكُمْ نِصْفُ مَا تَرَكَ
أَزْوَٰجُكُمْ إِن لَّمْ يَكُن لَّهُنَّ وَلَدٌ
فَإِن كَانَ لَهُنَّ وَلَدٌ فَلَكُمُ
ٱلرُّبُعُ مِمَّا تَرَكْنَ مِنۢ
بَعْدِ وَصِيَّةٍ يُوصِينَ بِهَآ
أَوْ دَيْنٍ وَلَهُنَّ ٱلرُّبُعُ مِمَّا
تَرَكْتُمْ إِن لَّمْ يَكُن لَّكُمْ وَلَدٌ
فَإِن كَانَ لَكُمْ وَلَدٌ فَلَهُنَّ
ٱلثُّمُنُ مِمَّا تَرَكْتُم مِّنۢ بَعْدِ
وَصِيَّةٍ تُوصُونَ بِهَآ أَوْ دَيْنٍ

---

in financial distress, any brother, sister, brother's wife, nephew, and other relatives who seem to be in need of support. If there are no such relatives bequests can be made either to other needy people or for charitable purposes. In short, the Law has fixed regulations for the distribution of two-thirds or more of one's inheritance, out of which the legal heirs are to receive their shares according to the regulations laid down by the Law. A maximum of one-third of the inheritance has been left to the discretion of the person concerned, who can dispose of it by means of bequest in light of his particular family circumstances. If anyone makes either an inequitable bequest or misuses his discretion so as to hurt the legitimate rights of others, it is permissible for the members of the family to rectify the situation either by mutual agreement or by requesting a judge to

And if the man or woman has no heir in the direct line, but has a brother or sister, then each of these shall inherit one-sixth; but if they are more than two, then they shall inherit one-third of the inheritance,[23] after the payment of the bequest that might have been made or any debts outstanding against the deceased, providing that the bequest causes no injury.[24] This is a commandment from Allah; Allah is All-Knowing, All-Forbearing.[25]

وَإِن كَانَ رَجُلٌ يُورَثُ كَلَٰلَةً
أَوِ ٱمْرَأَةٌ وَلَهُۥٓ أَخٌ أَوْ أُخْتٌ فَلِكُلِّ
وَٰحِدٍ مِّنْهُمَا ٱلسُّدُسُ ۚ فَإِن كَانُوٓا۟
أَكْثَرَ مِن ذَٰلِكَ فَهُمْ شُرَكَآءُ
فِى ٱلثُّلُثِ ۚ مِنۢ بَعْدِ وَصِيَّةٍ يُوصَىٰ بِهَآ
أَوْ دَيْنٍ غَيْرَ مُضَآرٍّ ۚ وَصِيَّةً مِّنَ ٱللَّهِ ۗ
وَٱللَّهُ عَلِيمٌ حَلِيمٌ ﴿١٢﴾

---

intervene. For further details see my booklet *Yatīm Pōté kī Wirāthat kā Mas'alah*, Lahore, 1954.

21. This is in response to those feeble-minded people who do not fully appreciate God's law of inheritance and try to fill, with the help of their limited intellect, what they see as gaps in God's Laws.

22. Whether a man has one wife or several wives the share of the wife/wives is one-eighth of the inheritance when the deceased has issue, and one-fourth when he has no issue. The share of the wives, whether one-fourth or one-eighth, will be distributed equally among them.

23. The remaining five-sixths or two-thirds of the inheritance goes to the legal heirs, if any. Where there are no legal heirs, the person concerned is entitled to make a bequest with regard to the remaining part of the inheritance.

Commentators are agreed that the sisters and brothers mentioned here mean half-brothers and half-sisters, i.e. those who have kinship with the deceased on the mother's side. Injunctions affecting full brothers and sisters, and half-brothers and half-sisters on the father's side are mentioned towards the end of the present *sūrah*. (See verse 176 below, and nn. 219 ff. – Ed.)

24. 'Bequests which cause injury' are those that entail depriving deserving kin of their legitimate rights. Similarly, the debt which causes injury is

(13) These are the bounds set by Allah. Allah will make the man who obeys Allah and His Messenger enter the Gardens beneath which rivers flow. He will abide there for ever. That is the mighty triumph. (14) And he who disobeys Allah and His Messenger and transgresses the bounds set by Him – him shall Allah cause to enter the Fire. There he will abide. A humiliating chastisement awaits him.[25a]

تِلْكَ حُدُودُ اللَّهِ ۚ وَمَن يُطِعِ
اللَّهَ وَرَسُولَهُۥ يُدْخِلْهُ جَنَّـٰتٍ
تَجْرِى مِن تَحْتِهَا الْأَنْهَـٰرُ
خَـٰلِدِينَ فِيهَا ۚ وَذَٰلِكَ الْفَوْزُ
الْعَظِيمُ ﴿١٣﴾ وَمَن يَعْصِ اللَّهَ
وَرَسُولَهُۥ وَيَتَعَدَّ حُدُودَهُۥ يُدْخِلْهُ
نَارًا خَـٰلِدًا فِيهَا وَلَهُۥ عَذَابٌ
مُّهِينٌ ﴿١٤﴾

---

the fake debt which one falsely admits to owing, and any other device to which one resorts merely in order to deprive the rightful heirs of their shares in inheritance. This kind of injury has been declared to be a major sin in a tradition from the Prophet (peace be on him). According to another tradition the Prophet (peace be on him) said that even if a man worked all his life, like the men of Paradise, yet ended his life's record by making a wrongful bequest, he would be consigned to Hell. (Ibn Kathīr, vol. 2, p. 218.) Such an act of deliberate injury and calculated effort designed to deprive people of their due rights is always a sin, but it is mentioned by God particularly in the case of *kalālah* (the person who leaves behind neither parents nor descendants). (For *kalālah* see nn. 219 ff. below – Ed.) The reason for this seems to be that a man who has neither issue nor parents is often prone to squander his property and somehow prevent his distant relatives from receiving any share in the inheritance.

25. God's knowledge is referred to here for two reasons. First, to stress that if a man violates God's Law he will not be able to escape from the grip of God, for He is Omniscient. Second, to emphasize that the shares in inheritance fixed by God are absolutely sound, for God knows better than His creatures where their true interests lie. Reference is also made to God's forbearance. This is in order to point out that harshness could not characterize the laws laid down by God in respect of inheritance since He Himself is not harsh. On the contrary, the aim of God's laws is to prevent people suffering inconvenience and hardship.

25a. This is a terrifying verse in which those who either tamper with God's laws of inheritance or violate the legal bounds categorically laid down

(15) As for those of your women who are guilty of immoral conduct, call upon four from amongst you to bear witness against them. And if four men do bear witness, confine those women to their houses until either death takes them away or Allah opens some way for them. (16) Punish both of those among you who are guilty of this sin, then if they repent and mend their ways, leave them alone. For Allah is always ready to accept repentance. He is All-Compassionate.[26]

وَٱلَّٰتِي يَأۡتِينَ ٱلۡفَٰحِشَةَ مِن
نِّسَآئِكُمۡ فَٱسۡتَشۡهِدُواْ عَلَيۡهِنَّ
أَرۡبَعَةٗ مِّنكُمۡۖ فَإِن شَهِدُواْ
فَأَمۡسِكُوهُنَّ فِي ٱلۡبُيُوتِ حَتَّىٰ
يَتَوَفَّىٰهُنَّ ٱلۡمَوۡتُ أَوۡ يَجۡعَلَ ٱللَّهُ لَهُنَّ
سَبِيلٗا ١٥ وَٱلَّذَانِ يَأۡتِيَٰنِهَا
مِنكُمۡ فَـَٔاذُوهُمَاۖ فَإِن تَابَا
وَأَصۡلَحَا فَأَعۡرِضُواْ عَنۡهُمَآۗ إِنَّ ٱللَّهَ
كَانَ تَوَّابٗا رَّحِيمًا ١٦

---

by God in His Book are warned of unending punishment. It is lamentable that, in spite of these very stern warnings, Muslims have occasionally been guilty of breaching God's laws with the same boldness and insolence as that of the Jews. Disobedience to God's law of inheritance has occasionally assumed the proportion of open rebellion against Him. In some instances, women have been disinherited altogether. In others, the eldest son has been declared the only legal heir. There are also instances where the entire system of inheritance distribution has been replaced by the system of joint family property. In still other instances, the shares of women have been made equal to those of men. In our time a few Muslim states, in imitation of the West, even contrived a new form of disobedience. This consists of imposing death duties so that governments, too, become one of the heirs of the deceased, an heir whose share God had altogether failed to mention! This is despite the fact that under Islamic dispensation governments may assume control of a dead man's inheritance only if it is either unclaimed or if the person concerned has specifically so bequeathed part of his inheritance.

26. In these two verses (15–16) the first, preliminary directives for the punishment for unlawful sexual intercourse are stated. The first verse deals with women. The punishment laid down was to confine them until further directives were revealed. The second verse (i.e. 16) relates to both sexes. The injunction lays down that they should be punished – that is, they should be beaten and publicly reproached. Later, another injunction was revealed

(17) (And remember that) Allah's acceptance of repentance is only for those who commit evil out of ignorance and then soon repent. It is towards such persons that Allah turns graciously. Allah is All-Knowing, All-Wise. (18) But of no avail is repentance of those who do evil until death approaches any one of them and then he says: 'Now I repent.' Nor is the repentance of those who die in the state of unbelief of any avail to them. For them We have kept in readiness a painful chastisement.[27]

إِنَّمَا ٱلتَّوْبَةُ عَلَى ٱللَّهِ لِلَّذِينَ يَعْمَلُونَ
ٱلسُّوٓءَ بِجَهَٰلَةٍ ثُمَّ يَتُوبُونَ مِن قَرِيبٍ
فَأُو۟لَٰٓئِكَ يَتُوبُ ٱللَّهُ عَلَيْهِمْ ۗ وَكَانَ
ٱللَّهُ عَلِيمًا حَكِيمًا ﴿١٧﴾ وَلَيْسَتِ
ٱلتَّوْبَةُ لِلَّذِينَ يَعْمَلُونَ
ٱلسَّيِّـَٔاتِ حَتَّىٰٓ إِذَا حَضَرَ أَحَدَهُمُ
ٱلْمَوْتُ قَالَ إِنِّى تُبْتُ ٱلْـَٔـٰنَ وَلَا
ٱلَّذِينَ يَمُوتُونَ وَهُمْ كُفَّارٌ ۚ
أُو۟لَٰٓئِكَ أَعْتَدْنَا لَهُمْ عَذَابًا أَلِيمًا
﴿١٨﴾

(see *Sūrah al-Nūr* 24: 2) which laid down that both the male and female should be given a hundred lashes. These injunctions are necessarily of a preliminary nature since the people of Arabia were neither used to obeying the orders of any established government, the verdicts of any courts of law nor to following any legal code; it would therefore have been unwise to try to force acceptance of a penal code upon them so soon after the establishment of the Islamic state. In due course, the punishments for unlawful sexual intercourse, for slanderous accusations of unchastity against women, and for theft were laid down in their definitive form and served as the basis of that detailed penal code which was enforced by the Prophet (peace be on him) and the Rightly-Guided Caliphs.

The apparent difference between the contents of the two verses led al-Suddī to the misconceived belief that the first verse lays down the punishment for married women, and the second that for unmarried men and women. This is a tenuous explanation unsupported by any serious evidence and argument. Even less convincing is the opinion expressed by Abū Muslim al-Isfahānī that the first verse relates to lesbian relations between females, and the second to homosexual relations between males. It is strange that al-Isfahānī ignored the basic fact that the Qur'ān seeks merely to chart a broad code of law and morality and hence deals only with fundamental questions. It is inconsistent with the majestic style of the Qur'ān to discuss secondary details which have been left to people to decide

(19) Believers! It is not lawful for you to become heirs to women against their will.[28] It is not lawful that you should put constraint upon them that you may take away anything of what you have given them; (you may not put constraint upon them) unless they are guilty of brazenly immoral conduct.[29] Live with your wives in a good manner. If you dislike them in any manner, it may be that you dislike something in which Allah has placed much good for you.[30] (20) And if you decide to dispense with a wife in order to take another, do not take away anything of what you might have given the first one, even if you had given her a heap of gold. Would you take it back by slandering her and committing a manifest wrong?

يَـٰٓأَيُّهَا ٱلَّذِينَ ءَامَنُوا۟ لَا يَحِلُّ لَكُمْ
أَن تَرِثُوا۟ ٱلنِّسَآءَ كَرْهًا ۖ وَلَا تَعْضُلُوهُنَّ
لِتَذْهَبُوا۟ بِبَعْضِ مَآ ءَاتَيْتُمُوهُنَّ إِلَّآ
أَن يَأْتِينَ بِفَـٰحِشَةٍ مُّبَيِّنَةٍ ۚ
وَعَاشِرُوهُنَّ بِٱلْمَعْرُوفِ ۚ فَإِن
كَرِهْتُمُوهُنَّ فَعَسَىٰٓ أَن تَكْرَهُوا۟
شَيْـًٔا وَيَجْعَلَ ٱللَّهُ فِيهِ خَيْرًا كَثِيرًا
﴿١٩﴾ وَإِنْ أَرَدتُّمُ ٱسْتِبْدَالَ زَوْجٍ
مَّكَانَ زَوْجٍ وَءَاتَيْتُمْ
إِحْدَىٰهُنَّ قِنطَارًا فَلَا تَأْخُذُوا۟ مِنْهُ
شَيْـًٔا ۚ أَتَأْخُذُونَهُۥ بُهْتَـٰنًا وَإِثْمًا
مُّبِينًا ﴿٢٠﴾

---

through the exercise of their legal judgement. It is for this reason that when the problem of fixing a punishment for sodomy came up for consideration after the time of the Prophet (peace be on him), none of the Companions thought that the above-mentioned verse contained any relevant injunction.

27. The Arabic word *tawbah* means 'to return, to come back'.

A man's *tawbah* after he has sinned means that God's servant, who had turned away from his Master in disobedience, has repented, and has returned to obedience and service. On the other hand, *tawbah* on the part of God means that the attention of the Master, which had turned away from His erring servant, has once again turned towards him. In this verse, however, God makes it clear to His servants that *tawbah* is acceptable only from those who commit errors inadvertently and out of ignorance. Such persons will always find the door of God open for them whenever they turn to Him in repentance.

But this *tawbah* is not for those who pile sin upon sin throughout their lives in sheer indifference to God and who cry for pardon as soon as they see the angel of death approaching. The Prophet (peace be on him) has warned against this attitude in the following words: 'God accepts the repentance of a slave until the gurgling (of death) begins.' (Tirmidhī, 'Da'wāt', 98; Ibn Mājah, 'Zuhd', 30; Aḥmad b. Ḥanbal, *Musnad*, vol. 2, pp. 132 and 153, and vol. 3, pp. 425 – Ed.) For when the last leaf of a man's book of life has been turned, what opportunity remains for a man to return to righteous conduct? Likewise, if a person spends even the very last moment of his life in a state of disbelief and then on the threshold of the Next Life he comes to discover that the facts are quite contrary to what he had imagined, what sense is there for him to seek forgiveness?

28. This means that the relatives of the husband should not treat the widow of the deceased as if she were a part of the inheritance and begin imposing their will on her. Upon the death of her husband a woman becomes independent. As soon as her legally-prescribed period of waiting ends, she is free to go to wherever she likes and to marry anyone she wishes.

29. This permission is intended not in order to provide them with an excuse to misappropriate her property but to exercise a restraint on her conduct and prevent her from lewdness.

30. This means that if the wife is either not beautiful or has some shortcoming because of which she does not seem attractive enough to her husband, the latter should not suddenly decide, in a fit of rage and disgust, to part with her. Rather he should act with patience and forbearance. It often happens that a woman lacks physical attraction but has other qualities which are of much greater value for the success of married life. Hence if such a woman finds the opportunity to express her qualities, the same husband who initially felt revulsion towards her becomes captivated by her attractive conduct and character. Sometimes in the early stages of married life a husband dislikes certain things in his wife, and this initial dislike may even grow to revulsion. Were a man to be patient and allow all the potentialities of the woman to be realized, it would become evident to him that her merits outweighed her weaknesses. Hence a man's haste in taking the decision to rupture the matrimonial bond is not praiseworthy. Repudiation of marriage should be a man's last resort, a resort towards which he should turn only in unavoidable circumstances. The Prophet (peace be on him) has said: 'For God, divorce is the most reprehensible of all lawful things.' (Abū Dā'ūd, 'Ṭalāq', 3; Ibn Mājah, 'Ṭalāq', 1 – Ed.) In another tradition the Prophet (peace be on him) said: 'Marry and do not go about divorcing. For God does not like men and women who keep on changing partners merely for a change of taste.' (al-Ṭabrānī, cited by 'Ajlūnī in *Kashf al-Khifā'*, vol. 1, p. 304 – Ed.)

(21) How can you take it away after each one has enjoyed the other, and they have taken a firm covenant from you?[31]

(22) Do not marry the women whom your fathers married, although what is past is past.[32] This indeed was a shameful deed, a hateful thing, and an evil way.[33]

وَكَيْفَ تَأْخُذُونَهُۥ وَقَدْ أَفْضَىٰ
بَعْضُكُمْ إِلَىٰ بَعْضٍ وَأَخَذْنَ
مِنكُم مِّيثَٰقًا غَلِيظًا ﴿٢١﴾
وَلَا تَنكِحُوا۟ مَا نَكَحَ ءَابَآؤُكُم
مِّنَ ٱلنِّسَآءِ إِلَّا مَا قَدْ سَلَفَ ۚ
إِنَّهُۥ كَانَ فَٰحِشَةً وَمَقْتًا وَسَآءَ
سَبِيلًا ﴿٢٢﴾

31. The 'firm covenant' in this verse refers to marriage. For marriage is a firm covenant of fidelity. It is only because a woman has faith in the firmness of this covenant that she entrusts herself to a man. If a man decides of his own will to break it, he has no right to withdraw the amount he offered his wife by way of bridal-due at the time of entering into that covenant. (See *Towards Understanding the Qur'ān*, vol. I, *Sūrah* 2, n. 251.)

32. The Qur'ān rounds off all statements prohibiting the objectionable features of the social life of the *Jāhilīyah* period by condoning violations of those prohibitions prior to their revelation: 'What is past is past.' This has two meanings. First, that those concerned would not be punished for mistakes committed in their state of Ignorance, providing they rectified their conduct after the prohibitory injunction had been revealed. Second, that the prohibition of any ancient custom, usage and law did not mean that all acts which took place in the past would be nullified, and that all the consequences of those acts would be deemed void, and people absolved of all the obligations which ensued from them. If marriage with the step-mother, for instance, was prohibited it did not necessarily follow that the children of all such marriages which had been contracted in the past were to be reckoned illegitimate, and that the offspring from such marriages would be disinherited. Similarly, if a certain transaction was declared unlawful it did not mean that all such transactions which had taken place prior to the prohibition should be deemed void and that all the earnings of people accumulated through those transactions would be either seized or declared illegitimate property.

33. In Islamic law marrying women who fall in the prohibited degrees of marriage is a recognized criminal offence. According to traditions in the *Ḥadīth* collections of Abū Dā'ūd, Nasā'ī and Aḥmad b. Ḥanbal, people

(23) Forbidden to you are your mothers,[34] your daughters,[35] your sisters,[36] your father's sisters and your mother's sisters, your brother's daughters and your sister's daughters,[37] your milk-mothers, your milk-sisters,[38] the mothers of your wives,[39] and the step-daughters – who are your foster-children,[40] born of your wives with whom you have consummated the marriage; but if you have not consummated the marriage with them, there will be no blame upon you (if you marry their daughters). ▶

حُرِّمَتْ عَلَيْكُمْ أُمَّهَٰتُكُمْ
وَبَنَاتُكُمْ وَأَخَوَٰتُكُمْ وَعَمَّٰتُكُمْ
وَخَٰلَٰتُكُمْ وَبَنَاتُ ٱلْأَخِ وَبَنَاتُ
ٱلْأُخْتِ وَأُمَّهَٰتُكُمُ ٱلَّٰتِىٓ
أَرْضَعْنَكُمْ وَأَخَوَٰتُكُم مِّنَ
ٱلرَّضَٰعَةِ وَأُمَّهَٰتُ نِسَآئِكُمْ
وَرَبَٰٓئِبُكُمُ ٱلَّٰتِى فِى
حُجُورِكُم مِّن نِّسَآئِكُمُ
ٱلَّٰتِى دَخَلْتُم بِهِنَّ فَإِن لَّمْ تَكُونُوا۟
دَخَلْتُم بِهِنَّ فَلَا جُنَاحَ
عَلَيْكُمْ

guilty of this offence were punished by the Prophet (peace be on him) with death and confiscation of property. It appears from the tradition related by Ibn 'Abbās (found in the collection of Ibn Mājah), that the Prophet (peace be on him) had devised the following general rule: 'Kill whosoever commits sexual intercourse with a woman forbidden to him' (Ibn Mājah; 'Ḥudūd', 13, 35; also Aḥmad b. Ḥanbal, *Musnad*, vol. 1, p. 300 – Ed.) There is some disagreement, however, among jurists on this question. Aḥmad b. Ḥanbal is of the opinion that the convicted person should be put to death and his property confiscated. Abū Ḥanīfah, Mālik and Shāfi'ī are of the opinion that if a person commits sexual intercourse with a woman within the prohibited degrees he should be punished for adultery; and if he merely marries (but has not actually had sexual intercourse – Ed.) he should be subjected to severe punishment.

34. The word 'mother' applies to one's step-mother as well as to one's real mother. Hence the prohibition extends to both. This injunction also includes prohibition of the grandmother, both paternal and maternal.

There is disagreement on whether a woman with whom a father has had an unlawful sexual relationship is prohibited to his son or not. There are some among the early authorities who do not believe in such prohibition. But there are others who go so far as to say that a woman whom a father has touched with sexual desire becomes prohibited to the son. Likewise, there is disagreement among the scholars of the early period of Islam in regard to a woman with whom a person has had an illegitimate sexual relationship whether she is prohibited to his father or not. In the same way there has been disagreement in regard to a man with whom a mother or daughter has had an illegitimate sexual relationship, whether or not marriage with him is prohibited for both the mother and daughter. (See Jaṣṣāṣ, vol. 2, pp. 113 ff., and *Bidāyat al-Mujtahid*, vol. 2, pp. 33 f. – Ed.) There is a great deal of formal, legal discussion on this point. But even a little reflection makes it evident that if a man marries a woman who is at once the object of the desire of either his father or his son, and if a man marries a woman and is attracted to either her mother or daughter, this militates against the requirements of a righteous society. The spirit of the Law is opposed to the legal hair-splitting which makes a distinction between sexual relations that take place either within the marital framework or outside it, and between either touching or looking with desire and so on. The plain fact is that if the sexual passions of both the father and the son are focused on the same woman, or conversely, if the sexual passions of both the mother and daughter are focused on the same man, this situation is full of evil and mischief for family life and the Law can never tolerate it. The Prophet (peace be on him) has said: 'Whoever looks at the genitals of a woman, both the mother and daughter of that woman become prohibited for him.' In another tradition, the Prophet (peace be on him) said: 'God will not even care to look at the person who casts his look at the genitals of a woman as well as those of her daughter.' (Jaṣṣāṣ, *Aḥkām al-Qur'ān*, vol. IV, p. 141.) These traditions bring out the intent of the Law very clearly.

35. The injunction with regard to daughters applies to grand-daughters on both the paternal and maternal sides as well. There is disagreement, however, whether a daughter born of an illegitimate relationship becomes prohibited or not. According to Abū Ḥanīfah, Mālik and Aḥmad b. Ḥanbal such a daughter is prohibited in the same way as a daughter born in wedlock; Shāfi'ī, however, is of the opinion that such daughters are not prohibited. The very idea, however, of marrying a girl who was born of one's own semen would be repulsive to any decent person.

36. This applies to full sisters as well as to half-sisters.

37. In all these relationships, no distinction is made between the full and step-relationships. The sister of a man's father or mother, whether full sister or step-sister, is prohibited to him. Likewise, the daughters of a man's brothers and sisters are prohibited just as if they were one's own daughters. (See *Bidāyat al-Mujtahid*, vol. 2, pp. 31 ff. – Ed.)

38. There is consensus among Muslims that if a boy or girl is breast-fed by a woman, that woman attains the status of mother, and her husband the status of father. It is forbidden to marry relatives through milk where

the degree of relationship is such as to constitute a bar to marriage in the case of blood-relations. The basis of this rule is the saying of the Prophet (peace be on him): 'Whatever is rendered prohibited by descent (*nasab*) is likewise rendered prohibited by breast-feeding.' (Bukhārī, 'Shahādāt', 4, 7, 13, 14; Muslim, 'Riḍā'ah', 1–14, 26–30; etc. – Ed.) According to Abū Ḥanīfah and Mālik prohibition is established if a child suckles milk from a woman's breast equal to that minimum quantity which nullifies fasting. But according to Aḥmad b. Ḥanbal, it is established by three sucklings; and according to Shāfi'ī by five. There is also disagreement about the maximum age up to which breast-feeding leads to prohibition of marriage with the woman concerned.

In this connection, jurists have expressed the following opinions:

(1) Suckling is of legal significance only when it occurs before a child has been weaned, and when milk is its main source of nourishment. If a child suckles from a woman's breast after having been weaned, this is legally no different from drinking anything else. This is the opinion of Umm Salamah and Ibn 'Abbās, and a tradition to this effect has also been reported from 'Alī. This is also the view of al-Zuhrī, Ḥasan al-Baṣrī, Qatādah, 'Ikrimah and Awzā'ī.

(2) Prohibition is established by breast-feeding during the first two years of a child's life. This is the view of 'Umar, Ibn Mas'ūd, Abū Hurayrah and 'Abd Allāh b. 'Umar. Among jurists, Shāfi'ī, Aḥmad b. Ḥanbal, Abū Yūsuf, Muḥammad b. al-Ḥasan al-Shaybānī and Sufyān al-Thawrī followed this view; and according to a report, so did Abū Ḥanīfah. Mālik largely followed this view, but he was of the opinion that if breast-feeding took place a month or two after the age of two, the prohibition would still remain in effect.

(3) The generally-reported opinion of Abū Ḥanīfah and Zufar is that a bar to marriage is created by breast-feeding up to an age limit of two and a half years.

(4) Some other jurists are of the opinion that the prohibition comes into effect irrespective of the age when breast-feeding takes place. This opinion is based on the view that the effective cause of the prohibition is a woman's milk, rather than the age of the person fed. Hence, even in the case of an older person, the same prohibition would apply as in the case of an infant. This is the view of 'Ā'ishah and this has been supported on the basis of a tradition from 'Alī, which is presumably authentic. Among the jurists this opinion has been followed by 'Urwah b. al-Zubayr, 'Aṭā', Layth b. Sa'd and Ibn Ḥazm. (On this subject see Jaṣṣāṣ, vol. 2, pp. 124 ff.; and Ibn Rushd, *Bidāyat al-Mujtahid*, vol. 2, pp. 35 ff. – Ed.)

39. There is disagreement about prohibition in respect of the mother of the woman with whom one has merely contracted marriage (without having

It is also forbidden for you to take the wives of the sons who have sprung from your loins[41] and to take two sisters together in marriage,[42] although what is past is past. Surely Allah is All-Forgiving, All-Compassionate.[43]

وَحَلَٰٓئِلُ أَبْنَآئِكُمُ ٱلَّذِينَ مِنْ
أَصْلَٰبِكُمْ وَأَن تَجْمَعُوا۟
بَيْنَ ٱلْأُخْتَيْنِ إِلَّا مَا قَدْ سَلَفَ ۗ
إِنَّ ٱللَّهَ كَانَ غَفُورًا رَّحِيمًا ﴿٢٣﴾

---

consummated it). Abū Ḥanīfah, Mālik, Aḥmad b. Ḥanbal and Shāfi'ī believe that such a relationship is prohibited. 'Alī, however, holds the opinion that unless the marriage has been consummated the mother of one's wife does not become prohibited.

40. The prohibitive restriction in regard to such girls is not based on the consideration of their having been brought up in the house of a step-father. The reference to the child's upbringing in his house points to the delicacy of this relationship. The jurists are almost unanimous that it is prohibited to marry one's step-daughter irrespective of whether or not she has been raised in the step-father's house.

41. This restriction has been added because the widow of one's adopted son is, according to Islam, not prohibited. It is only the wife of one's own son who is prohibited. Likewise, the wives of grandsons (paternal and maternal) are prohibited to grandfathers (on both the mother's and father's side).

42. The Prophet (peace be on him) has taught that it is prohibited for a man to combine in marriage an aunt – whether maternal or paternal – with her niece. The guiding principle is that it is prohibited to have as wives two women who, if one were male, would be prohibited to each other. (See *Bidāyat al-Mujtahid*, vol. 2, p. 41 – Ed.)

43. This is an assurance that God would not call them to task for such misdeeds of the *Jāhilīyah* period as combining two sisters in matrimony, provided they abstained from doing so in the future. (See also n. 32 above.) For this reason a man with two sisters as his wives is required to divorce one of them when he embraces Islam.

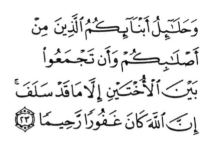

(24) And also forbidden to you are all married women (*muḥṣanāt*) except those women whom your right hands have come to possess (as a result of war).[44] This is Allah's decree and it is binding upon you.

۞ وَٱلْمُحْصَنَٰتُ مِنَ ٱلنِّسَآءِ إِلَّا
مَا مَلَكَتْ أَيْمَٰنُكُمْ ۖ كِتَٰبَ ٱللَّهِ
عَلَيْكُمْ ۚ

---

44. Women who come as captives of war, leaving their husbands behind in *Dār al-Ḥarb* (Domain of War), are not prohibited, for their marriage is nullified by virtue of their entry into *Dār al-Islām* (Domain of Islam). A man may marry such women and, if they happen to be his slave-girls, he may have sexual relations with them. There is disagreement, however, among jurists as to what should be done if both husband and wife have been taken captive together. Abū Ḥanīfah and the jurists of his school are of the opinion that their marriage should remain intact. Mālik and Shāfi'ī, on the other hand, argue that their matrimonial contract should be rendered void.

Many misunderstandings seem to persist about the right to have sexual relations with one's slave-girls. It is pertinent to call attention to the following regulations of Islam:

(1) Islam does not permit soldiers of the Islamic army to have sexual relations with women they capture in war. Islamic Law requires that such women should first be handed over to the government, which then has the right to decide what should be done with them. It may either set them free unconditionally, release them on payment of ransom, exchange them for Muslim prisoners of war held by the enemy or distribute them among the soldiers. A soldier may have sexual relations only with that woman who has been entrusted to him by the government.

(2) Even then, he may not have sexual relations with her until at least one menstrual period has expired; this is in order to establish that she is not already pregnant. If the woman concerned is pregnant one may not have sexual relations with her until after the birth of her child.

(3) It is not necessary for female captives of war to be People of the Book in order that sexual relations with them be permitted. The man to whom such a woman is entrusted has the right to have sexual relations with her regardless of her religious affiliations.

(4) Only that person to whom a female captive has been entrusted has the right to have sexual relations with her. Any child born to her will be

But it is lawful for you to seek out all women except these, offering them your wealth and the protection of wedlock rather than using them for the unfettered satisfaction of lust. And in exchange of what you enjoy by marrying them pay their bridal-due as an obligation. But there is no blame on you if you mutually agree to alter the settlement after it has been made. Surely Allah is All-Knowing, All-Wise. ▶

وَأُحِلَّ لَكُم مَّا وَرَآءَ ذَٰلِكُمْ أَن تَبْتَغُوا۟
بِأَمْوَٰلِكُم مُّحْصِنِينَ غَيْرَ مُسَٰفِحِينَ ۚ
فَمَا ٱسْتَمْتَعْتُم بِهِۦ مِنْهُنَّ فَـَٔاتُوهُنَّ
أُجُورَهُنَّ فَرِيضَةً ۚ وَلَا جُنَاحَ
عَلَيْكُمْ فِيمَا تَرَٰضَيْتُم بِهِۦ مِنۢ بَعْدِ
ٱلْفَرِيضَةِ ۚ إِنَّ ٱللَّهَ كَانَ عَلِيمًا
حَكِيمًا ﴿٢٤﴾

---

regarded as the legitimate child of her master, and will be entitled to all the rights laid down by the Law for one's issue. Moreover, once such a woman has given birth to a child she may not be sold to anyone, and on the death of her master she automatically becomes a free person.

(5) If the master allows the woman to marry someone else he ceases to have the right to sexual relations with her but retains the right to have her serve him in other ways.

(6) Although the Law has fixed the maximum number of wives at four, it has set no limit with regard to slave-girls. The Law does not lay down a limit in order to encourage people to accumulate huge armies of slave-girls, and thereby turn their homes into dens of sexual enjoyment. Rather the Law does not define the limit because the effects of war and the total number of female captives that would have to be disposed of after a certain war are unpredictable.

(7) In the same way as other rights of property are transferable, so are the proprietary rights regarding the captives of war that have been legally entrusted to a man by the state.

(8) Since the regular conferment of property rights is as legal an act as that of marriage, there is no basis for a person who feels no revulsion towards the idea of marriage to feel revulsion towards the idea of having sexual relations with a slave-girl duly entrusted to him.

(9) If a government confers proprietary rights to a man over a female captive of war it forfeits the right to withdraw those rights in the same

(25) And those of you who cannot afford to marry free, believing women (*muḥṣanāt*), then marry such believing women whom your right hands possess. Allah knows all about your faith. All of you belong to one another.[45] Marry them, then, with the leave of their guardians, and give them their bridal-due in a fair manner that they may live in the protection of wedlock rather than be either mere objects of unfettered lust or given to secret love affairs. Then if they become guilty of immoral conduct after they have entered into wedlock, they shall be liable to half the penalty to which free women (*muḥṣanāt*) are liable.[46] This relaxation is for those of you who fear to fall into sin by remaining unmarried.[47] But if you persevere, it is better for you. Allah is All-Forgiving, All-Compassionate.

وَمَن لَّمْ يَسْتَطِعْ مِنكُمْ طَوْلًا أَن
يَنكِحَ الْمُحْصَنَٰتِ الْمُؤْمِنَٰتِ
فَمِن مَّا مَلَكَتْ أَيْمَٰنُكُم مِّن
فَتَيَٰتِكُمُ الْمُؤْمِنَٰتِ ۚ وَاللَّهُ أَعْلَمُ
بِإِيمَٰنِكُم ۚ بَعْضُكُم مِّنۢ بَعْضٍ ۚ
فَانكِحُوهُنَّ بِإِذْنِ أَهْلِهِنَّ
وَءَاتُوهُنَّ أُجُورَهُنَّ بِالْمَعْرُوفِ
مُحْصَنَٰتٍ غَيْرَ مُسَٰفِحَٰتٍ وَلَا
مُتَّخِذَٰتِ أَخْدَانٍ ۚ فَإِذَآ أُحْصِنَّ
فَإِنْ أَتَيْنَ بِفَٰحِشَةٍ فَعَلَيْهِنَّ نِصْفُ
مَا عَلَى الْمُحْصَنَٰتِ مِنَ الْعَذَابِ ۚ
ذَٰلِكَ لِمَنْ خَشِىَ الْعَنَتَ مِنكُمْ ۚ
وَأَن تَصْبِرُوا خَيْرٌ لَّكُمْ ۗ وَاللَّهُ غَفُورٌ
رَّحِيمٌ ٢٥

way as the guardian (*walī*) of a woman ceases to have the right to withdraw his agreement to the marriage proposal after the marriage has been contracted.

(10) If a military commander permitted his soldiers to temporarily use the female captives as objects of sexual desire and distributed them among the soldiers for that purpose, such an act would be considered unlawful by Islamic Law. Such an act is not essentially different from fornication or adultery. For details see my book *Tafhīmāt*, vol. 2, pp. 366–84, and *Rasā'il wa Masā'il*, 6th edition, Lahore, 1976, vol. 3, pp. 102–4.

45. The difference between the status of people is relative. All Muslims are alike. If there is any true distinction its basis is a person's faith and

faith is not an exclusive privilege of the rich or so-called upper classes of the society. So it is possible for a slave-girl to be superior, in respect of her faith and morals, to a woman belonging to the elite of a society.

46. A superficial reading of this verse can lead to the mistaken conclusion, as Khawārij and others have done, that stoning is not the prescribed punishment for adultery. Such people ask: If stoning is the prescribed punishment for extra-marital sexual intercourse, then how is it possible to halve that punishment with regard to slave-girls? Such people have not noted carefully the wording of this verse. In this section (see verses 24–5) the term *muḥṣanāt* (protected women) is used in two different meanings. First, it is used in the sense of 'married women', that is, those who enjoy the protection of their husbands. Second, it is used in the sense of 'women belonging to families', i.e. those who enjoy the protection of families even though they may not be married. In the verse under discussion, the word *muḥṣanāt* is used in the latter sense, i.e. in the sense of women who enjoy the protection of families as opposed to slave-girls. At the same time, the word is also used in the first meaning, when slave-girls have acquired the protection accorded by the contract of marriage (*fa idhā uḥṣinna*), they will be liable to the punishment laid down in this verse if they have unlawful sexual intercourse.

It is therefore apparent that a free woman enjoys two kinds of protection. One is the protection of her family through which she remains protected even when she is not married. The second is the protection of her husband, which reinforces the protection of the family that she already enjoys. As long as the slave-girl remains a slave, she does not enjoy the protection of the family. However, when she is married she has the protection of her husband – and of her husband alone. This protection is partial. Even after marriage she is neither liberated from the bond of her master nor does she attain the status enjoyed by free women. The punishment prescribed for a married slave-girl is accordingly half the punishment of an unmarried free woman rather than half that of a married free woman.

This also explains that the punishment for unlawful sexual intercourse (*zinā*) laid down in *Sūrah al-Nūr* 24: 2 refers to the offence committed by unmarried free women alone, and it is in comparison with their punishment that the punishment of married slave women has been laid down as half. As for free married women, they deserve more severe punishment than the unmarried free women (*muḥṣanāt*) for they violate the double protection. Even though the Qur'ān does not specifically mention punishment by stoning it does allude to it in a subtle manner.

47. That is, if a man cannot afford to marry a free woman then he should marry a slave-girl with the permission of her master.

(26) Allah wants to make all this clear to you, and to guide you to the ways which the righteous have followed in the past. He will turn graciously towards you. Allah is All-Knowing, All-Wise.[48] (27) And Allah indeed wants to turn graciously towards you; but those who follow their lusts would want you to drift far away from the right way.[49] (28) Allah wants to lighten your burdens, for man was created weak.

يُرِيدُ ٱللَّهُ لِيُبَيِّنَ لَكُمْ وَيَهْدِيَكُمْ
سُنَنَ ٱلَّذِينَ مِن قَبْلِكُمْ وَيَتُوبَ
عَلَيْكُمْ وَٱللَّهُ عَلِيمٌ حَكِيمٌ ﴿٢٦﴾ وَٱللَّهُ
يُرِيدُ أَن يَتُوبَ عَلَيْكُمْ وَيُرِيدُ
ٱلَّذِينَ يَتَّبِعُونَ ٱلشَّهَوَٰتِ أَن
تَمِيلُوا۟ مَيْلًا عَظِيمًا ﴿٢٧﴾ يُرِيدُ ٱللَّهُ أَن
يُخَفِّفَ عَنكُمْ وَخُلِقَ ٱلْإِنسَـٰنُ
ضَعِيفًا ﴿٢٨﴾

---

48. Here a general reference is made to the directives embodied in this *sūrah*, as well as those revealed earlier in *Sūrah al-Baqarah* and which deal with social and collective matters. It is stressed that these directives reveal those lasting principles observed by the Prophets and their followers from the earliest times. It is merely out of His grace and benevolence that God liberated them from their state of Ignorance (*Jāhilīyah*) and opened to them the way of life of the righteous.

49. This refers to the hypocrites, the ultra-conservatives and the Jews who lived on the outskirts of Madina. Both the hypocrites and the conservatives were incensed at the reforms introduced by Islam, as these were diametrically opposed to the age-old customs and traditions of their society and culture. The reforms were numerous: a share of the inheritance was assigned to daughters; widows were liberated from bondage to the will of their husbands' families and were granted the freedom to marry whomever they wished after the expiry of the waiting-period (*'iddah*); marriage with one's step-mother and with two sisters together was prohibited; adopted sons were disinherited; and a foster-father's marriage with either the divorced or widowed wife of his adopted son was declared lawful.

These and other such reforms were so totally opposed to the customary laws of the Arabs that it was impossible for the elders and the blind devotees of the ways of their forefathers not to protest against them vehemently. They long continued to grumble against these injunctions. Mischievous people pointed to these innovations and exploited them by provoking people against the Prophet's movement of reform. For instance, they would meet those born as a result of the marriage which had been prohibited by

(29) Believers! Do not devour one another's possessions wrongfully; rather than that, let there be trading by mutual consent.[50] You shall not kill yourselves.[51] Surely Allah is ever Compassionate to you.[52] (30) And whoever does this by way of transgression and injustice him shall We surely cast into the Fire; that indeed is quite easy for Allah. (31) But if you avoid the major sins which you have been forbidden, We shall remit your (trivial) offences,[53] and cause you to enter an honourable abode.

يَٰٓأَيُّهَا ٱلَّذِينَ ءَامَنُوا۟ لَا
تَأْكُلُوٓا۟ أَمْوَٰلَكُم بَيْنَكُم
بِٱلْبَٰطِلِ إِلَّآ أَن تَكُونَ تِجَٰرَةً
عَن تَرَاضٍ مِّنكُمْ ۚ وَلَا تَقْتُلُوٓا۟ أَنفُسَكُمْ ۚ
إِنَّ ٱللَّهَ كَانَ بِكُمْ رَحِيمًا ﴿٢٩﴾ وَمَن
يَفْعَلْ ذَٰلِكَ عُدْوَٰنًا وَظُلْمًا فَسَوْفَ
نُصْلِيهِ نَارًا ۚ وَكَانَ ذَٰلِكَ عَلَى
ٱللَّهِ يَسِيرًا ﴿٣٠﴾ إِن تَجْتَنِبُوا۟ كَبَآئِرَ
مَا تُنْهَوْنَ عَنْهُ نُكَفِّرْ عَنكُمْ
سَيِّـَٔاتِكُمْ وَنُدْخِلْكُم مُّدْخَلًا
كَرِيمًا ﴿٣١﴾

Islam and try to infuriate them by saying that according to the new-fangled teachings of Muḥammad (peace be on him) the relationship between their parents was unlawful.

The Jews, on the other hand, had woven a complex network of laws and regulations for themselves. The result was that they had forbidden a great number of things which were, in fact, lawful. Additionally, they had introduced a number of superstitions into God's Law. It was argued that the simple and straightforward law of the Qur'ān was out of tune with the tastes and temperaments of both the religious leaders and the ordinary people. The Qur'ānic injunctions simply infuriated them and as soon as they came to know of any Qur'ānic law, they vehemently denounced it. They expected the Qur'ān to endorse and validate all the legal deductions and all the superstitions and myths of their forefathers, and to treat them as an integral part of the law of God. If the Qur'ān would not do so then they would refrain from recognizing it as the Book of God.

Let us take the following as an example. According to Jewish usage, a woman was considered completely unclean during her menstrual period. Hence, they neither ate the food she cooked, drank from the cup of water she offered nor even sat with her. It was even considered unwholesome to be touched by her. Thus for a few days every month a woman virtually became an untouchable in her own house. Owing to the influence of the Jews the same custom had found its way into the Arab families of Madina. When the Prophet (peace be on him) arrived in Madina, he was asked about this matter. In response to this query verse 222 of *Sūrah al-Baqarah* was revealed. In the light of the principle embodied in the verse the Prophet (peace be on him) made it clear that it was unlawful to have sexual intercourse with a woman during her menstrual period; but it was only that relationship, and no other, that was unlawful. (See Bukhārī, 'Ḥayḍ', 2, 3; Nasā'ī, 'Ḥayḍ', 9, 13, 16, 19, and 'Aḥkām', 13 – Ed.) This caused uproar among the Jews. They claimed that Muḥammad (peace be on him) was bent upon reversing all their legal injunctions to the extent that he wanted to legalize whatever they held as prohibited and prohibit whatever they held as lawful.

50. The expression 'wrongfully' embraces all transactions which are opposed to righteousness and which are either legally or morally reprehensible. By contrast, 'trade' signifies the mutual transfer of benefits between the parties concerned, such as that underlying those transactions in which one person provides whatever satisfies the needs of another person and is paid in return. 'Mutual consent' means that the exchange should be free of undue pressure, fraud and deception. Although bribery and interest apparently represent transactions based on mutual consent, closer examination reveals that such consent takes place by constraint and under pressure. In games of chance, too, the participants seem to consent freely to the outcome. This kind of consent, however, is due to the expectation entertained by the participants that they will win. No one takes part anticipating loss. Fraudulent transactions also seem to be based on the mutual consent of the parties concerned. That kind of consent, however, is based on the false assumption that no fraud is involved in the transaction. Nobody who knew that he would be subjected to fraud would consent to be a party to that transaction.

51. This can be considered either as complementary to the preceding sentence or as an independent statement. If it is complementary, it means that to consume the property of others by wrongful means is tantamount to courting one's own destruction; for such practices corrupt society on such a scale that even the most cunning are not spared their destructive consequences. This is in addition to the severe punishment that is bound to be meted out to such people in the Next Life.

Taken as an independent statement, it can mean either that one should not kill others or that one should not kill oneself. Both the words used and the sequence in which they have been placed by God in this verse make each of these three meanings feasible.

52. God wishes His creatures well; their well-being and salvation please Him, and it is out of benevolence that He has forbidden things harmful to human beings.

53. God is not overly exacting and severe in His judgements. He is not on the look out for trivial omissions and lapses on the part of His creatures

in order to punish them. God is prepared to condone minor omissions, and may even spare a man from being presented with a charge-sheet provided his record is free of major sins. But if a man's record is full of major transgressions, he will be required to explain all the sins he has committed – both major and minor.

We need at this stage to grasp the essential differences between major and minor sins. After reflecting on this question, in the light of the Qur'ān and *Sunnah*, it seems to me – and God alone knows what is absolutely correct – that three elements turn an act into a major sin:

(1) Violation of rights – be it either the rights of God, of parents, of other human beings or even of one's own self. The greater a person's rights, the greater is the sin in violating them. Hence sin is characterized in the Qur'ān as wrong-doing (*ẓulm*). It is for the same reason that associating others with God in His divinity is called the 'great wrong' in the Qur'ān. (See, for example, *Sūrah Luqmān* 31: 13 – Ed.)

(2) Insufficient fear of God, and arrogance and indifference towards Him, as a result of which man does not heed God's commandments, even wilfully violates them, and deliberately desists from carrying them out. The greater the brazenness, temerity and fearlessness with which one disobeys God, the more heinous is the sin in His eyes. It is for this reason that sin is also termed *ma'ṣiyah* (disobedience) and *fisq*. (See, for instance, *Sūrah al-Baqarah* 2: 26, 61; *Sūrah al-Ḥujurāt* 49: 11; *Sūrah al-Munāfiqūn* 63: 6; *Sūrah Hūd* 11: 59; *Sūrah Āl 'Imrān* 3: 112; *Sūrah al-Nisā'* 4: 42; *Sūrah al-Mā'idah* 5: 78; and *passim* for verbal forms derived from the word *ma'ṣiyah* and *fisq* – Ed.)

(3) Sin is aggravated by breaking those bonds and relationships on which the peace and tranquillity of social order rest. These bonds include the relationship between a man and his Lord, as well as that between a man and his fellow-beings. The more important a bond is, the greater is the harm done to the peace of human society when that bond is broken.

Likewise, the stronger the expectation that the sanctity of a certain bond will be honoured, the greater is the sin incurred through its desecration. Let us take the case of unlawful sexual intercourse in its various degrees. This act is inimical to the existence of a sound social order and is therefore a major sin. But in certain cases the sin becomes even graver. For instance, it is more serious if committed by a married person than by one who is unmarried. Similarly, unlawful sexual intercourse with a married woman is graver than with an unmarried woman. Again, to commit this act with one's neighbours is more heinous than with others, and to commit this act with women within the prohibited degrees, such as one's sister, daughter or mother, is far more abominable than with others. Further still, it is a much graver sin to commit such an act in places of worship than elsewhere. The difference in the degree of such sinfulness is based on the considerations we have mentioned above. Wherever the sanctity of a relationship is

(32) Do not covet what Allah has conferred more abundantly on some of you than others. Men shall have a share according to what they have earned, and women shall have a share according to what they have earned. Do ask of Allah His bounty. Allah has full knowledge of everything.[54]

وَلَا تَتَمَنَّوْا مَا فَضَّلَ ٱللَّهُ بِهِۦ بَعْضَكُمْ
عَلَىٰ بَعْضٍ ۚ لِّلرِّجَالِ نَصِيبٌ مِّمَّا
ٱكْتَسَبُوا۟ ۖ وَلِلنِّسَآءِ نَصِيبٌ مِّمَّا
ٱكْتَسَبْنَ ۚ وَسْـَٔلُوا۟ ٱللَّهَ مِن فَضْلِهِۦٓ ۗ
إِنَّ ٱللَّهَ كَانَ بِكُلِّ شَىْءٍ
عَلِيمًا ﴿٣٢﴾

---

normally respected, wherever there is a bond which deserves to be held sacred, and wherever the disruption of a particular relationship is likely to result in greater harm and corruption, the gravity of the sin increases. This is why in certain places the Qur'ān uses the term *fujūr* to denote sin. (See, for instance, *Sūrah al-Qiyāmah* 75: 5; *Sūrah al-Infiṭār* 82: 14; *Sūrah al-Shams* 91: 8 – Ed.)

54. This verse embodies a very important directive. By heeding it, man would be able to achieve a great measure of peace and tranquillity. God has not created all men alike. Some are handsome while others are ugly. The voices of some are sweet and those of others repulsive. Some are physically strong others are weak. Some have sound limbs others have inherent deformities. Some possess outstanding physical and mental abilities while others lack them. Some are born in favourable circumstances and others not. Some have been endowed with more resources than others. It is this diversity which gives variety to human civilization, and hence serves a useful purpose. Whenever man superimposes distinctions of his own over and above this natural inequality he disrupts the natural order of things, and paves the way for corruption. Likewise, when anyone attempts to obliterate all differences between human beings he in fact engages in a war against nature and inflicts wrongs of another kind.

Man is naturally inclined to feel uneasy whenever he sees someone else ahead of him. This is the root of jealousy and envy, of cut-throat competition and animosity, of mutual strife and conflict. These feelings often obsess a person to such a degree that whenever fair means do not prove effective, he resorts to unfair means to achieve his ambitions. In the present verse, God directs us not to allow this kind of mentality to take hold of us. The import of the directive is that one should not yearn for the good that God has bestowed on others. One should rather pray to God to bestow upon one the good which is in one's best interests according to God's wisdom and knowledge.

(33) And to everyone We have appointed rightful heirs to what the parents and near of kin might leave behind. As to those with whom you have made a solemn covenant, give them their share. Allah watches over all things.[55]

(34) Men are the protectors and maintainers of women[56] because Allah has made one of them excel over the other,[57] and because they spend out of their possessions (to support them).

وَلِكُلٍّ جَعَلْنَا مَوَٰلِيَ مِمَّا تَرَكَ
ٱلْوَٰلِدَانِ وَٱلْأَقْرَبُونَ وَٱلَّذِينَ
عَقَدَتْ أَيْمَٰنُكُمْ فَـَٔاتُوهُمْ
نَصِيبَهُمْ إِنَّ ٱللَّهَ كَانَ عَلَىٰ كُلِّ
شَىْءٍ شَهِيدًا ﴿٣٣﴾ ٱلرِّجَالُ
قَوَّٰمُونَ عَلَى ٱلنِّسَآءِ بِمَا فَضَّلَ
ٱللَّهُ بَعْضَهُمْ عَلَىٰ بَعْضٍ وَبِمَآ أَنفَقُوا۟
مِنْ أَمْوَٰلِهِمْ

The statement that 'men shall have a share according to what they have earned and women shall have a share according to what they have earned' seems to mean, to the best of my understanding, that men and women shall have their shares of good and evil, depending on the good and evil they have earned in using the resources bestowed upon them by God.

55. According to Arab customary law, those who concluded compacts of alliance and friendship also became mutual heirs. Likewise, an adopted son inherited from his foster-father. While abrogating this customary law, this verse reveals that inheritance goes to one's kin according to the rules for the distribution of inheritance laid down by God Himself. However, if a man has made commitments to people, he has the right to give away to them whatever he wishes during his lifetime.

56. A *qawwām* or *qayyim* is a person responsible for administering and supervising the affairs of either an individual or an organization, for protecting and safeguarding them and taking care of their needs.

57. The verb used here – a derivative of the root *fḍl* – is not used to mean that some people have been invested with superior honour and dignity. Rather it means that God has endowed one of the sexes (i.e. the male sex) with certain qualities which He has not endowed the other sex with, at least not to an equal extent. Thus it is the male who is qualified to function as head of the family. The female has been so constituted that she should live under his care and protection.

Thus righteous women are obedient and guard the rights of men in their absence under Allah's protection.[58] As for women of whom you fear rebellion, admonish them, and remain apart from them in beds, and beat them.[59] Then if they obey you, do not seek ways to harm them. Allah is Exalted, Great.

فَالصَّٰلِحَٰتُ قَٰنِتَٰتٌ
حَٰفِظَٰتٌ لِّلْغَيْبِ بِمَا حَفِظَ ٱللَّهُ ۚ
وَٱلَّٰتِى تَخَافُونَ نُشُوزَهُنَّ
فَعِظُوهُنَّ وَٱهْجُرُوهُنَّ فِى
ٱلْمَضَاجِعِ وَٱضْرِبُوهُنَّ ۖ فَإِنْ
أَطَعْنَكُمْ فَلَا تَبْغُوا۟ عَلَيْهِنَّ سَبِيلًا ۗ
إِنَّ ٱللَّهَ كَانَ عَلِيًّا كَبِيرًا ٣٤

---

58. It is reported in a tradition from the Prophet (peace be on him) that he said: 'The best wife is she who, if you look at her, will please you; who, if you bid her to do something, will obey; and who will safeguard herself and your property in your absence.' (Cited by Ibn Kathīr, and reported by Ṭabarī and Ibn Abī Ḥātim. See *Mukhtaṣar Tafsīr Ibn Kathīr*, 3 vols., ed. Muḥammad 'Alī al-Ṣābūnī, 7th edition, Beirut, 1402 A.H./1981 C.E.; vol. 1, p. 385 and n. 1 – Ed.) This tradition contains the best explanation of the above verse. It should be borne in mind, however, that obedience to God has priority over a woman's duty to obey her husband. If a woman's husband either asks her to disobey God or prevents her from performing a duty imposed upon her by God, she should refuse to carry out his command. Obedience to her husband in this case would be a sin. However, were the husband to prevent is wife from performing either supererogatory Prayer or Fasting – as distinct from the obligatory ones – she should obey him, for such acts would not be accepted by God if performed by a woman in defiance of her husband's wish. (See Abū Dā'ūd, 'Ṣawm', 73; Ibn Mājah, 'Ṣiyām', 53 – Ed.)

59. This does not mean that a man should resort to these three measures all at once, but that they may be employed if a wife adopts an attitude of obstinate defiance. So far as the actual application of these measures is concerned, there should, naturally, be some correspondence between the fault and the punishment that is administered. Moreover, it is obvious that wherever a light touch can prove effective one should not resort to sterner measures. Whenever the Prophet (peace be on him) permitted a man to administer corporal punishment to his wife, he did so with reluctance, and continued to express his distaste for it. And even in cases where it is necessary, the Prophet (peace be on him) directed men not to hit across the face, nor to beat severely nor to use anything that might leave marks on the body. (See Ibn Mājah, 'Nikāḥ', 3 – Ed.)

(35) If you fear a breach between the two, appoint an arbitrator from his people and an arbitrator from her people. If they both want to set things right,[60] Allah will bring about reconciliation between them. Allah knows all, is well aware of everything.[61]

وَإِنْ خِفْتُمْ شِقَاقَ بَيْنِهِمَا فَابْعَثُوا
حَكَمًا مِّنْ أَهْلِهِۦ وَحَكَمًا مِّنْ أَهْلِهَآ
إِن يُرِيدَآ إِصْلَٰحًا يُوَفِّقِ ٱللَّهُ بَيْنَهُمَآ
إِنَّ ٱللَّهَ كَانَ عَلِيمًا خَبِيرًا ﴿٣٥﴾

---

60. The statement: 'if they both want to set things right', may be interpreted as referring either to the mediators or to the spouses concerned. Every dispute can be resolved providing the parties concerned desire reconciliation, and the mediators too are keen to remove the misunderstandings between them and to bring them together.

61. Whenever the relationship between a husband and a wife starts to break down, an attempt should first be made to resolve the dispute at the family level, before it is aggravated and leads to the disruption of the matrimonial tie. The procedure to be followed is that two persons, one on behalf of each family, should be nominated to look into the matter together and devise means whereby the misunderstanding between the spouses may be brought to an end. Who should nominate these mediators? God has not specified this so as to allow people full freedom to choose the most convenient arrangement. The parties would be free, for instance, to decide that the mediators be nominated either by the spouses themselves or by the elders of their respective families. If the dispute is brought before the court, the latter also has the right to nominate mediators, representing the families of both parties, before referring the matter for judicial verdict.

There is disagreement among Muslim jurists about the extent of the mediators' authority. The Ḥanafī and Shāfi'ī schools are of the opinion that they normally have no authority to issue a binding verdict. All they may do is to recommend the solution they advocate, whereafter the spouses have the right either to accept or to reject it. The exception is if the spouses have nominated the mediators to act on their behalf in regard to either *ṭalāq* or *khul'*: they will then be bound by their verdict. This is the opinion of the Ḥanafī and Shāfi'ī schools. Another group of jurists argues that the authority of the mediators is confined to deciding how the spouses should reconcile their differences, and does not extend to the annulment of marriage. This is the opinion of Ḥasan al-Baṣrī and Qatādah, among others. Yet another group holds the opinion that the mediators have full authority both in respect of reconciliation and annulment of marriage. This is the

(36) Serve Allah and ascribe no partner to Him. Do good to your parents, to near of kin, to orphans, and to the needy, and to the neighbour who is of kin and to the neighbour who is a stranger, and to the companion by your side,[62] and to the wayfarer, and to those whom your right hands possess.

۞ وَاعْبُدُوا اللَّهَ وَلَا تُشْرِكُوا بِهِ
شَيْئًا وَبِالْوَالِدَيْنِ إِحْسَانًا وَبِذِي
الْقُرْبَىٰ وَالْيَتَامَىٰ وَالْمَسَاكِينِ
وَالْجَارِ ذِي الْقُرْبَىٰ وَالْجَارِ
الْجُنُبِ وَالصَّاحِبِ بِالْجَنْبِ
وَابْنِ السَّبِيلِ وَمَا مَلَكَتْ أَيْمَانُكُمْ

---

opinion of Ibn 'Abbās, Sa'īd b. Jubayr, Ibrāhīm al-Nakha'ī, al-Sha'bī, Muḥammad b. Sīrīn and several other authorities.

The precedents which have come down from early Islam, however, are the judgements of 'Uthmān and 'Alī. These indicate that they conferred upon the mediators the authority to issue judgements binding on both parties. When the dispute between 'Aqīl b. Abī Ṭālib and his wife Fāṭimah b. 'Utbah b. Rabī'ah came up for the judgement of 'Uthmān, he nominated Ibn 'Abbās and Mu'āwiyah b. Abī Sufyān from the families of the husband and the wife respectively. He also told them that if they thought that separation was preferable, they should declare the marriage annulled. In a similar dispute 'Alī nominated mediators and authorized them either to bring about reconciliation or annul the marriage, whichever they considered appropriate. This shows that the mediators do not have judicial authority as such. (See the commentaries of Ibn Kathīr and Jaṣṣāṣ on this verse – Ed.) Such authority, however, may be conferred upon them by the courts, in which case their decision will have the force of a judicial verdict.

62. The expression *al-ṣāḥib bi al-janb* (the companion by your side) embraces those with whom one has friendly relations of an abiding nature as well as those with whom one's relationship is transient: for instance, either the person who walks beside one on the way to the market or who sits beside one while buying things from the same shop or one's fellow traveller. Even this temporary relationship imposes certain claims on every refined and decent person – that he should treat him, as far as possible, in a kind and gracious manner and avoid causing him any inconvenience.

Allah does not love the arrogant and the boastful, (37) who are niggardly and bid others to be niggardly and conceal the bounty which Allah has bestowed upon them.[63] We have kept in readiness a humiliating chastisement for such deniers (of Allah's bounty). (38) Allah does not love those who spend out of their wealth to make a show of it to people when they believe neither in Allah nor in the Last Day. And he who has taken Satan for a companion has indeed taken for himself a very bad companion. (39) What harm would have befallen them if they had believed in Allah and the Last Day, and spent on charity what Allah had bestowed upon them as sustenance? For Allah indeed has full knowledge of them. (40) Indeed Allah wrongs none, not even as much as an atom's weight.

إِنَّ ٱللَّهَ لَا يُحِبُّ مَن كَانَ مُخۡتَالٗا
فَخُورًا ﴿٣٦﴾ ٱلَّذِينَ يَبۡخَلُونَ وَيَأۡمُرُونَ
ٱلنَّاسَ بِٱلۡبُخۡلِ وَيَكۡتُمُونَ
مَآ ءَاتَىٰهُمُ ٱللَّهُ مِن فَضۡلِهِۦۗ وَأَعۡتَدۡنَا
لِلۡكَٰفِرِينَ عَذَابٗا مُّهِينٗا ﴿٣٧﴾
وَٱلَّذِينَ يُنفِقُونَ أَمۡوَٰلَهُمۡ رِئَآءَ
ٱلنَّاسِ وَلَا يُؤۡمِنُونَ بِٱللَّهِ وَلَا بِٱلۡيَوۡمِ
ٱلۡأٓخِرِۗ وَمَن يَكُنِ ٱلشَّيۡطَٰنُ لَهُۥ قَرِينٗا فَسَآءَ
قَرِينٗا ﴿٣٨﴾ وَمَاذَا عَلَيۡهِمۡ لَوۡ ءَامَنُواْ بِٱللَّهِ
وَٱلۡيَوۡمِ ٱلۡأٓخِرِ وَأَنفَقُواْ مِمَّا رَزَقَهُمُ ٱللَّهُۚ
وَكَانَ ٱللَّهُ بِهِمۡ عَلِيمًا ﴿٣٩﴾ إِنَّ ٱللَّهَ لَا يَظۡلِمُ
مِثۡقَالَ ذَرَّةٖۖ

---

63. Concealing God's bounty is to live as if God had not bestowed that bounty. If anyone has considerable wealth and yet lives at a standard strikingly lower than that warranted by his income, if he shuns spending on himself and his family, and also on helping other creatures of God, and avoids providing financial support to any philanthropic cause, then he creates the false impression of being in a state of financial stringency. This is sheer ingratitude to God. The Prophet (peace be on him) is reported, according to a tradition, as saying: 'If God confers a bounty on somebody, He would like to see that benefaction displayed.' (Ibn Kathīr, vol. 4, p. 486 – Ed.) This means that a person's day-to-day life, his eating and drinking, his dress and his abode and his spending on others, all these should reflect God's bounty.

Whenever a man does good, He multiplies it two-fold, and bestows out of His grace a mighty reward. (41) Consider, then, when We shall bring forward witnesses from every community, and will bring you (O Muḥammad!) as a witness against them all.[64] (42) Those who disbelieved and disobeyed the Messenger will wish on that Day that the earth were levelled with them. They will not be able to conceal anything from Allah.

(43) Believers! Do not draw near to the Prayer while you are intoxicated[65] until you know what you are saying[66] nor while you are defiled[67] – save when you are travelling – until you have washed yourselves.[68] ▶

وَإِن تَكُ حَسَنَةً يُضَٰعِفْهَا وَيُؤْتِ
مِن لَّدُنْهُ أَجْرًا عَظِيمًا ﴿٤٠﴾ فَكَيْفَ
إِذَا جِئْنَا مِن كُلِّ أُمَّةٍ بِشَهِيدٍ
وَجِئْنَا بِكَ عَلَىٰ هَٰٓؤُلَآءِ شَهِيدًا ﴿٤١﴾
يَوْمَئِذٍ يَوَدُّ ٱلَّذِينَ كَفَرُوا۟ وَعَصَوُا۟
ٱلرَّسُولَ لَوْ تُسَوَّىٰ بِهِمُ ٱلْأَرْضُ وَلَا يَكْتُمُونَ
ٱللَّهَ حَدِيثًا ﴿٤٢﴾ يَٰٓأَيُّهَا ٱلَّذِينَ ءَامَنُوا۟
لَا تَقْرَبُوا۟ ٱلصَّلَوٰةَ وَأَنتُمْ سُكَٰرَىٰ
حَتَّىٰ تَعْلَمُوا۟ مَا تَقُولُونَ وَلَا جُنُبًا
إِلَّا عَابِرِى سَبِيلٍ حَتَّىٰ تَغْتَسِلُوا۟

64. The Prophet of each age will stand as a witness before God against his people; he will testify that he conveyed to them the true way of life, and showed them the right outlook and the fundamentals of moral conduct revealed to him by God. The testimony of the Prophet Muḥammad (peace be on him) will be to the same effect, and the Qur'ān indicates that he will stand as a witness to the period beginning with his advent as a Prophet right through to the Day of Judgement. (See *Towards Understanding the Qur'ān,* vol. I, *Sūrah* 3, n. 69.)

65. This is the second in the chronological sequence of injunctions concerning intoxicants. We came across the first injunction in *Sūrah al-Baqarah* 2: 219. In that verse God merely indicated that drinking wine was a great sin, making it clear that it was reprehensible in His sight. This was quite enough to make some Muslims give up liquor altogether, though many others still took intoxicating drinks: they sometimes stood up to pray while still under the influence of alcohol, so that they even made mistakes in their recitations. This second injunction was probably revealed at the

beginning of 4 A.H., making it forbidden, thenceforth, to pray in a state of intoxication. This led people to alter their drinking times. They drank only at those hours when there was no fear of their remaining under the influence of intoxicants when the time for Prayer came. The injunction embodying unconditional prohibition of intoxicants was revealed not long afterwards. (See *Sūrah al-Mā'idah* 5: 90–1.)

It should also be borne in mind that the word used in the verse is derived from *sukr*, which embraces not merely intoxicating liquors but everything which causes intoxication. The injunction contained in the verse is valid even now, for though the use of intoxicants as such has been completely prohibited, praying in a state of intoxication is a graver sin.

66. It is on this basis that the Prophet (peace be on him) directed anyone who is under the influence of sleep, and dozes off again and again during the Prayer, to stop praying and go to bed. (Ibn Kathīr, vol. 4, p. 494 – Ed.)

Some people argue, on the basis of this verse, that the Prayer of one who does not understand the Arabic text of the Qur'ān will not be accepted. Apart from taking things too far such a conclusion is not supported by the words in the text. The expression used by the Qur'ān is neither حتى تفقهوا nor even حتى تفهموا ما تقولون. On the contrary, the expression is حَتَّىٰ تَعْلَمُوا مَا تَقُولُونَ (i.e. until you *know* what you are saying, rather than 'until you *understand*' what you are saying). What is required is that while praying one should at least be conscious enough to know what one is uttering in the Prayer.

67. The term *janābah* denotes the state of major ritual impurity, and is derived from the root meaning: 'to ward off'. The word *ajnabī*, meaning foreigner or stranger, is also derived from the same root. In Islamic terminology, *janābah* denotes the state of ritual impurity (in both male and female) which results from the act of intercourse or from seminal emission (either from sexual stimulation or from a wet dream).

68. One group of jurists and Qur'ānic commentators interpret this verse to mean that one should not enter a mosque in the state of major ritual impurity (*janābah*), unless out of necessity. This is the opinion of 'Abd Allāh b. Mas'ūd, Anas b. Mālik, Ḥasan al-Baṣrī, Ibrāhīm al-Nakha'ī and others. Another group thinks that the reference here is to travel. In the opinion of this group, if a traveller is in the state of major ritual impurity he may resort to *tayammum* (i.e. symbolic ablution attained through wiping the hands and face with clean earth). (See *Sūrah al-Mā'idah* 5: 6 and also n. 70 below – Ed.) This group considers it permissible to stay in the mosque in this state provided one has performed ablution. This is the view of 'Alī, Ibn 'Abbās, Sa'īd b. Jubayr and some other authorities. The opinion that a traveller in the state of major impurity may perform ablution if he is unable to take a bath is supported by consensus, but while some authorities infer it from traditions others base it on the Qur'ānic verse mentioned above. (See Jaṣṣās, vol. 2, pp. 201–6; and Ibn Kathīr's commentary on this verse – Ed.)

If you are either ill or travelling or have satisfied a want of nature or have had contact with women[69] and can find no water, then betake yourselves to pure earth, passing with it lightly over your face and your hands.[70] Surely Allah is All-Relenting, All-Forgiving.

(44) Have you not seen those to whom a portion of the Book was given?[71] They purchased error for themselves, and wish that you too lose the right way? ►

وَإِن كُنتُم مَّرْضَىٰٓ أَوْ عَلَىٰ سَفَرٍ أَوْ جَآءَ
أَحَدٌ مِّنكُم مِّنَ ٱلْغَآئِطِ أَوْ لَٰمَسْتُمُ
ٱلنِّسَآءَ فَلَمْ تَجِدُوا۟ مَآءً فَتَيَمَّمُوا۟
صَعِيدًا طَيِّبًا فَٱمْسَحُوا۟ بِوُجُوهِكُمْ
وَأَيْدِيكُمْ إِنَّ ٱللَّهَ كَانَ عَفُوًّا غَفُورًا
﴿٤٣﴾ أَلَمْ تَرَ إِلَى ٱلَّذِينَ أُوتُوا۟ نَصِيبًا مِّنَ
ٱلْكِتَٰبِ يَشْتَرُونَ ٱلضَّلَٰلَةَ وَيُرِيدُونَ
أَن تَضِلُّوا۟ ٱلسَّبِيلَ ﴿٤٤﴾

---

69. There is disagreement as to what is meant here by the verb *lāmastum*, which literally means 'you touched'. 'Alī, Ibn 'Abbās, Abū Mūsá al-Ash'arī, Ubayy b. Ka'b, Sa'īd b. Jubayr, Ḥasan al-Baṣrī and several other leading jurists are of the opinion that it signifies sexual intercourse.* Abū Ḥanīfah and his school, and Sufyān al-Thawrī follow this view. But 'Abd Allāh b. Mas'ūd and 'Abd Allāh b. 'Umar hold that it signifies the act of touching, the mere placing of one's hand on a woman's body. This is the opinion adopted by Shāfi'ī. Other jurists take an intermediate position. Mālik, for instance, is of the opinion that if a man and a woman touch each other with sexual desire, their ablution is nullified, and if they want to perform the Prayer they are obliged to renew their ablution. He sees nothing objectionable, however, in the mere fact of a man touching a woman's body, or vice versa, provided the act is not motivated by sexual desire. (See Ibn Kathīr's commentary on this verse – Ed.)

70. The detailed rules of *tayammum* are as follows: A man who either needs to perform ablution or take a bath to attain the state of purity for ritual Prayer may resort to *tayammum* provided water is not available to him. Only then may he perform the Prayer. Permission to resort to *tayammum*, rather than make ablution with water or take a bath, is also extended to invalids whose health is likely to be harmed by the use of water.

---

*We have tried to convey both shades of meaning in the translation of the verse by using the expression 'have had contact with' instead of 'touched' – Ed.

Tayammum literally means 'to turn to, to aim at, to head for, to intend'. The relevance of the term in the Islamic religious context is that when water is either not available or when its use is likely to cause harm one should 'turn to' clean earth.

There is some disagreement among jurists about the manner of performing *tayammum*. According to some, one should strike one's palms on the clean earth, then gently wipe one's face, then strike one's hands again and gently wipe one's hands and arms up to the elbows. This is the view of Abū Ḥanīfah, Shāfi'ī, Mālik and the majority of jurists. Among the Companions and Successors, 'Alī, 'Abd Allāh b. 'Umar, Ḥasan al-Baṣrī, Sha'bī, Sālim b. 'Abd Allāh and many others are of the same opinion. Other jurists are of the view that it is sufficient to strike one's palms once on the clean earth, then wipe one's face and one's hands up to the wrist; it is not necessary to wipe the arms between the wrist and the elbow. This is the opinion of 'Aṭā', Makḥūl, Awzā'ī, and Aḥmad b. Ḥanbal, and is generally followed by the Ahl al-Ḥadīth. (Cf. Qurṭubī, *Aḥkam al-Qur'ān*, vol. 5, pp. 239–41.)

Tayammum is not necessarily performed by striking one's palms on earth proper. It is sufficient to strike the palms on anything which either has dust over it or anything consisting of the dry elements of the earth.

It may be asked how one attains purity by striking one's palms on the earth and then wiping one's hands and face with them. In fact *tayammum* is a useful psychological device to keep the sense of ritual purity and the sanctity of Prayer alive in man's mind even when water – the principal agent of purification – is not available. The value of *tayammum* is that even if a man is unable to use water – and no one knows how long this situation may persist – his sensitivity to cleanliness and purity will endure. He will continue to observe the regulation laid down by the Law in respect of cleanliness and purity, and the distinction between the states in which one may and may not perform the Prayer will not be erased.

71. The Qur'ān often characterizes the scholars of the People of the Book as those who 'were given a portion of the Book'. The reason for the use of this expression, in the first place, is that they caused a part of the divine revelation to be lost. Moreover, they had detached themselves from the spirit and purpose of the divine revelation which was available to them. Their concern with the Scripture was confined to verbal discussions, arguments about legal minutiae, and speculation about subtle and involved philosophical and theological questions. This had so alienated even their religious leaders and scholars from the true concept of religion that they lost true religious devotion and piety.

(45) Allah knows your enemies better and Allah suffices as a protector and Allah suffices as a helper. (46) Among those who have become Jews[72] there are some who alter the words from their context,[73] and make a malicious play with their tongues and seek to revile the true faith. They say: 'We have heard and we disobey' (*sami'nā wa 'aṣaynā*),[74] 'Do hear us, may you turn dumb' (*isma' ghayr musma'*),[75] and 'Hearken to us' (*rā'inā*). It would indeed have been better for them and more upright if they had said: 'We have heard and we obey' (*sami'nā wa aṭa'nā*)[76] and: 'Do listen to us, and look at us (with kindness)' (*wa isma' wa unẓurnā*). But Allah has cursed them because of their disbelief. Scarcely do they believe.

وَٱللَّهُ أَعْلَمُ بِأَعْدَآئِكُمْ ۚ وَكَفَىٰ بِٱللَّهِ وَلِيًّا
وَكَفَىٰ بِٱللَّهِ نَصِيرًا ﴿٤٥﴾ مِّنَ ٱلَّذِينَ هَادُوا۟
يُحَرِّفُونَ ٱلْكَلِمَ عَن مَّوَاضِعِهِۦ
وَيَقُولُونَ سَمِعْنَا وَعَصَيْنَا وَٱسْمَعْ
غَيْرَ مُسْمَعٍ وَرَٰعِنَا لَيًّۢا بِأَلْسِنَتِهِمْ
وَطَعْنًا فِى ٱلدِّينِ ۚ وَلَوْ أَنَّهُمْ قَالُوا۟ سَمِعْنَا
وَأَطَعْنَا وَٱسْمَعْ وَٱنظُرْنَا لَكَانَ خَيْرًا لَّهُمْ
وَأَقْوَمَ وَلَٰكِن لَّعَنَهُمُ ٱللَّهُ بِكُفْرِهِمْ
فَلَا يُؤْمِنُونَ إِلَّا قَلِيلًا ﴿٤٦﴾

---

72. It is to be noted that this expression means 'they *became* Jews', rather than 'they *were* Jews'. For, originally, they were nothing but Muslims, just as the followers of every Prophet are Muslims. Only later on did they become merely 'Jews'.

73. This signifies three things. First, that they tampered with the text of the Scripture. Second, that they misinterpreted the Scripture and thereby distorted the meanings of the verses of the Book. Third, that they came and stayed in the company of the Prophet (peace be on him) and his Companions and listened to the conversations which took place there, then went among other people and misreported what they had heard. They did this with the malicious intent of bringing the Muslims into disrepute and thereby preventing people from embracing Islam.

(47) O you who have been granted the Book! Do believe in what We have (now) revealed, which confirms the revelation which you already possess.[77] Do this before We alter countenances, turning them backwards, or lay a curse upon them as We cursed the Sabbath-men.[78] Bear in mind that Allah's command is done. (48) Surely Allah does not forgive that a partner be ascribed to Him,[79] although He forgives any other sins for whomever He wills.[80] He who associates anyone with Allah in His divinity has indeed forged a mighty lie and committed an awesome sin.

يَٰٓأَيُّهَا ٱلَّذِينَ أُوتُوا۟ ٱلْكِتَٰبَ ءَامِنُوا۟
بِمَا نَزَّلْنَا مُصَدِّقًا لِّمَا مَعَكُم مِّن قَبْلِ
أَن نَّطْمِسَ وُجُوهًا فَنَرُدَّهَا عَلَىٰٓ
أَدْبَارِهَآ أَوْ نَلْعَنَهُمْ كَمَا لَعَنَّآ أَصْحَٰبَ
ٱلسَّبْتِ ۚ وَكَانَ أَمْرُ ٱللَّهِ مَفْعُولًا ﴿٤٧﴾
إِنَّ ٱللَّهَ لَا يَغْفِرُ أَن يُشْرَكَ بِهِۦ وَيَغْفِرُ مَا دُونَ
ذَٰلِكَ لِمَن يَشَآءُ ۚ وَمَن يُشْرِكْ بِٱللَّهِ فَقَدِ
ٱفْتَرَىٰٓ إِثْمًا عَظِيمًا ﴿٤٨﴾

---

74. When the ordinances of God are announced to them, they loudly proclaim: 'Yes, we have heard', (*sami'nā*), but then they whisper: 'And we disobeyed' (*'aṣaynā*). Or else they pronounce *aṭa'nā* ('we obey') with such a twist of the tongue that it becomes indistinguishable from *'aṣaynā*.

75. Whenever they wanted to say something to the Prophet (peace be on him) they would say, *'isma'* (listen), but added to this the expression, '*ghayr musma'*' which had several meanings. It could either be a polite expression, meaning that he was worthy of such deep respect that one should say nothing to his dislike or it could have a malicious implication, meaning that he did not deserve to be addressed by anybody. It also meant the imprecation: 'May God turn you deaf.'

76. For an explanation of this see *Towards Understanding the Qur'ān*, vol. I, *Sūrah* 2, n. 108.

77. See *ibid., Sūrah* 3, n. 2.

78. See *ibid., Sūrah* 2, nn. 82 and 83.

(49) Have you not seen those who boast of their righteousness, even though it is Allah Who grants righteousness to whomsoever He wills? They are not wronged even as much as the husk of a date-stone (if they do not receive righteousness). (50) See how they forge lies about Allah! This in itself is a manifest sin.

(51) Have you not seen those to whom a portion of the Book was given? They believe in baseless superstitions[81] and *ṭāghūt* (false deities),[82] and say about the unbelievers that they are better guided than those who believe.[83] ►

أَلَمْ تَرَ إِلَى ٱلَّذِينَ يُزَكُّونَ أَنفُسَهُم ۚ بَلِ ٱللَّهُ
يُزَكِّى مَن يَشَآءُ وَلَا يُظْلَمُونَ فَتِيلًا ﴿٤٩﴾
ٱنظُرْ كَيْفَ يَفْتَرُونَ عَلَى ٱللَّهِ ٱلْكَذِبَ ۖ
وَكَفَىٰ بِهِۦٓ إِثْمًا مُّبِينًا ﴿٥٠﴾ أَلَمْ تَرَ إِلَى
ٱلَّذِينَ أُوتُوا۟ نَصِيبًا مِّنَ
ٱلْكِتَٰبِ يُؤْمِنُونَ بِٱلْجِبْتِ
وَٱلطَّٰغُوتِ وَيَقُولُونَ لِلَّذِينَ كَفَرُوا۟
هَٰٓؤُلَآءِ أَهْدَىٰ مِنَ ٱلَّذِينَ ءَامَنُوا۟
سَبِيلًا ﴿٥١﴾

79. Although the People of the Book claimed to follow the Prophets and the Divine Books they had, in fact, fallen a prey to polytheism.

80. The purpose of this verse is not to tell man that he may commit any sin as long as he does not associate others with God in His divinity. The object is rather to impress upon those who had begun to regard polytheism as a trivial matter that it constitutes the most serious offence in God's sight, an offence so serious that while other sins may be pardoned this will not. Jewish religious scholars were meticulous about questions of subsidiary importance, and devoted all their time to pondering over legal subtleties which their jurists had painstakingly elaborated by far-fetched deductions. Yet they treated polytheism so lightly that they neither abstained from it themselves nor tried to prevent their people from falling a prey to polytheistic ideas and practices nor found anything objectionable in establishing cordial relations with the polytheists nor in supporting them.

(52) Such are the ones whom Allah has cursed; and he whom Allah curses has none to come to his help. (53) Have they any share in the dominion (of Allah)? Had that been so, they would never have granted people even as much as the speck on a date-stone.[84] ▶

أُوْلَٰٓئِكَ ٱلَّذِينَ لَعَنَهُمُ ٱللَّهُ ۖ وَمَن يَلْعَنِ
ٱللَّهُ فَلَن تَجِدَ لَهُۥ نَصِيرًا ﴿٥٢﴾ أَمْ لَهُمْ نَصِيبٌ
مِّنَ ٱلْمُلْكِ فَإِذًا لَّا يُؤْتُونَ ٱلنَّاسَ
نَقِيرًا ﴿٥٣﴾

---

81. *Jibt* signifies 'a thing devoid of any true basis and bereft of all usefulness'. In Islamic terminology the various forms of sorcery, divination and soothsaying, in short all superstitions, are termed *jibt*. It is reported in a tradition that, 'to divine things from the cries of animals, or the traces of animals' paws, or the flight of birds, constitutes *jibt*'. Thus, *jibt* may be roughly translated as 'superstition'. (See Abū Dā'ūd, 'Ṭibb', 23; Aḥmad b. Ḥanbal, *Musnad*, vol. 3, p. 477 and vol. 5, p. 60 – Ed.)

82. For explanation see *Towards Understanding the Qur'ān*, vol. I, *Sūrah* 2, nn. 286 and 288.

83. The obstinacy of the Jewish religious scholars had reached such a point that they brazenly declared the followers of Muḥammad (peace be on him) to be in greater error than even the polytheists of Arabia. This was despite the fact that they knew that the Muslims stood for absolute monotheism while their opponents believed in that undisguised polytheism which has been so vehemently denounced throughout the Bible.

84. The Jews, who had judged the Muslims to be in error, are asked if they have some share in God's authority which entitles them to judge who is rightly guided and who is not. If the Jews really had any share in that authority, no one would receive so much as a penny from them, for their hearts are too small to even acknowledge the truth, let alone credit others with righteousness and goodness. This verse can also be understood somewhat differently so as to pose the following question to the Jews: 'Is it a matter of your possessing some dominion which you are reluctant to share with others?' Obviously, the question was merely one of acknowledging the Truth, and they were too grudging to credit others with it.

(54) Do they envy others for the bounty that Allah has bestowed upon them?[85] (Let them bear in mind that) We bestowed upon the house of Abraham the Book and Wisdom, and We bestowed upon them a mighty dominion,[86] (55) whereupon some of them believed, and others turned away.[87] (Those who turn away), Hell suffices for a blaze. (56) Surely We shall cast those who reject Our signs into the Fire; and as often as their skins are burnt out, We shall give them other skins in exchange that they may fully taste the chastisement. Surely Allah is All-Mighty, All-Wise. (57) And those who believe and do good deeds, We shall cause them to enter the Gardens beneath which rivers flow. There they shall abide for ever. There they shall have spouses purified and there We shall cause them to enter a shelter with plenteous shade.

أَمْ يَحْسُدُونَ ٱلنَّاسَ عَلَىٰ مَآ ءَاتَىٰهُمُ ٱللَّهُ
مِن فَضْلِهِۦ ۖ فَقَدْ ءَاتَيْنَآ ءَالَ إِبْرَٰهِيمَ
ٱلْكِتَـٰبَ وَٱلْحِكْمَةَ وَءَاتَيْنَـٰهُم مُّلْكًا
عَظِيمًا ﴿٥٤﴾ فَمِنْهُم مَّنْ ءَامَنَ بِهِۦ وَمِنْهُم
مَّن صَدَّ عَنْهُ ۚ وَكَفَىٰ بِجَهَنَّمَ سَعِيرًا ﴿٥٥﴾
إِنَّ ٱلَّذِينَ كَفَرُوا۟ بِـَٔايَـٰتِنَا سَوْفَ نُصْلِيهِمْ
نَارًا كُلَّمَا نَضِجَتْ جُلُودُهُم بَدَّلْنَـٰهُمْ
جُلُودًا غَيْرَهَا لِيَذُوقُوا۟ ٱلْعَذَابَ ۗ إِنَّ ٱللَّهَ
كَانَ عَزِيزًا حَكِيمًا ﴿٥٦﴾ وَٱلَّذِينَ ءَامَنُوا۟
وَعَمِلُوا۟ ٱلصَّـٰلِحَـٰتِ سَنُدْخِلُهُمْ
جَنَّـٰتٍ تَجْرِى مِن تَحْتِهَا ٱلْأَنْهَـٰرُ خَـٰلِدِينَ
فِيهَآ أَبَدًا ۖ لَّهُمْ فِيهَآ أَزْوَٰجٌ مُّطَهَّرَةٌ ۖ
وَنُدْخِلُهُمْ ظِلًّا ظَلِيلًا ﴿٥٧﴾

---

85. By implication, this query accurately portrays the state of mind of the Jews. They saw the Muslims being endowed with the grace and reward of God which they, notwithstanding their own unworthiness had expected to fall to their share. By virtue of the advent of a great Prophet among the *ummīs* of Arabia, a spiritual, moral and intellectual revolution had taken place which totally changed their practical life and ultimately led them to greatness and glory. It is this which aroused their spite and envy, and which was reflected in their unjustifiable remarks about the Muslims.

(58) Allah commands you to deliver trusts to those worthy of them; and when you judge between people, to judge with justice.[88] Excellent is the admonition Allah gives you. Allah is All-Hearing, All-Seeing.

۞إِنَّ ٱللَّهَ يَأْمُرُكُمْ أَن تُؤَدُّوا۟ ٱلْأَمَٰنَٰتِ
إِلَىٰٓ أَهْلِهَا وَإِذَا حَكَمْتُم بَيْنَ ٱلنَّاسِ أَن
تَحْكُمُوا۟ بِٱلْعَدْلِ ۚ إِنَّ ٱللَّهَ نِعِمَّا يَعِظُكُم بِهِۦٓ ۗ إِنَّ ٱللَّهَ
كَانَ سَمِيعًۢا بَصِيرًا ﴿٥٨﴾

---

86. This 'mighty dominion' refers to the position of world leadership and authority which a people attain by virtue of receiving the knowledge in the Book of God and acting according to its dictates.

87. This is in response to the malicious remarks of the Israelites. What is being said is that they had no reason to feel jealous since both the Israelites and Ishmaelites were offspring of the same Abraham. Now, the leadership of the world had been promised only to those children of Abraham who followed the Book and Wisdom revealed by God. The Book and Wisdom had been sent down earlier to the Israelites, and to their discredit they had turned away from them. The same Book and Wisdom had now been made available to the Ishmaelites and they had decided to greet it with faith and gratitude.

88. Here the Muslims are forewarned against the evils which had afflicted the Israelites. One of the fundamental mistakes committed by the Israelites was that in the time of their degeneration they had handed over positions of trust (i.e. religious and political leadership) to incompetent, mean, immoral, dishonest and corrupt people. The result was that corruption spread throughout the nation. The Muslims are directed to take heed of this, and to entrust positions of responsibility only to those who are capable of shouldering the burdens of such positions.

The other major weakness of the Israelites was that they completely lost their sense of justice. In their pursuit of either personal or national interests, honesty and good faith were often sacrificed. The Muslims, in the time of the Prophet (peace be on him), were themselves subjected to gross injustice at their hands. On the one side were the Prophet (peace be on him) and his followers, to whose purity of life and conduct the Jews were themselves witnesses. On the other side were those who worshipped idols, buried their daughters alive, married their step-mothers and circumambulated the Ka'bah naked. Despite this, these so-called People of the Book felt no shame in declaring that the latter were closer to righteousness than the Muslims.

After informing the Muslims of the iniquity of the Jews, God now warns them against committing similar injustices. They should rather declare what

(59) Believers! Obey Allah and obey the Messenger, and those from among you who are invested with authority; and then if you were to dispute among yourselves about anything refer it to Allah and the Messenger[89] if you indeed believe in Allah and the Last Day; that is better and more commendable in the end.[90]

يَٰٓأَيُّهَا ٱلَّذِينَ ءَامَنُوٓا۟ أَطِيعُوا۟ ٱللَّهَ وَأَطِيعُوا۟
ٱلرَّسُولَ وَأُو۟لِى ٱلْأَمْرِ مِنكُمْ ۖ فَإِن تَنَٰزَعْتُمْ
فِى شَىْءٍ فَرُدُّوهُ إِلَى ٱللَّهِ وَٱلرَّسُولِ إِن كُنتُمْ
تُؤْمِنُونَ بِٱللَّهِ وَٱلْيَوْمِ ٱلْءَاخِرِ ۚ ذَٰلِكَ خَيْرٌ
وَأَحْسَنُ تَأْوِيلًا ﴿٥٩﴾

---

is right in the face of friend and foe alike, and judge between people with equity and justice.

89. This verse is the cornerstone of the entire religious, social and political structure of Islam, and the very first clause of the constitution of an Islamic state. It lays down the following principles as permanent guidelines:

(1) In the Islamic order of life, God alone is the focus of loyalty and obedience. A Muslim is the servant of God before anything else, and obedience and loyalty to God constitute the centre and axis of both the individual and collective life of a Muslim. Other claims to loyalty and obedience are acceptable only insofar as they remain secondary and subservient, and do not compete with those owed to God. All loyalties which may tend to challenge the primacy of man's loyalty to God must be rejected. This has been expressed by the Prophet (peace be on him) in the following words: 'There may be no obedience to any creature in disobedience to the Creator.' (Muslim, 'Īmān', 37; Aḥmad b. Ḥanbal, *Musnad*, vol. 3, p. 472 – Ed.)

(2) Another basic principle of the Islamic order of life is obedience to the Prophet (peace be on him). No Prophet, of course, is entitled to obedience in his own right. Obedience to Prophets, however, is the only practical way of obeying God, since they are the only authentic means by which He communicates His injunctions and ordinances to men. Hence, we can obey God only if we obey a Prophet. Independent obedience to God is not acceptable, and to turn one's back on the Prophets amounts to rebellion against God. The following tradition from the Prophet (peace be on him) explains this: 'Whoever obeyed me, indeed obeyed God; and whoever disobeyed me, indeed disobeyed God.' (Bukhārī, 'Jihād', 109; 'I'tiṣām', 2; Muslim, 'Amārah', 32, 33; Nasā'ī, 'Bay'ah', 27; etc. – Ed.)

We shall see this explained in more detail a little further on in the Qur'ān.

(3) In the Islamic order of life Muslims are further required to obey fellow Muslims in authority. This obedience follows, and is subordinate to, obedience to God and the Prophet (peace be on him). Those invested with authority (*ulū al-amr*) include all those entrusted with directing Muslims in matters of common concern. Hence, persons 'invested with authority' include the intellectual and political leaders of the community, as well as administrative officials, judges of the courts, tribal chiefs and regional representatives. In all these capacities, those 'invested with authority' are entitled to obedience, and it is improper for Muslims to cause dislocation in their collective life by engaging in strife and conflict with them. This obedience is contingent, however, on two conditions: first, that these men should be believers; and second, that they should themselves be obedient to God and the Prophet (peace be on him).

These two conditions are not only clearly mentioned in this verse they have also been elucidated at length by the Prophet (peace be on him) and can be found in the *Ḥadīth*. Let us consider, for example, the following traditions:

> A Muslim is obliged to heed and to obey an order whether he likes it or not, as long as he is not ordered to carry out an act of disobedience to God (*ma'ṣiyah*). When ordered to carry out an act of disobedience to God he need neither heed nor obey.
>
> There is no obedience in sin; obedience is only in what is good (*ma'rūf*). (For these traditions see Bukhārī, 'Aḥkām', 4; 'Jihād', 108; Muslim, 'Amārah', 39; Tirmidhī, 'Jihād', 29; Ibn Mājah, 'Jihād', 40; Aḥmad b. Ḥanbal, *Musnad*, vol. 2, pp. 17 and 142 – Ed.)
>
> There will be rulers over you, some of whose actions you will consider good and others abominable. Who even disapproves of their abominable acts will be acquitted of all blame, and whoever resents them he too will remain secure (from all blame); not so one who approves and follows them in their abominable acts. They (i.e. the Companions) asked: 'Should we not fight against them?' The Prophet (peace be on him) said: 'No, not as long as they continue to pray.' (See Bukhārī, 'Jihād', 108 – Ed.)

This means that their abandonment of Prayer will be a clear sign of their having forsaken obedience to God and the Prophet (peace be on him). Thereafter it becomes proper to fight against them. In another tradition the Prophet (peace be on him) says:

> Your worst leaders are those whom you hate and who hate you; whom you curse and who curse you. We asked: 'O Messenger of God! Should we not rise against them?' The Prophet (peace be on him) said: 'No, not as long as they establish Prayer among you: not as long as they establish Prayer among you.' (See Muslim, 'Amārah', 65, 66; Tirmidhī, 'Fitan', 77; Dārimī, 'Riqāq, 78; Aḥmad b. Ḥanbal, *Musnad*, vol. 6, pp. 24, 28 – Ed.)

In this tradition the position is further clarified. The earlier tradition could have created the impression that it was not permissible to revolt against rulers as long as they observed their Prayers privately. But the latter tradition makes it clear that what is really meant by 'praying' is the establishment of the system of congregational Prayers in the collective life of Muslims. This means that it is by no means sufficient that the rulers merely continue observing their Prayers: it is also necessary that the system run by them should at least be concerned with the establishment of Prayer. This concern with Prayer is a definite indication that a government is essentially an Islamic one. But if no concern for establishing Prayer is noticed, it shows that the government has drifted far away from Islam making it permissible to overthrow it. The same principle is also enunciated by the Prophet (peace be on him) in another tradition, in which the narrator says: 'The Prophet (peace be on him) also made us pledge not to rise against our rulers unless we see them involved in open disbelief, so that we have definite evidence against them to lay before God' (Bukhārī and Muslim).

(4) In an Islamic order the injunctions of God and the way of the Prophet (peace be on him) constitute the basic law and paramount authority in all matters. Whenever there is any dispute among Muslims or between the rulers and the ruled the matter should be referred to the Qur'ān and the *Sunnah*, and all concerned should accept with sincerity whatever judgement results. In fact, willingness to take the Book of God and the *Sunnah* of His Messenger as the common point of reference, and to treat the judgement of the Qur'ān and the *Sunnah* as the last word on all matters, is a central characteristic which distinguishes an Islamic system from un-Islamic ones.

Some people question the principle that we should refer everything to the Book of God and the *Sunnah* of the Prophet (peace be on him). They wonder how we can possibly do so when there are numerous practical questions involved, for example, rules and regulations relating to municipal administration, the management of railways and postal services and so on which are not treated at all in these sources. This doubt arises, however, from a misapprehension about Islam. The basic difference between a Muslim and a non-Muslim is that whereas the latter feels free to do as he wishes, the basic characteristic of a Muslim is that he always looks to God and to His Prophet for guidance, and where such guidance is available, a Muslim is bound by it. On the other hand, it is also quite important to remember that when no specific guidance is available, a Muslim feels free to exercise his discretion because the silence of the Law indicates that God Himself has deliberately granted man the freedom to make his decision.

90. Since the Qur'ān is not merely a legal code, but also seeks to instruct, educate, admonish and exhort, the earlier sentence which enunciates a legal principle is followed by another which explains its underlying purpose and wisdom. Two things are laid down. First, that faithful adherence to

(60) (O Messenger!) Have you not seen those who claim to believe in the Book which has been revealed to you and in the Books revealed before you, and yet desire to submit their disputes to the judgement of *ṭāghūt* (the Satanic authorities who decide independently of the Law of Allah), whereas they had been asked to reject it.[91] And Satan seeks to make them drift far away from the right way. ▶

أَلَمْ تَرَ إِلَى ٱلَّذِينَ يَزْعُمُونَ أَنَّهُمْ ءَامَنُوا بِمَآ أُنزِلَ إِلَيْكَ وَمَآ أُنزِلَ مِن قَبْلِكَ يُرِيدُونَ أَن يَتَحَاكَمُوٓا إِلَى ٱلطَّٰغُوتِ وَقَدْ أُمِرُوٓا أَن يَكْفُرُوا بِهِۦ وَيُرِيدُ ٱلشَّيْطَٰنُ أَن يُضِلَّهُمْ ضَلَٰلَۢا بَعِيدًا ۝

the above four principles is a necessary requirement of faith. Anyone who claims to be a Muslim and yet disregards the principles of Islam involves himself in gross self-contradiction. Second, the well-being of Muslims lies in basing their lives on those principles. This alone can keep them on the straight path in this life, and will lead to their salvation in the Next.

It is significant that this admonition follows immediately after the section which embodies comments about the moral and religious condition of the Jews. Thus the Muslims were subtly directed to draw a lesson from the depths to which the Jews had sunk, as a result of their deviation from the fundamental principles of true faith just mentioned. Any community that turns its back upon the Book of God and the guidance of His Prophets, that willingly follows rulers and leaders who are heedless of God and His Prophets, and that obeys its religious and political authorities blindly without seeking authority for their actions either in the Book of God or in the practice of the Prophets, will inevitably fall into the same evil and corruption as the Israelites.

91. *Ṭāghūt* clearly signifies here a sovereign who judges things according to criteria other than the law of God. It also stands for a legal and judicial system which acknowledges neither the sovereignty of God nor the paramount authority of the Book of God. This verse categorically proclaims that to refer disputes to the judgement of a court of law which is essentially *ṭāghūt* contravenes the dictates of a believer's faith. In fact, true faith in God and His Book necessarily requires that a man should refuse to recognize the legitimacy of such courts. According to the Qur'ān, belief in God necessitates repudiation of the authority of *ṭāghūt*. To try to submit both to God and to *ṭāghūt* at the same time is hypocrisy.

(61) When they are told: 'Come to that which Allah has revealed, and come to the Messenger', you will notice the hypocrites turning away from you in aversion.[92] (62) But what happens when some misfortune visits them because of their own misdeeds? Then, they come to you swearing by Allah,[93] saying: 'We wanted nothing but to do good and to bring about conciliation (between the two parties)'. (63) As for them, Allah knows what is in their hearts. Leave them alone, admonish them, and say to them penetrating words about themselves. ▶

وَإِذَا قِيلَ لَهُمْ تَعَالَوْا إِلَىٰ مَا أَنزَلَ
اللَّهُ وَإِلَى الرَّسُولِ رَأَيْتَ الْمُنَافِقِينَ
يَصُدُّونَ عَنكَ صُدُودًا ﴿٦١﴾
فَكَيْفَ إِذَا أَصَابَتْهُم مُّصِيبَةٌ
بِمَا قَدَّمَتْ أَيْدِيهِمْ ثُمَّ جَاءُوكَ
يَحْلِفُونَ بِاللَّهِ إِنْ أَرَدْنَا إِلَّا إِحْسَانًا
وَتَوْفِيقًا ﴿٦٢﴾ أُولَٰئِكَ الَّذِينَ
يَعْلَمُ اللَّهُ مَا فِي قُلُوبِهِمْ فَأَعْرِضْ
عَنْهُمْ وَعِظْهُمْ وَقُل لَّهُمْ فِي
أَنفُسِهِمْ قَوْلًا بَلِيغًا ﴿٦٣﴾

---

92. This shows that the hypocrites were inclined to refer to the Prophet (peace be on him) those cases in which they expected a favourable decision. When they feared an adverse judgement they refused to refer to the Prophet (peace be on him). This continues to be the practice of many hypocrites even now. Whenever they feel that Islamic Law would further their interests they turn to it but when they feel it would militate against them they refer their disputes to whichever legal systems and courts of law, customs and usages they anticipate most likely to give them a favourable decision.

93. This may mean that when Muslims become aware of their hypocritical activities and they feel afraid of being caught, censured, and eventually punished, the hypocrites resort to every stratagem, including oaths, in order to assure people that they are true believers.

(64) (And tell them that) We never sent a Messenger but that he should be obeyed by the leave of Allah.[94] If whenever they wronged themselves they had come to you praying to Allah for forgiveness, and had the Messenger prayed for their forgiveness, they would indeed have found Allah All-Forgiving, All-Compassionate. (65) But no, by your Lord, they cannot become true believers until they seek your arbitration in all matters on which they disagree among themselves, and then find not the least vexation in their hearts over what you have decided, and accept it in willing submission.[95] ▶

وَمَآ أَرْسَلْنَا مِن رَّسُولٍ إِلَّا
لِيُطَاعَ بِإِذْنِ ٱللَّهِ ۚ وَلَوْ أَنَّهُمْ
إِذ ظَّلَمُوٓا۟ أَنفُسَهُمْ جَآءُوكَ
فَٱسْتَغْفَرُوا۟ ٱللَّهَ وَٱسْتَغْفَرَ لَهُمُ
ٱلرَّسُولُ لَوَجَدُوا۟ ٱللَّهَ تَوَّابًا رَّحِيمًا
﴿٦٤﴾ فَلَا وَرَبِّكَ لَا يُؤْمِنُونَ حَتَّىٰ
يُحَكِّمُوكَ فِيمَا شَجَرَ بَيْنَهُمْ ثُمَّ
لَا يَجِدُوا۟ فِىٓ أَنفُسِهِمْ حَرَجًا مِّمَّا
قَضَيْتَ وَيُسَلِّمُوا۟ تَسْلِيمًا ﴿٦٥﴾

94. This is to impress upon us that Prophets are not sent so that people may pay lip-service to their prophethood, and then obey whoever they wish. The purpose of sending Prophets is that people should follow the laws of God as brought and expounded by them rather than laws devised by man, and that they should obey the commands of God as revealed to the Prophets to the exclusion of the commands of others.

95. The application of the injunction embodied in this verse is not confined to the life-time of the Prophet (peace be on him). It will remain in force until the Day of Judgement. The guidance the Prophet (peace be on him) proclaimed on God's behalf, and the manner in which he followed God's direction and inspiration, will for ever remain the universal touchstone for Muslims. In fact, recognition of that guidance as the final authority is the criterion of true belief. This principle was pronounced by the Prophet (peace be on him) in the following words:

'None of you can become a believer until his desires become subservient to what I have brought (i.e. my teachings).' (Cited by al-Nawawī in *al-Arba'īn*, see the tradition no. 41, transmitted on the authority of Abū

(66) Had We enjoined upon them: 'Slay yourselves', or 'Leave your habitations', very few of them would have done it;[96] yet if they had done as they were admonished, it would have been better for them and would have strengthened them;[97] (67) whereupon We would indeed grant them from Us a mighty reward, (68) and guide them to a straight way.[98] ▶

وَلَوْ أَنَّا كَتَبْنَا عَلَيْهِمْ أَنِ ٱقْتُلُوٓا۟
أَنفُسَكُمْ أَوِ ٱخْرُجُوا۟ مِن دِيَٰرِكُم
مَّا فَعَلُوهُ إِلَّا قَلِيلٌ مِّنْهُمْ ۖ وَلَوْ أَنَّهُمْ
فَعَلُوا۟ مَا يُوعَظُونَ بِهِۦ لَكَانَ خَيْرًا لَّهُمْ
وَأَشَدَّ تَثْبِيتًا ﴿٦٦﴾ وَإِذًا لَّءَاتَيْنَٰهُم مِّن
لَّدُنَّآ أَجْرًا عَظِيمًا ﴿٦٧﴾ وَلَهَدَيْنَٰهُمْ
صِرَٰطًا مُّسْتَقِيمًا ﴿٦٨﴾

---

al-Qāsim Ismā'īl b. Muḥammad al-Iṣfahānī, *Kitāb al-Ḥujjah* with the opinion that it is a 'good' and 'sound' tradition, with a sound chain of transmission – Ed.)

96. As these people are not prepared to endure even minor losses and inconveniences in order to follow the law of God, they can never be expected to make big sacrifices. If asked either to lay down their lives or to give up their homes and families for the sake of the Truth they would fly straight back to unbelief and disobedience.

97. Had these people been able to free themselves of uncertainty, hesitation and ambivalence, and to resolve firmly to follow and obey the Prophet (peace be on him), their lives would have been spared the instability from which they suffer. Their way of thinking, their morals and their practical dealings would all have found permanent and stable foundations, and they would have enjoyed the blessings granted only to those who follow the one straight path with firmness and resolution. For one who is subject to indecision and hesitation, who keeps changing from one direction to another in a state of uncertainty, life is a continuous exercise in futility.

98. By giving up uncertainty, and deciding with complete faith and conviction to follow the Prophet (peace be on him), the straight path of their endeavours would have opened up before them. They would have been able to perceive clearly the channels into which their energies should be directed, so that each step they took would be a step towards the true goal.

(69) And he who obeys Allah and the Messenger – they shall be with those whom Allah has favoured – the Prophets, those steadfast in truthfulness, the martyrs, and the righteous.[99] How excellent will they be for companions![100] (70) That is a bounty from Allah, and Allah suffices to know the truth.

وَمَن يُطِعِ ٱللَّهَ وَٱلرَّسُولَ فَأُو۟لَٰٓئِكَ مَعَ
ٱلَّذِينَ أَنْعَمَ ٱللَّهُ عَلَيْهِم مِّنَ ٱلنَّبِيِّـۧنَ
وَٱلصِّدِّيقِينَ وَٱلشُّهَدَآءِ وَٱلصَّٰلِحِينَ ۚ
وَحَسُنَ أُو۟لَٰٓئِكَ رَفِيقًا ﴿٦٩﴾
ذَٰلِكَ ٱلْفَضْلُ مِنَ ٱللَّهِ ۚ وَكَفَىٰ
بِٱللَّهِ عَلِيمًا ﴿٧٠﴾

99. *Ṣiddīq* denotes someone who is utterly honest, someone whose devotion to truth has reached a very high point. Such a person is always upright and straightforward in his dealings. He supports nothing but right and justice and does so with sincerity. He opposes whatever is contrary to truth, and does not waver in his opposition to falsehood. His life is so unblemished and selfless that even enemies, let alone friends, expect of him unadulterated probity and justice.

The term *shahīd* (pl. *shuhadā'*) means 'witness'. It signifies one who attests to the truth of his faith with his whole life. He who lays down his life fighting for God is called a *shahīd* because by this sacrifice he confirms that his confession of faith was backed by a deep, genuine conviction of its truth, and that he valued it above his own life. The term *shahīd* is also applied to those outstandingly honest people who are so trustworthy that their testimony, on any matter, is accepted without hesitation.

Ṣāliḥ denotes one whose belief and thinking, motives and intentions, words and deeds, are based on righteousness. In short, he is a person whose life as a whole is oriented to righteousness.

100. He who enjoys, in this world, the company of the kind of people mentioned in this verse, and whom God judges worthy of the same company in the Hereafter is fortunate. The fact is that unless a man's natural sensitivity has atrophied, the companionship of corrupt and wicked people is a painful punishment even in this transient world, let alone that one should be subjected to the perpetual companionship of such people in the abiding life of the Hereafter. Good people have always longed for the company of like people, both in this world and the Next.

(71) Believers! Always be on your guard against encounters.[101] Then (as circumstance demands) either advance in detachments or advance in a body. (72) Among you there is such who lags behind,[102] then if some affliction strikes you, he says: 'Indeed Allah bestowed His favour upon me that I was not present with them.' (73) And if a bounty from Allah is given you, he says – and says as if there never was any affection between you and him – 'Oh, would that I had been with them, I would have come by a great gain.' (74) Let those who seek the life of the Next World in exchange for the life of this world fight in the way of Allah.[103] We shall grant a mighty reward to whoever fights in the way of Allah, whether he is slain or comes out victorious. ▶

يَـٰٓأَيُّهَا ٱلَّذِينَ ءَامَنُوا۟ خُذُوا۟ حِذْرَكُمْ
فَٱنفِرُوا۟ ثُبَاتٍ أَوِ ٱنفِرُوا۟ جَمِيعًا ﴿٧١﴾
وَإِنَّ مِنكُمْ لَمَن لَّيُبَطِّئَنَّ فَإِنْ أَصَـٰبَتْكُم
مُّصِيبَةٌ قَالَ قَدْ أَنْعَمَ ٱللَّهُ عَلَىَّ إِذْ لَمْ أَكُن
مَّعَهُمْ شَهِيدًا ﴿٧٢﴾ وَلَئِنْ أَصَـٰبَكُمْ
فَضْلٌ مِّنَ ٱللَّهِ لَيَقُولَنَّ كَأَن لَّمْ تَكُنۢ
بَيْنَكُمْ وَبَيْنَهُۥ مَوَدَّةٌ يَـٰلَيْتَنِى كُنتُ
مَعَهُمْ فَأَفُوزَ فَوْزًا عَظِيمًا ﴿٧٣﴾
۞ فَلْيُقَـٰتِلْ فِى سَبِيلِ ٱللَّهِ ٱلَّذِينَ
يَشْرُونَ ٱلْحَيَوٰةَ ٱلدُّنْيَا
بِٱلْـَٔاخِرَةِ ۚ وَمَن يُقَـٰتِلْ فِى سَبِيلِ
ٱللَّهِ فَيُقْتَلْ أَوْ يَغْلِبْ فَسَوْفَ نُؤْتِيهِ
أَجْرًا عَظِيمًا ﴿٧٤﴾

---

101. This discourse was revealed after the Battle of Uḥud, when the tribes living around Madina had been greatly encouraged by the defeat of the Muslims. Thus dangers seemed to surround the Muslims on all sides. Day in and day out news poured in about the hostile intentions of one tribe after another. Reports came in of attacks mounted now in one area, and then in another. The Muslims were again and again the victims of treachery. Their preachers were invited to preach and then put to the sword. Beyond Madina, neither their lives nor their property was secure. Consequently the Muslims had to prepare themselves for a fierce struggle, for a tremendous, all-out effort to ensure that the Islamic movement would not be crushed.

(75) How is it that you do not fight in the way of Allah and in support of the helpless – men, women and children – who pray: 'Our Lord, bring us out of this land whose people are oppressors and appoint for us from Yourself, a protector, and appoint for us from Yourself a helper'?[104] (76) Those who have faith fight in the way of Allah, while those who disbelieve fight in the way of *ṭāghūt* (Satan).[105] Fight, then, against the fellows of Satan. Surely Satan's strategy is weak.[106]

وَمَا لَكُمْ لَا تُقَٰتِلُونَ فِي سَبِيلِ ٱللَّهِ
وَٱلْمُسْتَضْعَفِينَ مِنَ ٱلرِّجَالِ وَٱلنِّسَآءِ
وَٱلْوِلْدَٰنِ ٱلَّذِينَ يَقُولُونَ رَبَّنَآ أَخْرِجْنَا
مِنْ هَٰذِهِ ٱلْقَرْيَةِ ٱلظَّالِمِ أَهْلُهَا وَٱجْعَل
لَّنَا مِن لَّدُنكَ وَلِيًّا وَٱجْعَل لَّنَا مِن لَّدُنكَ
نَصِيرًا ﴿٧٥﴾ ٱلَّذِينَ ءَامَنُوا۟ يُقَٰتِلُونَ فِي
سَبِيلِ ٱللَّهِ ۖ وَٱلَّذِينَ كَفَرُوا۟ يُقَٰتِلُونَ فِي
سَبِيلِ ٱلطَّٰغُوتِ فَقَٰتِلُوٓا۟ أَوْلِيَآءَ
ٱلشَّيْطَٰنِ ۖ إِنَّ كَيْدَ ٱلشَّيْطَٰنِ كَانَ
ضَعِيفًا ﴿٧٦﴾

---

102. Another meaning could be that such persons not only shirk the risks of fighting themselves but also go about spreading demoralization to discourage others from fighting in the name of God.

103. The point stressed here is that fighting in the cause of God cannot be conducted by people engrossed in the pursuit of worldly benefits. This is the task of those who seek to please God, who have complete faith in Him and in the Hereafter, who are prepared to sacrifice all opportunities of worldly success and prosperity, and of all worldly interests, hoping thereby to win God's good pleasure. Irrespective of what happens in the present world such sacrifices will not be wasted in the Hereafter. *Jihād* (struggle in the cause of God) is not for those who mainly care for worldly benefits.

104. This refers to those wronged, persecuted men, women and children of Makka and of the other tribes in Arabia who had embraced Islam, but were able neither to emigrate nor to protect themselves from the wrongs to which they were subjected. These helpless people suffered many forms of persecution, and prayed for deliverance from oppression.

105. This lays down a clear verdict of God. To fight in the cause of God in order that His religion be established on earth is the task of men of

(77) Have you not seen those who were told: 'Restrain you hands, and establish the Prayer, and pay the *Zakāh*'? But when fighting was enjoined upon them some of them feared men as one should fear Allah, or even more,[107] and said: 'Our Lord, why have You ordained fighting for us? Why did You not grant us a little more respite?' Say to them: 'There is little enjoyment in this world. The World to Come is much better for the God-fearing. And you shall not be wronged even to the extent of the husk of a date-stone.'[108] (78) Wherever you might be, death will overtake you even though you be in massive towers.

أَلَمْ تَرَ إِلَى ٱلَّذِينَ قِيلَ لَهُمْ كُفُّوٓا۟ أَيْدِيَكُمْ
وَأَقِيمُوا۟ ٱلصَّلَوٰةَ وَءَاتُوا۟ ٱلزَّكَوٰةَ فَلَمَّا كُتِبَ
عَلَيْهِمُ ٱلْقِتَالُ إِذَا فَرِيقٌ مِّنْهُمْ يَخْشَوْنَ
ٱلنَّاسَ كَخَشْيَةِ ٱللَّهِ أَوْ أَشَدَّ خَشْيَةً ۚ
وَقَالُوا۟ رَبَّنَا لِمَ كَتَبْتَ عَلَيْنَا ٱلْقِتَالَ
لَوْلَآ أَخَّرْتَنَآ إِلَىٰٓ أَجَلٍ قَرِيبٍ ۗ قُلْ مَتَٰعُ ٱلدُّنْيَا
قَلِيلٌ وَٱلْءَاخِرَةُ خَيْرٌ لِّمَنِ ٱتَّقَىٰ
وَلَا تُظْلَمُونَ فَتِيلًا ﴿٧٧﴾ أَيْنَمَا
تَكُونُوا۟ يُدْرِككُّمُ ٱلْمَوْتُ وَلَوْ كُنتُمْ فِى
بُرُوجٍ مُّشَيَّدَةٍ ۗ

---

faith, and whoever truly believes can never shirk this duty. To fight in the cause of *ṭāghūt* (authority in defiance of God) in order that the world may be governed by rebels against God is the task of unbelievers in which no believer can engage himself.

106. Satan and his comrades-in-arms ostensibly undertake tremendous preparations and contrive all kinds of ingenious machinations. True men of faith, however, should not be intimidated either by such preparations or by machinations. For, no matter what they do, they are doomed to fail.

107. This verse can be interpreted in three ways, and each meaning is equally valid:

First, that those who now shirked to fight in the cause of God were themselves initially eager to fight. They often approached the Prophet (peace be on him), saying that they were being wronged, beaten, persecuted and abused, that their patience was exhausted, and that they wanted permission to fight. They had then been told to be patient and continue to purify their souls by observing Prayers and dispensing *Zakāh*. At that time

And when some good happens to them, they say: 'This is from Allah'; whereas when some misfortune befalls them, they say: 'This is because of you'.[109] Say: 'All is from Allah.' What has happened to this people that they seem to understand nothing?

وَإِن تُصِبْهُمْ حَسَنَةٌ يَقُولُوا۟ هَٰذِهِۦ مِنْ
عِندِ ٱللَّهِ ۖ وَإِن تُصِبْهُمْ سَيِّئَةٌ يَقُولُوا۟
هَٰذِهِۦ مِنْ عِندِكَ ۚ قُلْ كُلٌّ مِّنْ عِندِ ٱللَّهِ ۖ فَمَالِ
هَٰٓؤُلَآءِ ٱلْقَوْمِ لَا يَكَادُونَ يَفْقَهُونَ
حَدِيثًا ٧٨

they had felt disconcerted by this counsel of patience. Later on, some of those very same people were to tremble at the first sight of the enemy and the dangers of warfare.

Second, that they remained highly 'religious' as long as they were asked merely to pray and pay *Zakāh*, which entailed no risk to their lives. But as soon as that phase was over and they were asked to expose themselves to danger, they began to shiver with fear.

Third, that in the former times the same people had unsheathed their swords for trivial causes. They had fought for loot and plunder, and engaged in feuds motivated by animal impulses, so much so that feuding had almost become their national pastime. At that time they had been told to abstain from bloodshed and to reform themselves by observing Prayers and dispensing *Zakāh*. When, later on, the same people were told that the time had come for them to fight in the cause of God, those who had shown themselves to be lions while fighting for their own selfish causes turned out to be as meek as lambs. The strong hands which had wielded the sword so firmly, and had used it so fiercely for the sake of either personal or tribal honour, or for Satan's sake, became almost paralysed.

Each of these three meanings applies to a different kind of person, but the actual words of the verse seem to apply equally to all who shirked fighting in the cause of God.

108. Were they to serve the religion of God and spend their energy in that cause, they would surely be rewarded by Him.

109. When such people encounter success and victory, they attribute it to the grace of God. They allow themselves to forget that this grace came to them through no one but the Prophet (peace be on him). When they are either beaten or face setbacks because of their own faults and weaknesses they gratuitously exonerate themselves and place the blame squarely on the Prophet (peace be on him).

(79) Whatever good hap-
pens to you is from Allah;
and whatever misfortune
smites you is because of your
own action. We have sent
you to mankind (O
Muḥammad!) as a Mes-
senger, and Allah is sufficient as a witness. (80) He
who obeys the Messenger
thereby obeys Allah; as for
he who turns away, We have
not sent you as a keeper over
them![110]

(81) They say (in your
presence): 'We obey', but
when they leave your pre-
sence a party of them meets
by night to plan against what
you have said. Allah takes
note of all their plots. So, let
them alone, and put your
trust in Allah. Allah is sufficient as a guardian. (82)
Do they not ponder about
the Qur'ān? Had it been
from any other than Allah,
they would surely have found
in it much inconsistency.[111]

مَّآ أَصَابَكَ مِنْ حَسَنَةٍ فَمِنَ ٱللَّهِ ۖ وَمَآ أَصَابَكَ مِن
سَيِّئَةٍ فَمِن نَّفْسِكَ ۚ وَأَرْسَلْنَٰكَ لِلنَّاسِ رَسُولًا ۚ
وَكَفَىٰ بِٱللَّهِ شَهِيدًا ﴿٧٩﴾ مَّن يُطِعِ ٱلرَّسُولَ
فَقَدْ أَطَاعَ ٱللَّهَ ۖ وَمَن تَوَلَّىٰ فَمَآ أَرْسَلْنَٰكَ
عَلَيْهِمْ حَفِيظًا ﴿٨٠﴾ وَيَقُولُونَ
طَاعَةٌ فَإِذَا بَرَزُوا۟ مِنْ عِندِكَ بَيَّتَ
طَآئِفَةٌ مِّنْهُمْ غَيْرَ ٱلَّذِى تَقُولُ ۖ وَٱللَّهُ
يَكْتُبُ مَا يُبَيِّتُونَ ۖ فَأَعْرِضْ عَنْهُمْ
وَتَوَكَّلْ عَلَى ٱللَّهِ ۚ وَكَفَىٰ بِٱللَّهِ وَكِيلًا ﴿٨١﴾
أَفَلَا يَتَدَبَّرُونَ ٱلْقُرْءَانَ ۚ وَلَوْ كَانَ مِنْ عِندِ
غَيْرِ ٱللَّهِ لَوَجَدُوا۟ فِيهِ ٱخْتِلَٰفًا
كَثِيرًا ﴿٨٢﴾

---

110. Such people are responsible for their own conduct. It is they rather than the Prophet (peace be on him) who will be censured. The task entrusted to the Prophet (peace be on him) was merely to communicate to them the ordinances and directives of God and he acquitted himself of it very well. It was not his duty to compel them to follow the right way, so that if they failed to follow the teachings communicated to them by the Prophet (peace be on him) the responsibility was entirely theirs. The Prophet (peace be on him) would not be questioned as to why they disobeyed.

111. The main reason for the attitude of the hypocrites and lukewarm believers was their lack of conviction that the Qur'ān came from God.

(83) Whenever they come upon any news bearing upon either security or causing consternation they go about spreading it, whereas if they were to convey it to either the Messenger or to those from among them who are entrusted with authority, it would come to the knowledge of those who are competent to investigate it.[112] But for Allah's bounty and mercy upon you, (weak as you were) all but a few of you would surely have followed Satan.

وَإِذَا جَآءَهُمْ أَمْرٌ مِّنَ ٱلْأَمْنِ
أَوِ ٱلْخَوْفِ أَذَاعُوا۟ بِهِۦ ۖ وَلَوْ رَدُّوهُ إِلَى
ٱلرَّسُولِ وَإِلَىٰٓ أُو۟لِى ٱلْأَمْرِ مِنْهُمْ
لَعَلِمَهُ ٱلَّذِينَ يَسْتَنۢبِطُونَهُۥ مِنْهُمْ ۗ
وَلَوْلَا فَضْلُ ٱللَّهِ عَلَيْكُمْ وَرَحْمَتُهُۥ
لَٱتَّبَعْتُمُ ٱلشَّيْطَٰنَ إِلَّا قَلِيلًا ﴿٨٣﴾

They did not believe that the Prophet (peace be on him) had received the messages and directives that he preached from God Himself. Hence, when they are censured for their hypocritical conduct, they are told that they do not reflect upon the Qur'ān. For the Qur'ān itself is a strong, persuasive testimony to its divine origin. It is inconceivable that any human being should compose discourses on different subjects under different circumstances and on different occasions, and that the collection of those discourses should then grow into a coherent, homogeneous and integrated work, no component of which is discordant with the others. It is also inconceivable that such a work would be permeated through and through with a uniform outlook and attitude, a work reflecting a remarkable consistency in the mood and spirit of its Author, and a work too mature ever to need revision.

112. This was a period of turbulence and upheaval and rumour was rife. Occasionally, baseless and exaggerated reports circulated and seized the whole of Madina and its outlying areas with alarm and consternation. At other times some cunning enemy tried to conceal the dangers threatening the Muslims by spreading soothing reports. A specially keen interest in rumours was taken by those who simply relished anything out of the ordinary, and who did not consider this life-and-death struggle between Islam and Ignorance to be a matter of crucial importance, and who were not aware of the far-reaching consequences of rumour-mongering. As soon as they heard something, they ran about spreading it everywhere. This rebuke is addressed to such people. They are warned against spreading

(84) (So, O Messenger!) Fight in the way of Allah – since you are responsible for none except yourself – and rouse the believers to fight, for Allah may well curb the might of the unbelievers. Indeed Allah is strongest in power and most terrible in chastisement. (85) He who intercedes in a good cause shall share in its good result, and he who intercedes in an evil cause shall share in its burden.[113] Allah watches over everything.

(86) When you are greeted with a salutation then return it with a better one, or at least the same.[114]

فَقَٰتِلْ فِى سَبِيلِ ٱللَّهِ لَا تُكَلَّفُ إِلَّا
نَفْسَكَ ۚ وَحَرِّضِ ٱلْمُؤْمِنِينَ ۖ عَسَى ٱللَّهُ أَن
يَكُفَّ بَأْسَ ٱلَّذِينَ كَفَرُوا۟ ۚ وَٱللَّهُ أَشَدُّ
بَأْسًا وَأَشَدُّ تَنكِيلًا ﴿٨٤﴾ مَّن
يَشْفَعْ شَفَٰعَةً حَسَنَةً يَكُن لَّهُۥ
نَصِيبٌ مِّنْهَا ۖ وَمَن يَشْفَعْ شَفَٰعَةً سَيِّئَةً
يَكُن لَّهُۥ كِفْلٌ مِّنْهَا ۗ وَكَانَ ٱللَّهُ عَلَىٰ كُلِّ
شَىْءٍ مُّقِيتًا ﴿٨٥﴾ وَإِذَا حُيِّيتُم بِتَحِيَّةٍ
فَحَيُّوا۟ بِأَحْسَنَ مِنْهَآ أَوْ رُدُّوهَآ ۗ

---

rumours and are directed to convey every report they receive to responsible quarters.

113. It is all a matter of choice and luck. One has the opportunity to struggle for the cause of God, and to urge others to strive for it in order to raise the banner of the Truth and be rewarded by God for so doing. Likewise, one also has the opportunity to expend one's energy trying to create misunderstanding among God's creatures and to demoralize people in their struggle for His cause thus incurring His chastisement.

114. At that time the relations between the Muslims and non-Muslims were strained to the limit. It was feared, therefore, that the Muslims might feel inclined to treat the latter discourteously. They are accordingly asked to pay at least as much respect and consideration to others as is paid to them – and preferably more. Good manners and courtesy are to be matched by the Muslims. In fact, the mission entrusted to the Muslims requires them to excel others in this respect. Harshness, irritability and bitterness are not becoming in a people whose main function is to preach a message and invite people to it; a people committed to guiding mankind towards righteousness. While harshness and bitterness may at best satisfy one's injured vanity, they are positively harmful to the cause that one seeks to promote.

Surely Allah takes good count of everything. (87) There is no god but Allah. He will certainly gather you all together on the Day of Resurrection – the Day regarding which there can be no doubt. Whose word can be truer than Allah's?[115]

(88) What has happened to you that you have two minds about the hypocrites[116] even though Allah has reverted them, owing to the sins that they earned?[117] Do you want to lead those to the right way whom Allah let go astray? And he whom Allah lets go astray, for him you can never find a way. ▶

إِنَّ ٱللَّهَ كَانَ عَلَىٰ كُلِّ شَيْءٍ حَسِيبًا ﴿٨٦﴾
ٱللَّهُ لَآ إِلَٰهَ إِلَّا هُوَ لَيَجْمَعَنَّكُمْ إِلَىٰ
يَوْمِ ٱلْقِيَٰمَةِ لَا رَيْبَ فِيهِ وَمَنْ أَصْدَقُ
مِنَ ٱللَّهِ حَدِيثًا ﴿٨٧﴾ ۞ فَمَا لَكُمْ فِي
ٱلْمُنَٰفِقِينَ فِئَتَيْنِ وَٱللَّهُ أَرْكَسَهُم بِمَا
كَسَبُوٓا۟ أَتُرِيدُونَ أَن تَهْدُوا۟ مَنْ
أَضَلَّ ٱللَّهُ وَمَن يُضْلِلِ ٱللَّهُ فَلَن تَجِدَ
لَهُۥ سَبِيلًا ﴿٨٨﴾

---

115. Whatever the unbelievers, polytheists and atheists may do does not impair God's godhead. That God is the One and Absolute Lord of all is a fact which none can alter. And a Day will come when He will gather together all human beings and will make them see the consequences of their deeds, and no one will be in a position to escape His retribution. God therefore does not require His good creatures to maltreat, on His behalf, those who are lost in error.

This is the link between the present verse and the one preceding it. The same verse also concludes the theme running through the last twenty verses or so (see verses 71 ff). The present verse outlines that a man can follow whichever course he deems fit, and expend his energy in any direction he likes, but ultimately all men will have to stand before the One True God for His judgement and will see the consequences of their deeds.

116. The problem of the hypocrites is discussed here. They had outwardly embraced Islam in Makka and in other parts of Arabia, but instead of migrating to the Domain of Islam they continued to live among their own people who were unbelievers, taking part in all their hostile machinations against Islam and the Muslims. It was not easy for the Muslims to decide how to deal with such people. Some were of the opinion that since they

(89) They wish that you should disbelieve just as they disbelieved so that you may all be alike. Do not, therefore, take from them allies until they emigrate in the way of Allah, but if they turn their backs (on emigration), seize them and slay them[118] wherever you come upon them. ▶

وَدُّواْ لَوْ تَكْفُرُونَ كَمَا كَفَرُواْ فَتَكُونُونَ
سَوَآءً فَلَا تَتَّخِذُواْ مِنْهُمْ أَوْلِيَآءَ حَتَّىٰ
يُهَاجِرُواْ فِي سَبِيلِ ٱللَّهِ فَإِن تَوَلَّوْاْ
فَخُذُوهُمْ وَٱقْتُلُوهُمْ حَيْثُ
وَجَدتُّمُوهُمْ

---

professed Islam, performed Prayers, fasted and recited the Qur'ān they could not be treated as unbelievers. Here God pronounces His judgement on this issue.

Unless the following is made clear at this point, the reader is likely to miss the real object of not only this verse but of all those verses in which believers who have failed to migrate are characterized as hypocrites. The fact is that after the Prophet (peace be on him) migrated to Madina the Muslims came to possess a piece of territory where they could fulfil the dictates of their faith. At that time all Muslims who suffered from the pressures and constraints imposed on them by the unbelievers, and who did not enjoy the freedom to practise their religion, were directed to migrate to Madina, the Domain of Islam. It was in these circumstances that all those believers who were in a position to migrate to Madina, but who failed to do so because their hearth and home, kith and kin, and their material interests were dearer to them than Islam, were declared hypocrites. Those who were not really in a position to migrate were reckoned as 'feeble' (see verse 98 below).

It is obvious that Muslims living in non-Islamic territories can be called hypocrites only when the Domain of Islam either extends a general invitation to all of them or at least leaves its doors open to them. In such circumstances, all Muslims who are neither engaged in trying to transform the non-Islamic territory into a Domain of Islam nor inclined to migrate to the latter despite their ability to do so, will be deemed hypocrites. But if the Domain of Islam neither invites them nor even keeps its doors open for them, then they obviously cannot be declared hypocrites merely because of their failure to migrate. Such persons would be considered hypocrites only if they did something too outrageous to be consistent with true faith.

117. God has returned them whence they came because of their duplicity, their excessive hankering after their material interests, and their preference for the good of this world over that of the Next. Those people

Take none of them for your ally or helper, (90) unless it be such of them who seek refuge with a people who are joined with you by a covenant,[119] or those who come to you because their hearts shrink from fighting either against you or against their own people. Had Allah so willed, He would certainly have given them power over you and they would have fought against you. If they leave you alone and do not fight against you and offer you peace, then Allah does not permit you to harm them. ►

وَلَا تَتَّخِذُوا مِنْهُمْ وَلِيًّا وَلَا نَصِيرًا ﴿٨٩﴾
إِلَّا الَّذِينَ يَصِلُونَ إِلَىٰ قَوْمٍ بَيْنَكُمْ وَبَيْنَهُم
مِّيثَاقٌ أَوْ جَاءُوكُمْ حَصِرَتْ
صُدُورُهُمْ أَن يُقَاتِلُوكُمْ أَوْ يُقَاتِلُوا
قَوْمَهُمْ ۚ وَلَوْ شَاءَ اللَّهُ لَسَلَّطَهُمْ عَلَيْكُمْ
فَلَقَاتَلُوكُمْ ۚ فَإِنِ اعْتَزَلُوكُمْ فَلَمْ يُقَاتِلُوكُمْ
وَأَلْقَوْا إِلَيْكُمُ السَّلَمَ فَمَا جَعَلَ اللَّهُ لَكُمْ
عَلَيْهِمْ سَبِيلًا ﴿٩٠﴾

---

had indeed tried to extricate themselves from the grip of unbelief and to advance towards Islam. To be a true Muslim calls for single-mindedness. It requires a willingness to sacrifice all interests and advantages that are in conflict with the interests of Islam. It requires a faith in the Hereafter strong enough to enable a man to cheerfully sacrifice all worldly advantages for the sake of his eternal happiness. Since those people lacked these qualities they retraced their steps. Could there be any doubt about the stuff they were made of?

118. This is the verdict on those hypocritical confessors of faith who belong to a belligerent, non-Muslim nation and actually participate in acts of hostility against the Islamic state.

119. The exception here does not relate to the injunction that they should not be taken as friends and supporters, but to the injunction that the believers should seize and slay them. What is meant is that if a hypocrite takes shelter among an unbelieving people with whom the Muslims have an agreement he should not be pursued into that territory. It is not permissible for Muslims of the Islamic state to kill a hypocrite in some neutral territory even if he merits execution. This is because of the sanctity of the agreement concluded by the Muslims rather than the sanctity of the hypocrite's blood.

(91) You will also find others who wish to be secure from you, and secure from their people, but who, whenever they have any opportunity to cause mischief, plunge into it headlong. If such people neither leave you alone nor offer you peace nor restrain their hands from hurting you, then seize them and slay them wherever you come upon them. It is against these that We have granted you a clear sanction.

(92) It is not for a believer to slay another believer unless by mistake.[120] And he who has slain a believer by mistake, his atonement is to set free from bondage a believing person[121] and to pay blood-money to his heirs,[122] unless they forgo it by way of charity. And if the slain belonged to a hostile people, but was a believer, then the atonement is to set free from bondage a believing person.

سَتَجِدُونَ ءَاخَرِينَ يُرِيدُونَ أَن يَأْمَنُوكُمْ
وَيَأْمَنُوا۟ قَوْمَهُمْ كُلَّ مَا رُدُّوٓا۟ إِلَى ٱلْفِتْنَةِ
أُرْكِسُوا۟ فِيهَا ۚ فَإِن لَّمْ يَعْتَزِلُوكُمْ وَيُلْقُوٓا۟ إِلَيْكُمُ
ٱلسَّلَمَ وَيَكُفُّوٓا۟ أَيْدِيَهُمْ فَخُذُوهُمْ
وَٱقْتُلُوهُمْ حَيْثُ ثَقِفْتُمُوهُمْ ۚ وَأُو۟لَٰٓئِكُمْ
جَعَلْنَا لَكُمْ عَلَيْهِمْ سُلْطَٰنًا مُّبِينًا ﴿٩١﴾
وَمَا كَانَ لِمُؤْمِنٍ أَن يَقْتُلَ مُؤْمِنًا
إِلَّا خَطَـًٔا ۚ وَمَن قَتَلَ مُؤْمِنًا خَطَـًٔا
فَتَحْرِيرُ رَقَبَةٍ مُّؤْمِنَةٍ وَدِيَةٌ مُّسَلَّمَةٌ
إِلَىٰٓ أَهْلِهِۦٓ إِلَّآ أَن يَصَّدَّقُوا۟ ۚ فَإِن
كَانَ مِن قَوْمٍ عَدُوٍّ لَّكُمْ وَهُوَ
مُؤْمِنٌ فَتَحْرِيرُ رَقَبَةٍ مُّؤْمِنَةٍ ۖ

120. The hypocritical confessors of Islam mentioned here are distinct from those whom the Muslims may kill. The reference here is to Muslims who are either residents of the Domain of Islam (*Dār al-Islām*) or to those who live in the Domain of War or of Unbelief (*Dār al-Ḥarb* or *Dār al-Kufr*) but against whom there is no proof of actual participation in the hostile activities with the enemies of Islam. In the time of the Prophet (peace be on him) there were many people who had embraced Islam and yet, because of genuine difficulties, were living among tribes hostile to Islam. It occasionally happened that, in attacking a hostile tribe, the Muslims inadvertently killed fellow Muslims living in its midst.

And if the slain belonged to a (non-Muslim) people with whom you have a covenant, then the atonement is to pay the blood-money to his heirs, and to set free from bondage a believing person.[123] But he who cannot (free a slave) should fast for two consecutive months.[124] This is the penance ordained by Allah.[125] Allah is All-Knowing, All-Wise. (93) And he who slays a believer wilfully his reward is Hell, where he will abide. Allah's wrath is against him and He has cast His curse upon him, and has prepared for him a great chastisement.

وَإِن كَانَ مِن قَوْمٍ بَيْنَكُمْ
وَبَيْنَهُم مِّيثَٰقٌ فَدِيَةٌ مُّسَلَّمَةٌ
إِلَىٰٓ أَهْلِهِۦ وَتَحْرِيرُ رَقَبَةٍ مُّؤْمِنَةٍ
فَمَن لَّمْ يَجِدْ فَصِيَامُ شَهْرَيْنِ
مُتَتَابِعَيْنِ تَوْبَةً مِّنَ ٱللَّهِ وَكَانَ
ٱللَّهُ عَلِيمًا حَكِيمًا ﴿٩٢﴾ وَمَن
يَقْتُلْ مُؤْمِنًا مُّتَعَمِّدًا
فَجَزَآؤُهُۥ جَهَنَّمُ خَٰلِدًا فِيهَا
وَغَضِبَ ٱللَّهُ عَلَيْهِ وَلَعَنَهُۥ وَأَعَدَّ
لَهُۥ عَذَابًا عَظِيمًا ﴿٩٣﴾

---

121. Since the person killed was a believer, expiation of the sin required the emancipation of a Muslim slave.

122. The Prophet (peace be on him) had fixed the blood-money at either 100 camels, 200 oxen or 2,000 head of cattle. If someone wished to pay this in another form the amount would be determined with reference to the market value of the articles mentioned above. For instance, for those who wished to pay blood-money in cash, the fixed amount in the time of the Prophet (peace be on him) was 800 dinars (8000 dirhams). In the time of Caliph 'Umar the amount of blood-money was fixed at 1000 golden dinars (12000 silver dirhams). It should be noted, however, that this amount relates to an unintentional rather than a deliberate homicide. (Regarding blood-money for unintentional homicide and injury see Abū Dā'ūd, 'Diyāt', 14–17; Tirmidhī, 'Diyāt', 1; Nasā'ī, 'Qasāmah', 34; Ibn Mājah, 'Diyāt', 6; Mālik b. Anas, *Muwaṭṭa'*, "Uqūl', 4; Aḥmad b. Ḥanbal, *Musnad*, vol. 1, pp. 384 and 450; vol. 2, pp. 178, 183, 186, 217, 224; vol. 4, p. 275. See also Ibn Rushd, *Bidāyat al-Mujtahid*, vol. 2, pp. 401 ff. – Ed.)

123. The legal injunctions embodied in this verse are as follows:

(1) If the victim was a resident of the Domain of Islam (*Dār al-Islām*) the killer is not only required to pay blood-money but also to emancipate a slave by way of expiation.

(94) Believers! When you go forth in the way of Allah, discern (between friend and foe), and do not say to him who offers you the greeting of peace: 'You are not a believer.'[126] If you seek the good of this worldly life, there lies with Allah abundant gain. After all, you too were such before, and then Allah was gracious to you.[127] Discern, then, for Allah is well aware of what you do.

يَـٰٓأَيُّهَا ٱلَّذِينَ ءَامَنُوٓا۟ إِذَا ضَرَبْتُمْ فِى
سَبِيلِ ٱللَّهِ فَتَبَيَّنُوا۟ وَلَا تَقُولُوا۟ لِمَنْ
أَلْقَىٰٓ إِلَيْكُمُ ٱلسَّلَـٰمَ لَسْتَ
مُؤْمِنًا تَبْتَغُونَ عَرَضَ ٱلْحَيَوٰةِ
ٱلدُّنْيَا فَعِندَ ٱللَّهِ مَغَانِمُ كَثِيرَةٌ ۚ
كَذَٰلِكَ كُنتُم مِّن قَبْلُ
فَمَنَّ ٱللَّهُ عَلَيْكُمْ فَتَبَيَّنُوٓا۟ ۚ
إِنَّ ٱللَّهَ كَانَ بِمَا تَعْمَلُونَ
خَبِيرًا ﴿٩٤﴾

---

(2) If the victim was a resident of the Domain of War (*Dār al-Ḥarb*) the killer is only required to emancipate a slave.

(3) If the victim was a resident of a non-Muslim country which had treaty relations with an Islamic state the killer is required to emancipate a slave and also to pay blood-money. The amount of the blood-money, however, depends on the terms stipulated in the treaty between the Muslims and the territory of the victim. (See Jaṣṣāṣ, vol. 2, pp. 238 ff. and 240 ff. – Ed.)

124. This means that he should observe fasting uninterrupted for the entire period. If a man breaks his fast for just one day without a legally valid reason he will be required to resume fasting anew.

125. This shows that what has been prescribed is an act of repentance and expiation rather than a penalty inflicted on a criminal. Penalization is essentially devoid of the spirit of repentance and of the urge to self-reform. A penalty is suffered under duress, usually with resentment, and leaves behind repugnance and bitterness. On the contrary, what God wants is that the believer who has committed a sin should wash the stain of it from his soul by supererogatory worship, by acts of charity, and by a meticulous fulfilment of all the duties incumbent upon him. Such a person is required to turn to God in remorse and repentance so that his sin may be pardoned and his soul secured against the recurrence of similar errors.

The word *kaffārah* signifies that which either covers or hides something. To declare that certain acts of charity constitute *kaffārah* means that those acts overlay the sin and cover it up, just as stains on a wall are covered up when it is painted.

126. In the early days of Islam the greeting *as-salām 'alaykum* ('peace be on you') was a distinguishing symbol of the Muslims. When a Muslim greeted another Muslim with this expression it signified that he was a member of the same community, that he was a friend and well-wisher, one who wished peace and security, from whom he need entertain no fear of hostility and towards whom, in return, he should not behave with hostility. The Islamic greeting occupied virtually the same position among Muslims as the passwords used by sentries to distinguish friend from foe. This was particularly important in those days because there were no distinctions in dress, language and so on by which Muslims could be conclusively marked off from their non-Muslim Arab compatriots.

The Muslims also encountered a strange problem on the battlefield. Whenever a Muslim was in danger of being harmed inadvertently by other Muslims during the fighting, he resorted to either the Islamic greeting (*as-salām 'alaykum*) or the Islamic creed 'There is no god save Allah' (لا إله إلا الله) in order to indicate that he was their brother-in-faith. The Muslims, however, often suspected this to be merely a ruse of the enemy and therefore sometimes disregarded the utterance of the Islamic greeting or of the Islamic creed, and killed such people and seized their belongings as booty. Although whenever the Prophet (peace be on him) came to know of such incidents, he severely reproached the people concerned, it, nevertheless, continued to take place. In the end God solved the problem by revelation. The purport of the verse is that no one has the right summarily to judge those who profess to be Muslims, and assume them to be lying for fear of their lives. At least two possibilities exist: the claim may either be true or it may be false. The truth can only be ascertained by proper investigation. While it is impossible to investigate a person's case properly during fighting and this may enable him to save his life by lying, it is equally possible that an innocent, true believer might be put to death by mistake. The error of letting an unbeliever go unpunished is preferable to that of killing a true believer.

127. The Muslims are now told that there was a time when they were scattered among different tribes of unbelievers. They were, therefore, forced to conceal the fact of being Muslims since they feared that they would be subjected to persecution and hardship. In those days they had nothing else besides their verbal profession to testify to their faith. Later on, some time before these verses were revealed, God benevolently enabled the Muslims to develop a collective entity of their own and thus to raise the banner of Islam in the face of strong opposition from the unbelievers. That the Muslims should fail to appreciate the hardships which other Muslims were enduring, and which they themselves had endured until not long before, and not to treat them with consideration and forbearance, did not seem an adequate way of thanking God for His benevolence.

(95) Those believers who sit at home, unless they do so out of a disabling injury, are not the equals of those who strive in the way of Allah with their possessions and their lives. Allah has exalted in rank those who strive with their possessions and their lives over those who sit at home; and though to each Allah has promised some good reward, He has preferred those who strive (in the way of Allah) over those who sit at home for a mighty reward.[128] (96) For them are ranks, forgiveness, and favours from Him. Allah is All-Forgiving, All-Compassionate.

لَّا يَسْتَوِي ٱلْقَٰعِدُونَ مِنَ ٱلْمُؤْمِنِينَ غَيْرُ
أُوْلِي ٱلضَّرَرِ وَٱلْمُجَٰهِدُونَ فِي سَبِيلِ ٱللَّهِ
بِأَمْوَٰلِهِمْ وَأَنفُسِهِمْۚ فَضَّلَ ٱللَّهُ ٱلْمُجَٰهِدِينَ
بِأَمْوَٰلِهِمْ وَأَنفُسِهِمْ عَلَى ٱلْقَٰعِدِينَ دَرَجَةًۚ
وَكُلًّا وَعَدَ ٱللَّهُ ٱلْحُسْنَىٰۚ وَفَضَّلَ ٱللَّهُ
ٱلْمُجَٰهِدِينَ عَلَى ٱلْقَٰعِدِينَ أَجْرًا عَظِيمًا
٩٥ دَرَجَٰتٍ مِّنْهُ وَمَغْفِرَةً وَرَحْمَةًۚ وَكَانَ
ٱللَّهُ غَفُورًا رَّحِيمًا ٩٦

128. 'Those who sit at home' (i.e. remain passive) does not refer either to those who had been ordered to fight but tried to look for excuses not to fight or to those who were individually obliged to take part in fighting because of the general summons of *Jihād* (fight in the cause of God) and yet shirked this duty. The reference here is to those who remained engrossed in personal concerns at a time when *Jihād* had become a collective obligation (*farḍ bi al-kifāyah*).* In the first case the person who fails to fight can only be a hypocrite, and God holds out no good promise for such a person unless there is good reason, for example, genuine disability. In the second case, however, what is required is the mobilization of a part rather than the entire military strength of the Islamic community. In such cases, if the recognized head (*imām*) of the Islamic community summons the people to come forward and undertake the expedition concerned, those who respond to that call are reckoned to be of superior merit to those who remain occupied with other pursuits however meritorious.

**Farḍ bi al-kifāyah* signifies a collective duty of the Muslim community so that if some people carry it out no Muslim is considered blameworthy; but if no one carries it out all incur a collective guilt – Ed.

(97) While taking the souls of those who were engaged in wronging themselves,[129] the angels asked: 'In what circumstances were you?' They replied: 'We were too weak and helpless in the land.' The angels said: 'Was not the earth of Allah wide enough for you to emigrate in it?'[130] For such men their refuge is Hell – an evil destination indeed; (98) except the men, women, and children who were indeed too feeble to be able to seek the means of escape and did not know where to go – (99) maybe Allah shall pardon these, for Allah is All-Pardoning, All-Forgiving.

إِنَّ ٱلَّذِينَ تَوَفَّىٰهُمُ ٱلْمَلَٰٓئِكَةُ ظَالِمِىٓ
أَنفُسِهِمْ قَالُوا۟ فِيمَ كُنتُمْ قَالُوا۟ كُنَّا
مُسْتَضْعَفِينَ فِى ٱلْأَرْضِ ۚ قَالُوٓا۟ أَلَمْ تَكُنْ
أَرْضُ ٱللَّهِ وَٰسِعَةً فَتُهَاجِرُوا۟ فِيهَا ۚ فَأُو۟لَٰٓئِكَ
مَأْوَىٰهُمْ جَهَنَّمُ ۖ وَسَآءَتْ مَصِيرًا ﴿٩٧﴾ إِلَّا
ٱلْمُسْتَضْعَفِينَ مِنَ ٱلرِّجَالِ وَٱلنِّسَآءِ
وَٱلْوِلْدَٰنِ لَا يَسْتَطِيعُونَ حِيلَةً وَلَا يَهْتَدُونَ
سَبِيلًا ﴿٩٨﴾ فَأُو۟لَٰٓئِكَ عَسَى ٱللَّهُ أَن يَعْفُوَ
عَنْهُمْ ۚ وَكَانَ ٱللَّهُ عَفُوًّا غَفُورًا ﴿٩٩﴾

129. The reference here is to those who stay behind along with the unbelievers, despite no genuine disability. They are satisfied with a life made up of a blend of Islamic and un-Islamic elements, even though they have had the chance to migrate to the *Dār al-Islām* and thus enjoy a full Islamic life. This is the wrong that they committed against themselves. What kept them satisfied with the mixture of Islamic and un-Islamic elements in their life was not any genuine disability but their love of ease and comfort, their excessive attachment to their kith and kin and to their properties and worldly interests. These concerns had exceeded reasonable limits and had even taken precedence over their concern for their religion (see also n. 116 above).

130. Those people who had willingly acquiesced to living under an un-Islamic order would be called to account by God and would be asked: If a certain territory was under the dominance of rebels against God, so that it had become impossible to follow His Law, why did you continue to live there? Why did you not migrate to a land where it was possible to follow the law of God?

(100) He who emigrates in the way of Allah will find in the earth enough room for refuge and plentiful resources. And he who goes forth from his house as a migrant in the way of Allah and His Messenger, and whom death overtakes, his reward becomes incumbent on Allah. Surely Allah is All-Forgiving, All-Compassionate.[131]

۞ وَمَن يُهَاجِرْ فِي سَبِيلِ ٱللَّهِ يَجِدْ فِي
ٱلْأَرْضِ مُرَٰغَمًا كَثِيرًا وَسَعَةً ۚ وَمَن يَخْرُجْ
مِنۢ بَيْتِهِۦ مُهَاجِرًا إِلَى ٱللَّهِ وَرَسُولِهِۦ
ثُمَّ يُدْرِكْهُ ٱلْمَوْتُ فَقَدْ وَقَعَ أَجْرُهُۥ عَلَى ٱللَّهِ ۗ
وَكَانَ ٱللَّهُ غَفُورًا رَّحِيمًا ﴿١٠٠﴾

---

131. It should be understood clearly that it is only permissible for a person who believes in the true religion enjoined by God to live under the dominance of an un-Islamic system on one of the following conditions. First, that the believer struggles to put an end to the hegemony of the un-Islamic system and to have it replaced by the Islamic system of life, as the Prophets and their early followers had done. Second, that he lacks the means to get out of his homeland and thus stays there, but does so with utmost disinclination and unhappiness.

If neither of these conditions exist, a believer who continues to live in a land where an un-Islamic order prevails, commits an act of continuous sin. To say that one has no Islamic state to go to does not hold water. For if no Islamic state exists, are there no mountains or forests from where one could eke out a living by eating leaves and drinking the milk of goats and sheep, and thus avoid living in a state of submission to unbelief.

Some people have misunderstood the tradition which says: 'There is no *hijrah* after the conquest of Makka' (Bukhārī, 'Ṣayd', 10; 'Jihād', 1, 27, 194; Tirmidhī, 'Siyar', 33; Nasā'ī, 'Bay'ah', 15, etc. – Ed.) This tradition is specifically related to the people of Arabia of that time and does not embody a permanent injunction. At the time when the greater part of Arabia constituted the Domain of Unbelief (*Dār al-Kufr*) or the Domain of War (*Dār al-Ḥarb*), and Islamic laws were being enforced only in Madina and its outskirts, the Muslims were emphatically directed to join and keep together. But when unbelief lost its strength and *elan* after the conquest of Makka, and almost the entire peninsula came under the dominance of Islam, the Prophet (peace be on him) declared that migration was no longer needed. This does not mean, however, that the duty to migrate was abolished for Muslims all over the world for all time to come regardless of the circumstances in which they lived.

(101) When you go forth journeying in the land, there is no blame on you if you shorten the Prayer,[132] (especially) if you fear that the unbelievers might cause you harm.[133] Surely the unbelievers are your open enemies.

وَإِذَا ضَرَبْتُمْ فِي ٱلْأَرْضِ فَلَيْسَ عَلَيْكُمْ
جُنَاحٌ أَن تَقْصُرُوا۟ مِنَ ٱلصَّلَوٰةِ إِنْ خِفْتُمْ
أَن يَفْتِنَكُمُ ٱلَّذِينَ كَفَرُوٓا۟ ۚ إِنَّ ٱلْكَٰفِرِينَ كَانُوا۟
لَكُمْ عَدُوًّا مُّبِينًا ﴿١٠١﴾

---

132. Shortening Prayers (*qaṣr*) while travelling in peace-time consists of praying two *rak'ahs* at those appointed times when one is normally required to pray four *rak'ahs*. The form of *qaṣr* during a state of war has not been specified. Prayers should, therefore, be performed as circumstances permit. People should pray in congregation if possible, otherwise individually. If it is not possible to turn towards the *qiblah*, one may keep the direction in which one happens to be facing. One may even pray while seated either on the back of an animal or on a vehicle. If actual bowing and prostrating are not possible, they may be performed with hand signals. If absolutely necessary, one may even pray while walking. One may also pray even though one's clothes are soiled with blood. If, in spite of these relaxations, a man still fails to manage to perform a Prayer within the prescribed time, he may defer it, following the precedent set by the Prophet (peace be on him) during the Battle of the Ditch.

There is disagreement as to whether one should also perform the *sunnah* (recommended) Prayers, or confine oneself to the obligatory ones. It is established that the practice of the Prophet (peace be on him) was to keep up the *sunnah* connected with the *fajr* (morning) Prayers, and with the *witr* in the *'ishā'* (evening) Prayers. At the other prescribed times, he performed only the obligatory Prayers. He did, however, perform the *nafl* (supererogatory) Prayers whenever he had the chance to do so, sometimes even while he was mounted. For this reason 'Abd Allāh b. 'Umar expressed the opinion that one ought not to perform the *sunnah* Prayers while travelling, except for the *sunnah* in the *fajr* Prayers. But a majority of scholars consider both the performance and the omission of these Prayers as equally permissible, leaving the matter entirely to the discretion of the individual. The opinion held by the Ḥanafī school, however, is that it is preferable for a traveller actually on the move to omit the *sunnah* Prayers, but when he makes an overnight stop and is at his ease (even though in the legal sense he may still be a traveller), their performance is preferable.

According to some eminent jurists, journeys on which one may resort to *qaṣr* are those characterized as being *fī sabīl Allāh* (in the cause of God), such as military expeditions, Pilgrimage, the quest for knowledge, and so on. This is the judgement of 'Abd Allāh b. 'Umar, 'Abd Allāh b. Mas'ūd and 'Aṭā'. On the other hand, Shāfi'ī and Aḥmad b. Ḥanbal are of the view that such permission extends to all journeys undertaken for lawful purposes, though not to those undertaken for unlawful purposes: indeed, if one travels for illegitimate purposes, one has no right whatever to benefit from the relaxation of *qaṣr*. Ḥanafī jurists, however, do not connect *qaṣr* with the purpose of the journey; they consider it lawful on all journeys, regardless of the purposes for which they are undertaken. They hold that a traveller may be either rewarded or punished by God, depending on his purpose in travelling. That, however, has nothing to do with the permissibility of *qaṣr*. (See the commentaries on the verse by Qurṭubī, Ibn Kathīr and Jaṣṣāṣ. See also Ibn Rushd, *Bidāyat al-Mujtahid*, vol. 1, p. 163 – Ed.)

Other eminent jurists have inferred from the words: 'And there is no blame on you . . . ' that *qaṣr* is not obligatory for a traveller: it is merely permitted. A person may avail himself of it if he chooses, and he may also perform his Prayers normally if he so wishes. This is the view of Shāfi'ī, even though he considers *qaṣr* recommended and holds its omission to be tantamount to failure to adopt the preferable alternative. According to Aḥmad b. Ḥanbal, however, while *qaṣr* is not obligatory, its omission falls under the category of disapproved acts. In Abū Ḥanīfah's opinion, *qaṣr* is obligatory, and according to one report, Mālik is of the same opinion. (See the commentaries on the verse by Qurṭubī, Jaṣṣāṣ and Ibn al-'Arabī. See also *al-Fiqh 'alá al-Madhāhib al-Arba'ah*, vol. 1, p. 471, and n. 1, pp. 471–3 and Ibn Rushd, vol. 1, p. 161 – Ed.) It is established by the *Ḥadīth* that the Prophet (peace be on him) always shortened his Prayers during his journeys. There is no reliable tradition to the effect that the Prophet (peace be on him) ever prayed four full *rak'ahs* in these circumstances. Ibn 'Umar states that he accompanied the Prophet (peace be on him) as well as Abū Bakr, 'Umar and 'Uthmān on their journeys, and never saw any of them fail to shorten their Prayers. A number of authentic traditions which have come down from Ibn 'Abbās and several other Companions corroborate this. When 'Uthmān prayed four *rak'ahs* in Miná on the occasion of *Ḥajj*, some Companions objected to his not shortening the Prayer. 'Uthmān convinced them that he had not made any mistake in so doing by arguing that he had got married in Makka and he had heard from the Prophet (peace be on him) that the place a person married in was in a sense his home. In that respect he was, therefore, not a traveller. (See the commentaries on the verse by Qurṭubī, Jaṣṣāṣ and Ibn Kathīr, and the chapters on 'Ṣalāt al-Qaṣr' in the major collections of *Ḥadīth* – Ed.)

In opposition to these numerous traditions are two from 'Ā'ishah which indicate that it is equally valid both to shorten the Prayers and to do them in full. These traditions, however, have weak links in their transmission and are also opposed to the authenticated practice of 'Ā'ishah herself. It is also true that there are intermediary states between travel and non-travel. During a temporary stop, it is quite proper for a man to shorten his Prayers on some occasions and on others to complete them. It depends upon the circumstances. It is probably in this context that 'Ā'ishah states that the

Prophet (peace be on him) sometimes shortened his Prayers and sometimes performed them in full.

The Qur'ānic expression in the verse 'there shall be no blame' also occurs in the Qur'ānic verse on the ritual of running between Ṣafā and Marwah (see *Sūrah al-Baqarah* 2: 158). The actual words used in both verses apparently mean that these acts were not blameworthy even though the running, as we know, is part of the prescribed rites of Pilgrimage and is obligatory. We can appreciate the significance of both these Qur'ānic verses if we remember that the purpose in each case is to dispel the misunderstanding that the acts concerned might either entail some sin or jeopardize a man's reward.

Another question in regard to *qaṣr* is: What is the minimum travelling distance in which Prayers may be shortened? The Ẓāhirī school recognizes no limit at all: any travelling validates the shortening of Prayers. According to Mālik, however, one may not shorten Prayers if the distance involved is either less than forty-eight miles (seventy-seven kilometers) or involves travelling for less than a day and a night. This is also the opinion of Aḥmad b. Ḥanbal and Ibn 'Abbās and a statement in support of it has also come down from Shāfi'ī. The Companion Anas considers it permissible to shorten Prayers if the travelling distance is fifteen miles. Awzā'ī, Zuhrī and 'Umar consider one day's travelling to be sufficient; Ḥasan al-Baṣrī says that the journey should be two days long, and Abū Yūsuf says that it should be more than two days. According to Abū Ḥanīfah, one may shorten the Prayers on any journey in which one has to travel for three days either on foot or by camel, i.e. a distance of eighteen farsakh. Ibn 'Umar, Ibn Mas'ūd and 'Uthmān agree with this view. (See the commentary on the verse by Qurṭubī and Jaṣṣāṣ. See also *al-Fiqh 'alá al-Madhāhib al-Arba'ah*, vol. 1, pp. 472 ff. and Ibn Rushd, vol. 1, pp. 163 ff. – Ed.)

If one stops over *en route* to one's destination, how long may one stay in one place and still be allowed to shorten one's Prayers? On this question, too, a variety of opinions have been expressed. Aḥmad b. Ḥanbal is of the opinion that if a man decides to stay for four days, he should perform his Prayers in full. Mālik and Shāfi'ī are of the opinion that a man may not shorten his Prayers if he decides to stay at a place for more than four days. Awzā'ī and Abū Ḥanīfah are respectively of the opinion that if a person intends to stay at a place for more than thirteen or fifteen days, he should pray in full. No categorical injunction has come down from the Prophet (peace be on him) on this matter. All jurists agree, however, that if a man has been held up somewhere and cannot proceed because of some constraint, he may shorten his Prayers indefinitely provided he is in a constant state of readiness to undertake the journey back to his home as soon as the constraint is removed. Instances are reported of Companions who continued to shorten their Prayers for two years in this kind of circumstance. Treating the situation of a prisoner as analogous to this, Aḥmad b. Ḥanbal holds that he may shorten his Prayers throughout the

(102) (O Messenger!) If you are among the believers and rise (in the state of war) to lead the Prayer for them,[134] let a party of them stand with you to worship, keeping their arms.[135] When they have performed their prostration, let them go behind you, and let another party who have not prayed, pray with you, remaining on guard and keeping their arms,[136] for the unbelievers love to see you heedless of your arms and your baggage so that they might swoop upon you in a surprise attack.

وَإِذَا كُنتَ فِيهِمْ فَأَقَمْتَ لَهُمُ
ٱلصَّلَوٰةَ فَلْتَقُمْ طَآئِفَةٌ مِّنْهُم مَّعَكَ
وَلْيَأْخُذُوٓا۟ أَسْلِحَتَهُمْ فَإِذَا سَجَدُوا۟
فَلْيَكُونُوا۟ مِن وَرَآئِكُمْ وَلْتَأْتِ
طَآئِفَةٌ أُخْرَىٰ لَمْ يُصَلُّوا۟ فَلْيُصَلُّوا۟
مَعَكَ وَلْيَأْخُذُوا۟ حِذْرَهُمْ وَأَسْلِحَتَهُمْ ۗ
وَدَّ ٱلَّذِينَ كَفَرُوا۟ لَوْ تَغْفُلُونَ عَنْ
أَسْلِحَتِكُمْ وَأَمْتِعَتِكُمْ فَيَمِيلُونَ
عَلَيْكُم مَّيْلَةً وَٰحِدَةً ۚ

---

period of his imprisonment. (For legal discussions on the questions discussed here see the commentaries on the verse by Ibn Kathīr, Jaṣṣāṣ, Qurṭubī and Ibn al-'Arabī. See also Ibn Rushd, vol. 1, pp. 160–5 – Ed.)

133. The Ẓāhirīs and Khawārij have interpreted this to signify that the injunction of shortening Prayers is confined to war-time alone and that it is against the Qur'ān to shorten Prayers while travelling in peace-time. But it is established by an authentic tradition that when 'Umar mentioned this misgiving to the Prophet (peace be on him), he said: 'This is a charitable gift to you from God, so accept His charitable gift.' (Muslim, 'Ṣalāt al-Musāfirīn', 12; Abū Dā'ūd, 'Ṣalāt al-Safar', 1; Aḥmad b. Ḥanbal, *Musnad*, vol. 3, pp. 129 and 190 – Ed.) It is more or less established by an overwhelmingly large number of traditions that the Prophet (peace be on him) shortened his Prayers in times of both war and peace. Ibn 'Abbās states categorically that the Prophet (peace be on him) left Madina with the intention of performing Pilgrimage to the Ka'bah, and during this journey he prayed two *rak'ahs* (instead of four) even though he could have nothing to fear except God. (See Nasā'ī, 'Taqṣīr al-Ṣalāh', 1 – Ed.) It is for this reason that I have added the word 'especially' in brackets to the text of the translation.

134. These words have led Abū Yūsuf and Ḥasan b. Ziyād to the view that Prayer in a state of insecurity was confined to the time of the Prophet (peace be on him) alone. There are numerous examples, however, where

a Qur'ānic injunction was addressed specifically to the Prophet (peace be on him), yet holds good for the succeeding periods. Moreover, it is established that many outstanding Companions also resorted to this form of Prayer, even after the death of the Prophet (peace be on him), and there are no reports of disagreement on this question among the Companions. (For discussion see Jaṣṣāṣ, vol. 2, pp. 261–3 and Ibn Rushd, vol. 1, p. 169 – Ed.)

135. This injunction regarding Prayer in a state of either fear or insecurity (*ṣalāt al-khawf*) refers to the time when an enemy attack is anticipated, but the fighting has not yet begun. When fighting is taking place the ruling of the Ḥanafī school is that Prayer may be deferred. Mālik and Thawrī are of the opinion that if it is not possible to bow and prostrate in Prayer, it is enough to perform these actions by means of signs. Shāfi'ī argues that should the need arise, one might even fight while still in the state of Prayer. It is an established fact that on four occasions during the Battle of the Ditch the Prophet (peace be on him) missed Prayers during the appointed times, but performed them subsequently in their correct sequence, even though the above-mentioned injunction regarding Prayer in the state of insecurity had already been revealed. (See Jaṣṣāṣ, vol. 2, pp. 263 ff. – Ed.)

136. The actual form of congregational Prayer in the state of insecurity depends, to a large extent, on the actual state of the hostilities. The Prophet (peace be on him) prayed variously under different conditions. A Muslim commander may use his discretion and adopt whichever of the following forms of Prayer seems to him most in keeping with the actual circumstances of the conflict:

(1) That a group of soldiers may pray behind the Prayer-leader, while the rest take their positions against the enemy. When one *rak'ah* is completed, the first group may disperse to be replaced in the Prayer by those who were at battle-stations, and who now complete the second *rak'ah* behind the leader. In this way the soldiers will have prayed one *rak'ah* each, and the leader two *rak'ahs*.

(2) That a group of soldiers may pray first and then another group may pray one *rak'ah* each behind the leader. Subsequently, each of the two groups comes, in turn, to complete the Prayer by performing one *rak'ah* individually. In this way, each of the two groups will have prayed one *rak'ah* congregationally and one *rak'ah* individually.

(3) That a group may pray two *rak'ahs* behind the leader, recite *tashahhud* and finish the Prayer by reciting the salutation. Then the second group may join the Prayer behind the leader and complete it with him. Thus the Prayer-leader will have prayed four *rak'ahs* and each of the two groups will have prayed two.

(4) That a group may pray one *rak'ah* behind the leader. When the leader rises to pray the second *rak'ah*, those who have been following him

But there shall be no blame upon you if you were to lay aside your arms if you are either troubled by rain or are sick; but remain on guard. Surely Allah has prepared a humiliating chastisement for the unbelievers.[137] (103) When you have finished the Prayer, remember Allah – standing, and sitting, and reclining. And when you become secure, perform the regular Prayer. The Prayer is enjoined upon the believers at stated times.

وَلَا جُنَاحَ عَلَيْكُمْ إِن كَانَ بِكُمْ
أَذًى مِّن مَّطَرٍ أَوْ كُنتُم مَّرْضَىٰٓ أَن
تَضَعُوٓا أَسْلِحَتَكُمْ ۖ وَخُذُوا حِذْرَكُمْ ۗ
إِنَّ ٱللَّهَ أَعَدَّ لِلْكَٰفِرِينَ عَذَابًا مُّهِينًا ﴿١٠٢﴾
فَإِذَا قَضَيْتُمُ ٱلصَّلَوٰةَ فَٱذْكُرُوا
ٱللَّهَ قِيَٰمًا وَقُعُودًا وَعَلَىٰ جُنُوبِكُمْ ۚ
فَإِذَا ٱطْمَأْنَنتُمْ فَأَقِيمُوا ٱلصَّلَوٰةَ ۚ إِنَّ
ٱلصَّلَوٰةَ كَانَتْ عَلَى ٱلْمُؤْمِنِينَ
كِتَٰبًا مَّوْقُوتًا ﴿١٠٣﴾

---

may complete the second *rak'ah* by themselves, including the recitation of the *tashahhud* and salutation. Then the second group joins the Prayer while the leader is in the second *rak'ah*. After the leader has finished his second *rak'ah* and his followers have prayed their first, the latter may rise and complete their Prayer by performing the second *rak'ah* by themselves. In this case, the leader should prolong his standing in the second *rak'ah* of the Prayer.

The first form has been reported by Ibn 'Abbās, Jābir b. 'Abd Allāh and Mujāhid. The second form has been reported by 'Abd Allāh b. Mas'ūd and is the basis of the Ḥanafī ruling on this matter. The third form of the Prayer has been adopted by Shāfi'ī and Mālik with slight modification. The basis of this ruling is a tradition from Sahl b. Abī Ḥathmah.*

There are certain other forms of Prayer in the state of insecurity, details of which can be found in larger works of Islamic Law.

137. This is to emphasize that the precautions recommended here are among the measures which ought to be adopted with a view to minimizing

---

* This tradition reports that the Prophet (peace be on him) led the Prayer of his Companions as prescribed for the state of insecurity. The Companions stood in two rows behind the Prophet (peace be on him). The Companions in the first row completed the first *rak'ah* with the Prophet (peace be on him), then rose and remained standing until those in the second row had prayed one *rak'ah*. The latter then rose and stepped forward and the ones standing ahead of them retreated behind them. Then the Prophet (peace be on him) prayed with this group one *rak'ah*, then sat down until the back row had prayed one *rak'ah*. Then the Prophet (peace be on him) recited the salutation (marking the end of the Prayer). See Muslim, 'Ṣalāt al-Musāfirīn' – Ed.

(104) Do not be faint of heart in pursuing these people:[138] if you happen to suffer harm they too are suffering just as you are, while you may hope from Allah what they cannot hope for.[139] Allah is All-Knowing, All-Wise.

(105) (O Messenger!) We have revealed to you this Book with the Truth so that you may judge between people in accordance with what Allah has shown you. So do not dispute on behalf of the dishonest,[140] (106) and seek forgiveness from Allah. Surely Allah is All-Forgiving, All-Compassionate. ▶

وَلَا تَهِنُوا۟ فِى ٱبْتِغَآءِ ٱلْقَوْمِ ۖ إِن تَكُونُوا۟
تَأْلَمُونَ فَإِنَّهُمْ يَأْلَمُونَ كَمَا
تَأْلَمُونَ ۖ وَتَرْجُونَ مِنَ ٱللَّهِ مَا لَا
يَرْجُونَ ۗ وَكَانَ ٱللَّهُ عَلِيمًا حَكِيمًا ﴿١٠٤﴾
إِنَّآ أَنزَلْنَآ إِلَيْكَ ٱلْكِتَـٰبَ بِٱلْحَقِّ
لِتَحْكُمَ بَيْنَ ٱلنَّاسِ بِمَآ أَرَىٰكَ ٱللَّهُ ۚ
وَلَا تَكُن لِّلْخَآئِنِينَ خَصِيمًا ﴿١٠٥﴾
وَٱسْتَغْفِرِ ٱللَّهَ ۖ إِنَّ ٱللَّهَ كَانَ غَفُورًا
رَّحِيمًا ﴿١٠٦﴾

losses and ensuring good results. Victory and defeat ultimately depend, however, on the will of God; so even while taking these precautionary measures one should feel sure that God will humiliate those who are trying to extinguish His light.

138. This refers to those unbelievers who adamantly opposed the cause of Islam and the establishment of the Islamic order.

139. It is astonishing that men of faith should not be prepared to endure the same degree of hardship for the sake of the Truth as unbelievers do for the sake of falsehood. This is strange insofar as the latter merely seek the transient benefits of worldly life whereas the faithful seek to please, and secure the proximity of the Lord of the Universe and look forward to everlasting rewards.

140. These and certain other verses which occur a little later on (see verses 113 ff.) deal with an important matter, related to an incident that took place around the time they were revealed. The incident involved a person called Ṭu'mah or Bashīr ibn Ubayriq of the Banū Ẓafar tribe of the

Anṣār. This man stole an Anṣārī's coat of mail. While the investigation was in progress, he put the coat of mail in the house of a Jew. Its owner approached the Prophet (peace be on him) and expressed his suspicion about Ṭu'mah. But Ṭu'mah, his kinsmen and many of the Banū Ẓafar colluded to ascribe the guilt to the Jew. When the Jew concerned was asked about the matter he pleaded that he was not guilty. Ṭu'mah's supporters, on the other hand, waged a vigorous propaganda campaign to save Ṭu'mah's skin. They argued that the wicked Jew, who had denied the Truth and disbelieved in God and the Prophet (peace be on him), was absolutely untrustworthy, and his statement ought to be rejected outright. The Prophet (peace be on him) was about to decide the case against the Jew on formal grounds and to censure the plaintiff for slandering Banū Ubayriq, but before he could do so, the whole matter was laid bare by a revelation from God. (For the traditions cited here, see the commentary of Ibn Kathīr on this verse – Ed.)

It is obvious that the Prophet (peace be on him) would have committed no sin if he had given judgement on the evidence before him. Judges are quite often faced with such situations. False evidence is given in order to obtain wrong verdicts. The time when this case came up for decision was a time of severe conflict between Islam and unbelief. Had the Prophet (peace be on him) issued a wrong judgement on the basis of the evidence before him, it would have provided the opponents of Islam with an effective weapon against the Prophet (peace be on him) as well as against the entire Islamic community, and even Islam itself. They could have spread the word that the Prophet (peace be on him) and his followers were not concerned about right and justice: it would have been claimed that they were guilty of the same prejudice and chauvinism against which they had themselves been preaching. It was specifically to prevent this situation that God intervened in this particular case.

In this and the following verses (105 ff.) the Muslims were strongly censured for supporting criminals for no other reason than either family or tribal solidarity and were told that they should not allow prejudice to interfere with the principle of equal justice for all. Man's instinctive honesty revolts against the idea of supporting one's own kin even when they are wrong, and denying others their legitimate rights.

(107) Do not plead for those who are dishonest to themselves;[141] Allah does not love him who betrays trust and persists in sin. (108) They can hide (their deeds) from men but they cannot hide (them) from Allah for He is with them even when they hold nightly counsels that are unpleasing to Allah. Allah encompasses all their doings. (109) You pleaded on their behalf in this worldly life but who will plead with Allah on their behalf on the Day of Resurrection, or who will be their defender there? (110) He who does either evil or wrongs himself, and then asks for the forgiveness of Allah, will find Allah All-Forgiving, All-Compassionate. (111) He who commits a sin, commits it only to his detriment. Surely Allah is All-Knowing, All-Wise. (112) But he who commits either a fault or a sin, and then casts it upon an innocent person, lays upon himself the burden of a false charge and a flagrant sin.

وَلَا تُجَٰدِلۡ عَنِ ٱلَّذِينَ يَخۡتَانُونَ
أَنفُسَهُمۡۚ إِنَّ ٱللَّهَ لَا يُحِبُّ مَن كَانَ
خَوَّانًا أَثِيمٗا ﴿١٠٧﴾ يَسۡتَخۡفُونَ مِنَ
ٱلنَّاسِ وَلَا يَسۡتَخۡفُونَ مِنَ ٱللَّهِ وَهُوَ
مَعَهُمۡ إِذۡ يُبَيِّتُونَ مَا لَا يَرۡضَىٰ مِنَ
ٱلۡقَوۡلِۚ وَكَانَ ٱللَّهُ بِمَا يَعۡمَلُونَ
مُحِيطًا ﴿١٠٨﴾ هَٰٓأَنتُمۡ هَٰٓؤُلَآءِ جَٰدَلۡتُمۡ
عَنۡهُمۡ فِي ٱلۡحَيَوٰةِ ٱلدُّنۡيَا فَمَن
يُجَٰدِلُ ٱللَّهَ عَنۡهُمۡ يَوۡمَ ٱلۡقِيَٰمَةِ أَم
مَّن يَكُونُ عَلَيۡهِمۡ وَكِيلٗا ﴿١٠٩﴾
وَمَن يَعۡمَلۡ سُوٓءًا أَوۡ يَظۡلِمۡ نَفۡسَهُۥ ثُمَّ
يَسۡتَغۡفِرِ ٱللَّهَ يَجِدِ ٱللَّهَ غَفُورٗا
رَّحِيمٗا ﴿١١٠﴾ وَمَن يَكۡسِبۡ إِثۡمٗا
فَإِنَّمَا يَكۡسِبُهُۥ عَلَىٰ نَفۡسِهِۦۚ وَكَانَ ٱللَّهُ
عَلِيمًا حَكِيمٗا ﴿١١١﴾ وَمَن يَكۡسِبۡ
خَطِيٓـَٔةً أَوۡ إِثۡمٗا ثُمَّ يَرۡمِ بِهِۦ بَرِيٓـٔٗا فَقَدِ
ٱحۡتَمَلَ بُهۡتَٰنٗا وَإِثۡمٗا مُّبِينٗا ﴿١١٢﴾

141. Whoever commits a breach of trust with others in fact commits a breach of trust with his own self first. For the powers of his head and heart have been placed at his disposal as a trust, and by misusing them he is forcing those powers to support him in acts which involve a breach of trust. In doing so the person concerned suppresses his conscience, which God has placed as a sentinel over his moral conduct, with the result that it is rendered incapable of preventing him from acts of wrong and iniquity. It

(113) (O Messenger!) But for Allah's favour and mercy upon you, a party of them had resolved to mislead you, yet they only misled themselves, and could not have harmed you in any way.[142] Allah revealed to you the Book and Wisdom, and He taught you what you knew not. Great indeed has been Allah's favour upon you.

(114) Most of their secret conferrings are devoid of good, unless one secretly enjoins in charity, good deeds, and setting the affairs of men right. We shall grant whoever does that seeking to please Allah a great reward. (115) As for him who sets himself against the Messenger and follows a path other than that of the believers even after true guidance had become clear to him, We will let him go to the way he has turned to,[143] and We will cast him into Hell – an evil destination.

وَلَوْلَا فَضْلُ ٱللَّهِ عَلَيْكَ وَرَحْمَتُهُۥ
لَهَمَّت طَّآئِفَةٌ مِّنْهُمْ أَن
يُضِلُّوكَ وَمَا يُضِلُّونَ إِلَّآ أَنفُسَهُمْ
وَمَا يَضُرُّونَكَ مِن شَىْءٍ وَأَنزَلَ ٱللَّهُ
عَلَيْكَ ٱلْكِتَٰبَ وَٱلْحِكْمَةَ وَعَلَّمَكَ
مَا لَمْ تَكُن تَعْلَمُ وَكَانَ فَضْلُ ٱللَّهِ
عَلَيْكَ عَظِيمًا ﴿١١٣﴾ ۞ لَّا خَيْرَ فِى
كَثِيرٍ مِّن نَّجْوَىٰهُمْ إِلَّا مَنْ أَمَرَ
بِصَدَقَةٍ أَوْ مَعْرُوفٍ أَوْ إِصْلَٰحٍ
بَيْنَ ٱلنَّاسِ وَمَن يَفْعَلْ ذَٰلِكَ
ٱبْتِغَآءَ مَرْضَاتِ ٱللَّهِ فَسَوْفَ نُؤْتِيهِ
أَجْرًا عَظِيمًا ﴿١١٤﴾ وَمَن يُشَاقِقِ ٱلرَّسُولَ
مِنۢ بَعْدِ مَا تَبَيَّنَ لَهُ ٱلْهُدَىٰ وَيَتَّبِعْ غَيْرَ
سَبِيلِ ٱلْمُؤْمِنِينَ نُوَلِّهِۦ مَا تَوَلَّىٰ وَنُصْلِهِۦ
جَهَنَّمَ وَسَآءَتْ مَصِيرًا ﴿١١٥﴾

---

is only after a man has already carried out this cruel suppression of conscience within himself that he is able to commit acts of sin and iniquity outwardly.

142. Even if some people succeeded in their design to obtain from the Prophet (peace be on him) a wrong judgement in their favour by presenting a false account of events, the real loss would have been theirs rather than the Prophet's (peace be on him). For the real criminals in the sight of God are the perpetrators of that fraud and not the Prophet (peace be on him) who might in good faith have delivered a verdict that actually did not

(116) Truly it is only associating others with Allah in His divinity that Allah does not forgive,[144] and forgives anything besides that to whomsoever He wills. Whoever associates others with Allah in His divinity has indeed strayed far away. (117) Rather than call upon Him, they call upon goddesses, and call upon a rebellious Satan[145] (118) upon whom Allah has laid His curse. He said (to Allah): 'I will take to myself an appointed portion of Your servants[146] (119) and shall lead them astray, and shall engross them in vain desires, and I shall command them and they will cut off the ears of the cattle,[147] and I shall command them and they will disfigure Allah's creation.'[148]

إِنَّ ٱللَّهَ لَا يَغْفِرُ أَن يُشْرَكَ بِهِۦ وَيَغْفِرُ
مَا دُونَ ذَٰلِكَ لِمَن يَشَآءُ ۚ وَمَن يُشْرِكْ
بِٱللَّهِ فَقَدْ ضَلَّ ضَلَٰلًۢا بَعِيدًا ﴿١١٦﴾ إِن
يَدْعُونَ مِن دُونِهِۦٓ إِلَّآ إِنَٰثًا وَإِن
يَدْعُونَ إِلَّا شَيْطَٰنًا مَّرِيدًا ﴿١١٧﴾
لَّعَنَهُ ٱللَّهُ ۘ وَقَالَ لَأَتَّخِذَنَّ
مِنْ عِبَادِكَ نَصِيبًا مَّفْرُوضًا ﴿١١٨﴾
وَلَأُضِلَّنَّهُمْ وَلَأُمَنِّيَنَّهُمْ وَلَءَامُرَنَّهُمْ
فَلَيُبَتِّكُنَّ ءَاذَانَ ٱلْأَنْعَٰمِ
وَلَءَامُرَنَّهُمْ فَلَيُغَيِّرُنَّ خَلْقَ ٱللَّهِ ۚ

---

conform to the facts. Whoever obtains a judgement in his favour by tricking the courts deludes himself into believing that by such tricks he can bring right to his side; right remains with its true claimant regardless of judgements obtained by fraud and deception. (See also *Towards Understanding the Qur'ān*, vol. I, *Sūrah* 2, n. 197.)

143. When, after revelation from God, the Prophet (peace be on him) delivered his verdict in favour of the innocent Jew rather than the dishonest Muslim, the latter was so seized by un-Islamic, egotistic and chauvinistic considerations that he left Madina, went straight to Makka to join the ranks of the enemies of Islam and of the Prophet (peace be on him), and undertook open opposition. The verse alludes to that incident.

144. In this and the following verses we are asked to consider coolly, the end result of obsession with rage and anger, and what kind of people

one chooses to identify with in place of the righteous people from whom one foolishly dissociates oneself.

145. No one sets up Satan as his 'god' in the sense that he makes him the object of his ritual worship and declares him to be God in so many words. The way to make Satan one's god is to entrust one's reins to him and let oneself be drawn helplessly in whichever direction he wants; the relationship between the two is, then, that of worshipper and worshipped. This shows that either absolute, unreserved obedience to or blind following of anybody is tantamount to 'worshipping' him, so that whoever indulges in this kind of absolute obedience is guilty of worshipping a 'god' other than the One True God.

146. This shows that Satan is determined to lay his claim to a portion of men's time, to their effort and labour, to their energies and capacities, to their material belongings, and to their offspring, and would somehow trick them into devoting a sizeable portion of all these in his cause.

147. The reference here is to a superstitious Arabian custom. It was customary among the Arabs that after a camel had given birth to five or ten young to slit her ears and let her go in the name of their deity; they considered it forbidden to put her to any work. Likewise, the male camel that had caused the birth of ten camels was consecrated to some deity. The slitting of ears symbolized this consecration.

148. To alter God's creation in some respect does not mean changing its original form. If that was meant, human civilization would have to be considered Satanic in its entirety. For civilization consists essentially of man's putting to use the resources endowed by God. Hence the alteration of God's creation, which is characterized as Satanic, consists in using a thing not for the purpose for which it was created by God. In other words, all acts performed in violation either of one's true nature or of the intrinsic nature of other things are the result of the misleading promptings of Satan. These include, for instance, sodomy, birth control, monasticism, celibacy, sterilization of either men or women, turning males into eunuchs, diverting females from the functions entrusted to them by nature and driving them to perform the functions for which men were created. These and numerous similar measures are enacted by Satan's disciples in this world, which amounts on their part, to saying that the laws of the Creator were faulty and that they would like to 'reform' them.

He who took Satan rather than Allah for his guardian has indeed suffered a manifest loss. (120) Satan makes promises to them and fills them with vain hopes,[149] but whatever he promises them is merely delusion. (121) For these people, their abode shall be Hell and from there they shall find no way of escape. (122) But those who believe and do good, We shall cause them to enter the Gardens beneath which rivers flow. Here they will abide for ever. This is Allah's promise in truth and whose word is truer than Allah's?

(123) It is neither your fancies nor the fancies of the People of the Book which matter. Whoever does evil shall reap its consequence and will find none to be his protector and helper against Allah. (124) Whoever does good and believes – whether he is male or female – such shall enter the Garden, and they shall not be wronged in the slightest.

وَمَن يَتَّخِذِ ٱلشَّيْطَٰنَ وَلِيًّا
مِّن دُونِ ٱللَّهِ فَقَدْ خَسِرَ
خُسْرَانًا مُّبِينًا ﴿١١٩﴾ يَعِدُهُمْ
وَيُمَنِّيهِمْ ۖ وَمَا يَعِدُهُمُ ٱلشَّيْطَٰنُ إِلَّا
غُرُورًا ﴿١٢٠﴾ أُو۟لَٰٓئِكَ مَأْوَىٰهُمْ جَهَنَّمُ
وَلَا يَجِدُونَ عَنْهَا مَحِيصًا ﴿١٢١﴾
وَٱلَّذِينَ ءَامَنُوا۟ وَعَمِلُوا۟
ٱلصَّٰلِحَٰتِ سَنُدْخِلُهُمْ جَنَّٰتٍ
تَجْرِى مِن تَحْتِهَا ٱلْأَنْهَٰرُ خَٰلِدِينَ
فِيهَآ أَبَدًا ۖ وَعْدَ ٱللَّهِ حَقًّا ۚ وَمَنْ أَصْدَقُ
مِنَ ٱللَّهِ قِيلًا ﴿١٢٢﴾ لَّيْسَ بِأَمَانِيِّكُمْ
وَلَآ أَمَانِىِّ أَهْلِ ٱلْكِتَٰبِ ۗ مَن
يَعْمَلْ سُوٓءًا يُجْزَ بِهِۦ وَلَا يَجِدْ لَهُۥ
مِن دُونِ ٱللَّهِ وَلِيًّا وَلَا نَصِيرًا ﴿١٢٣﴾
وَمَن يَعْمَلْ مِنَ ٱلصَّٰلِحَٰتِ مِن
ذَكَرٍ أَوْ أُنثَىٰ وَهُوَ مُؤْمِنٌ فَأُو۟لَٰٓئِكَ
يَدْخُلُونَ ٱلْجَنَّةَ وَلَا يُظْلَمُونَ
نَقِيرًا ﴿١٢٤﴾

---

149. Satanic operations are based on making attractive promises and raising high hopes. Whenever Satan wants to mislead men, whether individually or collectively, he tries to inspire them with utopian expectations. In some he inspires expectations of ecstatic pleasure and outstanding success in their individual lives. He inspires others with prospects for achieving national glory. To still others he promises the well-being of mankind. He makes people feel confident that they can arrive at the

(125) And whose way of life could be better than that of he who submits his whole being to Allah, does good, and follows exclusively the way of Abraham whom Allah took for a friend? (126) Whatever is in the heavens and in the earth belongs to Allah;[150] Allah encompasses everything.[151]

(127) They ask you to pronounce laws concerning women,[152] say: 'Allah pronounces to you concerning them,[153] and reminds you of the injunctions which were recited to you in the Book about female orphans whom you do not give what has been ordained for them[154] and whom you wish to marry (out of greed)',[155] and the commandments relating to the children who are weak and helpless.[156] Allah directs you to treat the orphans with justice. Allah is well aware of whatever good you do.

وَمَنْ أَحْسَنُ دِينًا مِّمَّنْ أَسْلَمَ وَجْهَهُۥ
لِلَّهِ وَهُوَ مُحْسِنٌ وَٱتَّبَعَ مِلَّةَ إِبْرَٰهِيمَ
حَنِيفًا ۗ وَٱتَّخَذَ ٱللَّهُ إِبْرَٰهِيمَ خَلِيلًا ﴿١٢٥﴾
وَلِلَّهِ مَا فِى ٱلسَّمَٰوَٰتِ وَمَا فِى ٱلْأَرْضِ ۚ
وَكَانَ ٱللَّهُ بِكُلِّ شَىْءٍ مُّحِيطًا
﴿١٢٦﴾ وَيَسْتَفْتُونَكَ فِى ٱلنِّسَآءِ ۖ قُلِ ٱللَّهُ
يُفْتِيكُمْ فِيهِنَّ وَمَا يُتْلَىٰ
عَلَيْكُمْ فِى ٱلْكِتَٰبِ فِى يَتَٰمَى ٱلنِّسَآءِ
ٱلَّٰتِى لَا تُؤْتُونَهُنَّ مَا كُتِبَ لَهُنَّ
وَتَرْغَبُونَ أَن تَنكِحُوهُنَّ
وَٱلْمُسْتَضْعَفِينَ مِنَ ٱلْوِلْدَٰنِ
وَأَن تَقُومُوا۟ لِلْيَتَٰمَىٰ بِٱلْقِسْطِ ۚ
وَمَا تَفْعَلُوا۟ مِنْ خَيْرٍ فَإِنَّ ٱللَّهَ كَانَ بِهِۦ
عَلِيمًا ﴿١٢٧﴾

---

ultimate truth without the aid of revealed knowledge. He deludes others into believing that God neither exists nor that there is any Life-after-Death. He comforts others with the belief that even if there is an After-life, they will be able to escape punishment through the intercession of certain persons. In short, Satan extends to different groups of people different promises and expectations with a view to seducing them.

150. To submit to God is the best course for man, for it conforms fully to ultimate reality. Since God is the Lord of the heavens and the earth and all that lies therein, the only right attitude for man is to give up his unlimited freedom and willingly commit himself to serve and obey God.

151. If man will neither submit to God nor stop acting in defiance of Him, he should bear in mind that he can never escape from God's grip, for His power encompasses him completely.

152. The actual query about women is not spelled out directly. The judgement pronounced a little later on in response to that query, however, makes it abundantly clear what the query was.

153. This is not a response to the query itself. Before attending to this, God once again emphasizes that people should implement His directives regarding orphans in general, and orphan girls in particular, as mentioned at the beginning of this *sūrah* (see verses 2 ff. above). This shows the importance of the rights of orphans in the sight of God. The protection of their rights, as we have pointed out, had already been stressed forcefully (see beginning of the *sūrah*, verses 1–14). But that was not deemed sufficient. Hence, when problems of family life came up for discussion, the question of the well-being of orphans automatically arose even before answering the questions people raised.

154. This alludes to verse 3 of this *sūrah*: 'And if you fear that you might not treat the orphans justly, then marry the women that seem good to you.'

155. The words of the text تَرْغَبُونَ أَن تَنكِحُوهُنَّ may be interpreted as: 'Whom you wish to marry (out of greed)' and also as 'Whom you do not wish to marry.' In explanation of this verse 'Ā'ishah states that, in those days, guardians of orphan girls who had any significant inheritance from their parents used to perpetrate many wrongs on their wards. If the girl was both rich and good looking, the guardian desired to marry her and exploit both her attractiveness and wealth without either having to make the bridal-due (*mahr*) or even having to undertake her maintenance. If the girl was ugly, the guardian would neither marry her nor allow her to get married, for she might thus get a husband who would support her claim to her legitimate rights. (See the commentary of Ibn Kathīr on this verse. The tradition is quoted by Ibn Kathīr from Bukhārī. See also n. 4 above – Ed.)

156. The reference here is to the injunctions regarding the protection of the rights of orphans at the beginning of the *sūrah* (see verses 1 ff. and 11 ff. above).

(128) If[157] a woman fears either ill-treatment or aversion from her husband it is not wrong for the husband and wife to bring about reconciliation among themselves (by compromising on their rights), for settlement is better.[158] Man's soul is always prone to selfishness,[159] but if you do good and are God-fearing, then surely Allah is aware of the things you do.[160] ▶

وَإِنِ ٱمْرَأَةٌ خَافَتْ مِنۢ بَعْلِهَا نُشُوزًا
أَوْ إِعْرَاضًا فَلَا جُنَاحَ عَلَيْهِمَآ أَن
يُصْلِحَا بَيْنَهُمَا صُلْحًا ۚ وَٱلصُّلْحُ خَيْرٌ ۗ
وَأُحْضِرَتِ ٱلْأَنفُسُ ٱلشُّحَّ ۚ وَإِن
تُحْسِنُوا۟ وَتَتَّقُوا۟ فَإِنَّ ٱللَّهَ كَانَ
بِمَا تَعْمَلُونَ خَبِيرًا ﴿١٢٨﴾

---

157. The actual response to the query begins here. In order to appreciate the response fully one would do well to consider the query itself. In the days of Ignorance a man was free to marry an unlimited number of women, who had virtually no rights. When the preliminary verses of the present *sūrah* were revealed (see especially verse 3) this freedom was circumscribed in two ways. First, the maximum number of wives was fixed at four. Second, justice (that is, equal treatment of wives) was laid down as a necessary condition for marrying more than one. This gives rise to the question whether a person is obligated by Islam to feel equally towards each of his wives, to love each to an equal degree, and treat them equally even in respect of sexual relationship. Such questions are especially relevant with regard to a husband one of whose wives might be, say, afflicted with either sterility, permanent sickness or who is incapable of sexual intercourse. Does justice demand that if he fails to live up to the standards of equality mentioned above that he should renounce his first wife in order to marry the second? Moreover, where the first wife is disinclined to agree to annulment of the marriage, is it appropriate for the spouses to make a voluntary accord between themselves, according to which the wife, towards whom the husband feels relatively less attracted, voluntarily surrenders some of her rights, prevailing upon her husband not to repudiate the marriage? Would such an act be against the dictates of justice?

It is to questions such as these that these verses are addressed.

158. It is better for the spouses to come to a mutual understanding so that the wife may remain with the same man with whom she has already spent part of her life.

159. The 'selfishness' on the part of the wife is that even though she is conscious of the causes which have contributed to her husband's aversion

(129) You will not be able to treat your wives with absolute justice not even when you keenly desire to do so. (It suffices in order to follow the Law of Allah that) you incline not wholly to one, leaving the other in suspense.[161] If you act rightly and remain God-fearing, surely Allah is All-Forgiving, All-Compassionate.[162] (130) But if the two separate, out of His plenty Allah will make each dispense with the other. Indeed Allah is All-Bounteous, All-Wise. ▶

وَلَن تَسْتَطِيعُوٓا۟ أَن تَعْدِلُوا۟ بَيْنَ
ٱلنِّسَآءِ وَلَوْ حَرَصْتُمْ ۖ فَلَا تَمِيلُوا۟
كُلَّ ٱلْمَيْلِ فَتَذَرُوهَا كَٱلْمُعَلَّقَةِ ۚ
وَإِن تُصْلِحُوا۟ وَتَتَّقُوا۟ فَإِنَّ ٱللَّهَ
كَانَ غَفُورًا رَّحِيمًا ﴿١٢٩﴾ وَإِن
يَتَفَرَّقَا يُغْنِ ٱللَّهُ كُلًّا مِّن سَعَتِهِۦ ۚ
وَكَانَ ٱللَّهُ وَٰسِعًا حَكِيمًا ﴿١٣٠﴾

towards her, she nevertheless expects from him the treatment that a husband accords to the wife that he loves. The 'selfishness' of the husband, on the other hand, lies in suppressing her unduly and curtailing her rights to an intolerable extent, merely because she is keen to continue to live with him even though she has lost her attraction for him.

160. Here, too, God urges the male, as He usually does in such matters, to be magnanimous. God urges a man to treat his wife, who has probably spent a considerable number of years with him as his companion, with kindliness and grace in spite of the aversion that he has come to feel for her. He also urges man to love God, for if He were to deprive him of His loving care and blessing in order to punish him for his shortcomings, what place would he have under the sun?

161. This means that it is not possible for a man to accord complete equality of treatment to two or more wives under all circumstances and in all respects. It is possible that one is ugly, the other beautiful; one is old, the other young; one is permanently sick, the other healthy; one is irritable, the other good-tempered. These and other differences are likely to make a person less attracted to one and more to the other. In such circumstances, the Law does not demand that one should necessarily maintain absolute equality between the wives in respect of love, emotional attachment and sexual relationship. What it does demand is that if a husband does not

(131) All that is in the heavens and all that is in the earth belongs to Allah. We enjoined upon those who were given the Book before you, and also yourselves, to have fear of Allah. But if you disbelieve, then bear in mind that all that is in the heavens and all that is in the earth belongs to Allah. Allah is Self-Sufficient, Most Praiseworthy. ▶

وَلِلَّهِ مَا فِي ٱلسَّمَٰوَٰتِ وَمَا فِي
ٱلْأَرْضِ ۗ وَلَقَدْ وَصَّيْنَا ٱلَّذِينَ أُوتُوا۟ ٱلْكِتَٰبَ
مِن قَبْلِكُمْ وَإِيَّاكُمْ أَنِ ٱتَّقُوا۟ ٱللَّهَ ۚ
وَإِن تَكْفُرُوا۟ فَإِنَّ لِلَّهِ مَا فِي ٱلسَّمَٰوَٰتِ
وَمَا فِي ٱلْأَرْضِ ۚ وَكَانَ ٱللَّهُ غَنِيًّا حَمِيدًا ﴿١٣١﴾

repudiate the marriage despite aversion for his wife, either because of his own desire or out of consideration for the desire of his wife, he should at least maintain a good relationship short of which his wife begins to feel as if she is without a husband. In such circumstances, while it is natural that a person should prefer one wife to the other, this should not go to the extent that the woman remains, as it were, in a state of suspension, as if she were without a husband at all.

Some people point out that in this verse the Qur'ān in one breath stipulates justice as the necessary condition for plurality of wives and in the other breath declares it to be impossible. On this ground they conclude that the Qur'ān has itself revoked the permission to marry more than one wife. There is, however, absolutely no justification for such an inference. Such an inference would have been justified had the Qur'ān merely said that 'You will not be able to treat your wives with (absolute) justice.' But this statement has been followed by the directive: ' . . . do not allow yourselves to incline wholly to one, leaving the other in suspense.' This leaves no grounds at all for the blind followers of Christian Europe to force an interpretation of their liking on the verse.

162. If a man does not deliberately inflict any wrong and tries earnestly to be just in his dealings God will pardon whatever minor shortcomings take place.

(132) And to Allah belongs all that is in the heavens and all that is in the earth; and Allah suffices for help and protection. (133) If He wills, He has the full power to remove you, O mankind, and bring in others in your place. (134) He who desires the reward of this world, let him know that with Allah is the reward of this world and also of the World to Come. Allah is All-Hearing, All-Seeing.[163]

وَلِلَّهِ مَا فِي السَّمَٰوَٰتِ وَمَا فِي الْأَرْضِ ۚ
وَكَفَىٰ بِاللَّهِ وَكِيلًا ﴿١٣٢﴾ إِن يَشَأْ
يُذْهِبْكُمْ أَيُّهَا النَّاسُ وَيَأْتِ
بِـَٔاخَرِينَ ۚ وَكَانَ اللَّهُ عَلَىٰ ذَٰلِكَ قَدِيرًا
﴿١٣٣﴾ مَّن كَانَ يُرِيدُ ثَوَابَ الدُّنْيَا فَعِندَ
اللَّهِ ثَوَابُ الدُّنْيَا وَالْـَٔاخِرَةِ ۚ وَكَانَ اللَّهُ
سَمِيعًا بَصِيرًا ﴿١٣٤﴾

---

163. In the Qur'ān God often rounds off His enunciation of laws by urging people to reform those aspects of family life and social order in which they are generally liable to commit injustice with admonitions designed to create in people the urge to follow those legal injunctions. Since in the preceding verse the believers were asked to treat women and orphans with justice and kindness it was deemed necessary to bring home to them the following points:

First, that people should not entertain the illusion that they have the power to make or mar the destinies of others, that if they were to withdraw their support, people would be left helpless. The fact is that the destinies of all lie in the Hand of God alone and He need not remain dependent upon any single person as the sole instrument for helping any particular creature. The resources of the Lord of the heavens and the earth are limitless and He also knows how to use those resources.

Second, that the followers of the Prophet (peace be on him) ought to heed the admonition that was made to them, just as it was made to the followers of the former Prophets: to fear God in all their actions. They are being told in effect that by following God's guidance they will secure their own well-being rather than be the source of any benefit to God, that they can do God no harm by disobeying Him, just as it did not lie in the power of the followers of the former Prophets to cause God any harm. The Lord of the Universe does not need people's obedience. If they disobey He may simply replace them with some other nation, and their dismissal will not diminish the majesty and splendour of His realm in the least.

Third, that God alone has the power to dispense the good of this world as well as that of the Hereafter, to lavish transient benefits as well as

(135) Believers! Be upholders of justice,[164] and bearers of witness to truth for the sake of Allah,[165] even though it may either be against yourselves or against your parents and kinsmen, or the rich or the poor: for Allah is more concerned with their well-being than you are. Do not, then, follow your own desires lest you keep away from justice. If you twist or turn away from (the truth), know that Allah is well aware of all that you do.

۞ يَـٰٓأَيُّهَا ٱلَّذِينَ ءَامَنُوا۟ كُونُوا۟ قَوَّٰمِينَ
بِٱلْقِسْطِ شُهَدَآءَ لِلَّهِ وَلَوْ عَلَىٰٓ أَنفُسِكُمْ
أَوِ ٱلْوَٰلِدَيْنِ وَٱلْأَقْرَبِينَ ۚ إِن يَكُنْ غَنِيًّا
أَوْ فَقِيرًا فَٱللَّهُ أَوْلَىٰ بِهِمَا ۖ فَلَا تَتَّبِعُوا۟
ٱلْهَوَىٰٓ أَن تَعْدِلُوا۟ ۚ وَإِن تَلْوُۥٓا۟ أَوْ
تُعْرِضُوا۟ فَإِنَّ ٱللَّهَ كَانَ بِمَا تَعْمَلُونَ
خَبِيرًا ﴿١٣٥﴾

abiding felicity. It all depends on a man's nature and the extent of his ambition what kind of benefit he seeks from God. If a man is infatuated with the fleeting benefits of this world, and is prepared to sacrifice the benefits of the everlasting life, then God will grant him only the good of this world and he will have no share in the good of the Hereafter. God's benevolence is like a river which never dries up, a river which is both capable of, and geared to, providing abundant water to all who need their tillage watered. It is short-sighted and unambitious to want one's fields to be irrigated only once, and to be prepared thereafter to face the prospect of eternal drought. Anyone with breadth of vision would commit himself to submit to God and obey Him, thereby earning the well-being of both worlds.

The section ends with the assertion that God is All-Seeing and All-Hearing. This means that God is fully aware of the actions of His creatures, and is unlike those negligent sovereigns who are blind in lavishing their favours. God governs the universe with full knowledge and awareness. He has an eye on the capacities and ambitions of all human beings and knows their qualities exactly. He is fully aware of the purposes to which people devote their efforts and energies. Anyone who wilfully decides to be disobedient to God should therefore not cherish hopes of receiving the favours reserved for those who obey Him.

164. It is not enough for believers to uphold justice themselves: they are expected to be its standard-bearers. They are supposed not merely to practise justice in their own dealings but to strive for its triumph. They

(136) Believers! Believe[166] in Allah and His Messenger and in the Book He has revealed to His Messenger, and in the Book He revealed before. And whoever disbelieves[167] in Allah, in His angels, in His Books, in His Messengers and in the Last Day, has indeed strayed far away. ▶

يَـٰٓأَيُّهَا ٱلَّذِينَ ءَامَنُوٓا۟ ءَامِنُوا۟ بِٱللَّهِ
وَرَسُولِهِۦ وَٱلْكِتَـٰبِ ٱلَّذِى نَزَّلَ
عَلَىٰ رَسُولِهِۦ وَٱلْكِتَـٰبِ ٱلَّذِىٓ
أَنزَلَ مِن قَبْلُ ۚ وَمَن يَكْفُرْ بِٱللَّهِ
وَمَلَـٰٓئِكَتِهِۦ وَكُتُبِهِۦ وَرُسُلِهِۦ وَٱلْيَوْمِ
ٱلْـَٔاخِرِ فَقَدْ ضَلَّ ضَلَـٰلًۢا بَعِيدًا ﴿١٣٦﴾

---

have to do all within their power to ensure that injustice is eradicated and replaced by equity and justice. A true believer is required to be the pillar supporting the establishment of right and justice.

165. The testimony of the believers should be solely for the sake of God. Their testimony should not be biased in favour of any of the parties concerned, they should not use any opportunity for personal aggrandizement, and they should not seek to please anyone but God.

166. To ask believers to believe might at first seem strange. The fact is, however, that belief as used here has two meanings. First, belief denotes that a man has preferred to acknowledge the soundness of true guidance, to distance himself from the fold of those who disbelieve, and to join the camp of the believers. Second, belief denotes faith, a man's believing in the truth with all his heart, with full earnestness and sincerity. It denotes man's sincere determination to mould his way of thinking, his taste and temperament, his likes and dislikes, his conduct and character, his friendship and enmity, and the direction of his efforts and striving, in conformity with the creed which he has resolved to embrace. This verse is addressed to all those who are 'believers' in the first sense of the term, and they are asked to change themselves into true believers, i.e. believers in the second sense.

167. *Kufr* has two meanings. One signifies categorical rejection. The other signifies that pretence of belief even when either one's heart is not convinced or one's conduct is flagrantly opposed to the demands of one's belief. Here the term *kufr* conveys both meanings, and the verse aims at impressing upon people that whichever kind of *kufr* they adopt in respect of the fundamental beliefs of Islam, it will only alienate them from the Truth, and lead them instead to falsehood, and ultimately to their tragic failure and destruction.

(137) Allah will neither forgive nor show the right way to those who believed, and then disbelieved, then believed, and again disbelieved, and thenceforth became ever more intense in their disbelief.[168] (138) Give tidings of painful chastisement to the hypocrites (139) who take the unbelievers for their allies in preference to the believers. Do they seek honour from them[169] whereas honour altogether belongs to Allah alone? ▶

إِنَّ ٱلَّذِينَ ءَامَنُوا۟ ثُمَّ كَفَرُوا۟ ثُمَّ ءَامَنُوا۟
ثُمَّ كَفَرُوا۟ ثُمَّ ٱزْدَادُوا۟ كُفْرًا لَّمْ يَكُنِ ٱللَّهُ
لِيَغْفِرَ لَهُمْ وَلَا لِيَهْدِيَهُمْ سَبِيلًا ﴿١٣٧﴾ بَشِّرِ
ٱلْمُنَٰفِقِينَ بِأَنَّ لَهُمْ عَذَابًا أَلِيمًا ﴿١٣٨﴾
ٱلَّذِينَ يَتَّخِذُونَ ٱلْكَٰفِرِينَ أَوْلِيَآءَ مِن
دُونِ ٱلْمُؤْمِنِينَ ۚ أَيَبْتَغُونَ عِندَهُمُ
ٱلْعِزَّةَ فَإِنَّ ٱلْعِزَّةَ لِلَّهِ جَمِيعًا ﴿١٣٩﴾

---

168. This refers to those for whom religion is no more than an object of casual entertainment, a toy with which they like to play as long as it suits their desires and fancies. One wave carries them to the fold of Islam and the next away to that of disbelief. Whenever Islam appears to suit their interests they become Muslims; and when the glamorous visage of the god of utility leaps up before their eyes they rush off to worship it. To such people God holds out neither the assurance of forgiveness nor of direction to true guidance. The statement that such people 'became even more intense in their disbelief' refers to those who are not content with not believing themselves, but also try to undermine the faith of others and to persuade them to disbelief, who engage in secret conspiracies as well as overt activities against Islam, and who devote their energies to the struggle aimed at exalting disbelief and degrading the true religion of God. This is a higher degree of disbelief, involving the progressive heaping of crime upon crime. It is obvious that the punishment for this must be greater than for simple disbelief.

169. The term *'izzah* denotes a position which is at once exalted and secure. In other words, the term signifies 'inviolable honour and glory'.

(140) Allah has enjoined upon you in the Book that when you hear the signs of Allah being rejected and scoffed at, you will not sit with them until they engage in some other talk, or else you will become like them.[170] Know well, Allah will gather the hypocrites and the unbelievers in Hell – all together. (141) These hypocrites watch you closely: if victory is granted to you by Allah, they will say: 'Were we not with you?' And were the unbelievers to gain the upper hand, they will say: 'Did we not have mastery over you, and yet we protected you from the believers?'[171] It is Allah Who will judge between you on the Day of Resurrection, and He will not allow the unbelievers, in any way, to gain advantage over the believers.

وَقَدْ نَزَّلَ عَلَيْكُمْ فِي ٱلْكِتَٰبِ أَنْ إِذَا
سَمِعْتُمْ ءَايَٰتِ ٱللَّهِ يُكْفَرُ بِهَا وَيُسْتَهْزَأُ
بِهَا فَلَا تَقْعُدُوا۟ مَعَهُمْ حَتَّىٰ يَخُوضُوا۟ فِى
حَدِيثٍ غَيْرِهِۦٓ ۚ إِنَّكُمْ إِذًا مِّثْلُهُمْ ۗ إِنَّ ٱللَّهَ
جَامِعُ ٱلْمُنَٰفِقِينَ وَٱلْكَٰفِرِينَ فِى
جَهَنَّمَ جَمِيعًا ﴿١٤٠﴾ ٱلَّذِينَ يَتَرَبَّصُونَ
بِكُمْ فَإِن كَانَ لَكُمْ فَتْحٌ مِّنَ ٱللَّهِ قَالُوٓا۟
أَلَمْ نَكُن مَّعَكُمْ وَإِن كَانَ لِلْكَٰفِرِينَ
نَصِيبٌ قَالُوٓا۟ أَلَمْ نَسْتَحْوِذْ عَلَيْكُمْ
وَنَمْنَعْكُم مِّنَ ٱلْمُؤْمِنِينَ ۚ فَٱللَّهُ يَحْكُمُ
بَيْنَكُمْ يَوْمَ ٱلْقِيَٰمَةِ ۗ وَلَن يَجْعَلَ
ٱللَّهُ لِلْكَٰفِرِينَ عَلَى ٱلْمُؤْمِنِينَ سَبِيلًا ﴿١٤١﴾

170. A person who professes Islam and yet enjoys the company of those who indulge in blasphemy against God, and who bears with equanimity their scoffing at God and His Messenger, is no different from the unbelievers mentioned here. (For the injunction in this verse, see also *Sūrah al-An'ām* 6: 68 below.)

171. This is typical of the hypocrites of every age. Such people try to avail themselves of all the benefits which can accrue from a verbal profession of Islam and identification with the Islamic community. They also try to secure the advantages to be obtained by associating with the unbelievers, by assuring them in every possible way about themselves that they are not 'fanatic Muslims', that their association with the Muslims is only nominal. On the other hand, they never fail to assure the unbelievers

(142) Behold, the hypocrites seek to deceive Allah, but it is they who are being deluded by Him. When they rise to Prayer, they rise reluctantly, and only to be seen by men. They remember Allah but little.[172] (143) They dangle between the one and the other (faith and disbelief), and belong neither to these nor to those completely. And he whom Allah lets go astray, for him you can find no way.[173]

إِنَّ ٱلْمُنَٰفِقِينَ يُخَٰدِعُونَ ٱللَّهَ وَهُوَ
خَٰدِعُهُمْ وَإِذَا قَامُوٓا۟ إِلَى ٱلصَّلَوٰةِ
قَامُوا۟ كُسَالَىٰ يُرَآءُونَ ٱلنَّاسَ
وَلَا يَذْكُرُونَ ٱللَّهَ إِلَّا قَلِيلًا ﴿١٤٢﴾
مُّذَبْذَبِينَ بَيْنَ ذَٰلِكَ لَآ إِلَىٰ هَٰٓؤُلَآءِ
وَلَآ إِلَىٰ هَٰٓؤُلَآءِ ۚ وَمَن يُضْلِلِ ٱللَّهُ فَلَن
تَجِدَ لَهُۥ سَبِيلًا ﴿١٤٣﴾

---

that their loyalties and concerns are the same as theirs, that in mental outlook, cultural orientation and taste they are in harmony with them, and that if a decisive conflict between Islam and unbelief were to take place, their weight will certainly be on the side of the latter.

172. In the time of the Prophet (peace be on him) no one, unless he prayed regularly, could be reckoned as belonging to the Islamic community. We know that secular associations consider the absence of any member from their meetings, without a valid excuse, a sign of lack of interest, and that in the event of continued absence, they cancel his membership. The early Islamic community did the same with those who absented themselves from congregational Prayers. In those days a person's absence from congregational Prayers was considered a clear indication of his indifference towards Islam: if he absented himself from them repeatedly he was no longer held to be a Muslim. In those days, therefore, even the worst hypocrites had to attend the five daily Prayers in the mosque. What distinguished a true believer from the hypocrite was that the former came to the mosque with devotion, fervour and eagerness, came there well before the appointed time for the Prayer, and did not rush out of the mosque as soon as the Prayer was over. In short, everything about him indicated that his heart was in the Prayer. Whereas the call to the Prayer for the hypocrite seemed like the announcement of an unavoidable calamity. When such a person set off for the mosque, he seemed to do so in spite of himself. He walked as if he were dragging the entire weight of his being. No wonder, then, that as soon as the Prayer was over, he escaped like a prisoner released from jail. His entire demeanour testified that the remembrance of God was not what he really had his heart in.

(144) Believers! Do not take the unbelievers as your allies in preference to the believers. Do you wish to offer Allah a clear proof of guilt against yourselves? (145) Surely the hypocrites shall be in the lowest depth of the Fire and you shall find none to come to their help, (146) except those who repent and mend their ways and hold fast to Allah and make their faith exclusive to Allah.[174] Those people shall be numbered with the believers and Allah will certainly bestow on the believers a great reward. (147) Why should Allah deal chastisement to you if you are grateful[175] to Him and believe? Allah is All-Appreciative,[176] All-Knowing.

يَٰٓأَيُّهَا ٱلَّذِينَ ءَامَنُوا۟ لَا تَتَّخِذُوا۟
ٱلْكَٰفِرِينَ أَوْلِيَآءَ مِن دُونِ ٱلْمُؤْمِنِينَ ۚ
أَتُرِيدُونَ أَن تَجْعَلُوا۟ لِلَّهِ عَلَيْكُمْ
سُلْطَٰنًا مُّبِينًا ﴿١٤٤﴾ إِنَّ ٱلْمُنَٰفِقِينَ
فِى ٱلدَّرْكِ ٱلْأَسْفَلِ مِنَ ٱلنَّارِ وَلَن
تَجِدَ لَهُمْ نَصِيرًا ﴿١٤٥﴾ إِلَّا ٱلَّذِينَ
تَابُوا۟ وَأَصْلَحُوا۟ وَٱعْتَصَمُوا۟ بِٱللَّهِ
وَأَخْلَصُوا۟ دِينَهُمْ لِلَّهِ فَأُو۟لَٰٓئِكَ مَعَ
ٱلْمُؤْمِنِينَ ۚ وَسَوْفَ يُؤْتِ ٱللَّهُ
ٱلْمُؤْمِنِينَ أَجْرًا عَظِيمًا ﴿١٤٦﴾ مَّا
يَفْعَلُ ٱللَّهُ بِعَذَابِكُمْ إِن
شَكَرْتُمْ وَءَامَنتُمْ ۚ وَكَانَ ٱللَّهُ
شَاكِرًا عَلِيمًا ﴿١٤٧﴾

173. Here an important fact has been stated about the person who remained unguided to the Truth despite his acquaintance with the Book of God and with the life of His Prophet (peace be on him). He was a person who was so disinclined to the Truth and so infatuated with error that even God let him go forth along the same erroneous direction that he had chosen for himself, a person on whom the door of true guidance had been shut and the way towards error had been made smooth by God. It is virtually beyond the power of human beings to direct such a person to the Truth.

We may be able to grasp this if we consider the case of man's livelihood. God controls all the sources of man's livelihood. Thus, anyone who receives any portion of livelihood receives it from God alone. At the same time, God grants every man livelihood through the means he has himself sought. If a man seeks his livelihood through lawful means and strives accordingly, God opens the door to honest living to him and closes the avenues of dishonest earnings in proportion to his earnestness. On the other hand, there is the person who is bent upon fattening himself on dishonest earnings and strives accordingly. God permits such a person to continue making an unlawful living, and no one has the power to help him secure an honest means of living.

The same applies to man's belief and conduct in this life. In this respect too, the ultimate control rests with God. No human being can proceed along any path, whether it be good or evil, unless God lets him proceed along it, and bestows upon him the means to do so. However, it is up to man himself to choose his own path, and after he has made the choice, God will let him proceed along it, and will even pave the way for him. If a person really cares about God, genuinely seeks the truth and earnestly tries to pursue the path charted by God, God permits him to follow his choice, and even provides the means necessary to proceed along his chosen path. On the other hand, God shuts the door of true guidance on the person who chooses error and strives to proceed only along wrong paths, and further enables him to follow the path of his choice. It is beyond the power of any human being to prevent such a person from thinking wrongly, acting wrongly and using up his energies in wrong directions. If a man loses the road to his success and is subsequently deprived of true guidance by God, in whose power does it lie, then, to restore to him his lost treasure?

174. To make one's faith exclusively to God means to concentrate one's loyalties, concerns, affections, and adorations on God, and not to allow any attachments to strike such deep roots in one's heart that one may cease to be capable of sacrificing them for His sake.

175. *Shukr* denotes an acknowledgement of benefaction and a feeling of gratitude. This verse states if a person does not behave ungratefully towards God then there is no reason why God should punish him.

The attitude of gratefulness to God consists of acknowledging His benefaction in one's heart, in confessing it in one's speech and by manifesting it in one's deeds. It is the sum-total of these which is termed *shukr*. This attitude requires: (1) that a person should ascribe the benefaction to its real source, letting no one share in either the gratitude or the acknowledgement of benevolence; (2) that his heart should be overflowing with love for, and loyalty to, the Benefactor, and that he should have no attachment to His opponents; (3) that he should obey the Benefactor and should not use His bounties contrary to His directives.

176. The word used here is *shākir* which we have translated as 'All-Appreciative'. In the context of the God-man relationship, when the word *shukr* is used in respect of God, it denotes 'appreciation of services'. When it is used in respect of man, it denotes his acknowledgement of God's benefaction and his sense of gratitude to Him. To say that God 'thanks' His creatures stresses that God is fully appreciative of the services which His servants have rendered and will recompense them liberally. This contrasts sharply with the attitude of human beings, who are generally slow

(148) Allah does not like speaking evil publicly unless one has been wronged. Allah is All-Hearing, All-Knowing. (149) (Even though you have the right to speak evil if you are wronged), if you keep doing good – whether openly or secretly – or at least pardon the evil (then that is the attribute of Allah). Allah is All-Pardoning and He has all the power to chastise.[177]

۞ لَّا يُحِبُّ ٱللَّهُ ٱلْجَهْرَ بِٱلسُّوٓءِ مِنَ
ٱلْقَوْلِ إِلَّا مَن ظُلِمَ ۚ وَكَانَ ٱللَّهُ سَمِيعًا
عَلِيمًا ﴿١٤٨﴾ إِن تُبْدُوا۟ خَيْرًا أَوْ تُخْفُوهُ
أَوْ تَعْفُوا۟ عَن سُوٓءٍ فَإِنَّ ٱللَّهَ كَانَ عَفُوًّا
قَدِيرًا ﴿١٤٩﴾

and uncharitable in appreciating the services rendered to them, and quick and severe in censuring people for their omissions. As for God, He is lenient and prone to overlook man's omissions. On the contrary, He rewards man manifold for his good deeds.

177. This verse embodies a moral directive of very high value to the Muslims. The hypocrites, the Jews and the polytheists were all bent on placing all kinds of obstacles in the way of the spread of Islam. They eagerly persecuted the Muslims and used all possible means, however malicious, against them. Such an attitude inevitably created anger and resentment. It was in the context of this storm of bitter feelings that God told the Muslims that He did not consider speaking ill of people as praiseworthy. No doubt the Muslims had been wronged, and if a wronged person speaks out against a wrong-doer, he is quite justified in doing so. Even though this is a person's right, it is more meritorious to continue to do good both in public and in private, and to ignore the misdeeds of others. For one's ideal should be to try to approximate to God's way as far as possible. God with whom one wants to be close is lenient and forbearing; He provides sustenance even to the worst criminals and seeks mitigating circumstances in even the most serious offences. In order to become close to God, one ought to be generous in spirit and full of tolerance.

(150) There are those who disbelieve in Allah and His Messengers and seek to differentiate between Allah and His Messengers, and say: 'We believe in some and deny others, and seek to strike a way between the two.' (151) It is they, indeed they, who are, beyond all doubt, unbelievers;[178] and for the unbelievers We have prepared a humiliating chastisement. (152) For those who believe in Allah and His Messengers, and do not differentiate between them, We shall certainly give them their reward.[179] Allah is All-Forgiving, All-Compassionate.[180]

(153) The People of the Book now ask of you to have a Book come down on them from heaven;[181] indeed they asked of Moses even greater things than this, for they said: 'Make us see Allah with our own eyes' – whereupon the thunderbolt suddenly smote them for their wickedness.[182]

إِنَّ ٱلَّذِينَ يَكۡفُرُونَ بِٱللَّهِ وَرُسُلِهِۦ
وَيُرِيدُونَ أَن يُفَرِّقُواْ بَيۡنَ ٱللَّهِ
وَرُسُلِهِۦ وَيَقُولُونَ نُؤۡمِنُ بِبَعۡضٍ
وَنَكۡفُرُ بِبَعۡضٍ وَيُرِيدُونَ
أَن يَتَّخِذُواْ بَيۡنَ ذَٰلِكَ سَبِيلًا ﴿١٥٠﴾
أُوْلَٰٓئِكَ هُمُ ٱلۡكَٰفِرُونَ حَقًّاۚ وَأَعۡتَدۡنَا
لِلۡكَٰفِرِينَ عَذَابًا مُّهِينًا ﴿١٥١﴾ وَٱلَّذِينَ
ءَامَنُواْ بِٱللَّهِ وَرُسُلِهِۦ وَلَمۡ يُفَرِّقُواْ بَيۡنَ
أَحَدٍ مِّنۡهُمۡ أُوْلَٰٓئِكَ سَوۡفَ يُؤۡتِيهِمۡ
أُجُورَهُمۡۚ وَكَانَ ٱللَّهُ غَفُورًا رَّحِيمًا ﴿١٥٢﴾
يَسۡـَٔلُكَ أَهۡلُ ٱلۡكِتَٰبِ أَن تُنَزِّلَ
عَلَيۡهِمۡ كِتَٰبًا مِّنَ ٱلسَّمَآءِۚ فَقَدۡ سَأَلُواْ
مُوسَىٰٓ أَكۡبَرَ مِن ذَٰلِكَ فَقَالُوٓاْ أَرِنَا ٱللَّهَ
جَهۡرَةً فَأَخَذَتۡهُمُ ٱلصَّٰعِقَةُ
بِظُلۡمِهِمۡۚ

---

178. Insofar as being an unbeliever is concerned, there is no difference between (1) those who believe neither in God nor in the Prophets, (2) those who believe in God but not in the Prophets, and (3) those who believe in some Prophets but reject others.

179. This means that only those who acknowledge God to be their sole object of worship and their only sovereign, and who commit themselves to follow all the Prophets, will merit reward for their acts in the Hereafter.

Then they took to worshipping the calf after clear signs had come to them.[183] Still, We forgave them, and conferred a manifest commandment upon Moses, (154) and We raised the Mount high above them and took from them a covenant[184] (to obey the commandment), and ordered them: 'Enter the gate in the state of prostration.'[185]

ثُمَّ ٱتَّخَذُوا۟ ٱلْعِجْلَ مِنۢ بَعْدِ مَا جَآءَتْهُمُ
ٱلْبَيِّنَـٰتُ فَعَفَوْنَا عَن ذَٰلِكَ ۚ وَءَاتَيْنَا
مُوسَىٰ سُلْطَـٰنًا مُّبِينًا ﴿١٥٣﴾ وَرَفَعْنَا
فَوْقَهُمُ ٱلطُّورَ بِمِيثَـٰقِهِمْ وَقُلْنَا لَهُمُ
ٱدْخُلُوا۟ ٱلْبَابَ سُجَّدًا

What that reward will be depends on the nature and extent of their acts of goodness. Those who do not either acknowledge the exclusive sovereignty of God or who rebelliously reject some Messengers of God and believe only in those whom they choose to, will not be rewarded, for in God's sight their apparently good acts are essentially not valid.

180. God will be lenient and forgiving in judging the conduct of those who believe in Him and the Prophets.

181. One of the odd demands which the Jews of Madina made to the Prophet (peace be on him) was that if he wanted them to accept his claim to prophethood he should have them either witness a book descending from the heavens or that each one of them should receive a writ from on high, confirming Muḥammad's prophethood and the absolute necessity of believing in him.

182. The purpose here is not to describe the details of any particular event, but merely to mention, in brief, the crimes of the Jews. Hence passing references are made to the main incidents in the national history of the Jews. The particular event referred to has been mentioned earlier in *Sūrah al-Baqarah*. (See *Towards Understanding the Qur'ān*, vol. I, *Sūrah* 2: 55; also n. 71.)

183. 'Clear signs' refer here to the signs which people had constantly witnessed from the time of Moses' appointment to his prophetic office, to the drowning of Pharaoh and the deliverance of the Israelites out of Egypt. It is clear that He Who had secured the deliverance of the Israelites from the clutches of the powerful Egyptian empire was not the calf, but God, the Lord of the Universe. One is simply staggered at the overpowering

And We said to them: 'Do not violate the law of the Sabbath', and took from them a firm covenant.[186] (155) (They have incurred Allah's wrath) for their breaking the covenant, and their rejection of the signs of Allah, and for slaying Prophets without right, and for saying: 'Our hearts are wrapped up in covers'[187] – even though in fact Allah has sealed their hearts because of their unbelief, so that they scarcely believe[188] – (156) and for their going so far in unbelief[189] as uttering against Mary a mighty calumny,[190] ►

وَقُلْنَا لَهُمْ لَا تَعْدُوا فِي السَّبْتِ وَأَخَذْنَا
مِنْهُم مِّيثَاقًا غَلِيظًا ﴿١٥٤﴾ فَبِمَا نَقْضِهِم
مِّيثَاقَهُمْ وَكُفْرِهِم بِآيَاتِ اللَّهِ وَقَتْلِهِمُ
الْأَنبِيَاءَ بِغَيْرِ حَقٍّ وَقَوْلِهِمْ قُلُوبُنَا غُلْفٌ
بَلْ طَبَعَ اللَّهُ عَلَيْهَا بِكُفْرِهِمْ فَلَا يُؤْمِنُونَ
إِلَّا قَلِيلًا ﴿١٥٥﴾ وَبِكُفْرِهِمْ وَقَوْلِهِمْ عَلَىٰ
مَرْيَمَ بُهْتَانًا عَظِيمًا ﴿١٥٦﴾

---

predisposition of the Jews to error, as evidenced by the fact that at that very juncture in their history when they had experienced the most illustrious signs of God's power and grace they bowed down before the image of the calf, rather than before God, their Benefactor.

184. This 'manifest commandment' refers to the commandments which had been handed over to Moses on tablets. (For a more detailed account of this incident see *Sūrah al-A'rāf* 7, verses 143 ff.) The covenant referred to here is that which had been entered into by the representatives of Israel in the valley of Mount Sinai. (For this see *Sūrah al-Baqarah* 2: 63 and *Sūrah al-A'rāf* 7: 171.)

185. See *Towards Understanding the Qur'ān*, vol. I, *Sūrah* 2: 58–9 and n. 75.

186. See *ibid., Sūrah* 2: 65 and nn. 82–3.

187. This statement of the Jews has already been mentioned in *Sūrah al-Baqarah* 2: 88. In fact, like all ignorant worshippers of falsehood, these people also boasted that their faith in the ideas and prejudices, customs and usages of their forefathers was so firm that they could never be made to forsake them. Whenever the Messengers of God tried to admonish them,

they have been told point-blank that no matter what argument or evidence the latter might adduce in support of their message, they would never be prepared to alter their viewpoint. (See *Towards Understanding the Qur'ān*, vol. I, *Sūrah* 2, n. 94.)

188. This is a parenthetical statement.

189. This marks the resumption of the main theme of the discourse.

190. The Jews had no grounds for suspicion regarding the miraculous birth of Jesus. The day he was born God made the entire Jewish people witness that it was the birth of an extraordinary person, and that his birth had taken place miraculously rather than as the result of an act of moral corruption. When this unmarried girl, of a highly esteemed and pious Israelite family, produced a new-born infant, thousands of people of all age groups thronged to her house out of curiosity. Instead of replying to their queries verbally, Mary pointed to the baby, indicating that he would himself reply. The wonder-struck crowd inquired if they were expected to direct their questions to the infant child who lay in the cradle. To their amazement the child addressed the crowd in a clear and eloquent style: 'I am indeed a servant of God, and to me has He vouchsafed Revelation, me has He made a Prophet'. (*Sūrah Maryam* 19: 30.)

Thus God demolished every basis for casting doubt on the birth of Jesus. When Jesus was young no one accused Mary of either unchastity or Jesus of being born illegitimately. When Jesus reached the age of thirty he launched his prophetic mission, censuring the Jews for their misdeeds and reproaching the rabbis and the Pharisees for their hypocrisy. He also called attention to the moral degeneration to which they had sunk, urging people to rise up and engage in the perilous struggle to establish the hegemony of God's religion. Such a struggle called for all kinds of sacrifices and involved confrontation with Satanic forces on all fronts. Once Jesus launched this mission these criminals decided to spare no weapon, however base, in their bid to silence this fearless voice of truth. It was at this point that they flung at Mary the accusation of unchastity and at Jesus that of illegitimate birth. They made these accusations despite full knowledge that both mother and child were absolutely chaste and innocent. That is why this accusation is not characterized as either a wrong or a falsehood. It is rather branded as disbelief (*kufr*) since the calumny was motivated chiefly by the desire to obstruct the path of true faith and not just to bring an innocent woman into disrepute.

(157) and their saying: 'We slew the Messiah, Jesus, son of Mary', the Messenger of Allah[191] – whereas[192] in fact they had neither slain him nor crucified him but the matter was made dubious to them[193] – and those who differed about it too were in a state of doubt! They have no definite knowledge of it, but merely follow conjecture;[194] and they surely slew him not, (158) but Allah raised him to Himself.[195] Allah is All-Mighty, All-Wise. ▶

وَقَوۡلِهِمۡ إِنَّا قَتَلۡنَا ٱلۡمَسِيحَ عِيسَى ٱبۡنَ مَرۡيَمَ
رَسُولَ ٱللَّهِ وَمَا قَتَلُوهُ وَمَا صَلَبُوهُ
وَلَٰكِن شُبِّهَ لَهُمۡۚ وَإِنَّ ٱلَّذِينَ ٱخۡتَلَفُواْ فِيهِ
لَفِي شَكّٖ مِّنۡهُۚ مَا لَهُم بِهِۦ مِنۡ عِلۡمٍ إِلَّا ٱتِّبَاعَ
ٱلظَّنِّۚ وَمَا قَتَلُوهُ يَقِينَۢا ﴿١٥٧﴾ بَل رَّفَعَهُ
ٱللَّهُ إِلَيۡهِۚ وَكَانَ ٱللَّهُ عَزِيزًا حَكِيمٗا ﴿١٥٨﴾

191. Their criminal boldness had reached such proportions that they attempted to put an end to the life of the one they themselves knew to be a Prophet, and subsequently went around boasting of this achievement. The least reflection on the incident of Jesus talking in his cradle (see the preceding note) makes it clear that there was no strong reason to doubt his prophethood. Moreover, the miracles of Jesus which they themselves witnessed (see *Sūrah Āl 'Imrān* 3: 49) had firmly established his claim to prophethood. Thus, whatever treatment they meted out to him was not based on any misconception, for they were fully aware that the person whom they were subjecting to criminal treatment had been appointed by God as the bearer of His message.

It seems strange that a people should recognize a man to be a Prophet in their hearts and still try to assassinate him. The ways of degenerate nations are indeed strange. Such people are absolutely unprepared to tolerate the existence of those who reproach them for their corruption and seek to prevent them from evil. Hence the reformers, including Prophets, who arise among corrupt nations are always persecuted; they are imprisoned and even put to death. The Talmud mentions that:

> Nebuchadnezzar laid waste the land of Israel . . . when the city had been captured, he marched with his princes and officers into the Temple . . . on one of the walls he found the mark of an arrow's head, as though somebody had been killed or hit nearby, and he asked: 'Who was killed here?' 'Zachariah, the son of Yohoyadah, the high priest', answered the people. 'He rebuked us incessantly on account

of our transgressions, and we tired of his words, and put him to death.' (*The Talmud Selections* by H. Polano, London, Frederick Warne & Co.)

The Bible also mentions that when the corrupt practices of Israel exceeded all limits, and Jeremiah warned them that God would have them overrun by other nations in punishment for their wickedness, his warning was greeted by the Jews with the accusation that he was a collaborator with the Chaldeans and hence a traitor. And under that pretext Jeremiah was sent to prison. In the same manner, about two and a half years before Jesus' crucifixion, John the Baptist suffered a cruel fate. On the whole the Jews knew him to be a Prophet, or at least acknowledged him to be one of the most religious people in the nation. But when he criticized the royal court of Herod, the King of Judah, he was first thrown into prison, and then, in response to the demand of a dancing girl, who was Herod's favourite 'mistress', his head was cut off.

If this record of the Jews is kept in mind, it does not seem surprising that, after having subjected Jesus – according to their belief – to crucifixion, they might have been overcome by jubilation and in a fit of self-congratulation might have boastfully exclaimed: 'Yes, we have put a Prophet of God to death!' (For similar incidents see *Towards Understanding the Qur'ān*, vol. I, *Sūrah* 2, n. 79 – Ed.)

192. This again is a parenthetical statement.

193. This verse categorically states that Jesus was raised on high before he could be crucified, and that the belief of both the Jews and the Christians that Jesus died on the cross is based on a misconception. As a result of a comparative study of the Qur'ānic and Biblical versions we are persuaded that, so far as the trial at the court of Pilate is concerned, it was probably Jesus who was tried. Pilate sentenced him to death after the Jews showed their deep hostility to Truth and righteousness by openly declaring that, in their view, the life of a thief was of higher value than that of a man with such a pure soul as Jesus. It was then that God raised Jesus up to heaven. The person the Jews subsequently crucified was someone else who, for one reason or another, was mistaken for the person of Jesus. The fact that the person who had actually been crucified was someone other than Jesus does not in any way detract from the guilt of those Jews, for in their minds it was Jesus whose head they were crowning with thorns, in whose face they were spitting, and whom they were subjecting to crucifixion.

We are not in a position now to find out how and why such a confusion arose. As no authentic source of information is available to us, it would be inappropriate to conjecture and speculate about the cause of the misapprehension which led the Jews to believe that they had crucified Jesus, the son of Mary, whereas he had already passed far beyond their grasp.

194. 'Those who differed' refers to the Christians. The Christians have dozens of different versions, rather than one universally agreed view, regarding the crucifixion of the Messiah. This in itself is an eloquent testimony that the Christians were doubtful about the actual event. Some of them held the view that the one who was crucified was someone other than Jesus and that Jesus himself in fact remained standing somewhere nearby, laughing at their folly. Others were of the opinion that the one who was crucified was certainly Jesus himself, but that he did not die on the cross and was still alive when brought down from it. Others asserted that though Jesus died on the cross, he later returned to life, met his disciples and conversed with them about ten times. Again, some believe that the human body of Jesus suffered death and was buried, while the spirit of godhead in him was taken up on high. Yet others believe that after his death the Messiah was resurrected physically and was subsequently taken up to heaven in physical form. Had the truth been fully known and well-established so many divergent views could not have gained currency.

195. This is the truth revealed by God. What is categorically asserted here is merely that the Jews did not succeed in killing the Messiah, but that God raised him unto Himself. The Qur'ān furnishes no detailed information about the actual form of this 'raising'. It neither states categorically that God raised him from the earthly sphere to some place in heaven in both body and soul, nor that his body died on earth and his soul alone was raised to heaven. Hence neither of the two alternatives can be definitely affirmed nor denied on the basis of the Qur'ān. If one reflects on the Qur'ānic version of the event one gets the impression that, whatever the actual form of this 'raising', the event was of an extraordinary character. This extraordinariness is evident from three things:

First, the Christians believed in the ascension of the Messiah in both body and soul, which was one of the reasons for large sections of people to believe in the godhead of Jesus. The Qur'ān does not refute that idea but employs the same term, *raf'* (i.e. 'ascension'), employed by the Christians. It is inconceivable that the Qur'ān, which describes itself as the 'Clear Book', would employ an expression that might lend support to a misconception it seeks to repudiate.

Second, one might assume that either the ascension of the Messiah was of the kind that takes place at every person's death or that this 'ascension' meant merely the exaltation of a Prophet's position, like that of Idrīs: 'And We raised him to an exalted station' (*Sūrah Maryam* 19: 57). Had it been so, this idea would have been better expressed by a statement such as: And indeed they did not kill the Messiah; Allah delivered him from execution and caused him to die a natural death. The Jews had wanted to slight him but Allah granted him an exalted position.

Third, if this *raf'* (exaltation, ascension) referred to in the verse: 'Allah raised him to Himself' was of an ordinary kind, the statement which follows, namely that 'Allah is All-Mighty, All-Wise', would seem altogether out of context. Such a statement is pertinent only in the context of an event which manifested, in a highly extraordinary manner, by the overwhelming power and wisdom of God.

The only Qur'ānic argument that can be adduced to controvert this view is the verse in which the expression *mutawaffīka* (see *Sūrah Āl 'Imrān* 3: 55) is employed. But as we have pointed out (see *Towards Understanding the Qur'ān*, vol. I, *Sūrah* 3, n. 51), this word can denote either God's taking a man unto Himself in soul or taking him unto Himself in both body and soul. Arguments based on the mere use of this word are not enough to repudiate the arguments we have already adduced. Some of those who insist on the physical death of Jesus support their argument by pointing out that there is no other example of the use of the word *tawaffá* for God's taking unto Himself a man in body as well as in soul. But this argument is not tenable since the ascension of Jesus was a unique event in human history and, therefore, the quest for another example of the use of this term in the same context is meaningless. What is worth exploring is whether or not the use of the word in such a sense is valid according to Arabic usage. If it is, we will have to say that the choice of this particular word lends support to belief in the ascension of Jesus.

If we reflect on this verse in the light of the assumption that Jesus died physically, it appears strange that the Qur'ān does not employ those terms which would exclude signifying the simultaneous physical and spiritual ascension of Jesus. On the contrary, the Qur'ān prefers a term which, since it is liable to both interpretations (i.e. it can mean both spiritual and physical ascension), lends support to belief in the physical ascension of Jesus, even though that notion was used as a basis to support the false belief in the godhead of Jesus.

Belief in the physical ascension of Jesus is further reinforced by those numerous traditions which mention the return of Jesus, son of Mary, to the world and his struggle against the Anti-Christ before the end of time. (For these traditions see our appendix to *Sūrah* 33.) These traditions quite definitively establish the second coming of Jesus. Now it is for anybody to judge which is more reasonable: Jesus' return to this world after his death, or his being alive somewhere in God's universe, and returning to this world at some point in time?

(159) There are none among the People of the Book but will believe in him before his death,[196] and he will be a witness against them on the Day of Resurrection.[197] (160) Thus,[198] We forbade them many clean things which had earlier been made lawful for them,[199] for the wrong-doing of those who became Jews, for their barring many from the way of Allah,[200] (161) and for their taking interest which had been prohibited to them,[201] and for their consuming the wealth of others wrongfully. And for the unbelievers among them We have prepared a painful chastisement.[202] ▶

وَإِن مِّنْ أَهْلِ ٱلْكِتَٰبِ إِلَّا لَيُؤْمِنَنَّ بِهِۦ
قَبْلَ مَوْتِهِۦ ۖ وَيَوْمَ ٱلْقِيَٰمَةِ يَكُونُ عَلَيْهِمْ
شَهِيدًا ﴿١٥٩﴾ فَبِظُلْمٍ مِّنَ ٱلَّذِينَ هَادُوا۟
حَرَّمْنَا عَلَيْهِمْ طَيِّبَٰتٍ أُحِلَّتْ لَهُمْ
وَبِصَدِّهِمْ عَن سَبِيلِ ٱللَّهِ كَثِيرًا ﴿١٦٠﴾
وَأَخْذِهِمُ ٱلرِّبَوٰا۟ وَقَدْ نُهُوا۟ عَنْهُ وَأَكْلِهِمْ
أَمْوَٰلَ ٱلنَّاسِ بِٱلْبَٰطِلِ ۚ وَأَعْتَدْنَا لِلْكَٰفِرِينَ
مِنْهُمْ عَذَابًا أَلِيمًا ﴿١٦١﴾

---

196. The death mentioned here could refer either to the death of Jesus or to the death of each and every person among 'the People of the Book'. The text lends itself to both meanings. We have adopted the first in our translation. If we accept the alternative meaning, the verse would mean: 'There is no one among the People of the Book who, before his death, will not believe in Jesus.' The expression, 'People of the Book' here refers to the Jews and possibly even to the Christians. In the light of this latter meaning, the purpose of the verse would be to affirm that at the time when the physical death of Jesus takes place, all the living 'People of the Book' would have come to believe in him (i.e. in his prophethood). Alternatively, the verse would mean that the prophethood of Jesus will become manifest to every person among the People of the Book just before he dies so that they will believe in him, but at a time when believing would be of no avail. Both these views have been supported by several Companions, Successors and outstanding scholars of Qur'ānic exegesis. The truth of the matter is best known to God alone.

197. This means that on the Day of Judgement Jesus will stand in the court of the Almighty and testify to the treatment meted out to him and to the message he brought. (For the nature of this testimony see *Sūrah al-Mā'idah* 5: 109 ff. below.)

198. After this parenthetical statement, the main discourse is once again resumed.

199. This may refer to the regulation mentioned in *Sūrah al-An'ām* 6: 146, that all beasts with claws, and the fat of both oxen and sheep, were prohibited to the Jews. It might also refer, however, to the highly elaborate set of prohibitions found in Judaic Law. To restrict the choice of alternatives in their life is indeed a kind of punishment for a people. (For a fuller discussion see *Sūrah al-An'ām* 6, n. 122 below.)

200. The Jews, on the whole, are not satisfied with their own deviation from the path of God. They have become such inherent criminals that their brains and resources seem to be behind almost every movement which arises for the purpose of misleading and corrupting human beings. And whenever there arises a movement to call people to the Truth, the Jews are inclined to oppose it even though they are the bearers of the Scripture and inheritors of the message of the Prophets. Their latest contribution is Communism – an ideology which is the product of a Jewish brain and which has developed under Jewish leadership. It seems ironical that the professed followers of Moses and other Prophets should be prominent as the founders and promoters of an ideology which, for the first time in human history, is professedly based on a categorical denial of, and an undying hostility to God, and which openly strives to obliterate every form of godliness. The other movement which in modern times is second only to Communism in misleading people is the philosophy of Freud. It is a strange coincidence that Freud too was a Jew.

201. The Torah categorically lays down the injunction: 'And if you lend money to any of my people with you who is poor, you shall not be to him as a creditor, and you shall not exact interest from him. If ever you take your neighbour's garment in pledge, you shall restore it to him before the sun goes down; for that is his only covering, it is his mantle for his body; in what else shall he sleep? And if he cries to me, I will hear, for I am compassionate' (Exodus 22: 25–7). This is one of several passages of the Torah which embody the prohibition of interest. The followers of the Torah, however, are most conspicuously engaged in transactions involving interest and have become notorious the world over for their meanness and hard-heartedness in monetary matters.

202. God has kept in store a painful punishment both in this world and in the Next for those Jews who have deviated from the course of true faith

(162) Those among them who are firmly rooted in knowledge and the believers, such do believe in what has been revealed to you and what was revealed before you.[203] (Those who truly believe) establish the Prayer and pay *Zakāh*, those who firmly believe in Allah and in the Last Day, to them We shall indeed pay a great reward.

لَّٰكِنِ ٱلرَّٰسِخُونَ فِي ٱلۡعِلۡمِ مِنۡهُمۡ
وَٱلۡمُؤۡمِنُونَ يُؤۡمِنُونَ بِمَآ أُنزِلَ إِلَيۡكَ وَمَآ
أُنزِلَ مِن قَبۡلِكَۚ وَٱلۡمُقِيمِينَ ٱلصَّلَوٰةَۚ
وَٱلۡمُؤۡتُونَ ٱلزَّكَوٰةَ وَٱلۡمُؤۡمِنُونَ
بِٱللَّهِ وَٱلۡيَوۡمِ ٱلۡأٓخِرِ أُوْلَٰٓئِكَ سَنُؤۡتِيهِمۡ
أَجۡرًا عَظِيمًا ١٦٢

---

and sincere obedience to God, and are steeped in rejection of faith and rebellion against God. The severe punishment which has befallen the Jews in this world is unique and should serve as a lesson for all. Two thousand years have gone by and they have remained scattered all over the world and have been treated everywhere as outcasts. There has been no period during the last two millennia when they have not been looked on ignominiously and there is no part of the world where they are respected despite their enormous riches. What is more, this nation has been left dangling between life and death, unlike other nations which once appeared on the stage of history and then vanished. Their condemnation to this state of suspension makes them a lesson for all nations till the end of time. It marks the tragic fate that meets a people who, despite enjoying the guidance of the Book of God, dare to defy God. It would seem that their punishment in the Hereafter must be even more severe than in the present world. (For the questions which arise about the validity of our view, in spite of the establishment of the state of Israel, see *Towards Understanding the Qur'ān*, vol. I, *Sūrah* 3: 112, n. 90.)

203. Those well acquainted with the true teachings of the Scriptures, and whose minds are free from prejudice, obduracy, blind imitation of their forefathers and bondage to animal desires, will be disposed to follow those teachings. Their attitude is bound to be altogether different from the general attitude of those Jews apparently immersed in unbelief and transgression. Such people realize, even at first glance, that the Qur'ānic teaching is essentially the same as that of the previous Prophets, and hence feel no difficulty in affirming it.

(163) (O Muḥammad!) We have revealed to you as We revealed to Noah and the Prophets after him,[204] and We revealed to Abraham, Ishmael, Isaac, Jacob and the offspring of Jacob, and Jesus and Job, and Jonah, and Aaron and Solomon, and We gave to David Psalms.[205]

۞ إِنَّآ أَوْحَيْنَآ إِلَيْكَ كَمَآ أَوْحَيْنَآ إِلَىٰ
نُوحٍ وَٱلنَّبِيِّـۧنَ مِنۢ بَعْدِهِۦ ۚ وَأَوْحَيْنَآ
إِلَىٰٓ إِبْرَٰهِيمَ وَإِسْمَٰعِيلَ وَإِسْحَٰقَ
وَيَعْقُوبَ وَٱلْأَسْبَاطِ وَعِيسَىٰ
وَأَيُّوبَ وَيُونُسَ وَهَٰرُونَ وَسُلَيْمَٰنَ ۚ
وَءَاتَيْنَا دَاوُۥدَ زَبُورًا ﴿١٦٣﴾

---

204. This emphasizes that Muḥammad (peace be on him) did not introduce any innovations, and that his essential message was no different from the earlier revelations. What Muḥammad (peace be on him) expounded was the same truth which had previously been expounded by the earlier Prophets in various parts of the world and at different periods of time. *Waḥy* means 'to suggest; to put something into someone's heart; to communicate something in secrecy; to send a message'.

205. The 'Psalms' embodied in the Bible are not the Psalms of David. The Biblical version contains many 'psalms' by others and they are ascribed to their actual authors. The 'psalms' which the Bible does ascribe to David do indeed contain the characteristic lustre of truth. The book called 'Proverbs', attributed to Solomon, contains a good deal of accretion, and the last two chapters, in particular, are undoubtedly spurious. A great many of these proverbs, however, do have a ring of truth and authenticity. Another book of the Bible is ascribed to Job. Even though it contains many gems of wisdom, it is difficult to believe that the book attributed to Job could in fact be his. For the portrayal of Job's character in that book is quite contrary to the wonderful patience for which he is applauded in the Qur'ān and for which he is praised in the beginning of the Book of Job itself. The Book of Job, quite contrary to the Qur'ānic portrayal of him, presents him as one who was so full of grievance and annoyance with God throughout the entire period of his tribulation that his companions had to try hard to persuade him that God was not unjust. In fact Job is shown in the Bible as one whom even his companions failed to convince that God was just.

In addition to these, the Bible contains seventeen other books of the Israelite Prophets. The greater part of these seem to be authentic. In Jeremiah, Isaiah, Ezekiel, Amos and certain other books, in particular, one often encounters whole sections which stir and move one's soul. These sections without doubt have the lustre of Divine revelation. While going through them one is struck by the vehemence of moral admonition, the powerful opposition to polytheism, the forceful exposition of monotheism,

(164) We revealed to the Messengers We have already told you of, and to the Messengers We have not told you of; and to Moses Allah spoke directly.[206] (165) These Messengers were sent as bearers of glad tidings and as warners[207] so that after sending the Messengers people may have no plea against Allah.[208] Allah is All-Mighty, All-Wise. (166) (Whether people believe or not) Allah bears witness that whatever He has revealed to you, He has revealed with His knowledge, and the angels bear witness to it too, though the witness of Allah is sufficient. (167) Those who denied this truth and barred others from the way of Allah have indeed strayed far. (168) Likewise, Allah will neither forgive those who denied the truth and took to wrong-doing nor will He show them any other way (169) save that of Hell wherein they will abide. And that is easy for Allah.

وَرُسُلًا قَدْ قَصَصْنَاهُمْ عَلَيْكَ مِن قَبْلُ
وَرُسُلًا لَّمْ نَقْصُصْهُمْ عَلَيْكَ ۚ وَكَلَّمَ
اللَّهُ مُوسَىٰ تَكْلِيمًا ﴿١٦٤﴾ رُّسُلًا
مُّبَشِّرِينَ وَمُنذِرِينَ لِئَلَّا يَكُونَ لِلنَّاسِ
عَلَى اللَّهِ حُجَّةٌ بَعْدَ الرُّسُلِ ۚ وَكَانَ اللَّهُ
عَزِيزًا حَكِيمًا ﴿١٦٥﴾ لَّٰكِنِ اللَّهُ يَشْهَدُ
بِمَا أَنزَلَ إِلَيْكَ ۖ أَنزَلَهُ بِعِلْمِهِ ۖ
وَالْمَلَائِكَةُ يَشْهَدُونَ ۚ وَكَفَىٰ بِاللَّهِ
شَهِيدًا ﴿١٦٦﴾ إِنَّ الَّذِينَ كَفَرُوا
وَصَدُّوا عَن سَبِيلِ اللَّهِ قَدْ ضَلُّوا
ضَلَالًا بَعِيدًا ﴿١٦٧﴾ إِنَّ الَّذِينَ كَفَرُوا
وَظَلَمُوا لَمْ يَكُنِ اللَّهُ لِيَغْفِرَ لَهُمْ وَلَا
لِيَهْدِيَهُمْ طَرِيقًا ﴿١٦٨﴾ إِلَّا طَرِيقَ
جَهَنَّمَ خَالِدِينَ فِيهَا أَبَدًا ۚ وَكَانَ ذَٰلِكَ
عَلَى اللَّهِ يَسِيرًا ﴿١٦٩﴾

---

and the strong denunciation of the moral corruption of the Israelites which characterize them. One inevitably senses that these books, the orations of Jesus embodied in the Gospels, and the glorious Qur'ān are like springs which have arisen from one and the same Divine source.

206. Revelation in the case of other Prophets meant either that they heard a voice or received a message from an angel. The privileged treatment accorded to Moses was that God communicated with him directly. This

(170) O men! Now that the Messenger has come to you bearing the Truth from your Lord, believe in him; it will be good for you. If you reject, know well that to Allah belongs all that is in the heavens and the earth.[209] Allah is All-Knowing, All-Wise.[210]

يَٰٓأَيُّهَا ٱلنَّاسُ قَدۡ جَآءَكُمُ ٱلرَّسُولُ بِٱلۡحَقِّ مِن رَّبِّكُمۡ فَـَٔامِنُواْ خَيۡرٗا لَّكُمۡۚ وَإِن تَكۡفُرُواْ فَإِنَّ لِلَّهِ مَا فِي ٱلسَّمَٰوَٰتِ وَٱلۡأَرۡضِۚ وَكَانَ ٱللَّهُ عَلِيمًا حَكِيمٗا ١٧٠

communication was similar to one that takes place between two persons, as is fully illustrated by the conversation reported in *Sūrah Ṭā Hā* 20: 11 ff. This unique privilege of Moses is mentioned in the Bible as well, and in much the same manner. It mentions that the Lord used to speak to Moses 'face to face, as a man speaks to his friend' (Exodus 33: 11).

207. It is emphasized that the essential function of all the Prophets was the same: to announce good tidings of salvation and felicity to those who believe in the teachings revealed by God and mend their conduct accordingly, and to warn those who persist in false beliefs and evil ways that they will have to face dire consequences.

208. God's purpose in sending the Prophets was to establish His plea against mankind. God did not want criminals to have any basis on which to plead that their actions were done in ignorance. Prophets were therefore sent to all parts of the world, and many Scriptures were revealed. These Prophets communicated knowledge of the Truth to large sections of people, and left behind Scriptures which have guided human beings in all ages. If anyone falls a prey to error, in spite of all this, the blame does not lie with God or the Prophets. The blame lies rather with those who have spurned God's message even after having received it, and with those who knew the Truth but failed to enlighten others.

209. By disobeying one cannot hurt the Lord of the heavens and the earth. One can only hurt one's own self.

210. They are being told that their Lord was not at all unaware of the wickedness in which they indulged, nor did He lack the capacity to deal severely with those who only violated His commands.

(171) People of the Book! Do not exceed the limits in your religion,[211] and attribute to Allah nothing except the truth. The Messiah, Jesus, son of Mary, was only a Messenger of Allah, and His command[212] that He conveyed unto Mary, and a spirit from Him (which led to Mary's conception).[213] So believe in Allah and in His Messengers,[214] and do not say: '(Allah is a) trinity.'[215] ▶

يَـٰٓأَهْلَ ٱلْكِتَـٰبِ لَا تَغْلُوا۟ فِى
دِينِكُمْ وَلَا تَقُولُوا۟ عَلَى ٱللَّهِ إِلَّا
ٱلْحَقَّ ۚ إِنَّمَا ٱلْمَسِيحُ عِيسَى ٱبْنُ مَرْيَمَ
رَسُولُ ٱللَّهِ وَكَلِمَتُهُۥٓ أَلْقَىٰهَآ إِلَىٰ
مَرْيَمَ وَرُوحٌ مِّنْهُ ۖ فَـَٔامِنُوا۟ بِٱللَّهِ وَرُسُلِهِۦ ۖ
وَلَا تَقُولُوا۟ ثَلَـٰثَةٌ ۚ

211. The expression 'People of the Book' refers here to the Christians and the word *ghulūw* denotes the tendency to exceed the limits of propriety in support of something. The fault of the Jews was that they had exceeded the limits of propriety in rejecting and opposing Jesus, whereas the crime of the Christians was that they had gone beyond the proper limits in their love for and devotion to Jesus.

212. What is meant by sending the 'command' to Mary is that God ordered Mary's womb to become impregnated without coming into contact with sperm. In the beginning the Christians were told that this was the secret of the fatherless birth of Jesus. Later on, under the misleading influence of Greek philosophy, they equated this with the 'Logos', which was subsequently interpreted as the Divine attribute of speech. The next step in this connection was the development of the notion that this Divine attribute entered into the womb of Mary and assumed the physical form of Jesus. Thus there developed among the Christians the false doctrine of the godhead of Jesus, and the false notion that out of His attributes God caused that of speech to appear in the form of Jesus.

213. Here Jesus himself is called 'a spirit from God'. The same idea is also expressed elsewhere in the Qur'ān: 'And We supported him with the spirit of holiness' (*Sūrah al-Baqarah* 2: 87). The import of both verses is that God endowed Jesus with a pure, impeccable soul. He was therefore an embodiment of truth, veracity, righteousness, and excellence. This is what the Christians had been told about Christ. But they exceeded the proper limits of veneration for Jesus. The 'spirit *from* God' became the 'spirit *of* God', and the 'spirit of holiness' was interpreted to mean God's

Give up this assertion; it would be better for you. Allah is indeed just one God. Far be it from His glory that He should have a son.[216] To Him belongs all that is in the heavens and in the earth.[217] Allah is sufficient for a guardian.[218]

ٱنتَهُوا۟ خَيْرًا لَّكُمْ ۚ إِنَّمَا ٱللَّهُ إِلَٰهٌ
وَٰحِدٌ ۖ سُبْحَٰنَهُۥٓ أَن يَكُونَ لَهُۥ
وَلَدٌ ۘ لَّهُۥ مَا فِى ٱلسَّمَٰوَٰتِ وَمَا فِى
ٱلْأَرْضِ ۗ وَكَفَىٰ بِٱللَّهِ وَكِيلًا ﴿١٧١﴾

---

own Spirit which became incarnate in Jesus. Thus, along with God and Jesus, there developed the third person of God – the Holy Ghost. It was this unjustified exaggeration which led the Christians to even greater error. Ironically, however, Matthew contains the statement that: 'But while he thought on these things, behold, the angel of the Lord appeared to him in a dream, saying, Joseph, thou son of David, fear not to take unto thee Mary thy wife: for that which is conceived in her is of the Holy Ghost.' (The Bible, Authorized version, p. 771.)

214. The followers of Christ are urged to acknowledge God as the only God and to believe in the prophethood of all the Prophets, and that Jesus was one of them. This was the teaching of Christ and a basic truth which his followers ought to recognize.

215. They are urged to abandon the trinitarian doctrine, regardless of the form in which it was found. The fact is that the Christians subscribe simultaneously to the unity and the trinity of God. The statements of Jesus on this question in the Gospels, however, are so categorical that no Christian can easily justify anything but the clear, straightforward doctrine that God is One and that there is no god but He. The Christians, therefore, find it impossible to deny that monotheism is the very core of true religion. But the original confusion that in Jesus the Word of God became flesh, that the Spirit of God was incarnate in him, led them to believe in the godhead of Jesus and of the Holy Ghost along with that of God. This gratuitous commitment gave rise to an insoluble riddle: how to combine monotheism with the notion of trinity. For over eighteen centuries Christian theologians have grappled with this self-created riddle. The concept of the trinity is capable of such a myriad of interpretations that literally dozens of sects have arisen as a result of its ambiguity. And it has been largely responsible for the various Christian churches indulging in mutual excommunication. Moreover, it is logically impossible to maintain belief in trinity without impairing belief in One God. This problem has arisen because of

(172) The Messiah neither did disdain to be a servant of Allah nor do the angels who are stationed near to Him; and whoever disdains to serve Him, and waxes arrogant, Allah will certainly muster them all to Him. (173) He will grant those who have believed and done good deeds their rewards in full, and will give them more out of His bounty. He will bestow upon those who have been disdainful and arrogant a painful chastisement; and they will find for themselves neither a guardian nor a helper besides Allah.

لَّن يَسْتَنكِفَ ٱلْمَسِيحُ أَن يَكُونَ
عَبْدًا لِّلَّهِ وَلَا ٱلْمَلَٰٓئِكَةُ ٱلْمُقَرَّبُونَ
وَمَن يَسْتَنكِفْ عَنْ عِبَادَتِهِۦ
وَيَسْتَكْبِرْ فَسَيَحْشُرُهُمْ إِلَيْهِ جَمِيعًا
﴿١٧٢﴾ فَأَمَّا ٱلَّذِينَ ءَامَنُوا۟ وَعَمِلُوا۟
ٱلصَّٰلِحَٰتِ فَيُوَفِّيهِمْ أُجُورَهُمْ
وَيَزِيدُهُم مِّن فَضْلِهِۦ ۖ وَأَمَّا ٱلَّذِينَ
ٱسْتَنكَفُوا۟ وَٱسْتَكْبَرُوا۟ فَيُعَذِّبُهُمْ
عَذَابًا أَلِيمًا وَلَا يَجِدُونَ لَهُم مِّن
دُونِ ٱللَّهِ وَلِيًّا وَلَا نَصِيرًا ﴿١٧٣﴾

---

the extravagance in which the Christians have indulged. The easiest course to get out of the morass is to give up the innovated belief in the godhead of Jesus and of the Holy Ghost, acknowledge God as the Only God, and accept Jesus as His Messenger rather than as God's partner in godhead.

216. This is the refutation of the fourth extravagance in which the Christians have indulged. Even if the reports embodied in the New Testament are considered authentic, the most that can be inferred from them (particularly those embodied in the first three Gospels) is that Jesus likened the relationship between God and His servants to that between a father and his children, and that he used to employ the term 'father' as a metaphor for God. But in this respect Jesus was not unique. From very ancient times the Israelites had employed the term 'father' for God. The Old Testament is full of examples of this usage. Jesus obviously employed this expression in conformity with the literary usage of his people. Moreover, he characterized God not merely as his own father but as the father of all men. Nevertheless, the Christians exceeded all reasonable limits when they declared Jesus to be the only begotten son of God. Their strange doctrine on this question is that since Jesus is an incarnation, an embodiment of the Word and Spirit of God, he is therefore the only son of God, who was sent to the earth in order to expiate the sins of humanity through his crucifixion. The Christians hold this to be their basic doctrine

(174) O men! A proof has come to you from your Lord, and We have sent down unto you a clear light. (175) Allah will surely admit those who believe in Him and hold fast to Him to His mercy and bounty, and will guide them on to a straight way to Himself.

يَـٰٓأَيُّهَا ٱلنَّاسُ قَدْ جَآءَكُم بُرْهَـٰنٌ مِّن
رَّبِّكُمْ وَأَنزَلْنَآ إِلَيْكُمْ نُورًا مُّبِينًا ﴿١٧٤﴾
فَأَمَّا ٱلَّذِينَ ءَامَنُوا۟ بِٱللَّهِ
وَٱعْتَصَمُوا۟ بِهِۦ فَسَيُدْخِلُهُمْ
فِى رَحْمَةٍ مِّنْهُ وَفَضْلٍ وَيَهْدِيهِمْ إِلَيْهِ
صِرَٰطًا مُّسْتَقِيمًا ﴿١٧٥﴾

---

even though they cannot produce one shred of evidence from the statements of Jesus himself. This doctrine was a later product of their fancies, an outcome of the extravagance in which they indulged as a result of their impression of the awe-inspiring personality of their Prophet.

God does not repudiate here the doctrine of expiation, for this is not an independent doctrine but a corollary of recognizing Jesus as the son of God, and is a mystical and philosophical answer to the query as to why the only begotten son of God died an accursed death on the cross. The doctrine of expiation automatically falls apart by repudiating the dogma that Jesus was the son of God and by dispelling the misapprehension that he was crucified.

217. This strongly emphasizes that the true relationship between God and His creatures is one between the Lord and His slave. This repudiates the idea that the relationship which exists is one between a father and his offspring.

218. God is Himself sufficiently powerful to govern His dominion and has no need of a son to assist Him.

(176) People[219] ask you to pronounce a ruling concerning inheritance from those who have left behind no lineal heirs (*kalālah*).[220] Say: 'Allah pronounces for you the ruling: should a man die childless but have a sister,[221] she shall have one half of what he has left behind; and should the sister die childless, his brother shall inherit her.[222] And if the heirs are two sisters, they shall have two-thirds of what he has left behind.[223] And if the heirs are sisters and brothers, then the male shall have the share of two females. Allah makes (His commandments) clear to you lest you go astray. Allah has full knowledge of everything.

يَسْتَفْتُونَكَ قُلِ ٱللَّهُ يُفْتِيكُمْ فِى
ٱلْكَلَٰلَةِ ۚ إِنِ ٱمْرُؤٌا۟ هَلَكَ لَيْسَ لَهُۥ وَلَدٌ
وَلَهُۥٓ أُخْتٌ فَلَهَا نِصْفُ مَا تَرَكَ ۚ
وَهُوَ يَرِثُهَآ إِن لَّمْ يَكُن لَّهَا وَلَدٌ ۚ فَإِن
كَانَتَا ٱثْنَتَيْنِ فَلَهُمَا ٱلثُّلُثَانِ مِمَّا تَرَكَ ۚ
وَإِن كَانُوٓا۟ إِخْوَةً رِّجَالًا وَنِسَآءً
فَلِلذَّكَرِ مِثْلُ حَظِّ ٱلْأُنثَيَيْنِ ۗ يُبَيِّنُ
ٱللَّهُ لَكُمْ أَن تَضِلُّوا۟ ۗ وَٱللَّهُ بِكُلِّ
شَىْءٍ عَلِيمٌۢ ﴿١٧٦﴾

219. This verse was revealed long after the revelation of the rest of this *sūrah*. According to certain traditions, this verse was the very last Qur'ānic verse to be revealed. (For these traditions, see Ibn Kathīr's comments on this verse – Ed.) Even if this is disputed, it shows at least that this verse was revealed in 9 A.H., whereas the Muslims had been reciting the present *sūrah*, *al-Nisā'*, for quite some time before that. It was for this reason that this verse was not included among the verses relating to inheritance mentioned at the beginning of the *sūrah*, but was attached to it at the end as an appendix.

220. There is disagreement about the meaning of the word *kalālah*. According to some scholars, it means one who dies leaving neither issue nor father nor grandfather. According to others, it refers to those who die without issue (regardless of whether succeeded by either father or grandfather). On this question 'Umar remained undecided up to the last. But the majority of jurists accept the opinion of Abū Bakr that the former meaning is correct. The Qur'ān also seems to support this, for here the sister of the *kalālah* has been apportioned half of the inheritance whereas,

had his father been alive, the sister would not have inherited from him at all. (For relevant traditions on the subject see the commentary on this verse by Ibn Kathīr. For legal discussion on the question see the commentaries of Jaṣṣāṣ and Qurṭubī – Ed.)

221. The apportioned shares in inheritance mentioned here are those of brothers and sisters, whether related through both parents or through a common father only. Abū Bakr gave this interpretation in one of his pronouncements and none of the Companions expressed any dissent. This view is, therefore, considered to be supported by consensus *(ijmā')*.

222. This means that if there is no other legal heir the brother will receive the entire inheritance. In the presence of other heirs (such as husband), the brother will receive all the residual inheritance after the other heirs have received their apportioned shares.

223. The same also applies to more than two sisters.

Sūrah 5

Al-Mā'idah

(Madinan Period)

Title

The title of this *sūrah* is derived from verse 112 in which the word 'repast' occurs: 'Jesus, son of Mary, has your Lord the power to send down unto us a repast (*mā'idah*) from the heaven?' Like the titles of the other *sūrahs* it does not indicate the subject matter discussed but serves to distinguish this *sūrah* from the others.

Period of Revelation

The *sūrah* has considerable internal evidence to show that it was revealed either about the end of 6 A.H. or in the early part of 7 A.H., after the conclusion of the Treaty of Ḥudaybīyah. This view is also corroborated by traditions.

In the month of Dhu al-Qa'dah 6 A.H., the Prophet (peace be on him), together with about 1,400 Muslims, set out for Makka with the intention of performing *'Umrah* (Minor Pilgrimage). In the spirit of petty revenge, the pagans of the Quraysh barred them from performing this rite despite the fact that this was one of the most time-honoured religious customs of Arabia. After considerable negotiation the Quraysh agreed to permit the Muslims to go to Makka the following year to visit the Ka'bah. It seemed necessary at this stage, therefore, to teach the Muslims the rules and regulations of the Pilgrimage so that they could perform it in a truly Islamic manner. It was also felt necessary to direct the Muslims not to commit excesses against the hostile pagans of Makka in retaliation for wrongfully preventing them from performing the *'Umrah*; the Muslims could easily have prevented many pagan tribes from visiting Makka. This was possible since the Domain of Islam (*Dār al-Islām*) lay along their routes to that city. The Muslims are being directed, however, not to do so.

This is the context of the opening discourse. The same question is taken up later (see verses 56 ff.), illustrating that a single theme runs throughout the first fourteen sections of the *sūrah* (i.e. verses 1–108). The other subjects discussed also seem to have been revealed during the same period.

The unbroken continuity of the narration suggests that the entire *sūrah* is one single discourse, revealed at the same time and in an integrated form. This cannot be altogether ruled out. It is also possible, however, that certain verses were revealed at another period, and were then knitted into the narrative so well that there is no indication that the *sūrah* comprises two or three distinct discourses.

Historical Context

A great many changes had occurred during the period separating the present revelation from that of *Sūrahs* 3 and 4. A few years earlier, after the Muslims had suffered a setback at the Battle of Uḥud, the tribes living around Madina had assumed a menacing posture. Islam, by this time, however, had become an apparently indestructible force and the Islamic state had come to occupy large tracts of land: up to Najd, as far as the borders of Syria and the coasts of the Red Sea, and the environs of Makka. The wounds inflicted upon the Muslims during the Battle of Uḥud, far from demoralizing them, had in fact proved a spur. Within three years the entire situation had changed. Thanks to the continuous struggle and bravery of the Muslims the strength of the hostile tribes within a radius of about 150 to 200 miles of Madina was broken. The Jewish menace, which had always loomed large over Madina, had been ended once and for all. The Quraysh had made their last desperate effort to crush Islam at the Battle of the Ditch (5 A.H.), and this had ended in a fiasco. As a result there was no doubt in the minds of the people of Arabia that the Islamic movement had become too strong to be crushed. Islam was no longer just a creed and a way of life which ruled over the hearts and minds of people: it had come to possess a State and this State governed the lives of the people living in its domain. The Muslims now had the power to live according to their convictions without hindrance and without it being possible for extraneous creeds, norms and laws to encroach upon their lives.

Moreover, during these few years the Muslims had developed their own particular cultural entity so that their morality, their family life and their social order distinguished them from others. In all parts of the Islamic state mosques were erected, people began to pray regularly in congregation, and leaders of congregational Prayers were appointed for different tribes and regions. The Islamic civil and criminal laws were expounded in considerable detail and were enforced by Muslim judges. Many old forms of business transactions were prohibited and new, reformed ones introduced. A new code of inheritance was promulgated. Marriage and divorce laws, regulations prescribing modesty of dress and appearance and forbidding promiscuity, and other rules relating to decency, for example, the necessity of obtaining permission to enter another person's house, and laws laying down punishments for extra-marital sexual intercourse, and for accusing innocent women of unchastity, were enforced. As a result the entire lifestyle of the Muslims – their food and dress, the manner of their speech and conversation, the way they met and dispersed – had become distinct. Once the non-Muslims of the time observed this distinctive way of life they became despondent of the fact that the Muslims might lose their identity and be re-assimilated into the former body-politic. Before the conclusion of the Treaty of Ḥudaybīyah, however, a major obstacle barred the spreading of the message of Islam – the continuous conflict between the Muslims and the Quraysh. This obstacle was removed by the Treaty of Ḥudaybīyah which, on the face of it, implied the Muslims' acknowledgement of their inferior status.

In point of fact, this treaty amounted to a significant victory for the Muslims because it not only secured them against aggression within the borders of their own state, but enabled them to freely carry the message of Islam to the neighbouring areas. This phase was inaugurated by the Prophet (peace be on him) who despatched letters to the rulers of Persia, Rome and Egypt, and to the tribal chiefs of the Arabs, and who sent missionaries in all directions to summon people to God's true religion.

Subject Matter

It is in this historical context that the *sūrah* addressed the following three major themes:

1. The first theme comprises additional injunctions and directives relating to the religious, social and political life of the Muslims. In this connection the rules of the Pilgrimage (*Ḥajj*) are elucidated and the Muslims are directed not to desecrate the symbols of (devotion to) Allah (*sha'ā'ir Allāh*); orders are given not to molest Pilgrims to the Ka'bah; in matters of eating and drinking the true distinction between the lawful and the unlawful is laid down and the superstitions and man-made restrictions of pre-Islamic times are swept aside; permission is granted to eat the food of the People of the Book and to marry their women; regulations concerning *wuḍū'* (ablution) and *tayammum* (a symbolic ablution attained by wiping parts of the body with earth) are promulgated; the penalties for rebellion, public mischief and theft are fixed; games of chance and the drinking of intoxicants are categorically prohibited; the expiation for breach of vows is enunciated and a few more provisions are added to the law of evidence.

2. The second theme is an admonition to the Muslims. The Muslims had by now achieved political power, and this often intoxicates people and thereby misleads them. Although their period of subjection to injustice was almost over they, nevertheless, were to be put to a more severe test. The Muslims are repeatedly urged, therefore, to remain committed to justice; to avoid the pitfalls of their predecessors, the People of the Book; to observe their commitment to obey God and follow His commandments, and thus avoid the catastrophic end which overtook the Jews and Christians who had thrown overboard their covenant with God. They are required to remain scrupulously bound by the ordinances of the Book of God and to shun hypocrisy in all their affairs.

3. The third theme of the *sūrah* is an admonition to the Jews and Christians. The strength of the Jews was by now shattered and all the Jewish settlements of Northern Arabia had come under the hegemony of the Muslims. Here they are once again warned about their evil conduct and asked to follow the Right Way. Moreover, since the Treaty of Ḥudaybīyah made it possible to propagate Islam in Arabia and in the neighbouring countries, the opportunity to address the Christians in detail and to bring home to them the falsity of their beliefs and to ask them to believe in the Prophet (peace be on him), is also seized. However, although those neighbouring nations that followed either idolatrous or Magian cults are not addressed directly there is enough for their guidance in what was said to their fellow travellers, the idolatrous people of Arabia, in the *sūrahs* revealed during the Prophet's stay in Makka.

In the name of Allah, the Merciful, the Compassionate.

(1) Believers! Honour your bonds![1] All grazing beasts of the flock[2] are permitted to you except those which are recited to you hereinafter, but you are not allowed to hunt in the state of *Iḥrām* (a state of pilgrim sanctity).[3] Indeed Allah decrees as He wills.[4]

بِسْمِ اللَّهِ الرَّحْمَٰنِ الرَّحِيمِ

يَا أَيُّهَا الَّذِينَ آمَنُوا أَوْفُوا بِالْعُقُودِ ۚ
أُحِلَّتْ لَكُمْ بَهِيمَةُ الْأَنْعَامِ إِلَّا مَا يُتْلَىٰ
عَلَيْكُمْ غَيْرَ مُحِلِّي الصَّيْدِ وَأَنْتُمْ حُرُمٌ ۗ إِنَّ اللَّهَ
يَحْكُمُ مَا يُرِيدُ ﴿١﴾

1. People should abide by the limitations and prohibitions laid down in this *sūrah* and elsewhere in the law of God. This brief introductory statement is followed by an enunciation of those prohibitions which people are required to observe.

2. The Arabic word *an'ām* (cattle) denotes camels, oxen, sheep and goats, whereas the word *bahīmah* means all grazing quadrupeds. Had God said that *an'ām* had been made lawful for them, this permission would have included only those animals to which the term *an'ām* is applicable. But the terms in which the injunction is conveyed are *bahīmat al-an'ām* (all grazing beasts of the flock). Hence the permission is of wider import and embraces all grazing quadrupeds of the cattle type, i.e. which do not possess canine teeth, which feed on plants rather than animals, and which resemble the cattle found in Arabia in other characteristics. This implies that the flesh of those animals which have canine teeth and are carnivorous is not permissible. This implication was elucidated by the Prophet (peace be on him) and is embodied in a tradition in which he prohibited those beasts which kill and eat other animals. Likewise, the Prophet (peace be on him) also prohibited birds with claws and those that feed on carrion. According to a tradition transmitted by Ibn 'Abbās: 'The Messenger of Allah (peace be on him) prohibited all beasts with canine teeth and all birds with claws.' (Bukhārī, 'Dhabā'iḥ', 28, 29; 'Ṭibb', 53; Abū Dā'ūd, 'Aṭ'imah', 32; Tirmidhī, 'Aṭ'imah', 9, 11; Muslim, 'Ṣayd', 11–16; Nasā'ī, 'Ṣayd wa Dhabā'iḥ', 28, 30, 33; Ibn Mājah, 'Ṣayd', 13; etc. – Ed.)

3. *Iḥrām* is the name of the simple apparel worn at the time of Pilgrimage. In every direction around the Ka'bah, there are certain fixed points beyond which no Pilgrim may proceed without donning this special Pilgrim's garment in place of his normal clothes. This apparel consists of

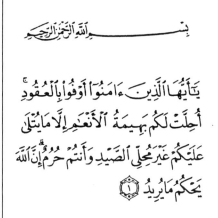

(2) Believers! Neither desecrate the symbols of (devotion to) Allah,[5] nor the holy month, nor the animals of offering, nor the animals wearing collars indicating they are for sacrifice, nor ill-treat those who have set out for the Holy House seeking from their Lord His bounty and good pleasure.[6]

يَٰٓأَيُّهَا ٱلَّذِينَ ءَامَنُوا۟ لَا تُحِلُّوا۟ شَعَٰٓئِرَ ٱللَّهِ
وَلَا ٱلشَّهْرَ ٱلْحَرَامَ وَلَا ٱلْهَدْىَ وَلَا ٱلْقَلَٰٓئِدَ
وَلَآ ءَآمِّينَ ٱلْبَيْتَ ٱلْحَرَامَ يَبْتَغُونَ فَضْلًا مِّن
رَّبِّهِمْ وَرِضْوَٰنًا

---

two sheets of untailored cloth, one of which is wrapped around the lower part of the body while the other is thrown over the upper part. This manner of dressing is termed *iḥrām* because once a man has assumed it he must treat as prohibited a number of things which are ordinarily lawful, for example either shaving or trimming the hair, or using perfumes and other items of toiletry and the gratification of sexual desires. These restrictions also extend to both killing and hunting, and to leading anyone else to either kill or hunt an animal.

4. God is the absolute sovereign and has absolute authority to issue whatever command He might will. His creatures do not have the right to complain about any of these orders. Even though wisdom (*ḥikmah*) underlies the ordinances of God, a true believer does not obey them because he considers them either appropriate or conducive to his best interests. He obeys them simply because they are the ordinances of his Lord. He holds unlawful all that God has declared unlawful, because God has so decreed it; whatever He has declared lawful is regarded as such for no other reason than that God, the Lord of all, has allowed His servants the use of it. Hence the Qur'ān establishes very firmly the principle that nothing except permission from the Lord – or lack of it – is to be taken into consideration in deciding what is lawful and what is not.

5. Whatever characteristically represents either a particular doctrine, creed, way of thought or conduct is recognized as its symbol. For example, official flags, uniforms of the armed forces, coins, notes and stamps are symbols used by governments so that their subjects – in fact all those who live within their sphere of influence – treat them with proper respect. Cathedrals, altars and crosses are symbols of Christianity. A special bunch of hair on the head, a special kind of bead-rosary and the temple are symbols of Hinduism. A turban, bracelet and *Kirpān* (a special dagger kept by the Sikhs) are symbols of the Sikh religion. The hammer and sickle are the symbols of Communism. The swastika has been the symbol of

Aryan racialism. The followers of these ideologies are required to treat these symbols with respect. If a man insults any symbol associated with a particular ideology it is regarded as an act of hostility; and if the person concerned is himself a follower of that ideology then that insult is considered tantamount to an abandonment of, and a revolt against it.

The expression *'sha'ā'ir Allāh'* refers to all those rites which, in opposition to polytheism and outright disbelief and atheism, are the characteristic symbols of an exclusive devotion to God. Muslims are required to respect these symbols, regardless of the people among whom they are found, provided their underlying spirit is one of godliness and that they have not been tainted by either polytheistic or pagan associations. Hence, whenever a Muslim encounters something in either the creed or practice of a non-Muslim, which embodies any element of devotion and service to the One True God, he will identify himself with it and show respect to the symbols which represent it. For this true element in their religious life constitutes the point of agreement between them and the Muslims. The point of dispute is not that they serve God, but that they associate others in that service.

It should be recalled that this directive to treat the symbols of God with due respect was given at a time when a state of belligerency existed between the Muslims and the polytheists of Arabia, and Makka was under the occupation of the latter. Polytheistic tribes from all over Arabia used to visit the Ka'bah for Pilgrimage, and the routes of many of these tribes were within the reach of the Muslims if they decided to attack. It was in such circumstances that the Muslims were told that, even though those people were polytheists, they should not be molested if they were proceeding towards the 'House of God'; that they should not be attacked during the months of Pilgrimage; and that the animals which they were carrying for sacrificial offering should not be touched. The element of godliness which persisted in their otherwise distorted religious life deserved to be respected.

6. Following a general directive that the symbols of God should be treated with proper respect a few such symbols are mentioned specifically lest war fever lead even to the desecration of religious rites and symbols. The enumeration of these particular symbols does not mean that respect is due to these alone.

But once you are free from Pilgrimage obligations, you are free to hunt.[7] Do not let your wrath against the people who have barred you from the Holy Mosque move you to commit undue transgressions;[8] rather, help one another in acts of righteousness and piety, and do not help one another in sin and transgression. Fear Allah. Surely Allah is severe in retribution.

(3) Forbidden to you are carrion,[9] blood, the flesh of swine, the animal slaughtered in any name other than Allah's,[10] the animal which has either been strangled, killed by blows, has died of a fall, by goring or that devoured by a beast of prey – unless it be that which you yourselves might have slaughtered while it was still alive[11] – and that which was slaughtered at the altars.[12–13] ▶

وَإِذَا حَلَلْتُمْ فَاصْطَادُواْ وَلَا يَجْرِمَنَّكُمْ شَنَئَانُ قَوْمٍ أَن صَدُّوكُمْ عَنِ ٱلْمَسْجِدِ ٱلْحَرَامِ أَن تَعْتَدُواْ وَتَعَاوَنُواْ عَلَى ٱلْبِرِّ وَٱلتَّقْوَىٰ وَلَا تَعَاوَنُواْ عَلَى ٱلْإِثْمِ وَٱلْعُدْوَٰنِ وَٱتَّقُواْ ٱللَّهَ إِنَّ ٱللَّهَ شَدِيدُ ٱلْعِقَابِ ۝ حُرِّمَتْ عَلَيْكُمُ ٱلْمَيْتَةُ وَٱلدَّمُ وَلَحْمُ ٱلْخِنزِيرِ وَمَا أُهِلَّ لِغَيْرِ ٱللَّهِ بِهِ وَٱلْمُنْخَنِقَةُ وَٱلْمَوْقُوذَةُ وَٱلْمُتَرَدِّيَةُ وَٱلنَّطِيحَةُ وَمَا أَكَلَ ٱلسَّبُعُ إِلَّا مَا ذَكَّيْتُمْ وَمَا ذُبِحَ عَلَى ٱلنُّصُبِ

7. *Iḥrām* is also one of the symbols of God and violation of any of the prohibitions which should be observed in that state is an act of sacrilege. The prohibition of hunting while in the state of *iḥrām* is mentioned in connection with the desecration of the symbols of God. When *iḥrām* is over, the prohibitions become void, and one is permitted to hunt.

8. The unbelievers had prevented the Muslims from visiting the Ka'bah. In fact, in violation of the ancient usage of Arabia they had even deprived them of their right to make Pilgrimage. As a result, the Muslims felt inclined to prevent the pagan tribes from making their pilgrimage by not letting them pass along the routes to Makka which lay close to the Islamic domains,

and to attack their trading caravans during the time of Pilgrimage (*Ḥajj*). God prevented them from carrying out this plan through the revelation.

9. 'Carrion' signifies the animal which has died a natural death.

10. This refers to the practice of pronouncing the name of anyone or anything other than God and dedicating the animal, as an offering, to either a holy personage, god or goddess before slaughtering. (For details see *Towards Understanding the Qur'ān*, vol. I, *Sūrah* 2, n. 171.)

11. It is lawful to eat the flesh of an animal which may have suffered from any of the above-mentioned accidents providing it was still alive until slaughtered. This verse also makes it clear that the flesh of an animal becomes lawful only by slaughtering ritually, and that no other method of killing is valid. The words *dhabḥ* and *dhakāh* belong to the technical terminology of Islam and denote slitting the throat so that the blood is completely drained from the animal's body. The disadvantage of killing an animal by either guillotine or strangulation is that the greater part of the blood remains within the body, and at various places it sticks to the flesh and forms congealed lumps. If an animal is slaughtered by slitting the throat, on the other hand, the connection between mind and body remains intact for a short while, with the result that the blood is thoroughly drained out from all the veins and the flesh becomes fully cleansed of blood.

We have just come across the injunction prohibiting the eating of blood. So only that flesh which has been purged of blood is declared lawful.

12. The word *nuṣub* signifies all the places consecrated for offerings to others than the One True God, regardless of whether they are images of wood, stone or something else.

13. The division of objects of eating and drinking into lawful and unlawful is based on their moral rather than their medicinal properties. God has left matters relating to the physical world to be tackled by man's own effort and striving. It is for man himself to discover by his own efforts which items of food and drink provide him with healthy nourishment and which are useless and harmful. The Law (*Sharī'ah*) does not take upon itself to guide man in such matters. Had it undertaken such a task, perhaps one of the first things for it to do would have been to pronounce the prohibition of arsenic oxide. But one will notice that the Qur'ān and *Ḥadīth* mention neither arsenic oxide nor other things which either singly or jointly are fatal for man. The underlying considerations of the Law with regard to the various items of eating and drinking are their possible effects on man's morals and on the purity of his soul. This is in addition to the judgements that the Law makes with regard to the various means adopted by man in his quest for food – whether they are appropriate according to Islamic standards or not. It is impossible for man to determine what is beneficial and what is harmful for his morals; he has not been endowed

You are also forbidden to seek knowledge of your fate by divining arrows.[14] All these are sinful acts. This day the unbelievers have fully despaired of your religion. Do not fear them; but fear Me.[15]

وَأَن تَسْتَقْسِمُوا بِالْأَزْلَامِ ذَٰلِكُمْ
فِسْقٌ ۗ الْيَوْمَ يَئِسَ الَّذِينَ كَفَرُوا مِن
دِينِكُمْ فَلَا تَخْشَوْهُمْ وَاخْشَوْنِ ۚ

---

with the capacities needed to arrive at sound conclusions on these matters, and so he frequently stumbles into error. Hence the Law undertakes to guide him in these matters and these matters alone. Whatever has been prohibited by Islam has been prohibited because of its bad effects on human morals, because of its repugnance to spiritual purity, and because of its association with false beliefs. Things which have been declared lawful have been so declared because they are untainted by these evils.

It may be asked why God did not specify the considerations underlying the prohibition of various things for this would have afforded us very valuable insights. In reply, it must be pointed out that it is impossible for us to fully grasp such considerations. The kind of questions we face are for instance: What are the corrupting effects of the consumption of either blood or the flesh of swine and carrion on our morals? The extent to which this corruption affects our morals, and the way in which certain things affect our morals is a matter that we are incapable of investigating, for we do not possess the means of weighing and measuring the moral properties of various things. To mention some of these bad effects would carry little weight with the sceptic, for how could he test the soundness of statements on such questions? Hence, God considers faith rather than man's own judgement as the main basis for observing the standards of lawfulness and prohibition. Whoever is fully convinced that the Qur'ān is the Book of God, that the Prophet (peace be on him) was designated by Him, and that God is All-Knowing and All-Wise, will necessarily commit himself to observe the restrictions enjoined by God regardless of whether he is able to grasp the wisdom underlying them or not. Whoever lacks this basic conviction will avoid only those evils which are fully evident to human beings, and will remain a prey to all those which have not yet become apparent but which in fact are intrinsically harmful.

14. The things which are prohibited in this verse fall into the following categories:

(1) Polytheistic divination, which is a form of omen-seeking whereby knowledge either about one's future or about matters beyond human perception, is sought from gods and goddesses. The polytheists of Makka had consecrated the idol Hubal in the Ka'bah for this purpose. Seven

arrows had been placed at its altars and on each of them different words and sentences had been inscribed. Whenever people were faced with the question whether a certain course was wise or not, or they wanted to trace something lost, or sought a judgement in a murder case, or had other similar problems, they would approach the oracle of Hubal, present him with an offering as his fee, and pray to Hubal to issue a verdict on the question concerned. Then the oracle would draw arrows, and the inscription on the arrow which fell to a person's lot was deemed to represent the verdict of Hubal.

(2) Superstitious divination, which has also been prohibited, means that instead of deciding the problems of life in a rational way one should decide them on fanciful grounds. Or it could mean deciding matters by arbitrary interpretation of accidental events, or to have one's future prophesied by means which have not been reasonably established as adequate for obtaining knowledge about the future. This includes geomancy, astrology, fortune-telling and the numerous other methods adopted to determine omens.

(3) Games of chance are also prohibited and include all those transactions in which what one receives depends on chance and other purely accidental factors rather than on rational considerations such as either due payment or recompense for services rendered. This applies, for instance, to lotteries where the holder of an arbitrarily-drawn number receives a huge amount of money which has been obtained from thousands of other people. It also applies to crossword puzzles were the award of prizes does not depend on the actual correctness of the solution (since several correct solutions are possible) but on accidental conformity with the particular solution which is arbitrarily chosen as the only correct one by the sponsors of the puzzle.

After prohibiting each of these three categories, the only kind of lot-drawing which Islam permits is that which one resorts to when obliged to make a decision either in favour of one of numerous permissible options or in favour of one out of two or more equally legitimate claimants. For instance, two persons have an equal claim over a thing which neither of them is prepared to relinquish, and at the same time there is no reasonable basis for preferring one to the other. In such a case, with the consent of the claimants, the matter may be settled by drawing lots. The Prophet (peace be on him) himself used to resort to drawing lots when he had to make a decision between two equal claimants, and when preferring one of them would cause distress and grievance to the other. (For such instances see Aḥmad b. Ḥanbal, *Musnad*, vol. 4, p. 373; Bukhārī, 'Nikāḥ', 97 and 'Shahādāt', 30; Muslim, 'Faḍā'il al-Ṣaḥābah', 88; Ibn Mājah, 'Aḥkām', 20, etc. – Ed.)

15. 'This day', here, does not signify a particular day or specific date. It refers to that period of time when these verses were revealed. In our own usage, too, expressions like 'today' or 'this day' often have the sense

This day I have perfected for you your religion, and have bestowed upon you My bounty in full measure, and have been pleased to assign for you Islam as your religion. (Follow, then, the lawful and unlawful bounds enjoined upon you.)[16] As for he who is driven by hunger, without being wilfully inclined to sin, surely Allah is All-Forgiving, All-Compassionate.[17]

ٱلْيَوْمَ أَكْمَلْتُ لَكُمْ دِينَكُمْ وَأَتْمَمْتُ
عَلَيْكُمْ نِعْمَتِى وَرَضِيتُ لَكُمُ ٱلْإِسْلَـٰمَ
دِينًا ۚ فَمَنِ ٱضْطُرَّ فِى مَخْمَصَةٍ غَيْرَ
مُتَجَانِفٍ لِّإِثْمٍ ۙ فَإِنَّ ٱللَّهَ غَفُورٌ
رَّحِيمٌ ﴿٣﴾

of the 'present time'. 'This day the unbelievers have fully despaired of your religion' refers to the fact that the Muslims' religion had developed into a full-fledged system of life, reinforced by the authority and governmental power which it had acquired. The unbelievers who had hitherto resisted its establishment now despaired of destroying Islam and of forcing the believers back to their former state of Ignorance. The believers therefore no longer needed to fear men: they should fear God alone instead. Indeed, the Muslims were repeatedly asked to fear God, for they would not be treated lightly if they failed to carry out His commands, especially as there was no longer any justifiable excuse for such failure. If they still violated the law of God, there could be no basis for supposing that they did so under constraint: it must mean that they simply had no intention of obeying Him.

16. The 'perfection of religion' mentioned in this verse refers to making it a self-sufficient system of belief and conduct, and an order of social life providing its own answers to the questions with which man is confronted. This system contains all necessary guidance for man, either by expounding fundamental principles from which detailed directives can be deduced or by spelling out such directives explicitly so that in no circumstances would one need to look for guidance to any extraneous source.

The bounty referred to in the statement: 'I have bestowed upon you My bounty in full measure', is the bounty of true guidance.

The statement: 'I have been pleased to assign for you Islam as your religion' means that, since the Muslims had proved by their conduct and their striving that they were honest and sincere about the commitment they had made to God in embracing Islam – the commitment to serve and obey Him – He had accepted their sincerity and created conditions in which they were no longer yoked in bondage to anyone but Him. Thus the Muslims

(4) They ask you what has been made lawful to them. Say: 'All clean things have been made lawful to you,[18] and such hunting animals as you teach, training them to hunt, teaching them the knowledge Allah has given you – you may eat what they catch for you[19] – but invoke the name of Allah on it.[20] Have fear of Allah (in violating His Law). Allah is swift in His reckoning.'

يَسْـَٔلُونَكَ مَاذَآ أُحِلَّ لَهُمْ قُلْ أُحِلَّ لَكُمُ
ٱلطَّيِّبَٰتُ وَمَا عَلَّمْتُم مِّنَ ٱلْجَوَارِحِ
مُكَلِّبِينَ تُعَلِّمُونَهُنَّ مِمَّا عَلَّمَكُمُ ٱللَّهُ فَكُلُوا۟
مِمَّآ أَمْسَكْنَ عَلَيْكُمْ وَٱذْكُرُوا۟ ٱسْمَ ٱللَّهِ عَلَيْهِ
وَٱتَّقُوا۟ ٱللَّهَ إِنَّ ٱللَّهَ سَرِيعُ ٱلْحِسَابِ ﴿٤﴾

were not prevented from living in submission to God out of extraneous constraints just as there were no constraints preventing them from subscribing to true beliefs. Having recounted these favours, God does not point out what should be the proper response to those favours. But the implication is obvious: the only appropriate response on the part of the believers must be unstinting observance of the law of God out of gratitude to Him.

According to authentic traditions this verse was revealed in 10 A.H. on the occasion of the Prophet's Farewell Pilgrimage. The context however, seems to indicate that it was revealed soon after the conclusion of the Treaty of Ḥudaybīyah (i.e. in 6 A.H.). All parts of the discourse in which this verse occurs are so tightly interwoven and so closely inter-connected that it hardly seems conceivable that it should have been inserted here several years later. My own estimate – and true knowledge of this lies with God alone – is that this verse was originally revealed in its present context (i.e. commenting upon the conditions prevailing at the time of the Treaty of Ḥudaybīyah). It is conceivable that the true significance of the verse was not then fully appreciated. But later on, when Islam prevailed over the whole of Arabia and the power of Islam reached a high point, God once again revealed this sentence to His Messenger and ordered him to proclaim it.

17. See *Towards Understanding the Qur'ān*, vol. I, *Sūrah* 2, n. 172.

18. There is a certain subtlety in how the query is answered. Religious-minded people often fall into a prohibitionist mentality by tending to regard as unlawful everything not expressly declared as lawful. This makes them excessively fastidious and over-suspicious, and inclined to ask for a complete list of all that is lawful and permitted. The Qur'ān's response to

this question seems to be aimed, in the first place, at the reform of this mentality. The questioners want a list of what is lawful so they can treat everything else as prohibited, but the Qur'ān provides them with a list of what is prohibited and then leaves them with the guiding principle that all 'clean things' are lawful. This means a complete reversal of the old religious outlook according to which everything that has not been declared lawful is considered prohibited. This was a great reform, and it liberated human life from many unnecessary constraints. Henceforth, except for a few prohibitions, the lawful domain embraced virtually everything.

The lawfulness of things has been tied, however, to the stipulation of their being clean so that no one can argue for the lawfulness of things which are unclean. The question which arises at this point is: How are we to determine which things are clean? The answer is that everything is clean apart from those things which can be reckoned unclean either according to any of the principles embodied in the Law or which are repellent to man's innate sense of good taste or which civilized human beings have generally found offensive to their natural feelings of cleanliness and decency.

19. The expression 'hunting animals' signifies hounds, cheetahs, hawks and all those beasts and birds which men use in hunting. It is a characteristic of animals which have been trained to hunt that they hold the prey for their masters rather than devour it. It is for this reason that while the catch of these trained animals is lawful, that of others is prohibited.

There is some disagreement among the jurists as to the hunting animals whose catch is lawful. Some jurists are of the opinion that if the hunting animal, whether bird or beast, eats any part of the game, it becomes prohibited since the act of eating signifies that the animal hunted for its own sake rather than for the sake of its master. This is the doctrine of Shāfi'ī. Other jurists hold that the prey is not rendered unlawful even if the hunting animal has eaten part of the game; even if it has devoured one-third of the animal, the consumption of the remaining two-thirds is lawful, irrespective of whether the hunting animal is a bird or a beast. This is the view of Mālik. A third group of jurists is of the opinion that if the hunting animal which has eaten part of the game is a beast it becomes prohibited, but not so if the hunting animal is a bird. The reason for this distinction is that hunting beasts can be trained to hold the game for their master whereas experience shows that hunting birds are not fully capable of receiving such instruction. This is the opinion of Abū Ḥanīfah and his disciples. 'Alī, however, is of the opinion that it is unlawful to eat the catch of hunting birds because they cannot be trained to refrain from eating the game and to hold it merely for the sake of their master. (See the commentaries of Ibn Kathīr, Jaṣṣāṣ, Ibn al-'Arabī and Qurṭubī on this verse. See also Ibn Rushd, *Bidāyat al-Mujtahid*, vol. 2, pp. 440 ff. – Ed.)

20. They should pronounce the name of God at the time of dispatching animals to the hunt. It is mentioned in a tradition that 'Adī b. Ḥātim asked

(5) This day all good things have been made lawful to you. The food of the People of the Book is permitted to you, and your food is permitted to them.[21] And permitted to you are chaste women, be they either from among the believers or from among those who have received the Book before you,[22] provided you become their protectors in wedlock after paying them their bridal-due, rather than go around committing fornication and taking them as secret-companions. The work of he who refuses to follow the way of faith will go waste, and he will be among the utter losers in the Hereafter.[23]

ٱلْيَوْمَ أُحِلَّ لَكُمُ ٱلطَّيِّبَٰتُ ۖ وَطَعَامُ ٱلَّذِينَ
أُوتُوا۟ ٱلْكِتَٰبَ حِلٌّ لَّكُمْ وَطَعَامُكُمْ حِلٌّ
لَّهُمْ ۖ وَٱلْمُحْصَنَٰتُ مِنَ ٱلْمُؤْمِنَٰتِ وَٱلْمُحْصَنَٰتُ
مِنَ ٱلَّذِينَ أُوتُوا۟ ٱلْكِتَٰبَ مِن قَبْلِكُمْ إِذَآ
ءَاتَيْتُمُوهُنَّ أُجُورَهُنَّ مُحْصِنِينَ غَيْرَ
مُسَٰفِحِينَ وَلَا مُتَّخِذِىٓ أَخْدَانٍ ۗ وَمَن
يَكْفُرْ بِٱلْإِيمَٰنِ فَقَدْ حَبِطَ عَمَلُهُۥ وَهُوَ
فِى ٱلْءَاخِرَةِ مِنَ ٱلْخَٰسِرِينَ ﴿٥﴾

---

the Prophet (peace be on him) whether he could use hounds for hunting. The Prophet (peace be on him) replied: 'If you have pronounced the name of God while dispatching your trained hound, eat what he has caught for you. And if it has eaten from the game, then do not eat for I fear that the hound had caught the game for itself.' Then he inquired what should be done if one had pronounced the name of God while dispatching one's own hound, but later found another hound close to the prey. The Prophet (peace be on him) replied: 'Do not eat that, for you have pronounced the name of God on your own hound, but not on the other one.' (For relevant traditions see Bukhārī, 'Dhabā'iḥ', 4, 10; Ibn Mājah, 'Ṣayd', 3; Aḥmad b. Ḥanbal, *Musnad*, vol. 1, p. 231 and vol. 4, p. 195 – Ed.) The verse under discussion makes it clear that it is necessary to pronounce the name of God while dispatching a hound to the hunt. If a man later finds the prey alive he should slaughter it. But if he does not find it alive it will still be lawful to eat it since the name of God has already been pronounced. The same rule applies with regard to shooting arrows in hunting.

21. The food of the People of the Book includes the animals slaughtered by them. The rule that 'our food is lawful to them and theirs lawful to

us' signifies that there need be no barriers between us and the People of the Book regarding food. We may eat with them and they with us. But this general proclamation of permission is preceded by a reiteration of the statement: 'All good things have been made lawful to you.' This indicates that if the People of the Book either do not observe those principles of cleanliness and purity which are considered obligatory by the Law or if their food includes prohibited items, then one should abstain from eating them. If, for instance, they either slaughter an animal without pronouncing the name of God or if they slaughter it in the name of anyone else but God it is not lawful for us to eat that animal. Likewise, if intoxicating drinks, the flesh of swine, and any other prohibited thing is found on their dining table we may not justify our partaking of such items on the ground that the persons concerned are People of the Book.

The same applies to those non-Muslims who are not People of the Book, except for one difference – that whereas the animals slaughtered by the People of the Book are lawful provided they have pronounced the name of God at the time of slaughtering them, we are not permitted to eat the animals killed by non-Muslims who are not People of the Book.

22. This expression signifies the Jews and the Christians. Of non-Muslim women, Muslims may marry only Christians and Jews, and of them only those who have been characterized as *muḥṣanāt* (i.e. 'well-protected women').

There are differences among jurists as to the detailed application of this rule. The view of Ibn 'Abbās is that the expression 'People of the Book' here signifies only those People of the Book who are subjects of the Domain of Islam (*Dār al-Islām*). It is also unlawful to marry Jewish and Christian women who are either living in the Domain of War (*Dār al-Ḥarb*) or in the Domain of Disbelief (*Dār al-Kufr*). The Ḥanafī jurists hold a slightly different opinion. Although they disapprove of marrying such women, it is not considered unlawful. Sa'īd b. al-Musayyib and Ḥasan al-Baṣrī are of the opinion that the verse warrants general application and hence there is no need to differentiate between those who are *ahl al-Dhimmah* (the non-Muslim subjects of the Islamic State) and those who are not.

There is also disagreement among the jurists about the connotation of the term *muḥṣanāt*. 'Umar considered this word to signify only those women who are chaste and possess good moral character, and hence *ahl al-Kitāb* women who are of loose character are excluded from this permission. This is also the opinion of Ḥasan al-Baṣrī, Ṣha'bī and Ibrāhīm al-Nakha'ī and of the Ḥanafī jurists. But Shāfi'ī considers this expression to have been used as an antonym of 'slave women', and hence it signifies all those *ahl al-Kitāb* women who are not slaves. (Cf. the commentaries of Ibn Kathīr, Ibn al-'Arabī and Qurṭubī – Ed.)

23. The declaration that marriage to *ahl al-Kitāb* women is permitted is immediately followed by this warning which, in effect, means that those who avail themselves of this permission ought to be mindful of their faith

(6) Believers! When you stand up for Prayer wash your faces and your hands up to the elbows, and wipe your heads, and wash your feet up to the ankles.[24] And if you are in the state of ritual impurity, purify yourselves (by taking a bath).[25] But if you are either ill, travelling, have satisfied a want of nature or have had contact with women and find no water then have recourse to clean earth and wipe your faces and your hands therewith.[26] Allah does not want to lay any hardship upon you; rather He wants to purify you and complete His favours upon you[27] so that you may give thanks.

يَٰٓأَيُّهَا ٱلَّذِينَ ءَامَنُوٓا۟ إِذَا قُمْتُمْ إِلَى
ٱلصَّلَوٰةِ فَٱغْسِلُوا۟ وُجُوهَكُمْ
وَأَيْدِيَكُمْ إِلَى ٱلْمَرَافِقِ وَٱمْسَحُوا۟
بِرُءُوسِكُمْ وَأَرْجُلَكُمْ إِلَى
ٱلْكَعْبَيْنِ ۚ وَإِن كُنتُمْ جُنُبًا فَٱطَّهَّرُوا۟ ۚ
وَإِن كُنتُم مَّرْضَىٰٓ أَوْ عَلَىٰ سَفَرٍ أَوْ جَآءَ
أَحَدٌ مِّنكُم مِّنَ ٱلْغَآئِطِ أَوْ لَٰمَسْتُمُ
ٱلنِّسَآءَ فَلَمْ تَجِدُوا۟ مَآءً فَتَيَمَّمُوا۟
صَعِيدًا طَيِّبًا فَٱمْسَحُوا۟ بِوُجُوهِكُمْ
وَأَيْدِيكُم مِّنْهُ ۚ مَا يُرِيدُ ٱللَّهُ لِيَجْعَلَ
عَلَيْكُم مِّنْ حَرَجٍ وَلَٰكِن يُرِيدُ
لِيُطَهِّرَكُمْ وَلِيُتِمَّ نِعْمَتَهُۥ عَلَيْكُمْ
لَعَلَّكُمْ تَشْكُرُونَ ٦

---

and morals. They are urged to beware of infatuation with disbelieving women lest they also become enamoured of the ideas and beliefs which they cherish, thereby allowing their faith to dissipate. They are warned against adopting social patterns and modes of conduct inconsistent with the true requirements of their faith.

24. The explanation of this injunction by the Prophet (peace be on him) indicates that washing of the face includes rinsing one's mouth and inhaling water into the nostrils. Unless this is done the washing of the face is not considered complete. Likewise, since the ears are part of the head, 'wiping the head' includes wiping one's hands over the external and internal parts of the ears as well. Moreover, before starting to wash the other parts one should first wash one's hands so that the instruments of washing are themselves clean.

(7) Remember Allah's favour upon you[28] and His covenant which He made with you when you said: 'We have heard and we obey.' So do fear Allah. Allah has full knowledge even of that which is hidden in the breasts of people. (8) Believers! Be upright bearers of witness for Allah,[29] and do not let the enmity of any people move you to deviate from justice. Act justly, that is nearer to God-fearing. And fear Allah. Surely Allah is well aware of what you do.

وَاذْكُرُوا نِعْمَةَ اللَّهِ عَلَيْكُمْ
وَمِيثَاقَهُ الَّذِي وَاثَقَكُم بِهِ إِذْ قُلْتُمْ
سَمِعْنَا وَأَطَعْنَا ۖ وَاتَّقُوا اللَّهَ ۚ إِنَّ اللَّهَ
عَلِيمٌ بِذَاتِ الصُّدُورِ ﴿٧﴾ يَا أَيُّهَا
الَّذِينَ آمَنُوا كُونُوا قَوَّامِينَ لِلَّهِ
شُهَدَاءَ بِالْقِسْطِ ۖ وَلَا يَجْرِمَنَّكُمْ
شَنَآنُ قَوْمٍ عَلَىٰ أَلَّا تَعْدِلُوا ۚ اعْدِلُوا
هُوَ أَقْرَبُ لِلتَّقْوَىٰ ۖ وَاتَّقُوا اللَّهَ ۚ إِنَّ
اللَّهَ خَبِيرٌ بِمَا تَعْمَلُونَ ﴿٨﴾

---

25. *Janābah* (the state of major ritual impurity) – whether caused by the sexual act or merely by seminal discharge – renders it unlawful to perform the ritual Prayer and to touch the Qur'ān (for further details see *Sūrah* 4, nn. 67–9 above).

26. For explanation see *Sūrah* 4, nn. 69–70 above.

27. Just as purity of the soul is a blessing, so is cleanliness of the body. God's favour to man can be completed only when he has received comprehensive direction in respect of both spiritual purity and physical cleanliness.

28. The 'favour' mentioned here denotes illuminating the Straight Way, and entrusting to the believers the task of guidance and leadership of the whole world.

29. See *Sūrah* 4, nn. 164–5 above.

(9) Allah has promised those who believe and do righteous deeds forgiveness from sins and a great reward. (10) As for those who disbelieve and give the lie to Our signs, they are destined for the Blazing Flame.

(11) Believers! Remember Allah's favour upon you. When a certain people decided to stretch their hands against you, He restrained their hands from you.[30] Do fear Allah. Men of faith should put their trust in Allah alone.

وَعَدَ ٱللَّهُ ٱلَّذِينَ ءَامَنُوا۟ وَعَمِلُوا۟
ٱلصَّٰلِحَٰتِ ۙ لَهُم مَّغْفِرَةٌ وَأَجْرٌ
عَظِيمٌ ﴿٩﴾ وَٱلَّذِينَ كَفَرُوا۟
وَكَذَّبُوا۟ بِـَٔايَٰتِنَآ أُو۟لَٰٓئِكَ أَصْحَٰبُ
ٱلْجَحِيمِ ﴿١٠﴾ يَٰٓأَيُّهَا ٱلَّذِينَ ءَامَنُوا۟
ٱذْكُرُوا۟ نِعْمَتَ ٱللَّهِ عَلَيْكُمْ إِذْ
هَمَّ قَوْمٌ أَن يَبْسُطُوٓا۟ إِلَيْكُمْ أَيْدِيَهُمْ
فَكَفَّ أَيْدِيَهُمْ عَنكُمْ ۖ وَٱتَّقُوا۟ ٱللَّهَ ۚ
وَعَلَى ٱللَّهِ فَلْيَتَوَكَّلِ ٱلْمُؤْمِنُونَ ﴿١١﴾

---

30. This alludes to the incident reported by Ibn 'Abbās when a group of Jews invited the Prophet (peace be on him) and a number of his close Companions to dinner. They had in fact hatched a plot to pounce upon the guests and thus undermine the very foundation of Islam. But by the grace of God the Prophet (peace be on him) came to know of the plot at the eleventh hour and did not go. Since the following section is addressed to the Children of Israel, this incident is alluded to here in order to mark the transition to a new subject.

The discourse which begins here has two purposes. The first is to warn the Muslims against following the ways of their predecessors, the People of the Book. The Muslims are told, therefore, that the Israelites and the followers of Jesus had made a covenant with God in the past, in the manner that the Muslims had recently done so. The Muslims should, therefore, take heed lest they also break their covenant and fall a prey to error and misguidance as their predecessors had done.

The second is to sensitize the Jews and Christians to the errors they have committed and invite them to the true religion.

(12) Surely Allah took a covenant with the Children of Israel, and We raised up from them twelve of their leaders,[31] and Allah said: 'Behold, I am with you; if you establish Prayer and pay *Zakāh* and believe in My Prophets and help them,[32] and lend Allah a good loan,[33] I will certainly efface from you your evil deeds,[34] and will surely cause you to enter the Gardens beneath which rivers flow. ►

۞ وَلَقَدْ أَخَذَ ٱللَّهُ مِيثَـٰقَ بَنِىٓ
إِسْرَٰٓءِيلَ وَبَعَثْنَا مِنْهُمُ ٱثْنَىْ عَشَرَ
نَقِيبًا ۖ وَقَالَ ٱللَّهُ إِنِّى مَعَكُمْ ۖ لَئِنْ
أَقَمْتُمُ ٱلصَّلَوٰةَ وَءَاتَيْتُمُ ٱلزَّكَوٰةَ
وَءَامَنتُم بِرُسُلِى وَعَزَّرْتُمُوهُمْ
وَأَقْرَضْتُمُ ٱللَّهَ قَرْضًا حَسَنًا
لَّأُكَفِّرَنَّ عَنكُمْ سَيِّـَٔاتِكُمْ
وَلَأُدْخِلَنَّكُمْ جَنَّـٰتٍ تَجْرِى مِن
تَحْتِهَا ٱلْأَنْهَـٰرُ

31. The word *naqīb* in Arabic denotes supervisor and censor. There were twelve tribes among the Israelites and each tribe was required to appoint one of its members as a *naqīb*, to look after their affairs and try to prevent them from becoming victims of irreligiousness and moral corruption. Although the Book of Numbers in the Bible does mention these twelve men, it does not seem to convey the sense of their being religious and moral mentors, as the term *naqīb* employed by the Qur'ān does. The Bible simply mentions them as the chiefs and dignitaries of their tribes.

32. The assurance of God's support is made conditional upon their continuous response to the call of God and for support of His Prophets.

33. This expression signifies spending one's wealth for the sake of God. Since God has promised to return to man every penny that he spends in His way along with His reward, which will be several-fold, the Qur'ān characterizes this spending as a loan to God. This spending is considered a loan provided it is a 'good loan', that is, provided the money spent in the cause of God has been acquired by legitimate means and has been spent in accordance with the laws of God and with sincerity and earnestness.

34. To efface someone's evil deeds signifies two things. First, that if a man decides to follow the Straight Path and strives to follow God's directives in both thought and action his soul will be purged of many evils and his way of life will gradually become free of corruption. Second, if, in spite of this reform, weaknesses still persist in a man's life he is assured that God will not punish him and will have his failing erased from his record. For God is not too exacting over trivial errors, providing a man has sincerely accepted the basic guidance and reformed his character.

Whosoever of you disbelieves thereafter has indeed gone astray from the right way.'[35] (13) Then, for their breach of the covenant We cast them away from Our mercy and caused their hearts to harden. (And now they are in such a state that) they pervert the words from their context and thus distort their meaning, and have forgotten a good portion of the teaching they were imparted, and regarding all except a few of them you continue to learn that they committed acts of treachery. Pardon them, then, and overlook their deeds. Surely Allah loves those who do good deeds.

فَمَن كَفَرَ بَعْدَ ذَٰلِكَ
مِنكُمْ فَقَدْ ضَلَّ سَوَآءَ ٱلسَّبِيلِ
﴿١٢﴾ فَبِمَا نَقْضِهِم مِّيثَٰقَهُمْ لَعَنَّٰهُمْ
وَجَعَلْنَا قُلُوبَهُمْ قَٰسِيَةً
يُحَرِّفُونَ ٱلْكَلِمَ عَن مَّوَاضِعِهِۦ
وَنَسُوا۟ حَظًّا مِّمَّا ذُكِّرُوا۟ بِهِۦ وَلَا تَزَالُ
تَطَّلِعُ عَلَىٰ خَآئِنَةٍ مِّنْهُمْ إِلَّا قَلِيلًا مِّنْهُمْ
فَٱعْفُ عَنْهُمْ وَٱصْفَحْ إِنَّ ٱللَّهَ يُحِبُّ
ٱلْمُحْسِنِينَ ﴿١٣﴾

35. That is, they once found the 'right way' and then allowed it to be lost and thus put themselves on the road to perdition. We have translated the Qur'ānic expression *'sawā' al-sabīl'* as the 'right way' for the sake of brevity. A better rendering could be, 'the highroad of balance and moderation', but even this would fail to bring out the meaning fully.

In order to grasp the full significance of what is being said here one should bear in mind that in himself man constitutes a microcosm of society. He has innumerable powers and potentialities, myriad desires, feelings and inclinations, and a host of divergent urges. Social life consists of a huge network of complex relationships, and with the growth of civilization and culture the complexity of these relationships increases. There is also a rich fund of resources in the world and there are countless possibilities for their utilization; as a result, man is confronted with a plethora of choices and problems.

The fact that man has inherent limitations means that he is incapable of viewing in one sweep and in a balanced way the entire span of existence. Hence, man is in no position to prescribe for his kind a judicious way of life – a way of life wherein justice is done to all his powers and capacities; in which a wholesome balance is maintained between all his inherent potentialities; in which all his urges are given their due; in which his two-fold need for inner satisfaction and external self-realization is fully met; in which various aspects of human life are taken into proper consideration, giving birth to an integrated scheme with a built-in capacity to harmonize the multifarious strains and stresses of social life; in which material resources are fully exploited in the best interests of both the individual and society and within the framework of equity, justice and righteousness. When man takes upon himself the task of prescribing the guidelines for his life and becomes his own law-maker, his mind tends to become preoccupied with one specific aspect of human life, with one of the numerous demands of his nature, with one of the myriad problems calling for solution. His mental involvement is liable to be so intense that he adopts – consciously or otherwise – an unjust attitude towards all the other aspects, requirements and problems of human life. Consequently, when such opinions are imposed, the balance which ought to prevail in man's life is disrupted and he begins to swing either towards one extreme or the other. Gradually, this deviation assumes intolerable proportions. A reaction sets in, and justice is demanded for the neglected aspects of human life. Still, human life remains deprived of justice. The reason for this failure is that man's reaction to imbalance is itself devoid of balance. The new dispensation in turn persists in excessive preoccupation with either one specific aspect, problem or requirement of human life at the expense of all the others. Thus human life is denied judicious and balanced progress. Man continues to stumble hither and thither; from one form of self-destruction to another. All courses of life charted by man himself are winding and crooked. They move in the wrong direction, reach the wrong end and then turn back in another wrong direction.

Among these numerous ways – all false – there is just one way that lies exactly in the middle. This way alone does full justice to all of man's various potentialities and urges, to all his instincts and predispositions, to all the multifarious claims of both the body and the spirit; in short, to all aspects of his life. In this way there is no crookedness; it is the one course of life in which nothing is given either too much consideration or too little, and nothing suffers inequity and injustice. Man's very nature thirsts for such a way, and the succession of revolts against false ways of life is merely a manifestation of his constant quest for this right and straight way. Left to himself, man is incapable of charting this way. It is God alone Who can direct him to it; and indeed the Prophets were sent for this very purpose.

The Qur'ān designates this way as *sawā' al-sabīl* ('the right way') in the present verse and elsewhere as *al-ṣirāṭ al-mustaqīm* ('the straight way'). (See *Towards Understanding the Qur'ān*, vol. I, *Sūrah* 1, verse 5, and n. 8.) This is the road which goes amidst the countless winding and crooked paths of life; the road which leads man, disregarding all the curved and crooked paths, straight on to his success, right from this world to the Hereafter. Whoever goes along it enjoys rectitude in this world and success and felicity in the Next, but whoever loses this road is bound to become a victim of false beliefs and false ways of conduct and thus comes to have a wrong orientation in life. This will lead him to Hell, where all bent and crooked paths end. The following illustrates man's dilemma.

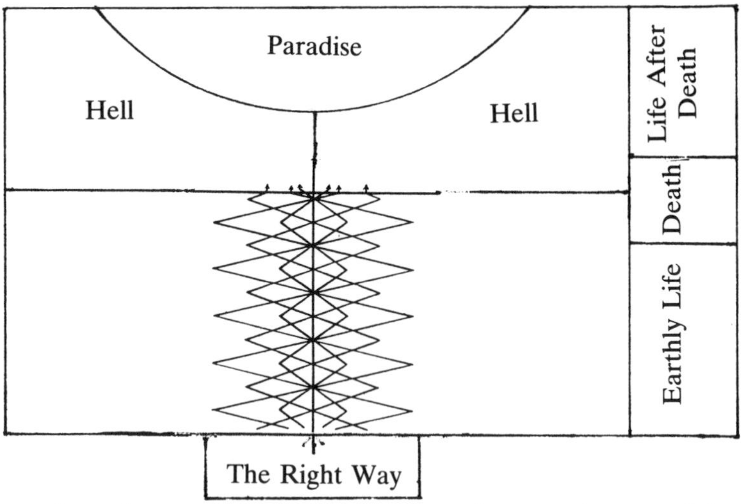

In modern times some philosophers have been so impressed by this constant swinging in human life, from one extreme to another, as to have mistakenly argued that the dialectical process is the natural course of human life. They conclude, therefore, that the only way for human life to progress is that a thesis should first swing it in one direction, and then an antithesis swing it in the opposite direction, after which there will emerge a synthesis which constitutes the course of human progress. These curved lines from one extreme to the other do not indicate the correct course of human progress. Rather they represent the tragic stumblings which again and again obstruct the true progress of human life. Every extreme thesis sets life on a certain course and continues to pull it in that direction for some time. When human life is thus thrown off its 'right course' the result is that certain realities of life – which had not received their due – rise up in revolt, and this revolt often assumes the form of an antithesis. This revolt begins to pull life in the opposite direction. As the 'right way' is approached the conflicting ideas – the thesis and antithesis – begin to effect some kind of mutual compromise, leading to the emergence of a synthesis. This synthesis comprises many elements conducive to the good of mankind. But since societies which do not submit to the guidance of the Prophets are deprived both of the signposts that might indicate the 'right way' and of faith to help steady man's feet thereon this synthesis does not permit human life to maintain the golden mean. Its momentum is so powerful that it once more pushes life to the opposite extreme. At this point, certain realities are once again denied their due, with the result that another antithesis emerges in reaction to the iniquities of the earlier ideology. Had the light of the Qur'ān been available to these short-sighted philosophers, and had they been able to perceive the 'right way' envisaged by the Qur'ān, they would have realized that this was the true course of human progress.

(14) We also took a covenant from those who said: 'We are Christians';[36] but they forgot a good portion of the teaching they had been imparted with. Wherefore We aroused enmity and spite between them till the Day of Resurrection, and ultimately Allah will tell them what they had contrived.

وَمِنَ ٱلَّذِينَ قَالُوٓا۟ إِنَّا نَصَٰرَىٰٓ
أَخَذْنَا مِيثَٰقَهُمْ فَنَسُوا۟ حَظًّا مِّمَّا
ذُكِّرُوا۟ بِهِۦ فَأَغْرَيْنَا بَيْنَهُمُ ٱلْعَدَاوَةَ
وَٱلْبَغْضَآءَ إِلَىٰ يَوْمِ ٱلْقِيَٰمَةِ ۚ
وَسَوْفَ يُنَبِّئُهُمُ ٱللَّهُ بِمَا
كَانُوا۟ يَصْنَعُونَ ﴿١٤﴾

36. Some are of the opinion that the word Naṣārá (meaning Christians) is derived from Nāṣirah (Nazareth), the birth-place of the Messiah. In fact this word is not derived from Nāṣirah (Nazareth) but from the word *nuṣrah,* and the basis of this derivation is the question posed by the Messiah to his disciples: 'Who are my supporters (*anṣārī*) in the way of God?' In response to this they had said: 'We are the supporters (*anṣār*) (in the way) of God.' Christian authors have been misled by the resemblance between the words Nāṣirah and Naṣārá into believing that the name of the sect founded in the early history of Christianity, and contemptuously characterized as either Nazarenes or Ebonites served as the basis of the Qur'ānic designation of the Christians. But here the Qur'ān categorically states that they had declared that they were 'Naṣārá' and it is obvious that the Christians never called themselves 'Nazarenes'.

In this connection it should be recalled that Jesus never called his followers 'Christians' for he had not come to found a new religion named after him. His mission was to revive the religion of Moses and of all the Prophets who preceded him as well as of the one who was to appear after him. Hence, he neither formed any cult divorced from the Israelites and the followers of the Mosaic Law nor designated his followers by any distinctive name. Likewise, his early followers neither considered themselves to be separate from the Israelite community nor developed into an independent group nor adopted any distinctive symbol and name. They worshipped in the temple of Jerusalem along with other Jews and considered themselves to be followers of the Mosaic Law (see Acts 3: 1–10; 21: 14–15, 21). Later on the process of alienation began to operate on both sides. On the one hand, Paul, one of the followers of Jesus, declared independence from the Mosaic Law holding that faith in Christ was all that one needed for salvation. On the other hand, the Jewish rabbis declared the followers of Christ to be heretics and excommunicated them. Despite this, for some time the new sect had no distinct appellation of its own. The

(15) People of the Book! Now Our Messenger has come to you: he makes clear to you a good many things of the Book which you were wont to conceal, and also passes over many things.[37] There has now come to you a light from Allah, and a clear Book (16) through which Allah shows to all who seek to please Him the paths leading to safety.[38] He brings them out, by His leave, from darkness to light and directs them on to the straight way.

يَٰٓأَهۡلَ ٱلۡكِتَٰبِ قَدۡ جَآءَكُمۡ
رَسُولُنَا يُبَيِّنُ لَكُمۡ كَثِيرٗا مِّمَّا
كُنتُمۡ تُخۡفُونَ مِنَ ٱلۡكِتَٰبِ
وَيَعۡفُواْ عَن كَثِيرٖۚ قَدۡ
جَآءَكُم مِّنَ ٱللَّهِ نُورٞ
وَكِتَٰبٞ مُّبِينٞ ﴿١٥﴾ يَهۡدِي بِهِ
ٱللَّهُ مَنِ ٱتَّبَعَ رِضۡوَٰنَهُۥ سُبُلَ
ٱلسَّلَٰمِ وَيُخۡرِجُهُم مِّنَ ٱلظُّلُمَٰتِ
إِلَى ٱلنُّورِ بِإِذۡنِهِۦ وَيَهۡدِيهِمۡ إِلَىٰ
صِرَٰطٖ مُّسۡتَقِيمٖ ﴿١٦﴾

---

followers of Christ variously described themselves as 'disciples', as 'brethren', as 'those who believed', and as 'saints' (see Acts 2: 44; 4: 32; 9: 26; 11: 29; 13: 52; 15: 1; 23: 1 and Romans 15: 25 and Colossians 1: 2). The Jews sometimes designated them as 'Galileans' and as 'the sect of Nazarenes' (see Acts 24: 5; Luke 13: 2). These nicknames, which were originally contrived in order to ridicule them, referred to Nazareth, the home town of Jesus in the district of Galilee. These names, however, did not gain sufficient popularity to become the permanent names of the followers of Christ. They were called 'Christians' for the first time by the people of Antioch in 43 A.D. or 44 A.D. when Paul and Barnabas went there and began to preach their religion (Acts 11: 26). This appellation was flung at them by the opponents of the followers of Christ precisely in order to tease them by using an appellation which was unacceptable to them. But when their enemies began to call them consistently by this name their leaders reacted by saying that if they were called Christians because of their allegiance to Christ they had no reason to be ashamed of it (1 Peter 4: 16). It was thus that the followers of Christ also gradually began to call themselves by the same name which had originally been conferred upon them sarcastically. In the course of time the Christians ceased to realize that theirs had originally been a derogatory appellation chosen for them by outsiders rather than by themselves.

The Qur'ān, therefore, does not refer to the followers of Christ as Christians. It reminds them rather that they belong to those who responded to the query of Jesus: 'Who are my supporters (*anṣārī*) in the way of God?'

(17) Indeed those who said: 'Christ, the son of Mary, he is indeed God', disbelieved.[39] Say (O Muḥammad!): 'Who could have overruled Allah had He so willed to destroy Christ, the son of Mary, and his mother, and all those who are on earth?' For to Allah belongs the dominion of the heavens and the earth and all that is between them; He creates what He wills.[40] Allah is All-Powerful.

لَّقَدْ كَفَرَ ٱلَّذِينَ قَالُوٓا۟ إِنَّ ٱللَّهَ
هُوَ ٱلْمَسِيحُ ٱبْنُ مَرْيَمَ ۚ قُلْ فَمَن
يَمْلِكُ مِنَ ٱللَّهِ شَيْـًٔا إِنْ أَرَادَ
أَن يُهْلِكَ ٱلْمَسِيحَ ٱبْنَ مَرْيَمَ
وَأُمَّهُۥ وَمَن فِى ٱلْأَرْضِ جَمِيعًا ۗ
وَلِلَّهِ مُلْكُ ٱلسَّمَٰوَٰتِ وَٱلْأَرْضِ
وَمَا بَيْنَهُمَا ۚ يَخْلُقُ مَا يَشَآءُ ۚ وَٱللَّهُ عَلَىٰ
كُلِّ شَىْءٍ قَدِيرٌ ﴿١٧﴾

by saying that they were his *anṣār* (supporters) in God's cause. (See *Sūrah al-Ṣaff* 61: 14 – Ed.) It is an irony of fate that far from feeling grateful at being referred to by a dignified appellation Christian missionaries take offence at the fact that the Qur'ān designates them as *Naṣārá* rather than as 'Christians'.

37. God discloses some of the dishonest and treacherous dealings of theirs where He deems it necessary in order to strengthen the cause of the true religion, and ignores the disclosure of those which are not truly indispensable.

38. The word 'safety' here denotes safety from false perception and outlook, safety from misdeeds and their consequences. Whoever seeks guidance from the Book of God and from the example of the Messenger (peace be on him) can find out how to keep himself safe from errors at each of life's crossroads.

39. The original mistake committed by the Christians in declaring Jesus to be a combination of human and divine essences turned Jesus into a mystery for them, and the more the Christian scholars tried to solve this mystery by resorting to conjecture and rhetorical extravagance the more involved the whole matter became. Those who were more impressed by the humanity of Jesus stressed his being the son of God and considered him to be one of the three gods. Those who were more impressed by the divinity of Jesus considered him to be none other than God, stressing that he was the human incarnation of God, and worshipped him as God. Those

(18) The Jews and the Christians say: 'We are Allah's children and His beloved ones.' Ask them: 'Why, then, does He chastise you for your sins?' You are the same as other men He has created. He forgives whom He wills and chastises whom He wills. And to Allah belongs the dominion of the heavens and the earth, and all that is between them. To Him is the eventual return.

وَقَالَتِ ٱلْيَهُودُ وَٱلنَّصَٰرَىٰ نَحْنُ أَبْنَٰٓؤُا۟
ٱللَّهِ وَأَحِبَّٰٓؤُهُۥ ۚ قُلْ فَلِمَ يُعَذِّبُكُم
بِذُنُوبِكُم ۖ بَلْ أَنتُم بَشَرٌ مِّمَّنْ خَلَقَ ۚ
يَغْفِرُ لِمَن يَشَآءُ وَيُعَذِّبُ مَن يَشَآءُ ۚ
وَلِلَّهِ مُلْكُ ٱلسَّمَٰوَٰتِ وَٱلْأَرْضِ
وَمَا بَيْنَهُمَا ۖ وَإِلَيْهِ ٱلْمَصِيرُ ﴿١٨﴾

---

who tried to strike a middle path spent all their efforts hammering out subtle verbal formulations of the Trinity that would allow people to consider the Messiah to be God and man at one and the same time, to affirm that God and the Messiah are independent and simultaneously constitute an inseparable whole (see *Sūrah* 4, nn. 212, 213, 215 above).

40. This statement hints at the childishness of those who have been misled into believing that the Messiah himself is God either because of his miraculous birth or because of his flawless moral character or because of the miracles which he performed. The Messiah is merely a sign of the innumerable wonders of God's creation; a sign which somehow dazzled the eyes of those superficial people. Had their perception been wider they would have been able to see that there are even more inspiring examples of His creation and infinite power. If anything their attitude was indicative of the intellectual puerility of those who were so overawed by the excellence of a creature as to mistake him for the Creator. Those whose intelligence penetrates through the excellence of creatures, who look upon them merely as signs of the magnificent power of God, and who are led by such observations to a reinforcement of faith in the Creator are truly wise.

(19) People of the Book! After a long interlude during which no Messengers have appeared there has come to you Our Messenger to elucidate the teaching of the true faith lest you say: 'No bearer of glad tidings and no warner has come to us.' For now there indeed has come to you a bearer of glad tidings and a warner. Allah is All-Powerful.[41]

(20) Remember when Moses said to his people: 'My people, remember Allah's favour upon you when He raised Prophets amongst you and appointed you rulers, and granted to you what He had not granted to anyone else in the world.[42] ▶

يَٰٓأَهۡلَ ٱلۡكِتَٰبِ قَدۡ جَآءَكُمۡ رَسُولُنَا يُبَيِّنُ
لَكُمۡ عَلَىٰ فَتۡرَةٖ مِّنَ ٱلرُّسُلِ أَن تَقُولُواْ
مَا جَآءَنَا مِنۢ بَشِيرٖ وَلَا نَذِيرٖۖ فَقَدۡ جَآءَكُم
بَشِيرٞ وَنَذِيرٞۗ وَٱللَّهُ عَلَىٰ كُلِّ شَيۡءٖ قَدِيرٞ
﴿١٩﴾ وَإِذۡ قَالَ مُوسَىٰ لِقَوۡمِهِۦ يَٰقَوۡمِ
ٱذۡكُرُواْ نِعۡمَةَ ٱللَّهِ عَلَيۡكُمۡ إِذۡ جَعَلَ
فِيكُمۡ أَنۢبِيَآءَ وَجَعَلَكُم مُّلُوكٗا وَءَاتَىٰكُم
مَّا لَمۡ يُؤۡتِ أَحَدٗا مِّنَ ٱلۡعَٰلَمِينَ ﴿٢٠﴾

---

41. In the present context this sentence is extremely eloquent and subtle. It signifies that the same God who had sent warners and bearers of glad tidings to men in the past has now sent Muḥammad (peace be on him) with the same task. At the same time it also means that they should not treat the message of this warner and bearer of glad tidings lightly. They should bear in mind that if they disregard the injunctions of God, He can chastise them as He wills, for He is All-Powerful and All-Mighty.

42. This refers to the glory the Israelites enjoyed before the time of Moses. There had appeared among them such great Prophets as Abraham, Isaac, Jacob and Joseph. Moreover, from the time of Joseph they were able to achieve very considerable power and authority in Egypt. For a considerable period they were the greatest rulers of the civilized world, reigning supreme in Egypt and the surrounding territories. People are generally inclined to regard the time of Moses as the starting point for the rise of the Israelites. The Qur'ān, however, states categorically that the truly glorious period of their history had passed long before Moses, and that Moses himself drew the attention of his people to that period as their time of glory.

(21) My people! Enter the holy land which Allah has ordained for you;[43] and do not turn back for then you will turn about losers.'[44] (22) They answered: 'Moses, therein live a ferocious people: we will not enter unless they depart from it; but if they do depart from it then we will surely enter it.' (23) Two from among these who were frightened but upon whom Allah had bestowed His favour[45] said: 'Enter upon them through the gate – for if you do enter – you will be the victors. And put your trust in Allah if indeed you are men of faith.' (24) Nevertheless they said: 'O Moses! Never shall we enter it as long as they are there. Go forth, then, you and your Lord, and fight, both of you. As for us, we will sit here.'

يَٰقَوْمِ ٱدْخُلُوا۟ ٱلْأَرْضَ ٱلْمُقَدَّسَةَ ٱلَّتِى
كَتَبَ ٱللَّهُ لَكُمْ وَلَا تَرْتَدُّوا۟ عَلَىٰٓ أَدْبَارِكُمْ
فَتَنقَلِبُوا۟ خَٰسِرِينَ ﴿٢١﴾ قَالُوا۟ يَٰمُوسَىٰٓ
إِنَّ فِيهَا قَوْمًا جَبَّارِينَ وَإِنَّا لَن نَّدْخُلَهَا
حَتَّىٰ يَخْرُجُوا۟ مِنْهَا فَإِن يَخْرُجُوا۟ مِنْهَا
فَإِنَّا دَٰخِلُونَ ﴿٢٢﴾ قَالَ رَجُلَانِ مِنَ
ٱلَّذِينَ يَخَافُونَ أَنْعَمَ ٱللَّهُ عَلَيْهِمَا
ٱدْخُلُوا۟ عَلَيْهِمُ ٱلْبَابَ فَإِذَا دَخَلْتُمُوهُ
فَإِنَّكُمْ غَٰلِبُونَ وَعَلَى ٱللَّهِ فَتَوَكَّلُوٓا۟ إِن
كُنتُم مُّؤْمِنِينَ ﴿٢٣﴾ قَالُوا۟ يَٰمُوسَىٰٓ
إِنَّا لَن نَّدْخُلَهَآ أَبَدًا مَّا دَامُوا۟ فِيهَا
فَٱذْهَبْ أَنتَ وَرَبُّكَ فَقَٰتِلَآ إِنَّا
هَٰهُنَا قَٰعِدُونَ ﴿٢٤﴾

43. This signifies Palestine which had been the homeland of Abraham, Isaac and Jacob. After their exodus from Egypt, God ordered the Israelites to go forth to Egypt and conquer it.

44. This statement of Moses refers to the second year after they had come out of Egypt when he and his people lived in tents in the wilderness of Paran. This desert lies in the Sinai peninsula adjacent to the northern borders of Arabia and the southern borders of Palestine.

45. This could have two meanings: either that two of those who feared the high-handed people of the Promised Land made that statement or that two of those who feared God did so. (However, most Qur'ānic commentators subscribe to the latter meaning – Ed.)

(25) Thereupon Moses said: 'My Lord! I have control over none but my own self and my brother; so distinguish between us and the transgressing people.' (26) Allah said: 'This land will now be forbidden to them for forty years and they will remain wandering about on the earth.[46] Do not grieve over the condition of these transgressing people.'[47]

قَالَ رَبِّ إِنِّى لَآ أَمْلِكُ إِلَّا نَفْسِى
وَأَخِى فَافْرُقْ بَيْنَنَا وَبَيْنَ ٱلْقَوْمِ
ٱلْفَٰسِقِينَ ﴿٢٥﴾ قَالَ فَإِنَّهَا مُحَرَّمَةٌ
عَلَيْهِمْ أَرْبَعِينَ سَنَةً يَتِيهُونَ فِى
ٱلْأَرْضِ فَلَا تَأْسَ عَلَى ٱلْقَوْمِ
ٱلْفَٰسِقِينَ ﴿٢٦﴾

46. The details of this incident are found in the Bible in Numbers, Deuteronomy and Joshua. The essence of the story is that Moses sent twelve heads of Israel to spy out Palestine. They returned after forty days and said: 'We came to the land to which you sent us; it flows with milk and honey. Yet the people who dwell in the land are strong, and the cities are fortified and very large; and besides, we saw the descendants of Anak there . . . and all the people that we saw in it are men of great stature. And there we saw the Nephilim (the sons of Anak, who come from the Nephilim); and we seemed to ourselves like grasshoppers, and so we seemed to them.' Then all the congregation cried out: 'Would that we had died in the land of Egypt; or would that we had died in this wilderness; why does the Lord bring us into this land, to fall by the sword? Our wives and our little ones will become a prey; would it not be better for us to go back to Egypt?' At this they were censured for cowardice by two of the twelve heads who had spied out Palestine, Joshua and Caleb. Caleb suggested that they should go and seize Palestine. Then both of them said: 'If the Lord delights in us, He will bring us into this land and give it to us, a land which flows with milk and honey. Only do not rebel against the Lord; and do not fear the people of the land . . . for the Lord is with us; do not fear them' (Numbers 14: 1–9). But the congregation responded to this by crying out that both ought to be stoned. This so provoked the wrath of God that He commanded that their bodies would fall dead in the wilderness and that of all their numbers numbered from twenty years old and upward, who had murmured against Him, none would come into the promised land except Caleb and Joshua; that only after an entire generation had passed away and a new generation had sprung up would they be enabled to conquer Palestine. Because of this divine decree, it took the people of Israel thirty-eight years to reach Transjordan from Paran. During this period all those who had left Egypt in their youth had perished. After the conquest of Transjordan Moses died (*Ibid.*, 14: 10 ff.).

WANDERINGS OF THE ISRAELITES IN THE SINAI PENINSULA

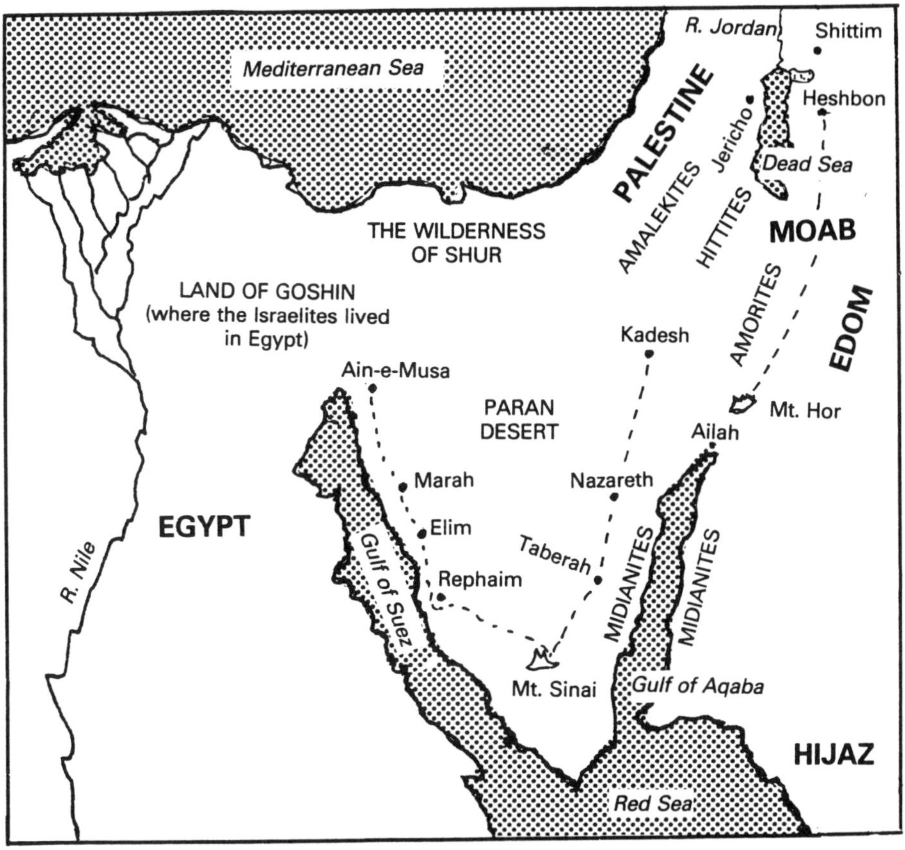

The Prophet Moses (peace be on him) led the Israelites out of Egypt and brought them to Mount Sinai by way of Marah, Elim and Rephaim in the Sinai Peninsula. Here he stayed for a little over a year and received most of the Commandments of the Torah. Then he was commanded to lead the Israelites towards Palestine and conquer it, for that land was to be given to them as an inheritance. So, he led them through Taberah and Nazareth and came to the desert of Paran from where he despatched a deputation of prominent Israelites to spy out Palestine. The deputation returned after forty days and made their report at Kadesh. Except for the encouraging picture presented by Joshua and Caleb, the report made by the other members was so disappointing that the Israelites cried out in disgust and refused to march on to Palestine. Thereupon God decreed that they would wander for forty years in the wilderness and none of their older generation except Joshua and Caleb would see Palestine. Thus, the Israelites wandered homeless in the wilderness of Paran, Shur and Zin, fighting and struggling against the Amalekites, the Amorites, the Edomites, the Midianites and the Moabites. When the forty years was about to end, the Prophet Aaron (peace be on him) died in Mount Hor, near the border of Edom. At about this time the Prophet Moses (peace be on him) entered Moab at the head of the Israelites, conquered the whole area and reached Heshbon and Shittim. After him Joshua, his first successor, crossed the River Jordan from the east and captured Jericho, the first Palestinian city to fall to the Israelites. Later on the whole of Palestine was conquered by them within a short period.

Ailah (present-day Aqaba) on this map is the place where probably the well-known incident of the Sabbath-breakers, as mentioned in Sūrah al-Baqarah 2: 65 and Sūrah al-A'rāf 7: 166, took place.

(27) Narrate to them in all truth the story of the two sons of Adam. When they made an offering and it was accepted from one of them and was not accepted from the other, the latter said: 'I will surely kill you.' Thereupon the former said: 'Allah accepts offerings only from the God-fearing.[48] (28) Even if you stretch forth your hand against me to kill, I will not stretch forth my hand to kill you.[49] Surely, I fear Allah, the Lord of the entire universe. ▶

۞ وَٱتۡلُ عَلَيۡهِمۡ نَبَأَ ٱبۡنَيۡ ءَادَمَ بِٱلۡحَقِّ
إِذۡ قَرَّبَا قُرۡبَانٗا فَتُقُبِّلَ مِنۡ أَحَدِهِمَا
وَلَمۡ يُتَقَبَّلۡ مِنَ ٱلۡأٓخَرِ قَالَ لَأَقۡتُلَنَّكَۖ
قَالَ إِنَّمَا يَتَقَبَّلُ ٱللَّهُ مِنَ ٱلۡمُتَّقِينَ ٢٧
لَئِنۢ بَسَطتَ إِلَيَّ يَدَكَ لِتَقۡتُلَنِي مَآ أَنَا۠
بِبَاسِطٖ يَدِيَ إِلَيۡكَ لِأَقۡتُلَكَۖ إِنِّيٓ
أَخَافُ ٱللَّهَ رَبَّ ٱلۡعَٰلَمِينَ ٢٨

Later on during the caliphate* (*sic*) of Joshua the Israelites became capable of conquering Palestine.

47. The purpose of referring to this event becomes clear if we reflect upon the context. It seems to be to bring home to the Israelites that the punishment to which they would be subjected if they adopted a rebellious attitude towards Muḥammad (peace be on him) would be even more severe than the one to which they had been subjected in the time of Moses.

48. God's refusal to accept the sacrifice of one of the two brothers was not due to any wrong the other brother might have committed but to his own lack of piety. Hence, rather than attempt to kill his brother he should be concerned with cultivating piety.

49. This does not mean that his brother assured him that when the latter stepped forward to kill him he would keep his hands tied and stretch out his own neck to be cut down rather than defend himself. What this statement amounts to is an assurance on the part of the first brother that, even though the other was intent on killing him, he himself had no such intention. In other words, he assured his brother that even though the latter was busy planning his murder he would not take the initiative in killing him despite his knowledge of the latter's intent.

---

*In view of the fact that the followers of all the Prophets are Muslims, the author has used a peculiarly Islamic term – caliphate, rather than kingship, etc. – to signify the predominantly religious (or shall we say, Islamic) quality of his rule and to distinguish it from systems of government not animated by the religious spirit – Ed.

(29) I would desire that you be laden with my sin and with your sin,[50] and thus become among the inmates of the Fire. That indeed is the right recompense of the wrong-doers.' (30) At last his evil soul drove him to the murder of his brother, and he killed him, whereby he himself became one of the losers. (31) Thereupon Allah sent forth a raven who began to scratch the earth to show him how he might cover the corpse of his brother. So seeing he cried: 'Woe unto me! Was I unable even to be like this raven and find a way to cover the corpse of my brother?'[51] Then he became full of remorse at his doing.[52]

إِنِّيٓ أُرِيدُ أَن تَبُوٓأَ بِإِثۡمِي وَإِثۡمِكَ فَتَكُونَ
مِنۡ أَصۡحَٰبِ ٱلنَّارِۚ وَذَٰلِكَ جَزَٰٓؤُاْ
ٱلظَّٰلِمِينَ ٢٩ فَطَوَّعَتۡ لَهُۥ نَفۡسُهُۥ قَتۡلَ
أَخِيهِ فَقَتَلَهُۥ فَأَصۡبَحَ مِنَ ٱلۡخَٰسِرِينَ
٣٠ فَبَعَثَ ٱللَّهُ غُرَابٗا يَبۡحَثُ فِي
ٱلۡأَرۡضِ لِيُرِيَهُۥ كَيۡفَ يُوَٰرِي سَوۡءَةَ
أَخِيهِۚ قَالَ يَٰوَيۡلَتَىٰٓ أَعَجَزۡتُ أَنۡ أَكُونَ
مِثۡلَ هَٰذَا ٱلۡغُرَابِ فَأُوَٰرِيَ سَوۡءَةَ
أَخِيۖ فَأَصۡبَحَ مِنَ ٱلنَّٰدِمِينَ ٣١

Righteousness does not demand at all that when a man is subjected to wrongful aggression he should surrender to the aggressor rather than defend himself. Righteousness, however, demands that a man should not take the initiative and try to kill someone even though he knows him to be bent on killing him. He should rather wait for the act of aggression to be initiated by the other person. And this is exactly what was intended by the statement of the righteous son of Adam.

50. The righteous son of Adam told his brother that rather than both of them becoming sinners by trying to kill each other, he would prefer to see the entire sin fall on the lot of the one who was intent on the murder – the sin of the aggressor's attempt to murder, as well as the sin of any injury that might be inflicted on him in self-defence.

51. In this way God made this errant son of Adam realize his ignorance and folly. Once his attention turned to self-appraisal, his regret was not confined to realizing that in his effort to hide his brother's corpse he proved to be even less efficient than the raven. He also began to feel how foolish he was to have killed his own brother. The later part of the sentence indicates this remorse.

(32) Therefore We ordained for the Children of Israel[53] that he who slays a soul unless it be (in punishment) for murder or for spreading mischief on earth shall be as if he had slain all mankind; and he who saves a life shall be as if he had given life to all mankind.[54] And indeed again and again did Our Messengers come to them with clear directives; yet many of them continued to commit excesses on earth.

مِنْ أَجْلِ ذَٰلِكَ كَتَبْنَا عَلَىٰ بَنِيٓ
إِسْرَٰٓءِيلَ أَنَّهُۥ مَن قَتَلَ نَفْسًۢا بِغَيْرِ
نَفْسٍ أَوْ فَسَادٍ فِي ٱلْأَرْضِ
فَكَأَنَّمَا قَتَلَ ٱلنَّاسَ جَمِيعًا
وَمَنْ أَحْيَاهَا فَكَأَنَّمَآ أَحْيَا
ٱلنَّاسَ جَمِيعًاۚ وَلَقَدْ جَآءَتْهُمْ
رُسُلُنَا بِٱلْبَيِّنَٰتِ ثُمَّ إِنَّ كَثِيرًا
مِّنْهُم بَعْدَ ذَٰلِكَ فِي ٱلْأَرْضِ
لَمُسْرِفُونَ ﴿٣٢﴾

---

52. The purpose of mentioning this particular incident is to reproach the Jews subtly for the plot they had hatched to assassinate the Prophet (peace be on him) and some of his illustrious Companions (see n. 30 above). The resemblance between the two incidents is evident.

God honoured some of the illiterate people of Arabia and disregarded the ancient People of the Book because the former were pious while the latter were not. But rather than reflect upon the causes of their rejection by God, and do something to overcome the failings which had led to that rejection, the Israelites were seized by the same fit of arrogant ignorance and folly which had once seized the criminal son of Adam, and resolved to kill those whose good deeds had been accepted by God. It was obvious that such acts would contribute nothing towards their acceptance by God. They would rather earn them an even greater degree of God's disapproval.

53. Since the same qualities which had been displayed by the wrong-doing son of Adam were manifest in the Children of Israel, God strongly urged them not to kill human beings and couched His command in forceful terms. It is a pity that the precious words which embody God's ordinance are to be found nowhere in the Bible today. The Talmud, however, does mention this subject in the following words:

> To him who kills a single individual of Israel, it shall be reckoned as if he had slain the whole race and he who preserves a single individual of Israel, it shall be reckoned in the Book of God as if he had preserved the whole world.

The Talmud also mentions that in trials for murder, the Israelite judges used to address the witnesses as follows:

(33) Those who wage war against Allah and His Messenger, and go about the earth spreading mischief[55] – indeed their recompense is that they either be done to death, or be crucified, or have their hands and feet cut off from the opposite sides or be banished from the land.[56] Such shall be their degradation in this world; and a mighty chastisement lies in store for them in the World to Come (34) except for those who repent before you have overpowered them. Know well that Allah is All-Forgiving, All-Compassionate.[57]

إِنَّمَا جَزَٰٓؤُا۟ ٱلَّذِينَ يُحَارِبُونَ ٱللَّهَ
وَرَسُولَهُۥ وَيَسْعَوْنَ فِى ٱلْأَرْضِ فَسَادًا
أَن يُقَتَّلُوٓا۟ أَوْ يُصَلَّبُوٓا۟ أَوْ تُقَطَّعَ
أَيْدِيهِمْ وَأَرْجُلُهُم مِّنْ خِلَـٰفٍ
أَوْ يُنفَوْا۟ مِنَ ٱلْأَرْضِ ۚ ذَٰلِكَ
لَهُمْ خِزْىٌ فِى ٱلدُّنْيَا ۖ وَلَهُمْ فِى
ٱلْـَٔاخِرَةِ عَذَابٌ عَظِيمٌ ﴿٣٣﴾ إِلَّا
ٱلَّذِينَ تَابُوا۟ مِن قَبْلِ أَن تَقْدِرُوا۟
عَلَيْهِمْ ۖ فَٱعْلَمُوٓا۟ أَنَّ ٱللَّهَ غَفُورٌ
رَّحِيمٌ ﴿٣٤﴾

Whoever kills one person, merits punishment as if he had slain all the men in the world.

54. This means that the survival of human life depends on everyone respecting other human beings and in contributing actively to the survival and protection of others. Whosoever kills unrighteously is thus not merely guilty of doing wrong to one single person, but proves by his act that his heart is devoid of respect for human life and of sympathy for the human species as such. Such a person, therefore, is an enemy of all mankind. This is so because he happens to be possessed of a quality which, were it to become common to all men, would lead to the destruction of the entire human race. The person who helps to preserve the life of even one person, on the other hand, is the protector of the whole of humanity, for he possesses a quality which is indispensable to the survival of mankind.

55. The 'land' signifies either the country or territory wherein the responsibility of establishing law and order has been undertaken by an Islamic state. The expression 'to wage war against Allah and His Messenger' denotes war against the righteous order established by the Islamic state.

It is God's purpose, and it is for this very purpose that God sent His Messengers, that a righteous order of life be established on earth; an order that would provide peace and security to everything found on earth; an order under whose benign shadow humanity would be able to attain its perfection; an order under which the resources of the earth would be exploited in a manner conducive to man's progress and prosperity rather than to his ruin and destruction. If anyone tried to disrupt such an order, whether on a limited scale by committing murder and destruction and robbery and brigandry or on a large scale by attempting to overthrow that order and establish some unrighteous order instead, he would in fact be guilty of waging war against God and His Messenger. All this is not unlike the situation where someone tries to overthrow the established government in a country. Such a person will be convicted of 'waging war against the state' even though his actual action may have been directed against an ordinary policeman in some remote part of the country, and irrespective of how remote the sovereign himself is from him.

56. These penalties are mentioned here in brief merely to serve as guidelines to either judges or rulers so they may punish each criminal in accordance with the nature of his crime. The real purpose is to indicate that for any of those who live in the Islamic realm to attempt to overthrow the Islamic order is the worst kind of crime, for which any of the highly severe punishments may be imposed.

57. If they give up subversion and abandon their endeavour to disrupt or overthrow the righteous order, and their subsequent conduct shows that they have indeed become peace-loving, law-abiding citizens of good character, they need not be subjected to the punishments mentioned here even if any of their former crimes against the state should come to light. If their crime involves violation of the rights of other men they may not be absolved from their guilt. If, for instance, they have either killed a person, seized someone's property or committed any other crime against human life or property they will be tried according to the criminal law of Islam. They will not, however, be accused of either rebellion and high treason or of waging war against God and His Messenger.

(35) Believers! Fear Allah and seek the means to come near to Him,[58] and strive hard in His way;[59] maybe you will attain true success. (36) For those who disbelieved – even if they had all that is in the earth, and the like of it with it, and offered it all as ransom from chastisement on the Day of Resurrection, it will not be accepted of them – a painful chastisement lies in store for them. (37) They will wish to come out of the Fire, but they will not. Theirs will be a long-lasting chastisement.

يَٰٓأَيُّهَا ٱلَّذِينَ ءَامَنُوا۟ ٱتَّقُوا۟ ٱللَّهَ
وَٱبْتَغُوٓا۟ إِلَيْهِ ٱلْوَسِيلَةَ وَجَٰهِدُوا۟
فِى سَبِيلِهِۦ لَعَلَّكُمْ تُفْلِحُونَ
﴿٣٥﴾ إِنَّ ٱلَّذِينَ كَفَرُوا۟ لَوْ أَنَّ لَهُم
مَّا فِى ٱلْأَرْضِ جَمِيعًا وَمِثْلَهُۥ مَعَهُۥ
لِيَفْتَدُوا۟ بِهِۦ مِنْ عَذَابِ يَوْمِ ٱلْقِيَٰمَةِ
مَا تُقُبِّلَ مِنْهُمْ ۖ وَلَهُمْ عَذَابٌ أَلِيمٌ ﴿٣٦﴾
يُرِيدُونَ أَن يَخْرُجُوا۟ مِنَ ٱلنَّارِ وَمَا هُم
بِخَٰرِجِينَ مِنْهَا ۖ وَلَهُمْ عَذَابٌ مُّقِيمٌ ﴿٣٧﴾

---

58. People are urged to solicit all means which might bring them close to God and enable them to please Him.

59. The English imperative 'strive hard' does not do full justice to the actual word used in the Qur'ān: *jāhidū*. The verbal form *mujāhadah* signifies and carries the nuance of doing something in defiance of, or in opposition to someone. The true sense of the Qur'ānic injunction 'strive hard' in the way of Allah is that the Muslims ought to use all their strength and engage in vigorous struggle against those forces which either forcefully prevent them from living in obedience to God or force them to live in obedience to others than God. It is this struggle which is likely to lead man to his true success and bring him to a close relationship with God.

This verse directs the believer to engage in a ceaseless, multifrontal struggle. On one side is the accursed Satan with his horde. Then comes the animal spirit of man, with its defiant and refractory desires. Then there are many men who have turned away from God, but with whom one is linked by social, cultural and economic ties. Then there are false religious, cultural and social systems which rest on rebellion against God and which force man to worship falsehood rather than Truth. These rebellious forces use different means to achieve their end, but those ends are always the same – to make men serve them rather than God. But man's true progress and his attainment of close communion with God depends entirely on his total obedience to God, on his serving God unreservedly in the inner as well as in the external aspects of his life. He cannot achieve this objective

(38) As for the thief – male or female – cut off the hands of both.[60] This is a recompense for what they have done, and an exemplary punishment from Allah. Allah is All-Mighty, All-Wise. ►	وَٱلسَّارِقُ وَٱلسَّارِقَةُ فَٱقْطَعُوٓا۟ أَيْدِيَهُمَا جَزَآءًۢ بِمَا كَسَبَا نَكَـٰلًا مِّنَ ٱللَّهِ ۗ وَٱللَّهُ عَزِيزٌ حَكِيمٌ ﴿٣٨﴾

without engaging in simultaneous combat with all the forces which are defiant and rebellious towards God, carrying on an unceasing struggle against them and trampling down all obstructions to his advancement along God's path.

60. The injunction is to cut off one not both hands. There is consensus among jurists that in the event of the first theft the right hand should be cut off.

This punishment has been laid down for theft alone. The Prophet (peace be on him) declared: 'There is no cutting off of a hand for he who embezzles.' (Abū Dā'ūd, 'Ḥudūd', 14; Tirmidhī, 'Ḥudūd', 18; Ibn Mājah, 'Ḥudūd', 36; Nasā'ī, 'Qaṭ' al-Sāriq', 13 – Ed.) This shows that the punishment prescribed for theft does not cover acts involving embezzlement and other dishonest practices. It is applicable only to acts involving the seizure, by stealth, of someone else's property.

The Prophet (peace be on him) also instructed that the punishment of cutting off a hand should not be applied in cases where the value of the article stolen is less than that of a shield. In the time of the Prophet (peace be on him) according to a tradition from Ibn 'Abbās, this was ten dirhams; according to a tradition from Ibn 'Umar, it was three dirhams; according to a tradition from Anas b. Mālik, it was five dirhams; and according to another tradition from 'Ā'ishah, it was a quarter of a dinar. Owing to this discrepancy, there is disagreement among jurists regarding the minimum value of the goods stolen which merits the punishment of cutting off a hand. This value, according to Abū Ḥanīfah, is ten dirhams whereas according to Mālik, Shāfi'ī and Aḥmad b. Ḥanbal, it is one quarter of a dinar (three dirhams). (For traditions on objects and amounts of things on which the hand of the thief is to be cut off, see Bukhārī, 'Ḥudūd', 13; Muslim, 'Ḥudūd', 1–7; Abū Dā'ūd, 'Ḥudūd', 12, 13; Tirmidhī, 'Ḥudūd', 16; Nasā'ī, 'Qaṭ' al-Sāriq', 5, 8–10 – Ed.)

Moreover, there are several things the theft of which would not necessitate cutting off a hand. The Prophet (peace be on him) directed, for instance, that no hand should be cut off if the stolen article was food. According to a tradition from 'Ā'ishah: '(The hand of) the thief was not cut off during the time of the Messenger of Allah for the theft of trivial

(39) But he who repents after he has committed wrong, and makes amends, Allah will graciously turn to him.[61] Truly Allah is All-Forgiving, All-Compassionate. (40) Do you not know that to Allah belongs the dominion of the heavens and the earth? He chastises whom He wills and forgives whom He wills. Allah is All-Powerful.

فَمَن تَابَ مِنۢ بَعْدِ ظُلْمِهِۦ وَأَصْلَحَ
فَإِنَّ ٱللَّهَ يَتُوبُ عَلَيْهِ ۗ إِنَّ ٱللَّهَ غَفُورٌ
رَّحِيمٌ ﴿٣٩﴾ أَلَمْ تَعْلَمْ أَنَّ ٱللَّهَ لَهُۥ مُلْكُ
ٱلسَّمَٰوَٰتِ وَٱلْأَرْضِ يُعَذِّبُ مَن
يَشَآءُ وَيَغْفِرُ لِمَن يَشَآءُ ۗ وَٱللَّهُ عَلَىٰ
كُلِّ شَىْءٍ قَدِيرٌ ﴿٤٠﴾

---

things.' (Aḥmad b. Ḥanbal, *Musnad*, vol. 3, p. 464; Dārimī, 'Ḥudūd', 4, 7 – Ed.) Furthermore, 'Alī and 'Uthmān gave the judgement – and none of the Companions disagreed with it – that a person's hand should not be cut off for stealing birds. 'Umar and 'Alī did not cut off the hands of those who had stolen from the public treasury, and on this question no disagreement on the part of any Companion has been reported. On these grounds the founders of the schools of Islamic Law exempted certain things from the application of this penal injunction.

According to Abū Ḥanīfah a man's hand should not be cut off for stealing vegetables, fruit, meat, cooked food, grain which is not stored in a barn, and instruments of music and play. Likewise, he is of the opinion that a hand should not be cut off for either stealing animals grazing in the forest or for stealing from the public treasury. The founders of the other schools of Islamic Law have also exempted the stealing of certain things from the punishment of cutting off a hand. But this exemption does not mean that the guilty parties should receive no punishment at all. (See the commentaries of Ibn Kathīr, Ibn al-'Arabī, Qurṭubī and Jaṣṣāṣ on this verse. See also Ibn Rushd, *Bidāyat al-Mujtahid*, vol. 2, pp. 441 ff. – Ed.)

61. Forgiveness on the part of Allah does not mean that the hand of the thief should not be cut off. It means rather that one who repents and becomes righteous by purging his soul of the sin of stealing will be spared the wrath of God, Who will remove the stain of that sin from him. But if after his hand has been cut off the person concerned does not purge himself of evil intent and continues to nurture the same impure feelings which led to his stealing and thus to the cutting off of his hand, it is evident that even though his hand has been severed from his body, stealing remains ingrained in his soul. The result will be that he will continue to merit God's wrath as he did before his hand was cut off. The Qur'ān therefore directs the thief to seek pardon from God and to try to reform himself. For the hand of

(41) O Messenger! Do not be grieved on account of those who vie with one another in disbelieving:[62] even though they be those who say with their mouths: 'We believe' even though their hearts have no faith; or they be Jews who have their ears eagerly turned to falsehood[63] and spy for other people who did not chance to come to you,[64] who pervert the words of Allah, taking them out of their proper context in order to distort their meaning.[65] ▶

۞ يَٰٓأَيُّهَا ٱلرَّسُولُ لَا يَحْزُنكَ
ٱلَّذِينَ يُسَٰرِعُونَ فِى ٱلْكُفْرِ مِنَ
ٱلَّذِينَ قَالُوٓا۟ ءَامَنَّا بِأَفْوَٰهِهِمْ وَلَمْ
تُؤْمِن قُلُوبُهُمْ ۛ وَمِنَ ٱلَّذِينَ هَادُوا۟ ۛ
سَمَّٰعُونَ لِلْكَذِبِ
سَمَّٰعُونَ لِقَوْمٍ ءَاخَرِينَ لَمْ يَأْتُوكَ ۖ
يُحَرِّفُونَ ٱلْكَلِمَ مِنۢ بَعْدِ مَوَاضِعِهِۦ ۖ

that thief was cut off for the sake of the judicious administration of human society and the cutting off of a hand did not automatically purify the soul of the person on whom the punishment was carried out. Purity of soul can be achieved only by repentance and turning oneself to God. Traditions mention that after the hand of a thief had been cut off in compliance with the Prophet's order, he was summoned by the Prophet (peace be on him) himself who said to him: 'Say: "I seek pardon from God, and to Him do I turn in repentance."' The thief uttered these words as directed by the Prophet (peace be on him) who then prayed for the thief, saying: 'O God, accept his repentance.' (Abū Dā'ūd, 'Ḥudūd', 8 – Ed.)

62. This verse refers to those who devoted all their capacities and efforts to ensure that the *status quo ante* of *Jāhilīyah* remained intact, and that the reformative mission of Islam should fail to set right the corruption that had come down to them from the past. Disregarding all moral scruples, these people used the vilest methods against the Prophet (peace be on him). They deliberately suppressed the truth and resorted to lying, deceit, treachery and low cunning in order to frustrate the mission of the Prophet (peace be on him) who was engaged in a tireless struggle actuated by absolute selflessness and benevolence, and who sought the welfare of all human beings, including that of his opponents. All this naturally hurt the Prophet (peace be on him). A sincere person must feel heartbroken when he sees men of low moral character, driven by ignorance, blind selfishness and bigotry, resort to vile methods in opposition to his mission, which is actuated by charity and goodwill towards all men. Hence the purpose of God's directive here is not to ask the Prophet (peace be on him) to abstain

They say to people: 'If such and such teaching is given to you, accept it; if you are not given that, then beware!'[66] You can be of no avail to him whom Allah wills to fall into error.[67] Those are the ones whose hearts Allah does not want to purify.[68] For them there is degradation in this world and a mighty chastisement in the Next.

يَقُولُونَ إِنْ أُوتِيتُمْ هَٰذَا فَخُذُوهُ
وَإِن لَّمْ تُؤْتَوْهُ فَاحْذَرُوا ۚ وَمَن يُرِدِ اللَّهُ
فِتْنَتَهُ فَلَن تَمْلِكَ لَهُ مِنَ اللَّهِ
شَيْئًا ۚ أُولَٰئِكَ الَّذِينَ لَمْ يُرِدِ اللَّهُ
أَن يُطَهِّرَ قُلُوبَهُمْ ۚ لَهُمْ فِي الدُّنْيَا
خِزْيٌ ۖ وَلَهُمْ فِي الْآخِرَةِ عَذَابٌ
عَظِيمٌ ﴿٤١﴾

---

from this natural feeling of grief but rather that he should not allow such feelings to undermine his morale and that he should persevere in his task. As for the opponents of the Prophet (peace be on him), in view of their low morals, their mean conduct was not at all contrary to expectations.

63. This has two meanings. First, that since such people are slaves to their desires they cannot have the least interest in the Truth, falsehood alone gratifies them. It is with falsehood alone that they like to fill their ears, for nothing else quenches the thirst of their souls. Second, it is the same love of falsehood which motivates them when they come and spend some time in the company of the Prophet (peace be on him) and the Muslims. They want to distort whatever they see or hear, to taint the facts with their fabrications, and then circulate them among those who have had no contact with the Prophet (peace be on him) and the Muslims in order to scandalize them.

64. This also has two meanings. First, that they socialized with the Prophet (peace be on him) and the Muslims in order to pry into their affairs and communicate them to the enemy. Second, that they went about collecting information to try to slander them. Their objective was to create misgivings about the Prophet (peace be on him) and the Muslims among those who were unacquainted with them.

65. They deliberately tamper with those injunctions of the Torah that do not accord with their desires, and by altering the meanings of the words occurring in the text they deduce laws that suit their interests.

66. This refers to the Jews who went about telling the ignorant masses that they should follow the teachings of the Prophet (peace be on him) only if they conformed to the teachings of the Jews.

(42) They are listeners of falsehood and greedy devourers of unlawful earnings.[69] If they come to you you may either judge between them or turn away from them. And were you to turn away from them they shall not be able to harm you; and were you to judge between them judge with justice. Surely Allah loves the just.[70] (43) Yet how will they appoint you a judge when they have the Torah with them, wherein there is Allah's judgement – and still they turn away from it?[71] The fact is, they are not believers.

سَمَّٰعُونَ لِلۡكَذِبِ أَكَّٰلُونَ
لِلسُّحۡتِۚ فَإِن جَآءُوكَ فَٱحۡكُم بَيۡنَهُمۡ
أَوۡ أَعۡرِضۡ عَنۡهُمۡۖ وَإِن تُعۡرِضۡ عَنۡهُمۡ
فَلَن يَضُرُّوكَ شَيۡـٔٗاۖ وَإِنۡ حَكَمۡتَ
فَٱحۡكُم بَيۡنَهُم بِٱلۡقِسۡطِۚ إِنَّ ٱللَّهَ
يُحِبُّ ٱلۡمُقۡسِطِينَ ﴿٤٢﴾ وَكَيۡفَ
يُحَكِّمُونَكَ وَعِندَهُمُ ٱلتَّوۡرَىٰةُ فِيهَا حُكۡمُ
ٱللَّهِ ثُمَّ يَتَوَلَّوۡنَ مِنۢ بَعۡدِ ذَٰلِكَۚ
وَمَآ أُوْلَٰٓئِكَ بِٱلۡمُؤۡمِنِينَ ﴿٤٣﴾

---

67. God's will to put someone to the test means that God confronts one in whom He sees the growth of evil with the opportunities of doing just that, so that he experiences the struggle between good and evil. If the person is not yet fully inclined towards evil, his moral health improves and his latent potentialities for resisting evil are revived. But if he has become excessively inclined towards evil, and goodness has been totally crushed from within his being, then every such test is bound to entangle him still more tightly in evil. The well-wisher is now powerless to rescue him.

It might be added that not only individuals but also nations are put to this kind of test.

68. God did not will that their hearts be purified for they themselves did not want them to be purified. It is not God's way to deprive of purity those who love it and strive for it; but God does not wish to purify those who do not seek their own purification.

69. Here pointed reference is made to judges and jurisconsults who accept false evidence and invent reports in order to issue verdicts contrary to justice and in favour of either those who bribe them or with whom their illegitimate interests lie.

70. Until then the Jews had not become full-fledged subjects of the Islamic state. Their relations with that state were based on agreements

according to which the Jews were to enjoy internal autonomy, and their disputes were to be decided by their own judges and in accordance with their own laws. They were not legally bound to place their disputes either before the Prophet (peace be on him) for adjudication or before the judges appointed by him. But in cases where it appeared against their interests to have their disputes judged according to their own religious law they approached the Prophet (peace be on him) in the hope that the Prophet might have a different ruling.

The particular case referred to here was that of a woman belonging to a respectable family, who was found to be involved in an unlawful sexual relationship with a man. The punishment for this in the Torah was that both be stoned to death (see Deuteronomy 22: 23–4). But the Jews did not want to enforce this punishment. Hence they deliberated among themselves and decided to put the case before the Prophet (peace be on him), with the reservation that his judgement be accepted only if it was other than stoning. The Prophet (peace be on him) decided that the punishment should, in fact, be stoning. When the Jews declined to accept the judgement, the Prophet (peace be on him) asked their rabbis what punishment had been prescribed for such a case in their religion. They replied that it was to strike the culprit with lashes, to blacken the face and to make the person concerned ride on a donkey. The Prophet (peace be on him) asked them under oath if the Torah had indeed prescribed that as punishment for adultery committed by married men and women. They repeated the same false reply. However, one of them called Ibn Ṣawriyā who, according to the Jews themselves, was the greatest living scholar of the Torah at that time, kept silent. The Prophet (peace be on him) asked him to state on oath in the name of God, Who had emancipated them from Pharaoh and had given them the Law, whether the punishment for adultery provided for in the Torah was what they had mentioned. He replied: 'Had you not put me under such a heavy oath, I would not have volunteered the correct information. The fact is that the prescribed punishment for adultery is indeed stoning, but when adultery became common among us our rulers adopted the rule that when respectable people committed adultery they were left unpunished, whereas when ordinary people were convicted they were punished by stoning. Later on when this caused resentment among the common people we altered the law of the Torah and adopted the rule that adulterers and adulteresses would be lashed, their faces would be blackened, and they would be made to ride on donkeys, seated in a backward-looking position.' This left the Jews with nothing to say and the adulterer and adulteress were, in accordance with the order of the Prophet (peace be on him), stoned to death. (Ibn Kathīr, *Tafsīr*, vol. 3, pp. 574–5 – Ed.)

71. In this verse, God unmasks completely the dishonesty of these people. It shows how these so-called religious people who had cast the spell of their religious piety and knowledge of the Scriptures over the whole

(44) Surely We revealed the Torah, wherein there is guidance and light. Thereby did Prophets – who had submitted themselves (to Allah) – judge for the Judaized folk;[72] and so did the scholars and jurists.[73] They judged by the Book of Allah for they had been entrusted to keep it, and bear witness to it. So (O Jews!) do not fear men but fear Me, and do not barter away My signs for a trivial gain. Those who do not judge by what Allah has revealed are indeed the unbelievers.

إِنَّآ أَنزَلْنَا ٱلتَّوْرَىٰةَ فِيهَا هُدًى وَنُورٌ
يَحْكُمُ بِهَا ٱلنَّبِيُّونَ ٱلَّذِينَ أَسْلَمُوا۟
لِلَّذِينَ هَادُوا۟ وَٱلرَّبَّـٰنِيُّونَ وَٱلْأَحْبَارُ
بِمَا ٱسْتُحْفِظُوا۟ مِن كِتَـٰبِ ٱللَّهِ
وَكَانُوا۟ عَلَيْهِ شُهَدَآءَ فَلَا
تَخْشَوُا۟ ٱلنَّاسَ وَٱخْشَوْنِ
وَلَا تَشْتَرُوا۟ بِـَٔايَـٰتِى ثَمَنًا قَلِيلًا وَمَن لَّمْ
يَحْكُم بِمَآ أَنزَلَ ٱللَّهُ فَأُو۟لَـٰٓئِكَ هُمُ
ٱلْكَـٰفِرُونَ ﴿٤٤﴾

---

of Arabia had set aside a categorical injunction of the book which they themselves recognized to be the Book of God, and which they professed to believe in. They had referred that judicial case to the Prophet (peace be on him) for his decision even though they vehemently denied his prophethood. This made it quite clear that there was nothing to which they subscribed sincerely. Their true religion consisted merely of worshipping their interests and desires. They were ready to turn their backs upon the very book which they recognized as the Book of God merely because some of its injunctions were unpalatable to them, and in such cases they did not mind approaching one whom they regarded as an imposter (may God be our refuge from such a blasphemy) in the hope that they might be able to obtain a judgement to their liking.

72. Here the verse tells the Jews that all the Prophets were *muslims* (submitters to God) whereas the Jews had deviated from *islām* (submission to God), and true to their chauvinistic sectarianism, were content with remaining merely 'Jews'.

73. *Rabbānī* = religious scholars, theologians.
Aḥbār = religious jurists.

(45) And therein We had ordained for them: 'A life for a life, and an eye for an eye, and a nose for a nose, and an ear for an ear, and a tooth for a tooth, and for all wounds, like for like.'[74] But whosoever forgoes it by way of charity, it will be for him an expiation.[75] Those who do not judge by what Allah has revealed are indeed the wrong-doers.

(46) And We sent Jesus, the son of Mary, after those Prophets, confirming the truth of whatever there still remained of the Torah. And We gave him the Gospel, wherein is guidance and light, and which confirms the truth of whatever there still remained of the Torah,[76] and a guidance and admonition for the God-fearing. ▶

وَكَتَبْنَا عَلَيْهِمْ فِيهَآ أَنَّ ٱلنَّفْسَ بِٱلنَّفْسِ
وَٱلْعَيْنَ بِٱلْعَيْنِ وَٱلْأَنفَ بِٱلْأَنفِ
وَٱلْأُذُنَ بِٱلْأُذُنِ وَٱلسِّنَّ بِٱلسِّنِّ
وَٱلْجُرُوحَ قِصَاصٌ فَمَن
تَصَدَّقَ بِهِۦ فَهُوَ كَفَّارَةٌ لَّهُۥ
وَمَن لَّمْ يَحْكُم بِمَآ أَنزَلَ ٱللَّهُ
فَأُو۟لَٰٓئِكَ هُمُ ٱلظَّٰلِمُونَ ﴿٤٥﴾
وَقَفَّيْنَا عَلَىٰٓ ءَاثَٰرِهِم بِعِيسَى ٱبْنِ مَرْيَمَ
مُصَدِّقًا لِّمَا بَيْنَ يَدَيْهِ مِنَ ٱلتَّوْرَىٰةِ
وَءَاتَيْنَٰهُ ٱلْإِنجِيلَ فِيهِ هُدًى وَنُورٌ
وَمُصَدِّقًا لِّمَا بَيْنَ يَدَيْهِ مِنَ ٱلتَّوْرَىٰةِ
وَهُدًى وَمَوْعِظَةً لِّلْمُتَّقِينَ ﴿٤٦﴾

74. Cf. Exodus 21: 23–5.

75. Whoever forgoes his right of retaliation does a good deed which will atone for many of his sins. The same is confirmed by a tradition of the Prophet (peace be on him) in which he said: 'Whoever receives an injury on his body, then pardons (the inflictor of the injury), his sins are atoned for to the measure of his pardoning.' (Aḥmad b. Ḥanbal, *Musnad*, vol. 5, pp. 316, 329 – Ed.)

76. The Messiah did not expound a new religion. That very religion which had been the religion of all the Prophets was also his religion, and it is towards that religion that he called people. He believed in the true teachings of the Torah which were extant in his time, and the Gospels (*Injīl*) confirm this (see, for example, Matthew 5: 17–18). The Qur'ān repeatedly stresses the fundamental fact that none of the Prophets of God,

(47) Let the followers of the Gospel judge by what Allah has revealed therein, and those who do not judge by what Allah has revealed are the transgressors.[77]	وَلْيَحْكُمْ أَهْلُ ٱلْإِنجِيلِ بِمَآ أَنزَلَ ٱللَّهُ فِيهِ ۚ وَمَن لَّمْ يَحْكُم بِمَآ أَنزَلَ ٱللَّهُ فَأُو۟لَٰٓئِكَ هُمُ ٱلْفَٰسِقُونَ ﴿٤٧﴾

no matter in which part of the world they appeared, denied the Prophets who had preceded them. On the contrary, each Prophet confirmed the message of his predecessors and sought to promote the mission which was the sacred legacy of them all. God did not reveal any of the Books in order to repudiate the previous ones; each confirmed and supported the preceding ones.

77. Here three judgements are issued against those who do not judge in accordance with the Law revealed by God. The first is that they are *kāfir* (unbelievers); the second, that they are *ẓālim* (wrong-doers); and the third, that they are *fāsiq* (transgressors). This clearly means that one who, in disregard of God's commandments and of the Laws revealed by Him, pronounces judgements according to man-made laws (whether made by himself or by others) is guilty of three major offences. First, his act amounts to rejecting the commandment of God, and this rejection is equivalent to *kufr* (infidelity, unbelief). Second, his act is contrary to justice, for only the laws made by God are in complete accord with the dictates of justice. Any judgement in contravention of God's injunctions amounts, therefore, to committing injustice (*ẓulm*). Third, when he enforces either his own or anyone else's law in disregard of the Laws of his Lord he steps out of the fold of subjection and obedience, and this constitutes *fisq* (transgression).

Kufr, ẓulm and *fisq* are essential elements in deviation from God's commandments. One finds them wherever there is deviation from the commandment of God. There is variation in the degree of deviation and hence in the degree of these three offences. Whoever passes judgement on something in opposition to an injunction of God, believing that injunction to be false, and holds either his own or anyone else's judgement to be sound, is an unbeliever (*kāfir*), wrong-doer (*ẓālim*) and transgressor (*fāsiq*). A man who is convinced that the injunctions of God are right but makes judgements contrary to them in practice is not an unbeliever in the sense that he ceases to remain a member of the Islamic community, but he is guilty of adulterating his faith by blending it with *kufr, ẓulm* and *fisq*. In the same manner, those who deviate from the injunctions of God in all matters are unbelievers, wrong-doers and transgressors. For those who are obedient in some respects and disobedient in others, the blending of faith and submission to God with the opposite attributes of unbelief, wrong-doing and transgression in their lives will be exactly in proportion to the mixture of their obedience to and their deviation from God's commands.

(48) Then We revealed the Book to you (O Muḥammad!) with Truth, confirming whatever of the Book was revealed before,[78] and protecting and guarding over it.[79] Judge, then, in the affairs of men in accordance with the Law that Allah has revealed, and do not follow their desires in disregard of the Truth which has come to you. For each of you We have appointed a Law and a way of life.[80] And had Allah so willed, He would surely have made you one single community; instead, (He gave each of you a Law and a way of life) in order to test you by what He gave you.

وَأَنزَلْنَآ إِلَيْكَ ٱلْكِتَٰبَ بِٱلْحَقِّ مُصَدِّقًا
لِّمَا بَيْنَ يَدَيْهِ مِنَ ٱلْكِتَٰبِ
وَمُهَيْمِنًا عَلَيْهِ فَٱحْكُم بَيْنَهُم بِمَآ
أَنزَلَ ٱللَّهُ وَلَا تَتَّبِعْ أَهْوَآءَهُمْ عَمَّا
جَآءَكَ مِنَ ٱلْحَقِّ لِكُلٍّ جَعَلْنَا مِنكُمْ
شِرْعَةً وَمِنْهَاجًا وَلَوْ شَآءَ ٱللَّهُ
لَجَعَلَكُمْ أُمَّةً وَٰحِدَةً وَلَٰكِن
لِّيَبْلُوَكُمْ فِى مَآ ءَاتَىٰكُمْ

Some commentators have attempted to restrict the application of these verses to the People of the Book alone. The verses, however, hardly lend themselves to such a restrictive interpretation. The best answer to such a restrictive interpretation has been given by the Companion Ḥudhayfah. When someone told him that these verses related merely to the Israelites, meaning that the unbelievers, wrong-doers and transgressors were only the Jews who passed judgement contrary to the injunctions revealed by God, Ḥudhayfah remarked: 'What good brothers these Israelites are to you! Whatever is bitter goes to them; whatever is sweet comes to you. Nay, by God, you will follow their way, your steps following theirs.'

78. This points to a fact of major significance. It could also have been said that the Qur'ān confirms all those parts of the earlier divine books which are still extant in their true and original form. But the sense has been conveyed by employing the word 'the Book' rather than 'the previous Books'. This expression reveals that the Qur'ān and all those Books sent down by God at various times and in different languages in reality constitute one and the same Book. Their Author is one and the same; their aim and purpose are the same; their teaching is the same; and the knowledge which they seek to impart to mankind is the same. The difference between these Books lies in their modes of expression, and this was necessarily so since

they were addressed to different audiences. It is, therefore, not merely that these divine books support rather than contradict each other but that they are actually different editions of one and the same book – 'the Book'.

79. In Arabic, *haymana, yuhayminu, hayamanah* signify 'to protect, to witness, to keep trust, to back and to support'. The expression *'haymana al-rajul al-shay'* means that the man protected and guarded the thing. Likewise, *'haymana al-ṭā'ir 'alá firākhih'* means that the bird took its young ones under the protection of its wings. Once 'Umar said to the people: *'Innī dā'in fa hayminū'* ('I am praying; support me by saying amen'). To say that the Qur'ān is *muhaymin* of *al-kitāb* means that it preserves all the true teachings of the earlier divine books; that it has secured them from loss. The Qur'ān also confirms those Books in that the contents of the Qur'ān testify to the truth of those parts which are indeed from God. The Qur'ān is, further, a witness over those Books in the sense that, with its help, the elements which embody true revelations from God can be distinguished from the accretions which have corrupted them. Whatever in these Books accords with the Qur'ān is from God, and whatever is not in conformity with it is from human beings.

80. This is a parenthetical phrase, the purpose of which is to elucidate a question which is likely to arise in the mind of the reader who has read the above section and might feel uneasy. The question is: Why do the religious laws propounded by the various Prophets differ in matters of detail even though the Prophets and their Books preach one and the same religion (*dīn*) and even confirm and support each other? Why is it that in regard to the prescribed forms of worship, the regulations concerning what is permitted and what is prohibited, and the detailed legal regulations governing the social and collective life, there is some disagreement among the various laws propounded by the different Prophets and the divine Books?

Vie, then, one with another in good works. Unto Allah is the return of all of you; and He will then make you understand the truth concerning the matters on which you disagreed.[81] ►	فَاسْتَبِقُوا الْخَيْرَٰتِ إِلَى اللَّهِ مَرْجِعُكُمْ جَمِيعًا فَيُنَبِّئُكُم بِمَا كُنتُمْ فِيهِ تَخْتَلِفُونَ ﴿٤٨﴾

81. This constitutes a detailed answer to the above question (see n. 80). It consists of the following points:

(1) It is a mistake to think that variations in religious laws result from a difference of source. It is God Himself Who altered the legal prescriptions to suit different nations at different times and in different circumstances.

(2) It was indeed possible, by divising one legal code for all human beings, for all men to have been made into one nation (*ummah*). But one of the many benevolent considerations keeping the religious laws of various Prophets different from one another was that God wanted this difference to become a means of testing people. Those who understand true religion, who have grasped its spirit and essence, and who are aware of the true importance of the different legal prescriptions, always recognize the Truth and accept it whatever its form. They have no hesitation in accepting the new ordinances of God in place of the old ones, in contrast to those who are not conversant with the spirit of true religion and who seem to identify it with a specific body of legal minutiae. Such people have overlaid God-given principles with their own legal deductions, and have subsequently fossilized this entire amalgam, seeking to preserve it in its entirety. They have grown so attached to it that, in order to preserve it, they spurn every directive which subsequently comes to them from God. In order to distinguish the people of the first category from those of the second God made the legal prescriptions of the various Prophets vary.

(3) The real purpose of all the divine religious laws is the attainment of goodness and righteousness. This purpose can be achieved only when a man obeys whatever commandment he receives from God at a particular time. The proper mode of conduct for people who keep their eyes fixed on this true purpose is to strive for God's good pleasure rather than quarrel about differences in the legal prescriptions of the various Prophets.

(4) The differences which have arisen because of the unjustified rigidity, prejudice, obduracy and erroneous attitudes of the human mind can be finally settled neither in the debating hall nor on the battlefield. The final judgement will be made by God Himself. Then the reality of everything will be fully uncovered, and it will be clear how much truth and falsehood underlay the squabbles which whole lives were wasted over.

(49) Therefore, judge between them (O Muḥammad!)[82] by what Allah has revealed and do not follow their desires, and beware lest they tempt you away from anything of what Allah has revealed to you. And if they turn away, then know well that Allah has indeed decided to afflict them for some of their sins. For surely many of them are transgressors. (50) (If they turn away from the Law of Allah) do they desire judgement according to the Law of Ignorance?[83] But for those who have certainty of belief whose judgement can be better than Allah's?

(51) Believers! Do not take the Jews and the Christians for your allies. They are the allies of each other. And among you he who takes them for allies, shall be regarded as one of them. Allah does not guide the wrong-doers.

وَأَنِ ٱحْكُم بَيْنَهُم بِمَآ أَنزَلَ ٱللَّهُ وَلَا تَتَّبِعْ
أَهْوَآءَهُمْ وَٱحْذَرْهُمْ أَن يَفْتِنُوكَ عَنۢ
بَعْضِ مَآ أَنزَلَ ٱللَّهُ إِلَيْكَ ۖ فَإِن تَوَلَّوْا۟ فَٱعْلَمْ
أَنَّمَا يُرِيدُ ٱللَّهُ أَن يُصِيبَهُم بِبَعْضِ ذُنُوبِهِمْ ۗ
وَإِنَّ كَثِيرًا مِّنَ ٱلنَّاسِ لَفَٰسِقُونَ ﴿٤٩﴾
أَفَحُكْمَ ٱلْجَٰهِلِيَّةِ يَبْغُونَ ۚ وَمَنْ أَحْسَنُ
مِنَ ٱللَّهِ حُكْمًا لِّقَوْمٍ يُوقِنُونَ ﴿٥٠﴾
۞ يَٰٓأَيُّهَا ٱلَّذِينَ ءَامَنُوا۟ لَا تَتَّخِذُوا۟ ٱلْيَهُودَ
وَٱلنَّصَٰرَىٰٓ أَوْلِيَآءَ ۘ بَعْضُهُمْ أَوْلِيَآءُ بَعْضٍ ۚ وَمَن
يَتَوَلَّهُم مِّنكُمْ فَإِنَّهُۥ مِنْهُمْ ۗ إِنَّ ٱللَّهَ لَا يَهْدِى
ٱلْقَوْمَ ٱلظَّٰلِمِينَ ﴿٥١﴾

82. Following this parenthetical clause, the previous subject is resumed.

83. The word *jāhilīyah* (literally 'ignorance') is used as an antonym to Islam. Islam is the way of *'ilm* (true knowledge), since it is God Himself Who has shown this way, and His knowledge embraces everything. In contrast is the way that diverges from Islam – the path of Ignorance (*jāhilīyah*). The pre-Islamic period in Arabia is designated as *jāhilīyah* because this was the era when human beings derived their norms from either superstitious beliefs, conjectures and imagination or from their desires. Whenever such an attitude is adopted, it is bound to be designated as Ignorance. The appellation *'jāhilīyah'* will apply to every aspect of life which is developed in disregard of the knowledge made available by God,

(52) Indeed you see those afflicted with the disease of hypocrisy race towards them, saying: 'We fear lest some misfortune overtakes us.'[84] And it may happen that Allah will either bring you a decisive victory or bring about something else from Himself[85] and then they will feel remorseful at their hypocrisy which they have kept concealed in their breasts – (53) while those who believe will exclaim: 'Are these the self-same people who solemnly swore by Allah that they were with you?' All their acts have gone to waste and now they are the losers.[86]

فَتَرَى ٱلَّذِينَ فِى قُلُوبِهِم مَّرَضٌ يُسَٰرِعُونَ
فِيهِمْ يَقُولُونَ نَخْشَىٰٓ أَن تُصِيبَنَا دَآئِرَةٌ ۚ
فَعَسَى ٱللَّهُ أَن يَأْتِىَ بِٱلْفَتْحِ أَوْ أَمْرٍ مِّنْ عِندِهِۦ
فَيُصْبِحُوا۟ عَلَىٰ مَآ أَسَرُّوا۟ فِىٓ أَنفُسِهِمْ
نَٰدِمِينَ ﴿٥٢﴾ وَيَقُولُ ٱلَّذِينَ ءَامَنُوٓا۟
أَهَٰٓؤُلَآءِ ٱلَّذِينَ أَقْسَمُوا۟ بِٱللَّهِ جَهْدَ أَيْمَٰنِهِمْ ۙ
إِنَّهُمْ لَمَعَكُمْ ۚ حَبِطَتْ أَعْمَٰلُهُمْ فَأَصْبَحُوا۟
خَٰسِرِينَ ﴿٥٣﴾

---

based only on man's partial knowledge blended with imagination, superstitious fancies, conjectures and desires.

84. The outcome of the conflict in Arabia between Islam and unbelief (*kufr*) had not crystallized. Although Islam had become a formidable force owing to the daring, courage and sacrifices of its followers, the forces opposed to it were also tremendously powerful. To an objective observer it must have seemed that either party had an equal chance of success, and so the hypocrites, apparently an integral part of the Muslim body politic, sought to maintain good relations with the Jews and the Christians as well. They expected refuge and protection from the Jews in case Islam was defeated. Moreover, the Jews and Christians held the greatest economic power in Arabia insofar as the banking system and the greenest and most fertile regions of Arabia were in their possession. For these reasons the hypocrites were keen to maintain good relations with them: they thought that to regard the conflict between Islam and unbelief as crucially important, and to sever their relations with all those currently in conflict with Islam, would be too great a risk both politically and economically.

85. They were looking for a conclusive victory, or at least something not far short of it, to inspire confidence that the conflict would end in favour of Islam.

(54) Believers! If any of you should ever turn away from your faith, remember that Allah will raise up a people whom He loves, and who love Him; a people humble towards the believers, and firm towards the unbelievers;[87] who will strive hard in the way of Allah and will not fear the reproach of the reproacher.[88] This is the favour of Allah which He grants to whom He wills. Allah is vast in resources, All-Knowing.

يَـٰٓأَيُّهَا ٱلَّذِينَ ءَامَنُوا۟ مَن يَرْتَدَّ مِنكُمْ عَن
دِينِهِۦ فَسَوْفَ يَأْتِى ٱللَّهُ بِقَوْمٍ يُحِبُّهُمْ وَيُحِبُّونَهُۥٓ
أَذِلَّةٍ عَلَى ٱلْمُؤْمِنِينَ أَعِزَّةٍ عَلَى ٱلْكَـٰفِرِينَ
يُجَـٰهِدُونَ فِى سَبِيلِ ٱللَّهِ وَلَا يَخَافُونَ لَوْمَةَ
لَآئِمٍ ۚ ذَٰلِكَ فَضْلُ ٱللَّهِ يُؤْتِيهِ مَن يَشَآءُ ۚ
وَٱللَّهُ وَٰسِعٌ عَلِيمٌ ٥٤

86. However much they might profess to follow Islam – by performing Prayers, by observing Fasts, by paying *Zakāh*, by taking part in wars in the cause of God – all was reduced to naught because they had not devoted themselves to the service of the One True God. In pursuit of their worldly ambitions they had split their souls into two, distributing half to God and half to those in rebellion against Him.

87. To be 'humble towards believers' signifies that a person should never use his strength against the believers. His native intelligence, shrewdness, ability, influence, wealth, physical prowess should not be used for the purpose of either suppressing, persecuting or causing harm to the Muslims. Among themselves, the Muslims should always find him gentle, merciful, sympathetic and mild tempered.

To be 'firm towards unbelievers', on the contrary, means that by virtue of the intensity of his faith, the sincerity of his conviction, his strict adherence to his principles, his strength of character and his insight and perspicacity born of faith, a man should be firm as a rock in his dealings with the opponents of Islam, so that they find it impossible to dislodge him. There should be no doubt in their minds that the believer would rather lay down his life than compromise his position by yielding to external pressures.

88. In following the religion of God, in implementing His injunctions, in judging things to be either right or wrong according to the criteria of the faith, the believer will be afraid of nothing. He will be impervious to opposition, reproach, denunciation, name-calling and scorn. Even when public opinion happens to be hostile, and his efforts to follow Islam single

(55) Only Allah, His Messenger, and those who believe and who establish Prayer, pay *Zakāh*, and bow (before Allah) are your allies. (56) All those who take Allah and His Messenger and those who believe as their allies, should remember that the party of Allah will be triumphant.

(57) Believers! Do not take for your allies those who make a mockery and sport of your faith, be they those given the Book before you or other unbelievers. Fear Allah if you indeed believe. (58) And when you call for Prayer, they take it for a mockery and sport.[89] That is because they are a people who do not understand.[90] (59) Say to them: 'People of the Book! Do you hate us for anything else except that we believe in Allah, and in the teaching which has been revealed to us and in the teaching which was revealed before? Indeed most of you are transgressors.' ▶

إِنَّمَا وَلِيُّكُمُ ٱللَّهُ وَرَسُولُهُۥ وَٱلَّذِينَ ءَامَنُوا۟ ٱلَّذِينَ
يُقِيمُونَ ٱلصَّلَوٰةَ وَيُؤْتُونَ ٱلزَّكَوٰةَ وَهُمْ
رَٰكِعُونَ ﴿٥٥﴾ وَمَن يَتَوَلَّ ٱللَّهَ وَرَسُولَهُۥ
وَٱلَّذِينَ ءَامَنُوا۟ فَإِنَّ حِزْبَ ٱللَّهِ هُمُ ٱلْغَٰلِبُونَ
﴿٥٦﴾ يَٰٓأَيُّهَا ٱلَّذِينَ ءَامَنُوا۟ لَا تَتَّخِذُوا۟ ٱلَّذِينَ
ٱتَّخَذُوا۟ دِينَكُمْ هُزُوًا وَلَعِبًا مِّنَ ٱلَّذِينَ أُوتُوا۟
ٱلْكِتَٰبَ مِن قَبْلِكُمْ وَٱلْكُفَّارَ أَوْلِيَآءَ ۚ وَٱتَّقُوا۟ ٱللَّهَ
إِن كُنتُم مُّؤْمِنِينَ ﴿٥٧﴾ وَإِذَا نَادَيْتُمْ إِلَى
ٱلصَّلَوٰةِ ٱتَّخَذُوهَا هُزُوًا وَلَعِبًا ۚ ذَٰلِكَ
بِأَنَّهُمْ قَوْمٌ لَّا يَعْقِلُونَ ﴿٥٨﴾ قُلْ يَٰٓأَهْلَ
ٱلْكِتَٰبِ هَلْ تَنقِمُونَ مِنَّآ إِلَّآ أَنْ ءَامَنَّا
بِٱللَّهِ وَمَآ أُنزِلَ إِلَيْنَا وَمَآ أُنزِلَ مِن قَبْلُ وَأَنَّ
أَكْثَرَكُمْ فَٰسِقُونَ ﴿٥٩﴾

---

him out for the scorn of the whole world, the man of faith will still follow the way which he recognizes in his heart to be true.

89. When they hear the call to Prayer the unbelievers make fun of it by mimicry, pervert its words to ridicule it, and utter disparaging and taunting remarks about it.

90. These are merely acts of stupidity on the part of unbelievers. Had they not been ignorant and foolish they would not have stooped to such base tactics, despite their significant differences with the Muslims on

(60) Then say to them: 'Shall I tell you about those whose retribution with Allah is even worse? They are the ones whom Allah has cursed, and who incurred His wrath and some of whom were changed into apes and swine, and who served the false deities. Such have an even worse rank and have strayed farther away from the right path.'[91]

(61) Whenever they come to you they say: 'We believe,' whereas, in fact, they come disbelieving, and go away disbelieving, and Allah knows all that they hide. (62) You will see many of them hastening towards sin and transgression and devouring unlawful earnings. Indeed what they do is evil. (63) Why is it that their scholars and jurists do not forbid them from sinful utterances and devouring unlawful earnings? Indeed they have been contriving evil.

قُلْ هَلْ أُنَبِّئُكُم بِشَرٍّ مِّن ذَٰلِكَ مَثُوبَةً عِندَ
ٱللَّهِ ۚ مَن لَّعَنَهُ ٱللَّهُ وَغَضِبَ عَلَيْهِ وَجَعَلَ
مِنْهُمُ ٱلْقِرَدَةَ وَٱلْخَنَازِيرَ وَعَبَدَ ٱلطَّٰغُوتَ ۚ
أُو۟لَٰٓئِكَ شَرٌّ مَّكَانًا وَأَضَلُّ عَن سَوَآءِ
ٱلسَّبِيلِ ﴿٦٠﴾ وَإِذَا جَآءُوكُمْ قَالُوٓا۟ ءَامَنَّا
وَقَد دَّخَلُوا۟ بِٱلْكُفْرِ وَهُمْ قَدْ خَرَجُوا۟ بِهِۦ ۚ
وَٱللَّهُ أَعْلَمُ بِمَا كَانُوا۟ يَكْتُمُونَ ﴿٦١﴾ وَتَرَىٰ
كَثِيرًا مِّنْهُمْ يُسَٰرِعُونَ فِى ٱلْإِثْمِ وَٱلْعُدْوَٰنِ
وَأَكْلِهِمُ ٱلسُّحْتَ ۚ لَبِئْسَ مَا كَانُوا۟
يَعْمَلُونَ ﴿٦٢﴾ لَوْلَا يَنْهَىٰهُمُ ٱلرَّبَّٰنِيُّونَ
وَٱلْأَحْبَارُ عَن قَوْلِهِمُ ٱلْإِثْمَ وَأَكْلِهِمُ
ٱلسُّحْتَ ۚ لَبِئْسَ مَا كَانُوا۟
يَصْنَعُونَ ﴿٦٣﴾

religious questions. After all, can any reasonable person be happy to see the people who call to the worship of God be ridiculed and mocked?

91. This alludes to the Jews whose history shows that they were subjected, over and over again, to the wrath and scourge of God. When they desecrated the law of the Sabbath the faces of many of them were distorted, and subsequently their degeneration reached such a low point that they took to worshipping Satan quite openly. The purpose of saying all this is to draw attention to their criminal boldness: while they had sunk to the lowest level of evil, transgression and moral decadence, they vigorously opposed all those who, thanks to their faith, lived a truly pious and righteous life.

(64) The Jews say: 'The Hand of Allah is fettered.'[92] It is their own hands which are fettered,[93] and they stand cursed for the evil they have uttered.[94] No! His Hands are outspread; He spends as He wills.

Surely the message that has been revealed to you from your Lord has increased many of them in their insurgence and unbelief,[95] and so We have cast enmity and spite among them until the Day of Resurrection. And as often as they kindle the fire of war, Allah extinguishes it; and they go about trying to spread mischief on earth, whereas Allah does not love those who spread mischief.

وَقَالَتِ ٱلْيَهُودُ يَدُ ٱللَّهِ مَغْلُولَةٌ غُلَّتْ أَيْدِيهِمْ
وَلُعِنُوا۟ بِمَا قَالُوا۟ بَلْ يَدَاهُ مَبْسُوطَتَانِ يُنفِقُ
كَيْفَ يَشَآءُ وَلَيَزِيدَنَّ كَثِيرًا مِّنْهُم
مَّآ أُنزِلَ إِلَيْكَ مِن رَّبِّكَ طُغْيَٰنًا وَكُفْرًا وَأَلْقَيْنَا
بَيْنَهُمُ ٱلْعَدَٰوَةَ وَٱلْبَغْضَآءَ إِلَىٰ يَوْمِ ٱلْقِيَٰمَةِ
كُلَّمَآ أَوْقَدُوا۟ نَارًا لِّلْحَرْبِ أَطْفَأَهَا ٱللَّهُ
وَيَسْعَوْنَ فِى ٱلْأَرْضِ فَسَادًا وَٱللَّهُ
لَا يُحِبُّ ٱلْمُفْسِدِينَ ﴿٦٤﴾

92. To say that someone's hands are tied, in Arabic usage, is to say that he is niggardly, that something prevents him from being generous and bountiful. Thus the Jewish observation does not mean that God's Hand is literally tied but that He is niggardly and miserly. For centuries the Jews had lived in humiliation and misery. Their past greatness had become legend, seemingly too remote ever to be restored, and so they would blasphemously lament that God had become a miser and that as the door to His treasury was now permanently locked, that He had nothing to offer them except suffering and calamity. This attitude, however, is not confined to the Jews. When confronted with trials and tribulations foolish people of other nations, too, are prone to utter such blasphemies rather than turn to God with humble prayer and supplication.

93. They accused God of the miserliness from which they themselves had suffered and had become notorious for.

94. If they entertained the hope that by such insolent and taunting expressions they might evoke God's munificence, and that His bounties would begin to shower upon them, they were dreaming of the impossible.

(65) Had the People of the Book only believed and been God-fearing, We should surely have effaced from them their evil deeds, and caused them to enter Gardens of Bliss. (66) Had the People of the Book observed the Torah and the Gospel, and all that had been revealed to them from their Lord, sustenance would have been showered over them from above and risen from beneath their feet.[96] Some among them certainly keep to the right path; but many of them do things which are evil.

وَلَوْ أَنَّ أَهْلَ ٱلْكِتَٰبِ ءَامَنُوا۟
وَٱتَّقَوْا۟ لَكَفَّرْنَا عَنْهُمْ سَيِّـَٔاتِهِمْ
وَلَأَدْخَلْنَٰهُمْ جَنَّٰتِ ٱلنَّعِيمِ ﴿٦٥﴾
وَلَوْ أَنَّهُمْ أَقَامُوا۟ ٱلتَّوْرَىٰةَ وَٱلْإِنجِيلَ وَمَآ
أُنزِلَ إِلَيْهِم مِّن رَّبِّهِمْ لَأَكَلُوا۟ مِن
فَوْقِهِمْ وَمِن تَحْتِ أَرْجُلِهِم ۚ مِّنْهُمْ أُمَّةٌ
مُّقْتَصِدَةٌ ۖ وَكَثِيرٌ مِّنْهُمْ سَآءَ
مَا يَعْمَلُونَ ﴿٦٦﴾

Indeed, such insolence was bound to have the opposite effect – to alienate them further from God's bounty, to cast them even further from His mercy.

95. Instead of learning any lessons from the Book of God, instead of recognizing their own mistakes and wrongs and then trying to make amends for them, instead of probing their miserable situation and then turning to reform, they reacted by launching a violent campaign of opposition to truth and righteousness. Rather than take to the right way as a result of being reminded of the forgotten lesson of righteousness, they attempted to suppress the voice which sought to remind them and others of such things.

96. In the Old Testament, Leviticus (chapter 26) and Deuteronomy (chapter 28) record a sermon of Moses in which he impresses upon Israel, in great detail, the bounties and blessings of God with which they would be endowed if they obeyed His commandments, and the afflictions, scourges and devastations that would descend upon them if they disobeyed Him and rejected the Book of God. That sermon of Moses is the best explanation of this verse of the Qur'ān.

(67) O Messenger! Deliver what has been revealed to you from your Lord, for if you fail to do that, you have not fulfilled the task of His messengership. Allah will certainly protect you from the evil of men. Surely Allah will not guide the unbelievers (to succeed against you). (68) Say to them: 'People of the Book! You have no solid ground to stand on unless you establish the Torah and the Gospel and all that had been revealed to you from your Lord.'[97] Indeed the message revealed to you from your Lord will aggravate insurgence and unbelief in many of them.[98] So do not grieve for those who disbelieve. (69) (Know well, none has an exclusive claim to the Truth.) For all those who believe in Allah and in the Last Day and do good deeds – be they either believers, Jews, Sabaeans or Christians – neither fear shall fall upon them, nor shall they have any reason to grieve.[99]

۞ يَٰٓأَيُّهَا ٱلرَّسُولُ بَلِّغْ مَآ أُنزِلَ إِلَيْكَ
مِن رَّبِّكَ ۖ وَإِن لَّمْ تَفْعَلْ فَمَا بَلَّغْتَ رِسَالَتَهُۥ ۚ
وَٱللَّهُ يَعْصِمُكَ مِنَ ٱلنَّاسِ ۗ إِنَّ ٱللَّهَ
لَا يَهْدِى ٱلْقَوْمَ ٱلْكَٰفِرِينَ ﴿٦٧﴾ قُلْ
يَٰٓأَهْلَ ٱلْكِتَٰبِ لَسْتُمْ عَلَىٰ شَىْءٍ حَتَّىٰ
تُقِيمُوا۟ ٱلتَّوْرَىٰةَ وَٱلْإِنجِيلَ وَمَآ أُنزِلَ
إِلَيْكُم مِّن رَّبِّكُمْ ۗ وَلَيَزِيدَنَّ كَثِيرًا
مِّنْهُم مَّآ أُنزِلَ إِلَيْكَ مِن رَّبِّكَ طُغْيَٰنًا
وَكُفْرًا ۖ فَلَا تَأْسَ عَلَى ٱلْقَوْمِ ٱلْكَٰفِرِينَ
﴿٦٨﴾ إِنَّ ٱلَّذِينَ ءَامَنُوا۟ وَٱلَّذِينَ هَادُوا۟
وَٱلصَّٰبِـُٔونَ وَٱلنَّصَٰرَىٰ مَنْ ءَامَنَ بِٱللَّهِ
وَٱلْيَوْمِ ٱلْءَاخِرِ وَعَمِلَ صَٰلِحًا فَلَا خَوْفٌ
عَلَيْهِمْ وَلَا هُمْ يَحْزَنُونَ ﴿٦٩﴾

97. By 'establishing the Torah and the Gospel' is meant observing them honestly and making them the law of life.

It should be noted here that the Scriptures which comprise the Bible consist of two kinds of writings. One was composed by the Jewish and Christian authors themselves. The second consists of those portions which have been recorded as either the injunctions of God or as the utterances of Moses, Jesus and other Prophets. Such portions are those in which it has been categorically stated that God said so and so, or that a particular Prophet said so and so. If we were to exclude the portions belonging to the first category and carefully study those belonging to the second we

(70) And We took a covenant from the Children of Israel and sent to them many Messengers. But whenever any Messenger brought to them something that did not suit their desires, they gave the lie to some of them and killed the others, (71) thinking that no harm would come from it. Thus they became blind and deaf (to the Truth). Thereafter Allah turned towards them in gracious forgiveness; but many of them became even more deaf and blind (to the Truth). Allah sees all that they do.

(72) And surely they disbelieved when they said: 'Christ, the son of Mary, is indeed God'; whereas Christ had said:

لَقَدْ أَخَذْنَا مِيثَٰقَ بَنِىٓ إِسْرَٰٓءِيلَ
وَأَرْسَلْنَآ إِلَيْهِمْ رُسُلًا ۖ كُلَّمَا جَآءَهُمْ
رَسُولٌۢ بِمَا لَا تَهْوَىٰٓ أَنفُسُهُمْ فَرِيقًا
كَذَّبُوا۟ وَفَرِيقًا يَقْتُلُونَ ﴿٧٠﴾
وَحَسِبُوٓا۟ أَلَّا تَكُونَ فِتْنَةٌ فَعَمُوا۟
وَصَمُّوا۟ ثُمَّ تَابَ ٱللَّهُ عَلَيْهِمْ ثُمَّ
عَمُوا۟ وَصَمُّوا۟ كَثِيرٌ مِّنْهُمْ ۚ وَٱللَّهُ
بَصِيرٌۢ بِمَا يَعْمَلُونَ ﴿٧١﴾ لَقَدْ
كَفَرَ ٱلَّذِينَ قَالُوٓا۟ إِنَّ ٱللَّهَ هُوَ
ٱلْمَسِيحُ ٱبْنُ مَرْيَمَ ۖ وَقَالَ ٱلْمَسِيحُ

---

would notice that their teachings are not perceptibly different from those of the Qur'ān. It is true that the second category has not altogether escaped the tamperings of translators, scribes and exegetes, and the errors of oral transmitters. Nevertheless, one cannot help feeling that the teachings embodied in the second category call man to the same pure monotheism as the Qur'ān, that they propound those very beliefs propounded by the Qur'ān and that they direct man to the same way of life as that to which the Qur'ān seeks to direct him. Hence, had the Jews and the Christians adhered to the teaching attributed in their Scriptures to God and the Prophets they would certainly have become a truth-loving and truth-oriented group of people and would have been able to see in the Qur'ān that very light which illuminates the earlier divine Scriptures. There would then have been no question of their abandoning their religion in order to follow the Prophet (peace be on him). To follow him would have caused neither break nor discontinuity; they would simply have gone one stage further along the same road.

98. Instead of reflecting on this seriously and dispassionately, they were seized by a fit of intransigence which intensified their opposition.

99. See *Towards Understanding the Qur'ān*, vol. I, *Sūrah* 2, verse 62, and n. 80.

'Children of Israel! Serve Allah, Who is your Lord and my Lord.' Allah has forbidden Paradise to those who associate anything with Him in His divinity and their refuge shall be the Fire. No one will be able to help such wrong-doers.

(73) Those who said: 'Allah is one of the Three', certainly they disbelieved, for there is no god save the One God. And if they do not give up this claim, all who have disbelieved among them shall be subjected to painful chastisement. (74) Will they not, then, turn to Allah in repentance, and ask for His forgiveness? Allah is All-Forgiving, All-Compassionate.

(75) The Messiah, son of Mary, was no more than a Messenger before whom many Messengers have passed away; and his mother adhered wholly to truthfulness, and they both ate food (as other mortals do). See how We make Our signs clear to them; and see where they are turning away![100]

يَٰبَنِىٓ إِسْرَٰٓءِيلَ ٱعْبُدُوا۟ ٱللَّهَ رَبِّى
وَرَبَّكُمْ ۖ إِنَّهُۥ مَن يُشْرِكْ بِٱللَّهِ فَقَدْ
حَرَّمَ ٱللَّهُ عَلَيْهِ ٱلْجَنَّةَ وَمَأْوَىٰهُ ٱلنَّارُ ۖ
وَمَا لِلظَّٰلِمِينَ مِنْ أَنصَارٍ ﴿٧٢﴾
لَّقَدْ كَفَرَ ٱلَّذِينَ قَالُوٓا۟ إِنَّ ٱللَّهَ
ثَالِثُ ثَلَٰثَةٍ ۘ وَمَا مِنْ إِلَٰهٍ إِلَّآ إِلَٰهٌ
وَٰحِدٌ ۚ وَإِن لَّمْ يَنتَهُوا۟ عَمَّا يَقُولُونَ
لَيَمَسَّنَّ ٱلَّذِينَ كَفَرُوا۟ مِنْهُمْ
عَذَابٌ أَلِيمٌ ﴿٧٣﴾ أَفَلَا يَتُوبُونَ
إِلَى ٱللَّهِ وَيَسْتَغْفِرُونَهُۥ ۚ وَٱللَّهُ
غَفُورٌ رَّحِيمٌ ﴿٧٤﴾ مَّا ٱلْمَسِيحُ
ٱبْنُ مَرْيَمَ إِلَّا رَسُولٌ قَدْ خَلَتْ مِن
قَبْلِهِ ٱلرُّسُلُ وَأُمُّهُۥ صِدِّيقَةٌ ۖ
كَانَا يَأْكُلَانِ ٱلطَّعَامَ ۗ ٱنظُرْ
كَيْفَ نُبَيِّنُ لَهُمُ ٱلْءَايَٰتِ ثُمَّ
ٱنظُرْ أَنَّىٰ يُؤْفَكُونَ ﴿٧٥﴾

100. In these few words the Christian doctrine of the divinity of Christ is repudiated. The nature of the Messiah is clear from the indications given here; he was merely a human being. He was one born from the womb of a woman, who had a known genealogy, who possessed a physical body, who was subject to all the limitations of a human being and who had all the

(76) Say: 'Do you serve, beside Allah, that which has no power either to harm or benefit you, whereas Allah alone is All-Hearing, All-Knowing?' (77) Say: 'People of the Book! Do not go beyond bounds in your religion at the cost of truth, and do not follow the caprices of the people who fell into error before, and caused others to go astray, and strayed far away from the right path.'[101]

قُلْ أَتَعْبُدُونَ مِن دُونِ ٱللَّهِ مَا لَا
يَمْلِكُ لَكُمْ ضَرًّا وَلَا نَفْعًا وَٱللَّهُ هُوَ
ٱلسَّمِيعُ ٱلْعَلِيمُ ﴿٧٦﴾ قُلْ يَٰٓأَهْلَ
ٱلْكِتَٰبِ لَا تَغْلُوا۟ فِى دِينِكُمْ
غَيْرَ ٱلْحَقِّ وَلَا تَتَّبِعُوٓا۟ أَهْوَآءَ قَوْمٍ قَدْ
ضَلُّوا۟ مِن قَبْلُ وَأَضَلُّوا۟ كَثِيرًا
وَضَلُّوا۟ عَن سَوَآءِ ٱلسَّبِيلِ ﴿٧٧﴾

---

attributes characteristic of human beings. He slept, ate, felt the discomfort of heat and cold and was so human that he was even put to the test by Satan. How could any reasonable person believe that such a being was either God or a partner or associate of God in His godhead? But the Christians continue to insist on the divinity of the Messiah, whose life has been portrayed in their own Scriptures as that of a human. The fact of the matter is that they do not believe at all in the historical Messiah. They have woven a Messiah out of their imagination and have deified that imaginary being.

101. This refers to those misguided nations from whom the Christians derived their false beliefs and ways, particularly to the Hellenistic philosophers under the spell of whose ideas the Christians had veered from the straight way they had originally followed. The beliefs of the early followers of the Messiah were mainly in conformity with the reality they had witnessed, and conformed to the teachings they had received from their guide and mentor. But they later resorted to an exaggerated veneration of Jesus, and interpreted their own beliefs in the light of the philosophical doctrines and superstitious ideas of the neighbouring nations. Thus they invented an altogether new religion not even remotely related to the original teachings of the Messiah. In this connection the observations of a Christian theologian, the Reverend Charles Anderson Scott are significant. In a lengthy article entitled 'Jesus Christ', published in the fourteenth edition of *Encyclopaedia Britannica*, he writes:

> . . . there is nothing in these three Gospels to suggest that their writers thought of Jesus as other than human, a human being specially endowed with the Spirit of God and standing in an unbroken relation

> to God which justified His being spoken of as the 'Son of God'. Even Matthew refers to Him as the carpenter's son and records that after Peter had acknowleged Him as Messiah he 'took Him aside and began to rebuke Him' (Matthew, xvi. 22). And in Luke the two disciples on the way to Emmaus can still speak of Him as 'a prophet mighty in deed and word before God and all the people' (Luke, xxiv. 19). It is very singular that in spite of the fact that before Mark was composed 'the Lord' had become the description of Jesus common among Christians, He is never so described in the second Gospel (nor yet in the first, though the word is freely used to refer to God). All three relate the Passion of Jesus with a fullness and emphasis of its great significance; but except the 'ransom' passage (Mark, x. 45) and certain words at the Last Supper there is no indication of the meaning which was afterwards attached to it. It is not even suggested that the death of Jesus had any relation to sin or forgiveness.

A little further on he writes:

> That He ranked Himself as a prophet appears from a few passages such as 'It cannot be that a prophet perish out of Jerusalem'. He frequently referred to Himself as the Son of Man; but while this must be maintained in face of influential opinions to the contrary, the result for our purpose is less important than we might expect, for the possible meanings of the phrase are as numerous as the sources from which it may possibly have been derived. They range from simple 'man' through 'man in his human weakness' and the representative 'Man' to the supernatural man from heaven foreshadowed in Daniel. If we had to postulate one source and one meaning for the phrase as used by Jesus of Himself, it would probably be found in Psalm lxxx., where the poignant appeal to God for the redemption of Israel runs out on the hope of a 'son of man whom thou madest strong for thyself'.

The same author adds:

> Certain words of Peter spoken at the time of Pentecost, 'A man approved of God', described Jesus as He was known and regarded by His contemporaries. He was 'found in fashion as a man', that is, in all particulars which presented themselves to outward observation He appeared and behaved as one of the human race. He 'was made man'. The Gospels leave no room for doubt as to the completeness with which these statements are to be accepted. From them we learn that Jesus passed through the natural stages of development, physical and mental, that He hungered, thirsted, was weary and slept, that He could be surprised and require information, that He suffered pain and died. He not only made no claim to omniscience, He distinctly waived it. This is not to deny that He had insight such as no other ever had, into human nature, into the hearts of men and the purposes and

methods of God. But there is no reason to suppose that He thought of the earth as other than the centre of the solar system, of any other than David as the author of the Psalms, or did not share the belief of His age that demons were the cause of disease. Indeed, any claim to omniscience would be not only inconsistent with the whole impression created by the Gospels, it could not be reconciled with the cardinal experiences of the Temptation, of Gethsemane and of Calvary. Unless such experiences were to be utterly unreal, Jesus must have entered into them and passed through them under the ordinary limitations of human knowledge, subject only to such modifications of human knowledge as might be due to prophetic insight or the sure vision of God.

There is still less reason to predicate omnipotence of Jesus. There is no indication that He ever acted independently of God, or as an independent God. Rather does He acknowledge dependence upon God, by His habit of prayer and in such words as 'this kind goeth not forth save by prayer'. He even repudiates the ascription to Himself of goodness in the absolute sense in which it belongs to God alone. It is a remarkable testimony to the truly historical character of these Gospels that though they were not finally set down until the Christian Church had begun to look up to the risen Christ as to a Divine Being, the records on the one hand preserve all the evidence of His true humanity and on the other nowhere suggest that He thought of Himself as God.

The same author also observes that:

He proclaimed that at and through the Resurrection Jesus had been publicly installed as Son of God with power; and if the phrase has not wholly lost its official Messianic connotation, it certainly includes a reference to the personal Sonship, which Paul elsewhere makes clear by speaking of Him as God's 'own Son' . . .

It may not be possible to decide whether it was the primitive community or Paul himself who first put full religious content into the title 'Lord' as used of Christ. Probably it was the former. But the Apostle undoubtedly adopted the title in its full meaning, and did much to make that meaning clear by transferring to 'the Lord Jesus Christ' many of the ideas and phrases which in the Old Testament had been specifically assigned to the Lord Jehovah. God 'gave unto Him that name that is above every name – the name of "Lord"'. At the same time by equating Christ with the Wisdom of God and with the Glory of God, as well as ascribing to Him Sonship in an absolute sense, Paul claimed for Jesus Christ a relation to God which was inherent and unique, ethical and personal, eternal. While, however, Paul in many ways and in many aspects, equated Christ with God, he definitely stopped short of speaking of him as 'God'.

In another article in *Encyclopaedia Britannica* (xiv edition), under the title 'Christianity', the Reverend George William Knox writes as follows about the fundamental beliefs of the Church:

> Its moulds of thought are those of Greek philosophy, and into these were run the Jewish teachings. We have thus a peculiar combination – the religious doctrines of the Bible, as culminating in the person of Jesus, run through the forms of an alien philosophy.
>
> *The Doctrine of the Trinity*. The Jewish sources furnished the terms Father, Son and Spirit. Jesus seldom employed the last term and Paul's use of it is not altogether clear. Already in Jewish literature it had been all but personified (Cf. the *Wisdom of Solomon*). Thus the material is Jewish, though already doubtless modified by Greek influence: but the problem is Greek; it is not primarily ethical nor even religious, but it is metaphysical. What is the ontological relationship between these three factors? The answer of the Church is given in the Nicene formula, which is characteristically Greek, . . .

Also significant in this connection are the following passages of another article in *Encyclopaedia Britannica* (xiv edition), entitled 'Church History':

> The recognition of Christ as the incarnation of the Logos was practically universal before the close of the 3rd century, but His deity was still widely denied, and the Arian controversy which distracted the Church of the 4th century concerned the latter question. At the Council of Nicaea in 325 the deity of Christ received official sanction and was given formulation in the original Nicene Creed. Controversy continued for some time, but finally the Nicene decision was recognised both in East and West as the only orthodox faith. The deity of the Son was believed to carry with it that of the Spirit, who was associated with Father and Son in the baptismal formula and in the current symbols, and so the victory of the Nicene Christology meant the recognition of the doctrine of Trinity as part of the orthodox faith.
>
> The assertion of the deity of the Son incarnate in Christ raised another problem which constituted the subject of dispute in the Christological controversies of the 4th and following centuries. What is the relation of the divine and human natures in Christ? At the Council of Chalcedon in 451 it was declared that in the person of Christ are united two complete natures, divine and human, which retain after the union all their properties unchanged. This was supplemented at the 3rd Council of Constantinople in 680 by the statement that each of the natures contains a will, so that Christ possesses two wills. The Western Church accepted the decisions of Nicaea, Chalcedon and Constantinople, and so the doctrines of the Trinity and of the two natures in Christ were handed down as orthodox dogma in West as well as East.
>
> Meanwhile in the Western Church the subject of sin and grace, and the relation of divine and human activity in salvation, received special

(78) Those of the Children of Israel who took to unbelief have been cursed by the tongue of David and Jesus, son of Mary, for they rebelled and exceeded the bounds of right. (79) They did not forbid each other from committing the abominable deeds they committed.[102] Indeed what they did was evil. ▶

لُعِنَ ٱلَّذِينَ كَفَرُوا۟ مِنۢ بَنِىٓ
إِسْرَٰٓءِيلَ عَلَىٰ لِسَانِ دَاوُۥدَ وَعِيسَى
ٱبْنِ مَرْيَمَ ۚ ذَٰلِكَ بِمَا عَصَوا۟
وَّكَانُوا۟ يَعْتَدُونَ ﴿٧٨﴾ كَانُوا۟
لَا يَتَنَاهَوْنَ عَن مُّنكَرٍ
فَعَلُوهُ ۚ لَبِئْسَ مَا كَانُوا۟
يَفْعَلُونَ ﴿٧٩﴾

> attention; and finally, at the 2nd Council of Orange in 529, after both Pelagianism and semi-Pelagianism had been repudiated, a moderate form of Augustinianism was adopted, involving the theory that every man as a result of the Fall is in such a condition that he can take no steps in the direction of salvation until he has been renewed by the divine grace given in baptism, and that he cannot continue in the good thus begun except by the constant assistance of that grace, which is mediated only by the Catholic Church.

It is evident from these statements of Christian scholars that it was exaggerated love and veneration of Christ which led the early Christians astray. This exaggeration and the use of expressions such as 'Lord' and 'Son of God' led to Jesus being invested with divine attributes and to the peculiar Christian notion of redemption, even though these could not be accommodated into the body of the teachings of Christ. When the Christians came to be infected with philosophical doctrines, they did not abandon the original error into which they had fallen, but tried to accommodate the errors of their predecessors through apologetics and rational explanations. Thus, instead of returning to the true teachings of Christ, they used logic and philosophy to fabricate one false doctrine after another.

It is to this error that the Qur'ān calls the Christians' attention in these verses.

102. The corruption of any nation begins with that of a few individuals. If the collective conscience of that nation is alive, the pressure of public opinion keeps those persons in check and prevents the nation as a whole from becoming corrupted. But if instead of censuring such individuals, the nation leaves them free to behave corruptly, the corruption originally confined to a few continues to spread till it engulfs the whole nation. It

(80) And now you can see many of them taking the unbelievers (instead of the believers) for their allies. Indeed they have prepared evil for themselves. Allah is angry with them, and they shall abide in chastisement. (81) For had they truly believed in Allah and the Messenger and what was sent down to him, they would not have taken unbelievers (instead of believers) for their allies.[103] But many of them have rebelled against Allah altogether.

(82) Of all men you will find the Jews and those who associate others with Allah in His divinity to be the most hostile to those who believe; and you will surely find that of all people they who say: 'We are Christians', are closest to feeling affection for those who believe. This is because there are worshipful priests and monks among them, and because they are not arrogant. ►

تَرَىٰ كَثِيرًا مِّنْهُمْ يَتَوَلَّوْنَ
ٱلَّذِينَ كَفَرُوا۟ لَبِئْسَ مَا قَدَّمَتْ لَهُمْ
أَنفُسُهُمْ أَن سَخِطَ ٱللَّهُ عَلَيْهِمْ وَفِى
ٱلْعَذَابِ هُمْ خَٰلِدُونَ ﴿٨٠﴾
وَلَوْ كَانُوا۟ يُؤْمِنُونَ بِٱللَّهِ وَٱلنَّبِىِّ
وَمَآ أُنزِلَ إِلَيْهِ مَا ٱتَّخَذُوهُمْ
أَوْلِيَآءَ وَلَٰكِنَّ كَثِيرًا مِّنْهُمْ
فَٰسِقُونَ ﴿٨١﴾ لَتَجِدَنَّ أَشَدَّ
ٱلنَّاسِ عَدَٰوَةً لِّلَّذِينَ ءَامَنُوا۟ ٱلْيَهُودَ
وَٱلَّذِينَ أَشْرَكُوا۟ وَلَتَجِدَنَّ
أَقْرَبَهُم مَّوَدَّةً لِّلَّذِينَ ءَامَنُوا۟
ٱلَّذِينَ قَالُوٓا۟ إِنَّا نَصَٰرَىٰ ذَٰلِكَ
بِأَنَّ مِنْهُمْ قِسِّيسِينَ وَرُهْبَانًا
وَأَنَّهُمْ لَا يَسْتَكْبِرُونَ ﴿٨٢﴾

---

was this which ultimately caused the degeneration of Israel. (For the curse against Israel in the words of David and Jesus see Psalms 10, 50 and Matthew 23.)

103. It seems natural that those who believe in God and the Prophets and the Scriptures, compared with the polytheists, would naturally be more sympathetic to those who at least share with them belief in God, in prophethood and in revelation (whatever their disagreements on other religious issues). It was ironic, therefore, that the Jews should openly support the polytheists in the struggle between polytheism and monotheism,

(83) And when they hear what has been revealed to the Messenger you see that their eyes overflow with tears because of the Truth that they recognize and they say: 'Our Lord! We do believe; write us down, therefore, with those who bear witness (to the Truth). (84) And why should we not believe in Allah and the Truth which has come down to us when we do fervently desire that our Lord include us among the righteous?' (85) So Allah rewarded them for these words with Gardens beneath which rivers flow so that they would abide there for ever. Such is the reward of the people who do good. (86) Those who disbelieved and gave the lie to Our signs are rightfully the inmates of the Blazing Flame.

۞ وَإِذَا سَمِعُوا مَا أُنزِلَ إِلَى الرَّسُولِ تَرَىٰ
أَعْيُنَهُمْ تَفِيضُ مِنَ الدَّمْعِ مِمَّا عَرَفُوا
مِنَ الْحَقِّ يَقُولُونَ رَبَّنَا آمَنَّا فَاكْتُبْنَا
مَعَ الشَّاهِدِينَ ﴿٨٣﴾ وَمَا لَنَا لَا نُؤْمِنُ
بِاللَّهِ وَمَا جَاءَنَا مِنَ الْحَقِّ وَنَطْمَعُ أَن
يُدْخِلَنَا رَبُّنَا مَعَ الْقَوْمِ الصَّالِحِينَ ﴿٨٤﴾
فَأَثَابَهُمُ اللَّهُ بِمَا قَالُوا جَنَّاتٍ تَجْرِي
مِن تَحْتِهَا الْأَنْهَارُ خَالِدِينَ فِيهَا
وَذَٰلِكَ جَزَاءُ الْمُحْسِنِينَ ﴿٨٥﴾
وَالَّذِينَ كَفَرُوا وَكَذَّبُوا بِآيَاتِنَا
أُولَٰئِكَ أَصْحَابُ الْجَحِيمِ ﴿٨٦﴾

---

and that their sympathies in the conflict between those who rejected prophethood and those who believed in it should lie expressly with the former. Despite all this, they brazenly claimed to be true believers in God, in the Prophets and in the Scriptures.

(87) Believers! Do not hold as unlawful the good things which Allah has made lawful to you,[104] and do not exceed the bounds of right.[105] Allah does not love those who transgress the bounds of right. (88) And partake of the lawful, good things which Allah has provided you as sustenance, and refrain from disobeying Allah in Whom you believe.

يَٰٓأَيُّهَا ٱلَّذِينَ ءَامَنُوا۟ لَا تُحَرِّمُوا۟ طَيِّبَٰتِ
مَآ أَحَلَّ ٱللَّهُ لَكُمْ وَلَا تَعْتَدُوٓا۟ ۚ إِنَّ ٱللَّهَ
لَا يُحِبُّ ٱلْمُعْتَدِينَ ﴿٨٧﴾ وَكُلُوا۟ مِمَّا
رَزَقَكُمُ ٱللَّهُ حَلَٰلًا طَيِّبًا ۚ وَٱتَّقُوا۟ ٱللَّهَ
ٱلَّذِىٓ أَنتُم بِهِۦ مُؤْمِنُونَ ﴿٨٨﴾

---

104. This verse embodies two directives. The first is that man should not attribute to himself the authority to proclaim things either lawful or unlawful according to his own wishes. Only that which God has held to be lawful *is* lawful, and only that which God has declared unlawful *is* unlawful. If men were to declare certain things either lawful or unlawful on their own authority, they would not be following the law of God but their own laws. The second directive is that they should not adopt the course of world-renunciation and abstention from worldly pleasures as the Christian monks, Hindu mendicants, Buddhist bhikshus and illuminist mystics did. Religious-minded and virtuous people have always tended to consider their physical and carnal desires an impediment to spiritual growth. They have considered suffering, deprivation from worldly pleasures and abstention from the means of worldly sustenance to be acts of goodness and indispensable for achieving proximity to God. Even some of the Companions leaned in this direction. The Prophet (peace be on him) once came to know that some Companions had resolved that they would fast without interruption, that instead of spending the night on their beds they would remain awake praying, that they would consume neither meat nor fat, and would have no (sexual) relations with women. The Prophet (peace be on him) addressed the people on this subject and said: 'I have not been commanded to do so. Even your own self has rights against you. So, fast on certain days and refrain from fasting on others. Stay awake praying at night and also sleep. Look at me, I sleep as well as stay awake (praying); sometimes I fast and sometimes I don't. I consume meat as well as fat. Whosoever dislikes my way does not belong to me.' He then added: 'What has happened to people that they have prohibited for themselves women, good food, perfumes, sleep and the pleasures of the world, whereas I have not taught you to become monks and priests. In my religion there is neither abstention from women nor from meat, neither seclusion nor withdrawal.

For the purposes of self-control my religion has fasting. As for monasticism, all its benefits can be derived from *jihād* (struggle in the way of God). Serve God and associate none with Him. Perform *Ḥajj* and *'Umrah*, establish Prayers, dispense *Zakāh* and observe the fasts of Ramaḍān. Those who were destroyed before you were destroyed because they were severe with themselves, and when they became severe with themselves God became severe with them as well. It is the remnants of such people who you see in the oratories and hermitages of monks.' (Ibn Kathīr, vol. 2, pp. 626 and 628–9 – Ed.)

There are traditions to the effect that the Prophet (peace be on him) once came to know that one of his Companions was always so preoccupied with worship and devotion that he did not approach his wife for long periods. The Prophet (peace be on him) called for him and directed him to go to his wife. On being told that he was fasting, the Prophet (peace be on him) asked him to break the fast and proceed to his wife. During the reign of 'Umar a lady once lodged the complaint that her husband fasted all day and prayed all night and had no relations with her. 'Umar appointed the famous Successor (*Tābi'ī*), Ka'b b. Thawr al-Azdī to look into the matter. He issued the judgement that the husband had the right to spend three nights in Prayer if he so wished, but every fourth night was the right of his wife. (*Fiqh al-Sunnah*, vol. 2, p. 164 – Ed.)

105. 'Do not exceed the bounds of right' has a broad signification. To hold the things which are lawful to be unlawful, and to shun the things declared by God to be clean as if they were unclean, is in itself an act of wrongful excess. It should be remembered, at the same time, that extravagant indulgence even in clean things is an act of wrongful excess. Likewise, to overstep the limits of the permissible is also an act of wrongful excess. God disapproves of all three kinds of excess.

(89) Allah does not take you to task for the oaths you utter vainly, but He will certainly take you to task for the oaths you have sworn in earnest. The expiation (for breaking such oaths) is either to feed ten needy persons with more or less the same food as you are wont to give to your families, or to clothe them, or to set free from bondage the neck of one man; and he who does not find the means shall fast for three days. This shall be the expiation for your oaths whenever you have sworn (and broken them.)[106] But do keep your oaths.[107] Thus does Allah make clear to you His commandments; maybe you will be grateful.

لَا يُؤَاخِذُكُمُ ٱللَّهُ بِٱللَّغْوِ فِىٓ أَيْمَـٰنِكُمْ
وَلَـٰكِن يُؤَاخِذُكُم بِمَا عَقَّدتُّمُ ٱلْأَيْمَـٰنَ ۖ
فَكَفَّـٰرَتُهُۥٓ إِطْعَامُ عَشَرَةِ مَسَـٰكِينَ
مِنْ أَوْسَطِ مَا تُطْعِمُونَ أَهْلِيكُمْ
أَوْ كِسْوَتُهُمْ أَوْ تَحْرِيرُ رَقَبَةٍ ۖ فَمَن لَّمْ يَجِدْ
فَصِيَامُ ثَلَـٰثَةِ أَيَّامٍ ۚ ذَٰلِكَ كَفَّـٰرَةُ
أَيْمَـٰنِكُمْ إِذَا حَلَفْتُمْ ۚ وَٱحْفَظُوٓا۟
أَيْمَـٰنَكُمْ ۚ كَذَٰلِكَ يُبَيِّنُ ٱللَّهُ لَكُمْ ءَايَـٰتِهِۦ
لَعَلَّكُمْ تَشْكُرُونَ ﴿٨٩﴾

---

106. Since some people had taken an oath prohibiting for themselves the things which He had permitted, God laid down this injunction regarding oaths made inadvertently. The injunction makes it unnecessary to feel bound by the terms of inadvertent oaths, and for which one will not be reproached by God. And if a person had deliberately made an oath which entails sin he should not abide by his oath and should expiate it (see *Towards Understanding the Qur'ān*, vol. I, *Sūrah* 2, nn. 243–4; for expiation see *Sūrah* 4, n. 125 above).

107. To be mindful of one's oaths has several meanings. First, one should make proper use of oaths and should not employ them either frivolously or sinfully. Second, when a person takes an oath, he should take care not to forget it lest he be led to break it. Third, when a man deliberately takes an oath regarding something sound in itself he should pay the penalty if he happens to violate it.

(90) Believers! Intoxicants, games of chance, idolatrous sacrifices at altars, and divining arrows[108] are all abominations, the handiwork of Satan. So turn wholly away from it that you may attain to true success.[109] (91) By intoxicants and games of chance Satan only desires to create enmity and hatred between you, and to turn you away from the remembrance of Allah and from Prayer. Will you, then, desist? (92) Obey Allah and obey the Messenger, and beware. But if you turn away, then know well that Our Messenger had merely to deliver the message clearly.

يَٰٓأَيُّهَا ٱلَّذِينَ ءَامَنُوٓا۟ إِنَّمَا ٱلْخَمْرُ وَٱلْمَيْسِرُ
وَٱلْأَنصَابُ وَٱلْأَزْلَٰمُ رِجْسٌ مِّنْ عَمَلِ
ٱلشَّيْطَٰنِ فَٱجْتَنِبُوهُ لَعَلَّكُمْ تُفْلِحُونَ ﴿٩٠﴾
إِنَّمَا يُرِيدُ ٱلشَّيْطَٰنُ أَن يُوقِعَ بَيْنَكُمُ
ٱلْعَدَٰوَةَ وَٱلْبَغْضَآءَ فِى ٱلْخَمْرِ وَٱلْمَيْسِرِ
وَيَصُدَّكُمْ عَن ذِكْرِ ٱللَّهِ وَعَنِ ٱلصَّلَوٰةِ ۖ فَهَلْ
أَنتُم مُّنتَهُونَ ﴿٩١﴾ وَأَطِيعُوا۟ ٱللَّهَ وَأَطِيعُوا۟
ٱلرَّسُولَ وَٱحْذَرُوا۟ ۚ فَإِن تَوَلَّيْتُمْ فَٱعْلَمُوٓا۟
أَنَّمَا عَلَىٰ رَسُولِنَا ٱلْبَلَٰغُ ٱلْمُبِينُ ﴿٩٢﴾

108. For 'altars' and divination by arrows see nn. 12 and 14 above. For games of chance see n. 14 above.

While divination by arrow-shooting essentially constitutes a game of chance there is nevertheless a certain difference between the two, since divination by arrow-shooting, in addition to being a game of chance, is also tainted with polytheistic beliefs and superstitions. As for games of chance, this expression is applied to those games and acts in which accidental factors are considered the criteria for acquisition, fortune-making and the division of goods and property.

109. In this verse four things are categorically prohibited: (1) intoxicants; (2) games of chance; (3) places consecrated for the worship of anyone else besides God, and altars for either sacrifices or offerings in the name of others than God; and (4) polytheistic divination by arrow-shooting. The last three items have already been explained. (See *Towards Understanding the Qur'ān*, vol. I, *Sūrah* 2: 219, n. 235 and *Sūrah* 5: 3, n. 14 above).

Two injunctions had already been revealed concerning the prohibition of intoxicants (See *Sūrahs* 2: 219 and 4: 43). Before the revelation of the last injunction, the Prophet (peace be on him) had warned the people that intoxicants were highly displeasing to God. Hinting at the possibility of their being prohibited, he advised people to dispose of intoxicants if they had any. A little later on the present verse was revealed and the Prophet

(93) There will be no blame on those who believe and do righteous deeds for whatever they might have partaken (in the past) as long as they refrain from things prohibited, and persist in their belief and do righteous deeds, and continue to refrain from whatever is forbidden and submit to divine commandments, and persevere in doing good, fearing Allah. Allah loves those who do good.

لَيْسَ عَلَى ٱلَّذِينَ ءَامَنُوا۟ وَعَمِلُوا۟
ٱلصَّٰلِحَٰتِ جُنَاحٌ فِيمَا طَعِمُوٓا۟ إِذَا
مَا ٱتَّقَوا۟ وَّءَامَنُوا۟ وَعَمِلُوا۟ ٱلصَّٰلِحَٰتِ
ثُمَّ ٱتَّقَوا۟ وَّءَامَنُوا۟ ثُمَّ ٱتَّقَوا۟ وَّأَحْسَنُوا۟ ۗ وَٱللَّهُ
يُحِبُّ ٱلْمُحْسِنِينَ ﴿٩٣﴾

(peace be on him) then proclaimed that those who had intoxicants should neither consume nor sell them, but rather destroy them. Intoxicating liquors were poured into the streets of Madina. When asked if such liquor might be offered to the Jews as a gift the Prophet (peace be on him) replied in the negative and said: 'He Who has prohibited it has also required it not to be given away as a gift.' Some people inquired whether it was permitted to make vinegar out of such liquor. The Prophet (peace be on him) told them not to do so, but to throw it away instead. Another person asked insistently whether or not an intoxicant could be used as medicine. The Prophet (peace be on him) replied that far from being a remedy for any malady it was in itself a malady. Others sought permission to consume intoxicating liquor on the plea that they lived in a very cold region and had to work very hard, and that the people of that region habitually drank intoxicants to combat exhaustion and cold. The Prophet (peace be on him) inquired if the drink concerned did cause intoxication. On being told that it did, he said that they should abstain from it. They pointed out that the people of their region would not accept this, to which the Prophet (peace be on him) replied that they should fight them.

It is reported by 'Abd Allāh Ibn 'Umar that the Prophet (peace be on him) said: 'God has cursed *khamr* (wine) and him who drinks it, him who provides it to others and him who buys or sells it, him who squeezes (the grapes) into wine and him who causes others to squeeze grapes (in order to make wine), him who carries it and him to whom it is carried.' (See Aḥmad b. Ḥanbal, *Musnad*, vol. 2, p. 97; vol. 1, p. 316; Abū Dā'ūd, 'Ashribah', 2 – Ed.)

According to another tradition the Prophet (peace be on him) instructed not to eat at the table where intoxicating drinks were being taken. In the beginning the Prophet (peace be on him) even forbade the use of vessels in which intoxicating drinks had either been made or served. Later on, when the prohibition of drinks was completely observed the Prophet (peace

(94) Believers! Allah will surely try you with a game which will be within the range of your hands and lances so that He might mark out those who fear Him, even though He is beyond the reach of human perception. A painful chastisement awaits whosoever transgresses after that the bounds set by Allah. (95) Believers! Do not kill game while you are in the state of pilgrim sanctity.[110] Whoever of you kills it wilfully there shall be a recompense, the like of what he has killed in cattle – as shall be judged by two men of equity among you – to be brought to the Ka'bah as an offering, or as an expiation the feeding of the needy, or its equivalent in fasting[111] in order that he may taste the grievousness of his deed. Allah has pardoned whatever has passed; but Allah will exact a penalty from him who repeats it. Allah is All-Mighty. He is fully capable of exacting penalties.

يَٰٓأَيُّهَا ٱلَّذِينَ ءَامَنُوا۟ لَيَبْلُوَنَّكُمُ ٱللَّهُ بِشَىْءٍ
مِّنَ ٱلصَّيْدِ تَنَالُهُۥٓ أَيْدِيكُمْ وَرِمَاحُكُمْ
لِيَعْلَمَ ٱللَّهُ مَن يَخَافُهُۥ بِٱلْغَيْبِ ۚ فَمَنِ ٱعْتَدَىٰ
بَعْدَ ذَٰلِكَ فَلَهُۥ عَذَابٌ أَلِيمٌ ﴿٩٤﴾ يَٰٓأَيُّهَا
ٱلَّذِينَ ءَامَنُوا۟ لَا تَقْتُلُوا۟ ٱلصَّيْدَ وَأَنتُمْ حُرُمٌ ۚ
وَمَن قَتَلَهُۥ مِنكُم مُّتَعَمِّدًا فَجَزَآءٌ مِّثْلُ
مَا قَتَلَ مِنَ ٱلنَّعَمِ يَحْكُمُ بِهِۦ ذَوَا عَدْلٍ
مِّنكُمْ هَدْيًۢا بَٰلِغَ ٱلْكَعْبَةِ أَوْ كَفَّٰرَةٌ طَعَامُ
مَسَٰكِينَ أَوْ عَدْلُ ذَٰلِكَ صِيَامًا لِّيَذُوقَ
وَبَالَ أَمْرِهِۦ ۗ عَفَا ٱللَّهُ عَمَّا سَلَفَ ۚ وَمَنْ عَادَ
فَيَنتَقِمُ ٱللَّهُ مِنْهُ ۗ وَٱللَّهُ عَزِيزٌ ذُو
ٱنتِقَامٍ ﴿٩٥﴾

---

be on him) withdrew the interdiction regarding the use of these vessels. (See Abū Dā'ūd, 'Aṭ'imah', 18; Tirmidhī, 'Adab', 43; Dārimī, 'Ashribah', 15; Aḥmad b. Ḥanbal, *Musnad*, vol. 1, p. 20; vol. 3, p. 339 – Ed.)

Though the word *khamr* in Arabic means literally 'the drink made from grapes', it was also used figuratively for intoxicating liquors made from wheat, barley, raisins, dates and honey. The Prophet (peace be on him) applied the prohibition of wine to all intoxicants. In this regard we find categorical statements from the Prophet (peace be on him) embodied in traditions: 'Every intoxicant is *khamr*, and every intoxicant is prohibited.'

'Every drink which causes intoxication is prohibited.' 'I forbid everything which intoxicates.' In a Friday sermon 'Umar defined *khamr* in the following manner: 'Whatever takes hold of the mind is *khamr.*' (See Bukhārī, 'Wuḍū'', 71; 'Maghāzī', 60, 'Ashribah', 4, 10, 'Adab', 8, 'Aḥkām', 22; Muslim, 'Ashribah', 67–9; Abū Dā'ūd, 'Ashribah', 5, 71; Ibn Mājah, 'Ashribah', 9, 13, 14; Dārimī, 'Ashribah', 8, 9; Muwaṭṭa', 'Ḍaḥāyā', 8; Aḥmad b. Hanbal, *Musnad*, vol. 1, pp. 274, 289, 350; vol. 2, pp. 16, 158, 171, 185, 429, 501; vol. 3, pp. 63, 66, 112, 119, 361; vol. 4, pp. 41, 416; vol. 6, pp. 36, 71, 72, 97, 131, 190 and 226 – Ed.)

The Prophet (peace be on him) also enunciated the following principle: 'If anything causes intoxication when used in large quantity, even a small quantity of it is prohibited.' 'If a large quantity of something causes intoxication, to drink even a palmful of it is prohibited.' (See Abū Dā'ūd, 'Ashribah', 5; Ibn Mājah, 'Ashribah', 10; Aḥmad b. Ḥanbal, *Musnad*, vol. 2, pp. 167, 179 and vol. 3, p. 343 – Ed.)

In the time of the Prophet (peace be on him) no specific punishment had been laid down for drinking. A person caught drunk would be struck with shoes, fists, and whips made of twisted cloth and palm sticks. The maximum number of lashes to which any culprit was subjected was forty. In the time of Abū Bakr the punishment continued to be forty lashes. In the time of 'Umar the punishment initially remained at forty lashes also, but when he saw people persist in drinking he fixed the punishment at eighty lashes after consulting the Companions. This was considered the prescribed legal punishment for drinking by Mālik and Abū Ḥanīfah, and even by Shāfi'ī according to one tradition. But Aḥmad b. Ḥanbal, and, according to a variant tradition, Shāfi'ī, considered the punishment to consist of forty lashes, and 'Alī is reported to have preferred this opinion.

According to Islamic Law, it is the bounden duty of an Islamic government to enforce this prohibition. In the time of 'Umar the shop of a member of the Thaqīf tribe, by the name of Ruwayshid, was burnt down because he carried on the sale of liquor. On another occasion a whole hamlet was set on fire because it had become a centre of illegal traffic in liquor.

110. When a person is in the state of pilgrim sanctity (*iḥrām*) it is prohibited for him both to hunt and to assist in hunting animals. Indeed, even if an animal has been hunted for him by someone else he may not eat it. However, if someone hunts an animal for himself and makes a gift of it to such a person, there is no harm in his eating it. There is an exception to this injunction and that is with regard to harmful animals. Snakes, scorpions, mad dogs and other such animals which cause injury to man may be killed even by one in the state of *iḥrām*. (See Bukhārī, 'Ṭalāq', 24; 'Ṣayd', 2; Abū Dā'ūd, 'Manāsik', 40, 41; Tirmidhī, 'Ḥajj', 27; 'Ṣayd', 26 – Ed.)

111. It would also be 'two men of equity' (*Sūrah al-Mā'idah* 5: 95) to judge as to the number of persons one should feed or the number of days one should fast by way of expiation for killing a certain animal.

(96) The game of the water and eating thereof[112] are permitted to you as a provision for you (who are settled) and for those on a journey; but to hunt on land while you are in the state of Pilgrim sanctity is forbidden for you. Beware, then, of disobeying Allah to Whom you shall all be mustered.

(97) Allah has appointed the Ka'bah, the Sacred House, as a means of support for (the collective life of) men, and has caused the holy month (of Pilgrimage), and the animals of sacrificial offering and their distinguishing collars to assist therein.[113]

أُحِلَّ لَكُمْ صَيْدُ ٱلْبَحْرِ وَطَعَامُهُۥ مَتَٰعًا
لَّكُمْ وَلِلسَّيَّارَةِ ۖ وَحُرِّمَ عَلَيْكُمْ صَيْدُ ٱلْبَرِّ
مَا دُمْتُمْ حُرُمًا ۗ وَٱتَّقُوا۟ ٱللَّهَ ٱلَّذِىٓ
إِلَيْهِ تُحْشَرُونَ ﴿٩٦﴾ ۞ جَعَلَ ٱللَّهُ
ٱلْكَعْبَةَ ٱلْبَيْتَ ٱلْحَرَامَ قِيَٰمًا لِّلنَّاسِ
وَٱلشَّهْرَ ٱلْحَرَامَ وَٱلْهَدْىَ وَٱلْقَلَٰٓئِدَ ۚ

---

112. Since one often runs out of provisions during a voyage and is left with no alternative but to catch sea creatures, fishing in the sea has been made lawful.

113. In Arabia, the Ka'bah was not merely a sacred place of worship. Thanks to its central position and its sanctity, it nurtured the economic and cultural life of the whole peninsula. Since the entire populace was drawn towards the Ka'bah for the performance of *Ḥajj* and *'Umrah*, their coming together brought about a measure of unity in the life of the Arabs which was otherwise rent with disunity. This enabled the people of various regions and tribes to establish social and cultural ties among themselves. Moreover, the security which reigned in the vicinity of the Ka'bah provided an impetus to creative literary activity, with the result that in the fairs held in the sacred territory, poets placed their poetic compositions before the audience, trying to excel one another. This led to the growth and flowering of their language and literature. Thanks, again, to the peace and security which reigned in the sacred territory, it became a major centre of trade and commerce. Moreover, since certain months of the year were regarded as sacred months in which there could be no bloodshed, the Arabs enjoyed peace and security for about a quarter of the year. It was during this period that caravans moved in freedom and with ease from one end of the peninsula to the other. The custom of consecrating animals for sacrifice,

This is so that you may know that Allah is aware of all that is in the heavens and all that is in the earth; and that Allah has knowledge of everything.[114] (98) Know well that Allah is severe in retribution, and that Allah is also All-Forgiving, All-Compassionate. (99) The Messenger is bound only to deliver the message, whereafter Allah knows well all that you disclose and all that you conceal. (100) (O Messenger!) Say to them: 'The bad things and the good things are not equal, even though the abundance of the bad things might make you pleased with them.[115] Men of understanding, beware of disobeying Allah; then maybe you will attain true success.'

ذَٰلِكَ لِتَعْلَمُوٓا۟ أَنَّ ٱللَّهَ يَعْلَمُ مَا فِى
ٱلسَّمَٰوَٰتِ وَمَا فِى ٱلْأَرْضِ وَأَنَّ
ٱللَّهَ بِكُلِّ شَىْءٍ عَلِيمٌ ﴿٩٧﴾ ٱعْلَمُوٓا۟
أَنَّ ٱللَّهَ شَدِيدُ ٱلْعِقَابِ وَأَنَّ ٱللَّهَ
غَفُورٌ رَّحِيمٌ ﴿٩٨﴾ مَّا عَلَى ٱلرَّسُولِ
إِلَّا ٱلْبَلَٰغُ ۗ وَٱللَّهُ يَعْلَمُ مَا تُبْدُونَ وَمَا
تَكْتُمُونَ ﴿٩٩﴾ قُل لَّا يَسْتَوِى ٱلْخَبِيثُ
وَٱلطَّيِّبُ وَلَوْ أَعْجَبَكَ كَثْرَةُ ٱلْخَبِيثِ ۚ
فَٱتَّقُوا۟ ٱللَّهَ يَٰٓأُو۟لِى ٱلْأَلْبَٰبِ
لَعَلَّكُمْ تُفْلِحُونَ ﴿١٠٠﴾

---

marked off from others by the collars around their necks, also facilitated the movement of caravans, for whenever the Arabs saw those animals with their collars signifying consecration for sacrifice, they bent their heads in reverence and no predatory tribe had the courage to molest them.

114. Were they to consider even the social and economic aspects of the life of their people, the existing arrangements would provide them with clear testimony to the fact that God has deep and thorough knowledge of the interests and requirements of His creatures, and that He can ensure immensely beneficial effects on many sectors of human life by just one single commandment. During the several centuries of anarchy and disorder which preceded the advent of the Prophet (peace be on him), the Arabs were themselves unaware of their own interests and seemed bent upon self-destruction. God, however, was aware of their needs and requirements and by merely investing the Ka'bah with a central position in Arabia He ensured their national survival. Even if they disregarded innumerable other facts and reflected on this alone they would become convinced that the

(101) Believers! Do not ask of the things which, if made manifest to you, would vex you;[116] for, if you should ask about them while the Qur'ān is being revealed, they will be made manifest to you. Allah has pardoned whatever happened in the past. He is All-Forgiving, All-Forbearing. (102) Indeed some people before you had asked such questions and in consequence fell into unbelief.[117]

يَٰٓأَيُّهَا ٱلَّذِينَ ءَامَنُوا۟ لَا تَسْـَٔلُوا۟
عَنْ أَشْيَآءَ إِن تُبْدَ لَكُمْ تَسُؤْكُمْ وَإِن
تَسْـَٔلُوا۟ عَنْهَا حِينَ يُنَزَّلُ ٱلْقُرْءَانُ تُبْدَ
لَكُمْ عَفَا ٱللَّهُ عَنْهَا ۗ وَٱللَّهُ غَفُورٌ حَلِيمٌ
﴿١٠١﴾ قَدْ سَأَلَهَا قَوْمٌ مِّن قَبْلِكُمْ
ثُمَّ أَصْبَحُوا۟ بِهَا كَٰفِرِينَ ﴿١٠٢﴾

---

injunctions revealed by God were conducive to their well-being, and that underlying them were a great many benefits and advantages for them which they themselves could neither have grasped nor achieved by their own contriving.

115. This verse enunciates a standard of evaluation and judgement quite distinct from the standards employed by superficial people. For the latter, for instance, a hundred dollars are worth more than five dollars, since a hundred is more than five. But, according to this verse, if those hundred dollars have been earned in a manner entailing the disobedience of God the entire amount becomes unclean. If, on the contrary, a man earns five dollars while obeying God then this amount is clean; and anything which is unclean, whatever its quantity, cannot be worth that which is clean. A drop of perfume is more valuable than a heap of filth; a palmful of clean water is much more valuable than a huge cauldron brimming with urine. A truly wise person should therefore necessarily be content with whatever he acquires by clean, permissible means, however small and humble its quantity may be. He should not reach out for what is prohibited, however large in quantity and glittering in appearance.

116. People used to ask the Prophet (peace be on him) many questions which were of no practical relevance to either religious or day-to-day affairs. Once, for instance, a person asked the Prophet (peace be on him) in the presence of a crowd: 'Who is my real father?' Likewise, many people used to ask unnecessary questions about legal matters. By these uncalled for inquiries they sought knowledge of matters which had for good reasons, been deliberately left undetermined by the Law-giver. In the Qur'ān, for example, Pilgrimage had been declared obligatory. A person who became

aware of this came to the Prophet (peace be on him) and inquired: 'Has it been made obligatory to perform it every year?' To this the Prophet (peace be on him) made no reply. When he inquired for the second time the Prophet (peace be on him) again stayed silent. On being asked for the third time, he said: 'Pity on you! Had I uttered "Yes" in reply to your question, it would have become obligatory to perform it every year. And then you would not have been able to observe it and would have been guilty of disobedience.' (See Bukhārī, 'Riqāq', 22; 'Zakāh', 53; 'I'tiṣām', 3; 'Adab', 6; Muslim, 'Aqḍiyah', 10, 11, 13, 14; Dārimī, 'Riqāq', 38; Muwaṭṭa', 'Kalām', 20; Aḥmad b. Ḥanbal, *Musnad*, vol. 2, pp. 327, 360, 367; vol. 4, pp. 246, 249, 250, 251, 255 – Ed.)

The Prophet (peace be on him) discouraged people from being over-inquisitive and unnecessarily curious about every question. We find in the *Ḥadīth* the following saying from the Prophet (peace be on him): 'The worst criminal among the Muslims is the one who inquired about something which had not been made unlawful, and then it was declared so, because of his inquiry.' (Bukhārī, 'I'tiṣām', 3; Muslim, 'Faḍā'il', 132, 133; Abū Dā'ūd, 'Sunnah', 6 – Ed.) According to another tradition the Prophet (peace be on him) said: 'God has imposed upon you certain obligations, do not neglect them; He has imposed certain prohibitions, do not violate them; He has imposed certain limits, do not even approach them; and He has remained silent about certain matters – and has not done so out of forgetfulness – do not pursue them.' (See *Towards Understanding the Qur'ān*, vol. I, *Sūrah* 2, n. 110 – Ed.)

In both these traditions an important fact has been called to our attention. In matters where the Law-giver has chosen to lay down certain injunctions only broadly, without any elaborate details, or quantitative specifications, He has done so not because of neglect or forgetfulness. Such seeming omissions are deliberate, and the reason thereof is that He does not desire to place limitations upon people, but prefers to allow them latitude and ease in following His commandments. Now there are some people who make unnecessary inquiries, cause elaborately prescribed, inflexibly determined and restrictive regulations to be added to the Law. Some others, in cases where such details are in no way deducible from the text, resort to analogical reasoning, thereby turning a broad general rule into an elaborate law full of restrictive details, and an unspecified into a specified rule. Both sorts of people put Muslims in great danger. For, in the area of belief, the more detailed the doctrines to which people are required to subscribe, the more problematic it becomes to do so. Likewise, in legal matters, the greater the restriction, the greater the likelihood of violation.

117. Some people first indulged in hair-splitting arguments about their laws and dogma, and thereby wove a great web of credal elaborations and legal minutiae. Then they became enmeshed in this same web and thus became guilty of dogmatic errors and the violation of their own religious laws. The people referred to here are the Jews, and the Muslims who

(103) Allah has neither appointed (cattle devoted to idols such as) *Baḥīrah, Sā'ibah, Waṣīlah* nor *Ḥām;*[118] but those who disbelieve forge lies against Allah and of them most have no understanding (and therefore succumb to such superstitions). (104) When they are asked: 'Come to what Allah has revealed, and come to the Messenger', they reply: 'The way of our forefathers suffices us.' (Will they continue to follow their forefathers) even though their forefathers might have known nothing, and might have been on the wrong way?

مَا جَعَلَ ٱللَّهُ مِنۢ بَحِيرَةٍ وَلَا سَآئِبَةٍ وَلَا
وَصِيلَةٍ وَلَا حَامٍ وَلَٰكِنَّ ٱلَّذِينَ كَفَرُوا۟
يَفْتَرُونَ عَلَى ٱللَّهِ ٱلْكَذِبَ وَأَكْثَرُهُمْ
لَا يَعْقِلُونَ ﴿١٠٣﴾ وَإِذَا قِيلَ لَهُمْ تَعَالَوْا۟
إِلَىٰ مَآ أَنزَلَ ٱللَّهُ وَإِلَى ٱلرَّسُولِ قَالُوا۟
حَسْبُنَا مَا وَجَدْنَا عَلَيْهِ ءَابَآءَنَآ أَوَلَوْ
كَانَ ءَابَآؤُهُمْ لَا يَعْلَمُونَ شَيْـًٔا وَلَا
يَهْتَدُونَ ﴿١٠٤﴾

---

followed in their footsteps and left no stone unturned, despite the warnings contained in the Qur'ān and in the sayings of the Prophet Muḥammad (peace be on him).

118. Just as, in the Indian subcontinent, cows, oxen and goats are set free after being consecrated either to God or to some idol or shrine or to some saintly person, and just as people consider it prohibited either to put them to work, to slaughter them or to derive any other kind of benefit from them, so the Arabs of the *Jāhilīyah* period also let loose certain animals after consecrating them. Such animals were variously named.

Baḥīrah was the name of a female camel which had already borne five young, the last of which was a male. The practice was to slit the ear of such a camel and then let her loose. Thereafter no one could ride her, use her milk, slaughter her or shear her hair. She was entitled to graze and drink water wherever she liked.

Sā'ibah was the name of either a male or female camel which had been let loose after consecration as a mark of gratitude in fulfilment of a vow taken for either the recovery from some ailment or delivery from some danger. In the same way the female camel which had borne ten times, and each time a female, was also let loose.

Waṣīlah. If the first kid born to a goat was a male, it was slaughtered in the name of the deities; but if it was a female, it was kept by the owners for themselves. If twins were born and one of them was a male and the

(105) Believers! Take heed of your own selves. If you are rightly guided, the error of he who strays will not harm you.[119] To Allah will all of you return; then He will let all of you know what you did.

يَـٰٓأَيُّهَا ٱلَّذِينَ ءَامَنُوا۟ عَلَيْكُمْ أَنفُسَكُمْ
لَا يَضُرُّكُم مَّن ضَلَّ إِذَا ٱهْتَدَيْتُمْ إِلَى
ٱللَّهِ مَرْجِعُكُمْ جَمِيعًا فَيُنَبِّئُكُم بِمَا
كُنتُمْ تَعْمَلُونَ ﴿١٠٥﴾

---

other a female goat, the male was not slaughtered but rather let loose in the name of the deities. This male goat was called *waṣīlah.*

Ḥām. If the young of camels in the second degree of descent had become worthy of riding they were let loose. Likewise, if ten offspring had been borne by a female camel she was also let loose, and called *ḥām.*

119. What is stressed here is that rather than occupying himself unduly with examining faults in the belief and conduct of others, a man should pay greater attention to a critical examination of his own conduct. His primary concern should be with his own faith and conduct. If a man is himself obedient to God, observes his duties to Him and to His creatures including his duty to promote what is good and forbid what is evil, and lives according to the dictates of righteousness and honesty, he has fulfilled his obligation and if others persist either in false beliefs or in moral corruption their errors cannot harm him.

This verse in no way means that a man should care only for his own salvation and should remain unconcerned with the reform of others. Abū Bakr removed this misconception in one of his sermons when he remarked: 'You recite this verse but interpret it erroneously. I have heard the Messenger of Allah (peace be on him) say that when people see corruption but do not try to change it; and when they see a wrong-doer commit wrong but do not prevent him from doing so, it is not unlikely that God's chastisement will seize them all. By God, it is incumbent upon you that you bid what is good and forbid what is evil or else God will grant domination upon you to those who are the worst among you. They will greatly chastise you and then when your righteous ones pray to God, their prayers will not be answered.'

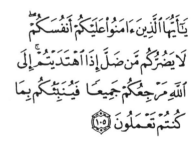

(106) Believers! When death approaches you, let two men of equity among you act as witnesses when you make your bequest;[120] or let two of those from others than yourselves* act as witnesses if you are on a journey when the affliction of death befalls you.[121] Then if any doubt occurs you shall detain both of them (in the mosque) after the Prayer, and they shall swear by Allah: 'We shall neither sell our testimony in return for any gain even though it concerns any near of kin nor shall we conceal our testimony which we owe to Allah, for then we should become among sinners.' (107) Then if it is discovered later that the two are guilty of such sin, then two others shall stand in their place from among those against whom the two had sinfully deposed, and swear by Allah: 'Our testimony is truer than the testimony of the other two, and we have not transgressed in our statement; for then indeed we would become wrong-doers.'

يَـٰٓأَيُّهَا ٱلَّذِينَ ءَامَنُوا۟ شَهَـٰدَةُ بَيْنِكُمْ إِذَا
حَضَرَ أَحَدَكُمُ ٱلْمَوْتُ حِينَ ٱلْوَصِيَّةِ
ٱثْنَانِ ذَوَا عَدْلٍ مِّنكُمْ أَوْ ءَاخَرَانِ مِنْ
غَيْرِكُمْ إِنْ أَنتُمْ ضَرَبْتُمْ فِى ٱلْأَرْضِ
فَأَصَـٰبَتْكُم مُّصِيبَةُ ٱلْمَوْتِ
تَحْبِسُونَهُمَا مِنۢ بَعْدِ ٱلصَّلَوٰةِ
فَيُقْسِمَانِ بِٱللَّهِ إِنِ ٱرْتَبْتُمْ لَا نَشْتَرِى
بِهِۦ ثَمَنًا وَلَوْ كَانَ ذَا قُرْبَىٰ وَلَا نَكْتُمُ
شَهَـٰدَةَ ٱللَّهِ إِنَّآ إِذًا لَّمِنَ ٱلْـَٔاثِمِينَ ﴿١٠٦﴾
فَإِنْ عُثِرَ عَلَىٰٓ أَنَّهُمَا ٱسْتَحَقَّآ إِثْمًا فَـَٔاخَرَانِ
يَقُومَانِ مَقَامَهُمَا مِنَ ٱلَّذِينَ ٱسْتَحَقَّ
عَلَيْهِمُ ٱلْأَوْلَيَـٰنِ فَيُقْسِمَانِ بِٱللَّهِ
لَشَهَـٰدَتُنَآ أَحَقُّ مِن شَهَـٰدَتِهِمَا وَمَا
ٱعْتَدَيْنَآ إِنَّآ إِذًا لَّمِنَ ٱلظَّـٰلِمِينَ ﴿١٠٧﴾

120. That is, pious, straightforward and trustworthy Muslims.

121. This shows that the testimony of non-Muslim witnesses in cases involving Muslims is appropriate only when no Muslim is available as a witness.

*That is, non-Muslims – Ed.

(108) Thus it is more likely that they will either bear the right testimony or else they will at least fear that their oaths may be rebutted by other oaths. Have fear of Allah and pay heed. Allah does not direct the disobedient to the right way.

(109) The Day[122] when Allah will gather together the Messengers[123] and say: 'What answer were you given?' They will reply: 'We have no real knowledge of it.[124] You alone fully know all that lies beyond the reach of human perception.' ▶

ذَٰلِكَ أَدْنَىٰٓ أَن يَأْتُوا۟ بِٱلشَّهَـٰدَةِ عَلَىٰ
وَجْهِهَآ أَوْ يَخَافُوٓا۟ أَن تُرَدَّ أَيْمَـٰنٌۢ بَعْدَ
أَيْمَـٰنِهِمْ ۗ وَٱتَّقُوا۟ ٱللَّهَ وَٱسْمَعُوا۟ ۗ وَٱللَّهُ
لَا يَهْدِى ٱلْقَوْمَ ٱلْفَـٰسِقِينَ ﴿١٠٨﴾ ۞ يَوْمَ
يَجْمَعُ ٱللَّهُ ٱلرُّسُلَ فَيَقُولُ مَاذَآ أُجِبْتُمْ ۖ
قَالُوا۟ لَا عِلْمَ لَنَآ ۖ إِنَّكَ أَنتَ عَلَّـٰمُ
ٱلْغُيُوبِ ﴿١٠٩﴾

122. This refers to the Day of Judgement.

123. The reference here is to the response of the world to the call of the Prophets.

124. This reply indicates that the Prophets would say that their knowledge was confined to that limited, outward response which they had encountered during their lifetimes. The true reaction to their call at various places and in different forms would only be known completely to God Himself.

(110) Imagine, then, when Allah will say:[125] 'Jesus, son of Mary, recall My favour upon you and your mother, and when I strengthened you with the spirit of holiness so that you talked to men in the cradle and also when you became of age; and when I taught you the Book and Wisdom, and the Torah and the Gospel; and when, by My leave, you fashioned from clay the likeness of a bird and you breathed into it, and by My leave it became a bird; you healed, by My leave, the blind from birth and the leprous; and when, by My leave, you caused the dead to come to life.[126] And recall when I restrained the Israelites from you when you came to them with clear proofs whereupon those of them who disbelieved said: "This is nothing but clear magic." ▶

إِذْ قَالَ ٱللَّهُ يَٰعِيسَى ٱبْنَ مَرْيَمَ ٱذْكُرْ
نِعْمَتِى عَلَيْكَ وَعَلَىٰ وَٰلِدَتِكَ إِذْ
أَيَّدتُّكَ بِرُوحِ ٱلْقُدُسِ تُكَلِّمُ
ٱلنَّاسَ فِى ٱلْمَهْدِ وَكَهْلًا ۖ وَإِذْ
عَلَّمْتُكَ ٱلْكِتَٰبَ وَٱلْحِكْمَةَ
وَٱلتَّوْرَىٰةَ وَٱلْإِنجِيلَ ۖ وَإِذْ تَخْلُقُ
مِنَ ٱلطِّينِ كَهَيْـَٔةِ ٱلطَّيْرِ بِإِذْنِى
فَتَنفُخُ فِيهَا فَتَكُونُ طَيْرًۢا بِإِذْنِى ۖ
وَتُبْرِئُ ٱلْأَكْمَهَ وَٱلْأَبْرَصَ
بِإِذْنِى ۖ وَإِذْ تُخْرِجُ ٱلْمَوْتَىٰ بِإِذْنِى ۖ
وَإِذْ كَفَفْتُ بَنِىٓ إِسْرَٰٓءِيلَ
عَنكَ إِذْ جِئْتَهُم بِٱلْبَيِّنَٰتِ فَقَالَ
ٱلَّذِينَ كَفَرُوا۟ مِنْهُمْ إِنْ هَٰذَآ إِلَّا سِحْرٌ
مُّبِينٌ ﴿١١٠﴾

125. The initial question would be addressed to all Prophets as such. Then each of them would be called upon to bear witness separately, as stated in several places in the Qur'ān. In this connection the question that will be addressed to Jesus is specifically mentioned here.

126. That is, with God's command Jesus brought people to life from the state of death.

(111) And recall when I revealed to the disciples to believe in Me and in My Messenger, they said: "We do believe, and we bear witness that we indeed are the ones who submit to Allah'"*[127] (112) Also recall when the disciples asked Jesus,[128] son of Mary: 'Jesus, son of Mary, has your Lord the power to send down to us a repast from the heaven?' Thereupon Jesus said: 'Fear Allah if you do indeed have faith.' (113) They said: 'We desire to partake of it that our hearts be satisfied and we know that you did speak the truth to us, and that we are its witnesses.'

وَإِذْ أَوْحَيْتُ إِلَى الْحَوَارِيِّـنَ أَنْ
ءَامِنُوا بِي وَبِرَسُولِي قَالُوٓا ءَامَنَّا
وَاشْهَدْ بِأَنَّنَا مُسْلِمُونَ ﴿١١١﴾ إِذْ قَالَ
الْحَوَارِيُّونَ يَٰعِيسَى ابْنَ مَرْيَمَ هَلْ
يَسْتَطِيعُ رَبُّكَ أَنْ يُنَزِّلَ عَلَيْنَا
مَآئِدَةً مِّنَ السَّمَآءِ قَالَ اتَّقُوا اللَّهَ
إِن كُنتُم مُّؤْمِنِينَ ﴿١١٢﴾ قَالُوا نُرِيدُ
أَن نَّأْكُلَ مِنْهَا وَتَطْمَئِنَّ قُلُوبُنَا
وَنَعْلَمَ أَن قَدْ صَدَقْتَنَا وَنَكُونَ
عَلَيْهَا مِنَ الشَّٰهِدِينَ ﴿١١٣﴾

127. Jesus is being told that the faith of the disciples in him was also the result of God's grace and succour, for he, himself, did not have the power to produce even one man of faith in that land of disbelief. It is also made clear that the true religion of the disciples of Jesus was Islam.

128. Since the disciples have been mentioned here, the continuity of the subject is interrupted momentarily in order to introduce another incident connected with the disciples. This clearly shows that those who had been directly instructed by Jesus considered him merely a human being and a slave of God; they had no conception of their master either being God or a partner of God or the son of God. Jesus had, rather, presented himself to them as a slave of God with no claims to divine authority.

One might feel inclined here to raise the question: What is the occasion for this parenthetical interjection in a conversation that is to take place on the Day of Judgement? This parenthesis, in my opinion, is not in fact part of such a conversation, but rather forms part of a discussion in this world regarding a conversation that will take place on the Day of Judgement. The conversation that will take place on the Day of Judgement is mentioned here precisely in order that the Christians may derive a lesson from it and

*That is, are Muslims – Ed.

(114) Jesus, son of Mary, then prayed: 'O Allah, our Lord, send down to us a repast from the heavens that shall be a festival for the first of us and for the last of us, and a sign from You. And provide us with sustenance, for You are the best Provider of sustenance.' (115) Allah said: 'I shall indeed send it down to you;[129] then, I shall afflict whoever among you who disbelieves with a chastisement wherewith I will afflict none in the worlds.' (116) And imagine when thereafter Allah will say: 'Jesus, son of Mary, did you say to people: "Take me and my mother for gods beside Allah?"[130] and he will answer: "Glory to You! It was not for me to say what I had no right to. Had I said so, You would surely have known it. You know all what is within my mind whereas I do not know what is within Yours. You, indeed You, know fully all that is beyond the reach of human perception. ▶

قَالَ عِيسَى ٱبْنُ مَرْيَمَ ٱللَّهُمَّ رَبَّنَآ أَنزِلْ
عَلَيْنَا مَآئِدَةً مِّنَ ٱلسَّمَآءِ تَكُونُ لَنَا
عِيدًا لِّأَوَّلِنَا وَءَاخِرِنَا وَءَايَةً مِّنكَ
وَٱرْزُقْنَا وَأَنتَ خَيْرُ ٱلرَّٰزِقِينَ ﴿١١٤﴾ قَالَ
ٱللَّهُ إِنِّى مُنَزِّلُهَا عَلَيْكُمْ فَمَن يَكْفُرْ بَعْدُ
مِنكُمْ فَإِنِّىٓ أُعَذِّبُهُۥ عَذَابًا لَّآ أُعَذِّبُهُۥٓ
أَحَدًا مِّنَ ٱلْعَٰلَمِينَ ﴿١١٥﴾ وَإِذْ قَالَ ٱللَّهُ
يَٰعِيسَى ٱبْنَ مَرْيَمَ ءَأَنتَ قُلْتَ لِلنَّاسِ
ٱتَّخِذُونِى وَأُمِّىَ إِلَٰهَيْنِ مِن دُونِ ٱللَّهِ
قَالَ سُبْحَٰنَكَ مَا يَكُونُ لِىٓ أَنْ أَقُولَ
مَا لَيْسَ لِى بِحَقٍّ إِن كُنتُ قُلْتُهُۥ فَقَدْ
عَلِمْتَهُۥ تَعْلَمُ مَا فِى نَفْسِى وَلَآ أَعْلَمُ مَا
فِى نَفْسِكَ إِنَّكَ أَنتَ عَلَّٰمُ ٱلْغُيُوبِ ﴿١١٦﴾

---

direct themselves to the right way. Hence, the mention of this incident regarding the disciples – even though it seems to interrupt the continuity of narration – is in no sense out of place.

129. The Qur'ān is silent on the question of whether this meal was sent down in response to this prayer. There is also no other authoritative basis to help us arrive at a clear conclusion. It is possible that the repast was actually sent down. It is also possible that the disciples withdrew their prayer after hearing the stern warning in response to it.

(117) I said to them nothing except what You commanded me, that is: 'Serve Allah, my Lord and your Lord.' I watched over them as long as I remained among them; and when You did recall me, then You Yourself became the Watcher over them. Indeed, You are Witness over everything. (118) If You chastise them, they are Your servants; and if You forgive them, You are the All-Mighty, the All-Wise."' (119) Thereupon Allah will say: 'This day truthfulness shall profit the truthful. For them are Gardens beneath which rivers flow. There they will abide for ever. Allah is well-pleased with them, and they well-pleased with Allah. That indeed is the mighty triumph.'

(120) To Allah belongs the dominion of the heavens and the earth and all that is in them and He has full power over everything.

مَا قُلْتُ لَهُمْ إِلَّا مَآ أَمَرْتَنِي بِهِۦٓ أَنِ ٱعْبُدُوا۟
ٱللَّهَ رَبِّي وَرَبَّكُمْ ۚ وَكُنتُ عَلَيْهِمْ شَهِيدًا
مَّا دُمْتُ فِيهِمْ ۖ فَلَمَّا تَوَفَّيْتَنِي كُنتَ أَنتَ
ٱلرَّقِيبَ عَلَيْهِمْ ۚ وَأَنتَ عَلَىٰ كُلِّ شَيْءٍ
شَهِيدٌ ﴿١١٧﴾ إِن تُعَذِّبْهُمْ فَإِنَّهُمْ عِبَادُكَ ۖ
وَإِن تَغْفِرْ لَهُمْ فَإِنَّكَ أَنتَ ٱلْعَزِيزُ
ٱلْحَكِيمُ ﴿١١٨﴾ قَالَ ٱللَّهُ هَٰذَا يَوْمُ يَنفَعُ
ٱلصَّٰدِقِينَ صِدْقُهُمْ ۚ لَهُمْ جَنَّٰتٌ تَجْرِي مِن
تَحْتِهَا ٱلْأَنْهَٰرُ خَٰلِدِينَ فِيهَآ أَبَدًا ۚ رَّضِيَ
ٱللَّهُ عَنْهُمْ وَرَضُوا۟ عَنْهُ ۚ ذَٰلِكَ ٱلْفَوْزُ ٱلْعَظِيمُ ﴿١١٩﴾
لِلَّهِ مُلْكُ ٱلسَّمَٰوَٰتِ وَٱلْأَرْضِ وَمَا فِيهِنَّ ۚ
وَهُوَ عَلَىٰ كُلِّ شَيْءٍ قَدِيرٌۢ ﴿١٢٠﴾

---

130. The Christians were not content merely with deifying Jesus and the Holy Spirit. They even turned Mary, the mother of Jesus, into a full-fledged object of worship. The Bible does not contain even the remotest suggestion that Mary was in any way either divine or superhuman. During the first three centuries after the Messiah, such a concept was totally alien to Christian thinking. Towards the end of the third century of the Christian era, however, some theologians of Alexandria employed, for the first time, the expression 'Mother of God' in connection with Mary. Subsequently, belief in Mary's divinity and the practice of Mariolatry began to spread among Christians. Even then, however, the Church was not prepared to

accord official approval to this belief and denounced the Mariolaters as heretics. It was not until the Council of Ephesus in 431 that the Church officially used the expression 'Mother of God' for Mary. The result was that Mariolatry began to spread fast within the Church itself, so much so that, by the time of the revelation of the Qur'ān, Mary had become so important a deity that she obscured even the Father, the Son and the Holy Ghost. Statues of Mary adorned the cathedrals. She became the object of rites and worship. People addressed their prayers to her. She was regarded as the one who responded to people's supplications, who heeded people's grievances and complaints, who relieved them in distress, who provided support and succour to the helpless. For a devout Christian there could be no greater source of comfort and inner strength than the belief that he enjoyed the support and patronage of the 'Mother of God'. In the preamble of his code, Justinian had declared Mary to be the defender and supporter of his empire, and his general, Marses, sought Mary's guidance on the battlefield. Heraclius, a contemporary of the Prophet (peace be on him), had a picture of Mary on his standard and he was confident that by her grace the standard would never be lowered. Several centuries later the Protestants argued strongly against Mariolatry during the movement which led to the Reformation. The Roman Catholic Church has, nevertheless, managed so far to cling to Mariolatry in one form or another.

Sūrah 6

Al-An'ām

(Makkan Period)

Title

The title refers to verses 136 ff., which dispel the superstitions common in Arabia regarding the unlawfulness of various types of cattle.

Period of Revelation

According to a tradition from Ibn 'Abbās, this *sūrah* was revealed as one piece in Makka. (Cf. the introduction to the *sūrah* by Qurṭubī and 'Ālūsī, and the traditions mentioned therein – Ed.) Asmā' bint Yazīd, the cousin of Mu'ādh b. Jabal, says: 'When this *sūrah* was being revealed to the Prophet (peace be on him) he was mounted on a she-camel, whose nose-string I was holding in my hand. The burden on the she-camel was so excessive that it seemed as if her bones would soon snap into pieces.' Traditions also mention that the Prophet (peace be on him) had this *sūrah* written down the very night it was revealed.

From a glance at the subjects discussed, it is evident that this *sūrah* must have been revealed during the last period of the Prophet's life in Makka. This seems to be confirmed by the tradition from Asmā' bint Yazīd (cited above), for she belonged to the *Anṣār* (Helpers) of Madina, and embraced Islam after the Prophet's migration to the city. Assuming that she visited the Prophet (peace be on him) in Makka, as an admirer, before having embraced Islam, this visit must have taken place during the very last year of the Prophet's stay in Makka. Before that stage, relations between the Prophet (peace be on him) and the people of Madina were not so close as to have occasioned a visit by a woman.

Background

At the time when this *sūrah* was revealed the Messenger of God (peace be on him) had already spent twelve years calling people to Islam. Resistance to this movement, and the persecution and oppression of the Muslims at the hands of the Quraysh, had reached their apogee. Many Muslims had even forsaken their homeland because of constant harassment and had settled in Abyssinia. The Prophet (peace be on him) himself had been deprived of the protection of his uncle, Abū Ṭālib, and the support of his wife, Khadījah, for both had by then passed away. Although cut off from all earthly support, the Prophet (peace be on him) continued to preach his message in the face of severe opposition. Thanks to these efforts, the righteous among the inhabitants of Makka and its environs began to embrace Islam. Nevertheless, the people as a whole seemed bent upon rejecting the message of the Prophet (peace be on him). As soon as a person showed the slightest inclination to Islam, he was derided and subjected to physical persecution and social and economic boycott. In this bleak situation, a faint ray of hope arose from Yathrib (later to be called Madina). A number of influential members of the Aws and Khazraj tribes of this city had already visited the Prophet (peace be on him) and had taken the oath of fealty at his hands. From then on Islam began to spread there without significant internal resistance. But few could have had the insight to appreciate in full measure the potentialities for the future in this modest beginning. As commonly perceived, Islam was then a moribund movement without material support, a movement whose leader was backed by no power except the feeble protection of his own family, a movement whose tiny band of helpless followers had been scattered like dry leaves and for no other reason than that they had abandoned the beliefs and way of life of their people.

Main Themes

Such were the conditions at the time when this *sūrah* was revealed, and its themes may be classified into the following categories:

(1) to repudiate polytheism and call men to pure monotheism;

(2) to preach belief in the Hereafter and refute the notion that there will be no life after the present one;
(3) to refute the pagan superstitions to which people had fallen a prey;
(4) to inculcate the principles on the basis of which Islam seeks to erect the structure of human society;
(5) to clarify the issues relating to objections raised against the message of the Prophet (peace be on him);
(6) to console the Prophet (peace be on him) and the Muslims in general who had begun to feel disconcerted, even heart-broken, by the fact that despite their long struggle their mission did not seem to be making effective headway; and
(7) to admonish and warn those who, in their heedlessness, inebriated folly and self-destructive ignorance, had adopted an attitude of denial and opposition to the Truth.

The *sūrah* does not deal separately with each of these subjects; it takes up one after the other and treats them in a different fashion on each occasion.

The Prophet's Life in Makka

Since in the following pages the reader will be studying a *sūrah* which was revealed during the Prophet's life in Makka, it seems pertinent to place before him a detailed background to the Makkan *sūrahs* as a whole.

The exact period of revelation of the Madinan *sūrahs* is more or less known to us. In fact, there are reliable traditions which refer to the revelation of individual verses as opposed to *sūrahs*. Our information regarding the Makkan *sūrahs*, however, is not abundant. There are very few *sūrahs* and verses for which we possess well-established and fully trustworthy traditions regarding their context and period of revelation. The reason is that the Makkan period of the Prophet's life was not recorded in such elaborate detail as the Madinan period. So instead of relying on direct, historical traditions and evidence we have to look at the internal evidence provided by the themes, contents and styles of different *sūrahs*, and on the direct and indirect allusions to their background. Such fragmentary evidence does not enable us to state with certainty the exact date or year in which a particular *sūrah* or verse was revealed. The most that we can do is to bear in mind the various pieces of evidence found in the Makkan *sūrahs*, to recall the main incidents in the Makkan period of the life of the Prophet (peace be on him), and then conclude, by comparing the two, which Makkan *sūrah* belongs to one and which to the other period of the Prophet's life in Makka.

When we review the life of the Prophet (peace be on him) in Makka, from this standpoint, it seems to be divided into four major periods.

The first period commenced with the entrustment of the Prophetic mission to Muḥammad (peace be on him) and lasted for about three years, concluding with the public announcement of his message. During this period the spreading of the message was secret and discreet. It was addressed to a select few, with the result that the Makkans, in general, were scarcely aware of it.

The second period lasted for about two years, that is, from the public announcement of his ministry until the beginning of persecution and oppression. The initial opposition turned into active resistance, then into a campaign of derision and lampooning, of slander, abuse and false propaganda, and of organized blocs of opposition. The result was that in the end those Muslims who were relatively poor, weak, and lacked support were badly harassed and even physically intimidated.

The third period opened with the start of persecution (the sixth year of prophethood) and lasted up till the death of the Prophet's uncle Abū Ṭālib, and his wife, Khadījah in the tenth year of prophethood. This period, therefore, lasted for about five or six years. During it, opposition turned into violent hostility and because of the persecution and cruelty perpetrated by the pagans of Makka a good many Muslims migrated to Abyssinia. The Prophet (peace be on him), his family, his Companions and the rest of the Muslims were subjected to economic and social boycott with the result that they were confined to the ravine known as Shi'b Abī Ṭālib.

The fourth period extended from the year 10 until the year 13 of prophethood. This was the period of utmost hardship and suffering for the Prophet (peace be on him) and his Companions. His life in Makka was made unbearable. When he went to Ṭā'if, that city offered him no shelter. On the occasion of *Ḥajj*, the Prophet (peace be on him) approached every single tribe with an appeal to accept his message, but the answer from each of them was a disappointing 'no'. The Makkans deliberated among themselves again and again as to what they should do with the Prophet (peace be on him): should they kill him, put him in prison, or should they banish him from their town? Ultimately, by the grace of God, the hearts of the *Anṣār* (Helpers) opened to Islam, and at their invitation the Prophet (peace be on him) migrated to Madina.

The *sūrahs* revealed in each of these four periods are distinct from those revealed in the other periods, both in terms of content and style. At various places we find allusions to incidents which throw a clear enough light on the background against which the different parts of the *sūrahs* were revealed. The characteristics of each period are, to a large extent, conspicuous in the respective *sūrah* sections. It is on the basis of such indications that we shall try to determine, in our introductory remarks to each Makkan *sūrah* in this work, the exact Makkan period in which it was revealed.

In the name of Allah, the Merciful, the Compassionate.

(1) All praise is for Allah alone, Who created the heavens and the earth, and brought into being light and darkness, and yet those who have rejected the call of the Truth ascribe others to be equals to their Lord.[1] (2) He it is Who has created you out of clay,[2] and then decreed a term (of life), and has also appointed another term, a term determined with Him.[3] Yet you are in doubt! (3) And He it is Who is One True God in the heavens and in the earth. He knows your deeds – both secret and open – and knows fully whatever you earn.

بِسۡمِ ٱللَّهِ ٱلرَّحۡمَٰنِ ٱلرَّحِيمِ

ٱلۡحَمۡدُ لِلَّهِ ٱلَّذِي خَلَقَ ٱلسَّمَٰوَٰتِ
وَٱلۡأَرۡضَ وَجَعَلَ ٱلظُّلُمَٰتِ وَٱلنُّورَۖ ثُمَّ
ٱلَّذِينَ كَفَرُواْ بِرَبِّهِمۡ يَعۡدِلُونَ ١
هُوَ ٱلَّذِي خَلَقَكُم مِّن طِينٖ ثُمَّ قَضَىٰٓ
أَجَلٗاۖ وَأَجَلٞ مُّسَمًّى عِندَهُۥۖ ثُمَّ أَنتُمۡ
تَمۡتَرُونَ ٢ وَهُوَ ٱللَّهُ فِي ٱلسَّمَٰوَٰتِ
وَفِي ٱلۡأَرۡضِ يَعۡلَمُ سِرَّكُمۡ وَجَهۡرَكُمۡ
وَيَعۡلَمُ مَا تَكۡسِبُونَ ٣

1. Remember that, although polytheists, the Arabs to whom these verses are addressed did acknowledge God as the Creator of the heavens and the earth, Who causes day to alternate with night, and Who has brought into existence the sun and the moon. None of them attributed any of these acts to either al-Lāt, al-Hubal, al-'Uzzá or any other deities. Why, then, should they prostrate themselves before others beside the Creator? Why should they offer their prayers and supplications to any but God? (See *Towards Understanding the Qur'ān,* vol. I, *Sūrah* 1, n. 2, and *Sūrah* 2, n. 163.)

The actual word that has been used in the original text for 'darkness' is in the plural. The contrast with the singular 'light' is significant: whereas light is one, there can be innumerable degrees of darkness, which is the absence of light.

(4) Yet every time a sign of their Lord comes to them, they turn away from it, (5) and thus they gave the lie to the Truth that has now come to them. Soon they will come upon some news concerning what they had mocked at.[4] (6) Have they not seen how many a people We have destroyed before them? People whom We had made more powerful in the earth than you are and upon them We showered from the heavens abundant rains, and at whose feet We caused the rivers to flow? And then (when they behaved ungratefully) We destroyed them for their sins, and raised other peoples in their place.

وَمَا تَأْتِيهِم مِّنْ ءَايَةٍ مِّنْ ءَايَٰتِ رَبِّهِمْ
إِلَّا كَانُوا۟ عَنْهَا مُعْرِضِينَ ﴿٤﴾ فَقَدْ كَذَّبُوا۟
بِٱلْحَقِّ لَمَّا جَآءَهُمْ ۖ فَسَوْفَ يَأْتِيهِمْ أَنۢبَٰٓؤُا۟
مَا كَانُوا۟ بِهِۦ يَسْتَهْزِءُونَ ﴿٥﴾ أَلَمْ يَرَوْا۟ كَمْ
أَهْلَكْنَا مِن قَبْلِهِم مِّن قَرْنٍ مَّكَّنَّٰهُمْ فِى
ٱلْأَرْضِ مَا لَمْ نُمَكِّن لَّكُمْ وَأَرْسَلْنَا
ٱلسَّمَآءَ عَلَيْهِم مِّدْرَارًا وَجَعَلْنَا ٱلْأَنْهَٰرَ
تَجْرِى مِن تَحْتِهِمْ فَأَهْلَكْنَٰهُم بِذُنُوبِهِمْ
وَأَنشَأْنَا مِنۢ بَعْدِهِمْ قَرْنًا ءَاخَرِينَ ﴿٦﴾

---

2. The elements composing the human organism are all, without exception, derived from the earth. Hence it is said that man has been created out of clay.

3. This alludes to the Hour of Judgement when human beings, regardless of the age in which they lived, will be brought back to life and summoned to render an account before their Lord.

4. The allusion here is to the Migration *(Hijrah)* and the numerous victories destined to follow it in quick succession. When this allusion was made, the unbelievers could not have guessed what kind of news they would receive, and even the Muslims could not have imagined those developments. In fact, the Prophet himself (peace be on him) was not fully aware of the possibilities which lay in store.

(7) (O Messenger!) Had We sent down to you a book inscribed on parchment, and had they even touched it with their own hands, the unbelievers would still have said: 'This is nothing but plain magic.' (8) They also say: 'Why has no angel been sent down to this Prophet?'[5] Had We sent down an angel, the matter would surely have long been decided and no respite would have been granted them.[6] (9) Had We appointed an angel, We would have sent him down in the form of a man – and thus We would have caused them the same doubt which they now entertain.[7]

وَلَوْ نَزَّلْنَا عَلَيْكَ كِتَٰبًا فِى قِرْطَاسٍ فَلَمَسُوهُ
بِأَيْدِيهِمْ لَقَالَ ٱلَّذِينَ كَفَرُوٓا۟ إِنْ هَٰذَآ إِلَّا
سِحْرٌ مُّبِينٌ ﴿٧﴾ وَقَالُوا۟ لَوْلَآ أُنزِلَ عَلَيْهِ
مَلَكٌ ۖ وَلَوْ أَنزَلْنَا مَلَكًا لَّقُضِىَ ٱلْأَمْرُ ثُمَّ
لَا يُنظَرُونَ ﴿٨﴾ وَلَوْ جَعَلْنَٰهُ مَلَكًا
لَّجَعَلْنَٰهُ رَجُلًا وَلَلَبَسْنَا عَلَيْهِم مَّا
يَلْبِسُونَ ﴿٩﴾

5. The unbelievers were saying that if Muḥammad (peace be on him) had indeed been endowed with prophethood, an angel should have been sent down from heaven to announce that he was the Messenger of God, and that people would be punished if they did not follow his directives. It was astonishing to these ignorant objectors that the Creator of the heavens and the earth should appoint someone as His Messenger and then leave him without protection against the physical hurts and insults that were flung at him. They would have expected the envoy of a Sovereign as great as the Creator of the universe to be accompanied by at least some heavenly constable, if not a large retinue, to protect him!

6. The unbelievers' objection is refuted by this remark. It warns them that the time available for accepting the true faith and bringing about the required reform in their lives will last only as long as Ultimate Reality remains concealed from human perception by the veil of the Unseen. Once that veil is removed, there will be no more respite: the summons to God's reckoning will have come. This earthly life is a test of whether a man is able to recognize the Ultimate Reality – even though it lies hidden from his sense perception – by the correct exercise of his reason and intellect, and of whether, having once recognized it, he is able to behave in

(10) And indeed before your time (O Muḥammad!) many a Messenger has been scoffed at; but those who mocked at them were encompassed by the Truth they had scoffed at. (11) Say: 'Go about journeying the earth, and behold the end of those who gave the lie (to the Truth).'[8]

(12) Ask them: 'To whom belongs all that is in the heavens and on the earth?'[9] Say: 'Everything belongs to Allah.' He has bound Himself to the exercise of mercy (and thus does not chastise you for your disobedience and excesses instantly). Surely He will gather you all together on the Day of Resurrection – the coming of which is beyond doubt; but those who have courted their own ruin are not going to believe.

وَلَقَدِ ٱسْتُهْزِئَ بِرُسُلٍ مِّن قَبْلِكَ
فَحَاقَ بِٱلَّذِينَ سَخِرُوا۟ مِنْهُم
مَّا كَانُوا۟ بِهِۦ يَسْتَهْزِءُونَ ﴿١٠﴾
قُلْ سِيرُوا۟ فِى ٱلْأَرْضِ ثُمَّ ٱنظُرُوا۟
كَيْفَ كَانَ عَٰقِبَةُ ٱلْمُكَذِّبِينَ
﴿١١﴾ قُل لِّمَن مَّا فِى ٱلسَّمَٰوَٰتِ وَٱلْأَرْضِ ۖ
قُل لِّلَّهِ ۚ كَتَبَ عَلَىٰ نَفْسِهِ ٱلرَّحْمَةَ ۚ
لَيَجْمَعَنَّكُمْ إِلَىٰ يَوْمِ ٱلْقِيَٰمَةِ
لَا رَيْبَ فِيهِ ۚ ٱلَّذِينَ خَسِرُوٓا۟
أَنفُسَهُمْ فَهُمْ لَا يُؤْمِنُونَ ﴿١٢﴾

---

conformity with that Reality by exercising control over his animal self and its lusts. This test necessarily requires that the Reality should remain concealed. Thereafter man will be confronted with the result of the test rather than by any further test. Until God has decided to bring the term of their test to a close, it is not possible to respond to such requests by sending angels to them in their true form. (See also *Towards Understanding the Qur'ān,* vol. I, *Sūrah* 2, n. 228.)

7. This is the second point in response to the unbelievers' objection. One possible form in which the angel could have appeared is in its true, non-terrestrial form. It has already been pointed out that the time for this has not arrived. Alternatively, angels could have come down in human form. But this would have left the unbelievers facing the same difficulty as they faced with regard to whether the Prophet Muḥammad (peace be on him) had been designated by God or not.

(13) And to Him belongs all that dwells in the night and the day. He is All-Hearing, All-Knowing. (14) Say: 'Shall I take for my guardian anyone other than Allah – the Originator of the heavens and earth; He Who feeds and Himself is not fed?'[10] Say: 'Surely I have been commanded to be the first among those who submit (to Allah) and not to be one of those who associate others with Allah in His divinity (even though others may do so).' ▶

۞ وَلَهُۥ مَا سَكَنَ فِى ٱلَّيۡلِ وَٱلنَّهَارِۚ وَهُوَ
ٱلسَّمِيعُ ٱلۡعَلِيمُ ﴿١٣﴾ قُلۡ أَغَيۡرَ ٱللَّهِ أَتَّخِذُ
وَلِيًّا فَاطِرِ ٱلسَّمَٰوَٰتِ وَٱلۡأَرۡضِ وَهُوَ يُطۡعِمُ
وَلَا يُطۡعَمُۗ قُلۡ إِنِّىٓ أُمِرۡتُ أَنۡ أَكُونَ
أَوَّلَ مَنۡ أَسۡلَمَۖ وَلَا تَكُونَنَّ مِنَ
ٱلۡمُشۡرِكِينَ ﴿١٤﴾

---

8. The archaeological remains and historical records of the ancient nations testify to how they met their tragic ends through turning away from truth and honesty and stubbornly persisting in their devotion to falsehood.

9. The subtlety of this expression should not go unnoticed. The unbelievers are asked to whom belongs whatever exists in either the heavens or on the earth. The inquirer then pauses to wait for the answer. Those questioned are themselves convinced that all belongs to God, yet while they dare not respond falsely, they are nevertheless not prepared to give the correct answer. Fearing that their response may be used as an argument against their polytheistic beliefs, they keep quiet. At this, the inquirer is told to answer the question himself and to say that all belongs to God.

10. This remark contains a subtle sarcasm. Far from providing sustenance to their followers, the beings whom the polytheists set up as deities beside the true God were dependent upon them for their sustenance. No Pharaoh can maintain the pomp and splendour connected with his godhead unless his subjects pay their tax dues and make him other offerings.

No deity can attract worshippers unless some of its devotees make an idol, place it in some magnificent temple, and decorate it lavishly. All these counterfeit gods are totally dependent upon their own servants. It is the Lord of the Universe alone Who is the True God, Whose godhead rests solely upon His own power; Who needs the help of no one, whereas no one can dispense with His.

(15) Say: 'Surely do I fear, if I disobey my Lord, the chastisement of an awesome Day. (16) Whosoever has been spared chastisement on that Day, Allah has bestowed His mercy upon him. That is the manifest triumph. (17) Should Allah touch you with affliction, there is none to remove it but He; and should He touch you with good, He has the power to do everything. (18) He has the supreme hold over His servants. He is All-Wise, All-Aware.

(19) Ask them: 'Whose testimony is the greatest?' Say: 'Allah is the witness between me and you;[11] and this Qur'ān was revealed to me that I should warn you thereby and also whomsoever it may reach.' Do you indeed testify that there are other gods with Allah?[12] Say: 'I shall never testify such a thing.'[13] Say: 'He is the One God and I am altogether averse to all that you associate with Him in His divinity.'

قُلۡ إِنِّيٓ أَخَافُ إِنۡ عَصَيۡتُ رَبِّي عَذَابَ
يَوۡمٍ عَظِيمٖ ١٥ مَّن يُصۡرَفۡ عَنۡهُ
يَوۡمَئِذٖ فَقَدۡ رَحِمَهُۥۚ وَذَٰلِكَ ٱلۡفَوۡزُ
ٱلۡمُبِينُ ١٦ وَإِن يَمۡسَسۡكَ ٱللَّهُ بِضُرّٖ
فَلَا كَاشِفَ لَهُۥٓ إِلَّا هُوَۖ وَإِن يَمۡسَسۡكَ
بِخَيۡرٖ فَهُوَ عَلَىٰ كُلِّ شَيۡءٖ قَدِيرٞ ١٧ وَهُوَ
ٱلۡقَاهِرُ فَوۡقَ عِبَادِهِۦۚ وَهُوَ ٱلۡحَكِيمُ
ٱلۡخَبِيرُ ١٨ قُلۡ أَيُّ شَيۡءٍ أَكۡبَرُ شَهَٰدَةٗۖ قُلِ
ٱللَّهُۖ شَهِيدُۢ بَيۡنِي وَبَيۡنَكُمۡۚ وَأُوحِيَ إِلَيَّ هَٰذَا
ٱلۡقُرۡءَانُ لِأُنذِرَكُم بِهِۦ وَمَنۢ بَلَغَۚ أَئِنَّكُمۡ
لَتَشۡهَدُونَ أَنَّ مَعَ ٱللَّهِ ءَالِهَةً أُخۡرَىٰۚ
قُل لَّآ أَشۡهَدُۚ قُلۡ إِنَّمَا هُوَ إِلَٰهٞ وَٰحِدٞ وَإِنَّنِي
بَرِيٓءٞ مِّمَّا تُشۡرِكُونَ ١٩

11. God Himself witnesses that the Prophet (peace be on him) has been designated by Him and that what he communicated was by His command.

12. In order to bear witness to something, mere guesswork and imagination are not sufficient. What is required is knowledge on the basis of which a person can state something with full conviction. Hence, the question means: Did they really have knowledge of anyone other than God who

(20) Those whom We have given the Book will recognize this just as they recognize their own offspring;[14] but those who have courted their own ruin will not believe.
(21) And who could be more wrong-doing than he who either foists a lie on Allah[15] or gives the lie to His signs?[16] Surely such wrong-doers shall not attain success.

ٱلَّذِينَ ءَاتَيْنَٰهُمُ ٱلْكِتَٰبَ يَعْرِفُونَهُۥ كَمَا
يَعْرِفُونَ أَبْنَآءَهُمُ ٱلَّذِينَ خَسِرُوٓا۟ أَنفُسَهُمْ
فَهُمْ لَا يُؤْمِنُونَ ﴿٢٠﴾ وَمَنْ أَظْلَمُ مِمَّنِ
ٱفْتَرَىٰ عَلَى ٱللَّهِ كَذِبًا أَوْ كَذَّبَ بِـَٔايَٰتِهِۦٓ إِنَّهُۥ
لَا يُفْلِحُ ٱلظَّٰلِمُونَ ﴿٢١﴾

---

could lay claim to man's worship and absolute service by dint of being the omnipotent sovereign, the one whose will prevailed throughout the universe?

13. The interlocutor is instructed to tell people that if they wanted to bear false witness and testify without knowledge, they could do so, but that he himself could not do something so unreasonable.

14. Those who have knowledge of the Scriptures know for sure that God is One alone and that no one shares His godhead with Him. It is true that one can spot one's own child even in the midst of a large crowd of children. The same can be said about those well-versed in the Scriptures. Even if the true concept of godhead were interspersed among numerous false beliefs and concepts about God, those well-versed in the scriptural lore would be able to recognize without doubt which doctrine was true.

15. This refers to those who asserted that there were also other beings which shared with God in His godhead, were possessed of divine attributes and powers, and rightly deserved to claim from man worship and absolute service. It is also a slander to claim that God has selected certain beings to be His chosen intimates and that He has commanded – or is at least agreeable to the idea – that they should be considered to possess divine attributes, and that people should serve and revere them as they would serve and revere God, their Lord.

(22) And on the Day when We shall gather them all together, We shall ask those who associated others with Allah in His divinity: 'Where, now, are your partners whom you imagined (to have a share in the divinity of Allah)?' (23) Then they will be able to play no mischief but will say (falsely): 'By Allah, our Lord, we associated none (with You in Your divinity).' (24) Behold, how they will lie against themselves and how their forged deities will forsake them!

وَيَوْمَ نَحْشُرُهُمْ جَمِيعًا ثُمَّ نَقُولُ لِلَّذِينَ
أَشْرَكُوٓا۟ أَيْنَ شُرَكَآؤُكُمُ ٱلَّذِينَ كُنتُمْ
تَزْعُمُونَ ﴿٢٢﴾ ثُمَّ لَمْ تَكُن فِتْنَتُهُمْ إِلَّآ
أَن قَالُوا۟ وَٱللَّهِ رَبِّنَا مَا كُنَّا مُشْرِكِينَ ﴿٢٣﴾
ٱنظُرْ كَيْفَ كَذَبُوا۟ عَلَىٰٓ أَنفُسِهِمْ ۚ وَضَلَّ
عَنْهُم مَّا كَانُوا۟ يَفْتَرُونَ ﴿٢٤﴾

---

16. By 'signs of God' are meant the signs found within man's own being, as well as those scattered throughout the universe. They also include the signs which are manifest from the lives and achievements of the Prophets, as well as those embodied in the Scriptures. All these point towards one and the same truth – that in the entire realm of existence there is one God alone and that all else are merely His subjects. Who could be more unjust than one who, in utter disregard of all these signs, invests others than the One True God with attributes of godhead, considering them to merit the same rights as God. And does so merely on grounds of either conjecture, or speculation or out of blind adherence to the beliefs of his forefathers although there is not so much as a shred of evidence founded on true knowledge, observation or experience in support of such beliefs. Such a person subjects truth and reality to grave injustice. He also wrongs his own self and everything else in this universe with which he has to deal on the basis of this false assumption.

(25) And of them there are some who appear to pay heed to you, but upon their hearts We have laid coverings so they understand it not; and in their ears, heaviness (so they hear not).[17] Even if they were to witness every sign, they would still not believe in it so much so that when they come to you, they dispute with you, those who disbelieve contend: 'This is nothing but fables of the ancient times.'[18] (26) As for others, they prevent them from embracing the Truth; and themselves, they flee from it (so as to harm you). But they court their own ruin, although they do not realize it. (27) If you could but see when they shall be made to stand by the Fire! They will plead: 'Would that we were brought back to life? Then we would not give the lie to the signs of our Lord and would be among the believers.' ▶

وَمِنْهُم مَّن يَسْتَمِعُ إِلَيْكَ وَجَعَلْنَا عَلَىٰ
قُلُوبِهِمْ أَكِنَّةً أَن يَفْقَهُوهُ وَفِىٓ ءَاذَانِهِمْ
وَقْرًا وَإِن يَرَوْاْ كُلَّ ءَايَةٍ لَّا يُؤْمِنُواْ بِهَآ
حَتَّىٰٓ إِذَا جَآءُوكَ يُجَٰدِلُونَكَ يَقُولُ ٱلَّذِينَ
كَفَرُوٓاْ إِنْ هَٰذَآ إِلَّآ أَسَٰطِيرُ ٱلْأَوَّلِينَ ٢٥
وَهُمْ يَنْهَوْنَ عَنْهُ وَيَنْـَٔوْنَ عَنْهُ وَإِن
يُهْلِكُونَ إِلَّآ أَنفُسَهُمْ وَمَا يَشْعُرُونَ ٢٦
وَلَوْ تَرَىٰٓ إِذْ وُقِفُواْ عَلَى ٱلنَّارِ فَقَالُواْ يَٰلَيْتَنَا
نُرَدُّ وَلَا نُكَذِّبَ بِـَٔايَٰتِ رَبِّنَا وَنَكُونَ
مِنَ ٱلْمُؤْمِنِينَ ٢٧

---

17. It is noteworthy that God attributes to Himself all that happens in the world as a result of the laws of nature. Since these laws were made by God Himself, the effects which result from their operation are also ultimately due to the will and permission of God. The refusal on the part of unbelievers to heed the call of the Truth even when it is clear and audible stems from their obstinacy, prejudice, mental rigidity and inertia. It is a law of nature that when a man is not prepared to rise above prejudice in his quest for the Truth, his heart closes to every truth which is opposed to his desires. We can describe this condition by saying that the heart of that person has become sealed and when God describes it He does so by saying

(28) No! They will say this merely because the Truth which they had concealed will become obvious to them;[19] or else if they were sent back, they would still revert to what was forbidden to them. (So this plea of theirs would be a lie too) for they are just liars. (29) They say now: 'There is nothing but the life of this world, and we shall not be raised from the dead.' (30) If you could but see when they will be made to stand before their Lord. He will say: 'Is not this the truth?' They will say: 'Yes indeed, by our Lord.' Whereupon He will say: 'Taste the chastisement, then, for your denying the Truth.'

بَلْ بَدَا لَهُم مَّا كَانُوا يُخْفُونَ مِن قَبْلُ ۖ وَلَوْ
رُدُّوا لَعَادُوا لِمَا نُهُوا عَنْهُ وَإِنَّهُمْ
لَكَاذِبُونَ ﴿٢٨﴾ وَقَالُوا إِنْ هِيَ إِلَّا حَيَاتُنَا
الدُّنْيَا وَمَا نَحْنُ بِمَبْعُوثِينَ ﴿٢٩﴾ وَلَوْ تَرَىٰ
إِذْ وُقِفُوا عَلَىٰ رَبِّهِمْ ۚ قَالَ أَلَيْسَ هَٰذَا
بِالْحَقِّ ۚ قَالُوا بَلَىٰ وَرَبِّنَا ۚ قَالَ فَذُوقُوا
الْعَذَابَ بِمَا كُنتُمْ تَكْفُرُونَ ﴿٣٠﴾

---

that He had sealed the heart of the person concerned. The explanation of this paradox is that whereas we describe merely an incident, God describes its ultimate cause.

18. Whenever ignorant people are called to the Truth they are liable to say that there is nothing novel about it, that it is merely a repetition of things that have come down from the past, as if in their view every truth must be new, and whatever is old must of necessity be false, although Truth has always been one and the same and will remain so. All those who have come forward to lead people in the light of God-given knowledge have been preaching one and the same Truth from time immemorial, and all those who will benefit from this valuable source of human knowledge in the future are bound to repeat the same old truths. Novelties can be invented only by those who, being bereft of the light of Divine guidance, are incapable of perceiving the eternal Truth, preferring to weave altogether new ideas out of their imagination and to put them forward as truth.

(31) Those who consider it a lie that they will have to meet Allah are indeed the losers so much so that when that Hour comes to them suddenly they will say: 'Alas for us, how negligent we have been in this behalf.' They will carry their burden (of sins) on their backs. How evil is the burden they bear! (32) The life of this world is nothing but a sport and a pastime,[20] and the life of the Hereafter is far better for those who seek to ward off their ruin. Will you not, then, understand?

قَدْ خَسِرَ ٱلَّذِينَ كَذَّبُوا۟ بِلِقَآءِ ٱللَّهِ ۖ حَتَّىٰٓ
إِذَا جَآءَتْهُمُ ٱلسَّاعَةُ بَغْتَةً قَالُوا۟
يَٰحَسْرَتَنَا عَلَىٰ مَا فَرَّطْنَا فِيهَا وَهُمْ
يَحْمِلُونَ أَوْزَارَهُمْ عَلَىٰ ظُهُورِهِمْ ۚ
أَلَا سَآءَ مَا يَزِرُونَ ﴿٣١﴾ وَمَا ٱلْحَيَوٰةُ
ٱلدُّنْيَآ إِلَّا لَعِبٌ وَلَهْوٌ ۖ وَلَلدَّارُ ٱلْءَاخِرَةُ
خَيْرٌ لِّلَّذِينَ يَتَّقُونَ ۗ أَفَلَا تَعْقِلُونَ ﴿٣٢﴾

19. At that moment such a statement on their part would not be indicative of either any true change of heart or of any genuinely revised judgement based on serious reflection and reasoning. It would rather be the result of direct observation of reality at a time when even the staunchest unbeliever would find it impossible to deny it.

20. This does not mean that earthly life has nothing serious about it and that it has been brought into being merely as a sport and pastime. What this observation means is that, compared with the true and abiding life of the Hereafter, earthly life *seems*, as it were, a sport, a transient pastime with which to amuse oneself before turning to serious business.

Earthly life has been likened to a sport and pastime for another reason as well. Since Ultimate Reality is hidden in this world, the superficially minded ones who lack true perception encounter many a thing which causes them to fall a prey to misconceptions. As a result of these misconceptions such persons indulge in a variety of actions which are so blatantly opposed to reality that their life seems to consist merely of sport and pastime. One who assumes the position of a king in this world, for instance, is no different from the person who plays the part of a king on the stage of a theatre. His head is bedecked with a crown and he goes about commanding people as if he were a king, even though he has no royal authority. He may later, if the director of the theatre wishes, be either dismissed from his royal office, put into prison or even be sentenced to death. Plays of this kind go on all

(33) (O Muḥammad!) We know indeed that the things they say grieve you, though in truth it is not you whom they give the lie to, but it is the signs of Allah that these wrong-doers reject.[21] (34) Messengers before you have been given the lie to, and they endured with patience their being given the lie to and being persecuted until the time when Our help reached them. None has the power to alter the words of Allah.[22] Indeed some account of the Messengers has already reached you. ▶

قَدْ نَعْلَمُ إِنَّهُۥ لَيَحْزُنُكَ ٱلَّذِى يَقُولُونَ ۖ فَإِنَّهُمْ
لَا يُكَذِّبُونَكَ وَلَٰكِنَّ ٱلظَّٰلِمِينَ
بِـَٔايَٰتِ ٱللَّهِ يَجْحَدُونَ ﴿٣٣﴾ وَلَقَدْ
كُذِّبَتْ رُسُلٌ مِّن قَبْلِكَ فَصَبَرُوا۟ عَلَىٰ
مَا كُذِّبُوا۟ وَأُوذُوا۟ حَتَّىٰٓ أَتَىٰهُمْ نَصْرُنَا ۚ
وَلَا مُبَدِّلَ لِكَلِمَٰتِ ٱللَّهِ ۚ وَلَقَدْ جَآءَكَ
مِن نَّبَإِى۟ ٱلْمُرْسَلِينَ ﴿٣٤﴾

---

over the world. Saints and man-made deities are deemed to respond to human supplications even though they do not have a shred of authority to do so. Again, some people try to unravel the Unseen even though to do so lies altogether beyond their reach. There are those who claim to provide sustenance to others despite the fact that they are themselves dependent on others for their own sustenance. There are still others who think that they have the power either to bestow honour and dignity on human beings or to degrade them, either to confer benefits or to harm them. Such people go about trumpeting their own glory but their own foreheads bear the stamp of their humble bondage to their Creator. By just one twist of fortune such people may fall off their pedestals and be trampled under the feet of those upon whom they have been imposing their God-like authority.

All these plays come to a sudden end with death. As soon as man crosses the boundaries of this world and steps into the Next, the reality will be fully manifest, all the misconceptions that he has entertained will be peeled away, and he will be shown the true worth of his beliefs and actions.

21. The fact is that before the Prophet Muḥammad (peace be on him) began to preach the message of God, all his people regarded him as truthful and trustworthy and had full confidence in his veracity. Only after he had begun to preach the message of God did they call him a liar. Even during this period none dared to say that the Prophet (peace be on him) had ever been guilty of untruthfulness in personal matters. Even his worst enemies

never accused him of lying in any worldly affairs. When they did accuse him of falsehood, they did so in respect of his prophetic mission. Abū Jahl, for instance, was one of his staunchest enemies. According to a tradition from 'Alī, Abū Jahl once said to the Prophet (peace be on him): 'We do not disbelieve you. We disbelieve your message.' On the occasion of the Battle of Badr, Akhnas b. Sharīq asked Abū Jahl, when they were alone, to confide whether he considered Muḥammad to be truthful or not. He replied: 'By God, Muḥammad is a veracious person. He has never lied in all his life. But if every honourable office – *liwā'* (standard-bearing in war), *siqāyah* (provision of water to the pilgrims), *ḥijābah* (guardianship of the Ka'bah), and *nubūwah* (prophethood) – were to fall to the share of the descendants of Quṣayy, what would be left for the rest of the Quraysh?'* (Ibn Kathīr, vol. 3, pp. 17–18 – Ed.)

Here God consoles the Prophet (peace be on him) by telling him that by charging him with falsehood the unbelievers were calling God untruthful. Since God has endured this accusation with mild forbearance, leaving them free to persist in their blasphemy, the Prophet (peace be on him) need not feel undue disquiet.

22. The point emphasized here is that no one has the power to change God's Law regarding the conflict between Truth and falsehood. Lovers of Truth must of necessity pass through trials and persecutions so as to be gradually tempered. Their endurance, their honesty of conviction, their readiness to sacrifice and to undertake all risks for their cause, the strength of their faith and the extent of their trust in God must be tested. They must pass through this phase of persecution to develop in themselves those qualities which can be developed nowhere else but on earth. They are also required to defeat the forces of Ignorance by virtue of their moral excellence and the nobility of their character. Only after they have established their moral superiority over their adversaries will God's help arrive. No one can secure that help beforehand.

*Before the advent of Islam these various functions were divided among the different clans of the Quraysh in Makka – Ed.

(35) Nevertheless, if their turning away grieves you, then seek – if you can – either a way down into the earth or a ladder to the heavens, and try to bring to them some sign.[23] Had Allah so willed, He would have gathered them all to the true guidance. Do not, then, be among the ignorant.[24] (36) Only they who listen can respond to the call of the Truth; as for the dead,[25] Allah will raise them and then to Him they will be returned.

وَإِن كَانَ كَبُرَ عَلَيْكَ إِعْرَاضُهُمْ فَإِنِ
ٱسْتَطَعْتَ أَن تَبْتَغِىَ نَفَقًا فِى ٱلْأَرْضِ
أَوْ سُلَّمًا فِى ٱلسَّمَآءِ فَتَأْتِيَهُم بِـَٔايَةٍ ۚ
وَلَوْ شَآءَ ٱللَّهُ لَجَمَعَهُمْ عَلَى ٱلْهُدَىٰ ۚ
فَلَا تَكُونَنَّ مِنَ ٱلْجَٰهِلِينَ ﴿٣٥﴾
۞ إِنَّمَا يَسْتَجِيبُ ٱلَّذِينَ يَسْمَعُونَ ۘ
وَٱلْمَوْتَىٰ يَبْعَثُهُمُ ٱللَّهُ ثُمَّ إِلَيْهِ يُرْجَعُونَ
﴿٣٦﴾

23. The Prophet (peace be on him) saw that even though he had spent a long time admonishing his people, they did not seem inclined to heed his call. As a result he sometimes wished for the appearance of some extraordinary sign of God that would undermine the stubbornness of his people and lead them to accept his guidance. This verse embodies God's response to the Prophet's desire. He is told not to be impatient. He must persist in his striving and continue to work in conformity with God's directive. Had it been God's purpose to work miracles, He would have done so. But God did not consider that to be either the appropriate method for bringing to a successful completion the required intellectual and moral revolution or for the evolution of a sound, healthy civilization. Well, then, if the Prophet (peace be on him) could not bear patiently with the attitude of stubbornness and rejection prevalent among his people, and if he thought it necessary to make them witness a tangible sign of God, let him muster all his strength and try to cleave the earth, or climb a ladder to the heaven and bring forth a miracle powerful enough to change the unbelief of the unbelievers into belief. He is told, however, that in this regard he should not expect God to fulfil his wish, for such things have no place in God's scheme.

24. Had it been required that all people should be driven to the Truth, there would have been no need to send Prophets, to reveal heavenly Books, to direct believers to engage in struggles against unbelievers, and to make the message of Truth pass through the necessary stages until fulfilment is reached. The result could have been achieved by a single sign of God's

(37) And they say: 'Why has no miraculous sign been sent down to him from his Lord?' Say: 'Surely Allah has the power to send down a sign, but most of them do not know.[26] ▶

وَقَالُوا۟ لَوْلَا نُزِّلَ عَلَيْهِ ءَايَةٌ مِّن رَّبِّهِۦ ۚ
قُلْ إِنَّ ٱللَّهَ قَادِرٌ عَلَىٰٓ أَن يُنَزِّلَ ءَايَةً
وَلَٰكِنَّ أَكْثَرَهُمْ لَا يَعْلَمُونَ ﴿٣٧﴾

---

creative will. God, however, did not want things to happen that way. He preferred the Truth to be set before people with its supporting arguments so that by a proper exercise of their rational judgement, they should recognize it for what it was and thereafter freely choose to embrace it as their faith. By moulding their lives in conformity with this Truth such people should demonstrate their moral superiority over the devotees of falsehood. They should continually attract men of sound morals by the force of their arguments, by the loftiness of their ideals, by the excellence of their principles and by the purity of their lives. They should thus reach their goal – the establishment of the hegemony of the true faith – by the natural and gradual escalation of strife against falsehood. God will guide them in the performance of this task and will provide them with whatever help they merit during the various stages of their struggle. But if anyone wishes to evade this natural course and wants God to obliterate corrupt ideas and to spread healthy ones in their stead, to root out a corrupt civilization and put a healthy one in its place by exercising His omnipotent will, let him know that this will not come about. The reason is that such is contrary to the scheme according to which God has created man as a responsible being, bestowed upon him a degree of power which he may exercise, granted him the freedom to choose between obedience and disobedience to God, awarded him a certain term of life in order to demonstrate his worth, and determined that at an appointed hour He will judge him for either reward or punishment in the light of his deeds.

25. 'Those who hear' refers to those whose consciences are alive, who have not atrophied their intellect and reason, and who have not closed their hearts to the Truth out of irrational prejudice and mental inflexibility. In contrast to such people are those who are characterized as 'dead' – who blindly follow the old familiar beaten tracks, and can never deviate from the ways they have inherited, even when these ways are plainly at variance with the Truth.

26. The word *āyah* here signifies a tangible miracle. The purpose of the verse is to point out that the reason for not showing a miraculous sign is not God's powerlessness. The true reason is something else which those people in their immaturity, have failed to comprehend.

(38) There is no animal that crawls on the earth, no bird that flies with its two wings, but are communities like you. We have neglected nothing in the Book (of decree). Then to their Lord will they all be mustered. (39) Those who gave the lie to Our signs are deaf and dumb and blunder about in darkness.[27] Allah causes whomsoever He wills to stray in error, and sets whomsoever He wills on the straight way.'[28] ▶

وَمَا مِن دَآبَّةٍ فِي ٱلْأَرْضِ وَلَا طَٰٓئِرٍ يَطِيرُ
بِجَنَاحَيْهِ إِلَّآ أُمَمٌ أَمْثَالُكُم مَّا فَرَّطْنَا فِي
ٱلْكِتَٰبِ مِن شَيْءٍ ثُمَّ إِلَىٰ رَبِّهِمْ
يُحْشَرُونَ ﴿٣٨﴾ وَٱلَّذِينَ كَذَّبُوا۟ بِـَٔايَٰتِنَا
صُمٌّ وَبُكْمٌ فِي ٱلظُّلُمَٰتِ مَن يَشَإِ ٱللَّهُ
يُضْلِلْهُ وَمَن يَشَأْ يَجْعَلْهُ عَلَىٰ صِرَٰطٍ
مُّسْتَقِيمٍ ﴿٣٩﴾

---

27. If they are concerned with miraculous signs in order to determine whether or not the message of the Prophet (peace be on him) is indeed true, then, let them look around with open and attentive eyes. If they actually do so they will find the world full of such signs. Let them take any species of animal or bird they like. They can reflect upon the superbness of its organic structure. They will notice how its instinctive urges are in complete conformity with its natural requirements. They will also observe how wonderfully adequate are the arrangements for providing it with nourishment; how marvellously well-determined are the limits within which it lives; how tremendously efficient is the system under which each living creature is protected, provided for, looked after and directed towards self-fulfilment; how strictly each one is fitted into the framework of the discipline devised for it, and how very smooth is the operation of the whole system of birth, procreation and death. Were one to reflect on this alone from among the innumerable signs of God, one would perceive fully how true the teaching of the Prophet (peace be on him) is concerning the unity and other attributes of God and how necessary it is to live a righteous life in conformity with the concept of God propounded by him. But their eyes were neither open to perceive the Truth nor their ears open to heed admonition. Instead, they remained ignorant, preferring to be entertained by the performance of wondrous feats.

(40) Say: 'What do you think
if some chastisement of Allah
or the Hour suddenly overtakes you: do you cry to any
other than Allah? Answer, if
you speak the truth. (41)
Lo, it is to Him alone that
you cry and then, if He so
wills, He removes the distress for which you had cried
to Him. Then you forget the
partners you had set up with
Allah.[29]

قُلْ أَرَءَيْتَكُمْ إِنْ أَتَىٰكُمْ عَذَابُ ٱللَّهِ
أَوْ أَتَتْكُمُ ٱلسَّاعَةُ أَغَيْرَ ٱللَّهِ تَدْعُونَ
إِن كُنتُمْ صَٰدِقِينَ ﴿٤٠﴾ بَلْ إِيَّاهُ تَدْعُونَ
فَيَكْشِفُ مَا تَدْعُونَ إِلَيْهِ إِن شَآءَ
وَتَنسَوْنَ مَا تُشْرِكُونَ ﴿٤١﴾

---

28. God's act of misguiding a man consists in not enabling one who cherishes his ignorance to observe the signs of God. The fact is that if a biased person – one who has no real love of the Truth – were to observe the signs of God, he might still fail to perceive it. Indeed, all those things which cause misconception and confusion would probably continue to alienate him from it. God's act of true guidance consists in enabling a seeker after the Truth to benefit from the sources of true knowledge, so that he constantly discovers sign after sign, leading him ultimately to the Truth.

A myriad of cases are encountered daily to illustrate this. We notice that a great many people pass inattentively over the countless signs of God that are scattered all over the world, and ignore even those signs which are manifest in human beings as well as in animals. It is little wonder, then, that they derive no lesson from all these signs. There are many who study zoology, botany, biology, geology, astronomy, physiology, anatomy and other branches of natural science. Others study history, archaeology and sociology. During the course of such studies they come across many signs of God which, if they cared to look at them in the correct perspective, might fill their hearts with faith. But since they commence their study with a bias, and are actuated only by the desire to acquire earthly advantages, they fail to discover the signs which could lead them to the Truth. On the contrary, each of those very signs of God contributes to pushing them towards atheism, materialism and naturalism. At the same time, the world is not empty of those truly wise ones who view the universe with open eyes. For them even the most ordinary phenomenon of the universe directs them to God.

29. Attention is now drawn towards another sign – one observable even in the lives of those who deny the Truth. When either some great calamity

(42) And We did indeed send Messengers to other nations before you and then We seized those nations with misfortune and hardship so that they might humble themselves (before Us). (43) But when misfortune befell them from Us why did they not humble themselves? Their hearts had hardened and Satan had made their deeds seem fair to them. (44) So, when they forgot what they had been reminded of, We opened the gates of all things so that while they rejoiced in what they had been granted We seized them suddenly and they were plunged into utter despair. (45) Thus the last remnant of those wrong-doing people was cut off. All praise is for Allah, the Lord of the entire universe, (for having punished them so).

وَلَقَدْ أَرْسَلْنَآ إِلَىٰٓ أُمَمٍ مِّن قَبْلِكَ
فَأَخَذْنَٰهُم بِٱلْبَأْسَآءِ وَٱلضَّرَّآءِ لَعَلَّهُمْ
يَتَضَرَّعُونَ ﴿٤٢﴾ فَلَوْلَآ إِذْ جَآءَهُم
بَأْسُنَا تَضَرَّعُوا۟ وَلَٰكِن قَسَتْ قُلُوبُهُمْ
وَزَيَّنَ لَهُمُ ٱلشَّيْطَٰنُ مَا كَانُوا۟
يَعْمَلُونَ ﴿٤٣﴾ فَلَمَّا نَسُوا۟ مَا
ذُكِّرُوا۟ بِهِۦ فَتَحْنَا عَلَيْهِمْ أَبْوَٰبَ
كُلِّ شَىْءٍ حَتَّىٰٓ إِذَا فَرِحُوا۟ بِمَآ أُوتُوٓا۟
أَخَذْنَٰهُم بَغْتَةً فَإِذَا هُم مُّبْلِسُونَ ﴿٤٤﴾
فَقُطِعَ دَابِرُ ٱلْقَوْمِ ٱلَّذِينَ ظَلَمُوا۟ ۚ
وَٱلْحَمْدُ لِلَّهِ رَبِّ ٱلْعَٰلَمِينَ ﴿٤٥﴾

befalls a man or when death starkly stares him in the face, it is only to God that he turns for refuge. On such occasions even the staunchest polytheists forget their false gods and cry out to the One True God, and even the most rabid atheists stretch out their hands in prayer to Him. This phenomenon is mentioned here in order to draw an instructive lesson. It shows that devotion to God and monotheism are ingrained in the human soul. No matter how overlaid this truth might be, some day it shakes off man's heedlessness and ignorance and manifests itself fully. It was the observation of this sign which had led 'Ikrimah, the son of Abū Jahl, to the true faith. For when Makka was conquered at the hands of the Prophet (peace be on him), 'Ikrimah fled to Jeddah and sailed from there towards Abyssinia. During the voyage the boat ran into a severe storm which threatened to capsize it. At first people began calling on their gods and

(46) Say (O Muḥammad!): What do you think? If Allah should take away your hearing and your sight and seal your hearts[30] – who is the god, other than Allah, who could restore them to you? Behold, how We put forth Our signs in diverse forms, and yet they turn away from them. (47) Say: 'If the chastisement of Allah were to overtake you unawares or openly shall any except the wrong-doing people be destroyed?' (48) We do not send Messengers except as bearers of glad tidings and warners. So, he who believes in their message and mends his conduct need have no fear and need not grieve; (49) whereas those who give the lie to Our signs, chastisement will visit them for their transgression.

قُلْ أَرَءَيْتُمْ إِنْ أَخَذَ ٱللَّهُ سَمْعَكُمْ وَأَبْصَٰرَكُمْ
وَخَتَمَ عَلَىٰ قُلُوبِكُم مَّنْ إِلَٰهٌ غَيْرُ ٱللَّهِ يَأْتِيكُم
بِهِ ٱنظُرْ كَيْفَ نُصَرِّفُ ٱلْءَايَٰتِ
ثُمَّ هُمْ يَصْدِفُونَ ﴿٤٦﴾ قُلْ أَرَءَيْتَكُمْ إِنْ
أَتَىٰكُمْ عَذَابُ ٱللَّهِ بَغْتَةً أَوْ جَهْرَةً
هَلْ يُهْلَكُ إِلَّا ٱلْقَوْمُ ٱلظَّٰلِمُونَ ﴿٤٧﴾
وَمَا نُرْسِلُ ٱلْمُرْسَلِينَ إِلَّا مُبَشِّرِينَ
وَمُنذِرِينَ فَمَنْ ءَامَنَ وَأَصْلَحَ فَلَا خَوْفٌ
عَلَيْهِمْ وَلَا هُمْ يَحْزَنُونَ ﴿٤٨﴾ وَٱلَّذِينَ كَذَّبُوا۟
بِـَٔايَٰتِنَا يَمَسُّهُمُ ٱلْعَذَابُ بِمَا كَانُوا۟
يَفْسُقُونَ ﴿٤٩﴾

goddesses. Later on, when the storm grew even worse and the passengers were sure that the boat would sink, they began to feel it was time to call on God alone, for He alone could save them. This opened the eyes of 'Ikrimah, whose heart cried out to him that if there was no effective helper for them in that situation, how could there be one elsewhere? He also recalled that this was precisely what the Prophet (peace be on him) had constantly told people, and that it was precisely because of this preaching that they had been engaged in unnecessary violent conflict with him. This was a turning-point in 'Ikrimah's life. He instantly made up his mind that if he survived the storm he would go straight to the Prophet Muḥammad (peace be on him) and place his hand in his, binding himself in allegiance. Thereafter he not only remained true to his word by becoming a Muslim, but spent the rest of his life struggling in the cause of Islam.

30. The expression 'sealing of hearts' means rendering people incapable of thinking and understanding things correctly.

(50) (O Muḥammad!) Say: 'I do not say to you I have the treasures of Allah. Nor do I have knowledge of what is beyond the reach of human perception. Nor do I say to you: I am an angel. I only follow what is revealed to me.'[31] Then ask them: 'Are the blind and the seeing alike?'[32] Do you not then reflect?

قُل لَّآ أَقُولُ لَكُمْ عِندِى خَزَآئِنُ ٱللَّهِ
وَلَآ أَعْلَمُ ٱلْغَيْبَ وَلَآ أَقُولُ لَكُمْ إِنِّى
مَلَكٌ ۖ إِنْ أَتَّبِعُ إِلَّا مَا يُوحَىٰٓ إِلَىَّ ۚ قُلْ هَلْ
يَسْتَوِى ٱلْأَعْمَىٰ وَٱلْبَصِيرُ ۚ أَفَلَا
تَتَفَكَّرُونَ ﴿٥٠﴾

31. Feeble-minded people have always entertained the foolish misconception that the more godly a man is, the more liberated he should be from the limitations of human nature. They expect a godly person to be able to work wonders. By a mere sign of his hand, whole mountains should be transmuted into gold. At his command, the earth should begin to throw up all its hidden treasures. He should have miraculous access to all relevant facts about people. He should be able to point out the locations of things which have been lost, and show how they can be retrieved. He should be able to predict whether or not a patient will survive his disease; whether a pregnant woman will deliver a boy or a girl. Moreover, he should be above all human disabilities and limitations. How can a genuinely godly person feel hunger or thirst? How can he be overcome by sleep? How can he have a wife and children? How can he engage in buying and selling to meet his material requirements? How can he be impelled by force of circumstances to resort to such mundane acts as making money? How can he feel the pinch of poverty and paucity of resources? False conceptions such as these dominated the minds of the contemporaries of the Prophet (peace be on him). When they heard of his claim, in order to test his veracity they asked him regarding things that lie beyond the ken of human perception and to work wonders, and blamed him when they saw him engaged in such acts as eating and drinking, and taking care of his wife and children, and walking about the bazaars like other ordinary human beings. It is misconceptions such as these that this verse seeks to remove.

32. The statement of a Prophet in such matters amounts to a testimony based on first-hand observation. For the truths which a Prophet propounds are those which he himself has observed and experienced and which have been brought within the range of his knowledge by means of revelation. On the contrary, those who are opposed to the truths propounded by the Prophets are blind since the notions they entertain are based either on

(51) And warn with this (revealed message) those who fear that they shall be mustered to their Lord, that there will be none apart from Allah to act as their protector and intercessor; then maybe they will become God-fearing.[33] (52) And do not drive away those who invoke their Lord in the morning and the evening, seeking His pleasure all the time.[34] You are by no means accountable for them just as they are by no means accountable for you. If you still drive them away, you will become among the wrong-doers.[35]

وَأَنذِرْ بِهِ ٱلَّذِينَ يَخَافُونَ أَن يُحْشَرُوٓا۟
إِلَىٰ رَبِّهِمْ ۙ لَيْسَ لَهُم مِّن دُونِهِۦ وَلِىٌّ
وَلَا شَفِيعٌ لَّعَلَّهُمْ يَتَّقُونَ ﴿٥١﴾ وَلَا تَطْرُدِ
ٱلَّذِينَ يَدْعُونَ رَبَّهُم بِٱلْغَدَوٰةِ وَٱلْعَشِىِّ
يُرِيدُونَ وَجْهَهُۥ ۖ مَا عَلَيْكَ مِنْ
حِسَابِهِم مِّن شَىْءٍ وَمَا مِنْ حِسَابِكَ
عَلَيْهِم مِّن شَىْءٍ فَتَطْرُدَهُمْ فَتَكُونَ
مِنَ ٱلظَّٰلِمِينَ ﴿٥٢﴾

guess-work and conjecture or on blind adherence to ideas hallowed by time. Thus the difference between a Prophet and his opponents is as that between a man who has sound vision and a man who is blind. Obviously the former is superior, by dint of this gift of knowledge from God rather than because he has access to hidden treasures, because of his knowledge of the unseen world, and because of his freedom from physical limitations.

33. Those who are too deeply immersed in the allurements of earthly life to think either of death or of their being brought to stand before God for His judgement can hardly benefit from such admonitions. Likewise, such admonitions can have no wholesome effect on those who cherish the illusion that because of their attachment to some holy personage who will intercede on their behalf, they will come to no harm in the Hereafter. The same applies to those who believe that someone has already obtained their redemption by expiating their sins. The Prophet (peace be on him) is therefore asked to disregard such persons and to attend to those who are conscious, those with no false illusions. Only these people are susceptible to admonitions and can be expected to reform themselves.

34. One of the objections raised by the chiefs and the affluent members of the Quraysh was that the Prophet (peace be on him) had gathered around him a host of slaves, clients (*mawālī*) and others belonging to the

(53) Thus We have made some of them a means for testing others[36] so that they should say: 'Are these the ones among us upon whom Allah has bestowed His favour?' Yes, does Allah not know well who are the thankful? (54) And when those who believe in Our signs come to you, say to them: 'Peace be upon you. Your Lord has made mercy incumbent upon Himself so that if anyone of you does a bad deed out of ignorance and thereafter repents and makes amends, surely you will find Him All-Forgiving, All-Compassionate.'[37] ▶

وَكَذَٰلِكَ فَتَنَّا بَعْضَهُم بِبَعْضٍ
لِّيَقُولُوٓاْ أَهَٰٓؤُلَآءِ مَنَّ ٱللَّهُ عَلَيْهِم مِّنۢ
بَيْنِنَآ ۗ أَلَيْسَ ٱللَّهُ بِأَعْلَمَ بِٱلشَّٰكِرِينَ
﴿٥٣﴾ وَإِذَا جَآءَكَ ٱلَّذِينَ يُؤْمِنُونَ
بِـَٔايَٰتِنَا فَقُلْ سَلَٰمٌ عَلَيْكُمْ ۖ كَتَبَ
رَبُّكُمْ عَلَىٰ نَفْسِهِ ٱلرَّحْمَةَ ۖ أَنَّهُۥ مَنْ
عَمِلَ مِنكُمْ سُوٓءًۢا بِجَهَٰلَةٍ ثُمَّ تَابَ
مِنۢ بَعْدِهِۦ وَأَصْلَحَ فَأَنَّهُۥ غَفُورٌ رَّحِيمٌ ﴿٥٤﴾

---

lower strata of society. They used to scoff at the fact that men of such humble social standing as Bilāl, 'Ammār, Ṣuhayb and Khabbāb had joined his ranks. They wondered if they happened to be the only chosen ones of the Quraysh in the sight of God! They not only poked fun at the financial distress of these people but also attacked them for any weakness of character they had before accepting Islam. They went about saying sarcastically that those who had been such and such in the past had now become part of the 'chosen' community.

35. That is, everyone is personally responsible for his deeds, whether good or bad. The Prophet (peace be on him) is told that he will neither have to explain to God the conduct of the converts nor will the latter be required to explain his conduct. They can neither usurp his good deeds, nor transfer their own misdeeds to his account. There is, therefore, no reason for the Prophet (peace be on him) to alienate those who approach him as seekers after Truth.

36. By enabling the poor and the indigent, the people who have a low station in society to precede others in believing, God has put those who wax proud of wealth and honour to a severe test.

(55) Thus We clearly set forth Our signs so that the way of the wicked might become distinct.[38]

(56) Say (O Muḥammad!): 'I have been forbidden to serve those to whom you call other than Allah.' Say: 'I do not follow your desires, for were I to do that, I would go astray and would not be of those who are rightly guided.' (57) Say: 'I take stand upon a clear evidence from my Lord and it is that which you have given the lie to. That which you desire to be hastened is not within my power.[39] Judgement lies with Allah alone. He declares the Truth, and He is the best judge.'

وَكَذَٰلِكَ نُفَصِّلُ الْآيَاتِ وَلِتَسْتَبِينَ
سَبِيلُ الْمُجْرِمِينَ ﴿٥٥﴾ قُلْ إِنِّي نُهِيتُ
أَنْ أَعْبُدَ الَّذِينَ تَدْعُونَ مِنْ دُونِ اللَّهِ ۚ
قُلْ لَا أَتَّبِعُ أَهْوَاءَكُمْ ۙ قَدْ ضَلَلْتُ
إِذًا وَمَا أَنَا مِنَ الْمُهْتَدِينَ ﴿٥٦﴾ قُلْ
إِنِّي عَلَىٰ بَيِّنَةٍ مِنْ رَبِّي وَكَذَّبْتُمْ
بِهِ ۚ مَا عِنْدِي مَا تَسْتَعْجِلُونَ
بِهِ ۚ إِنِ الْحُكْمُ إِلَّا لِلَّهِ ۖ يَقُصُّ الْحَقَّ ۖ
وَهُوَ خَيْرُ الْفَاصِلِينَ ﴿٥٧﴾

---

37. Several of those who came to believe in the Prophet (peace be on him) had committed many serious sins before they embraced Islam. Even though their lives had altogether changed following their conversion, the opposition continued to play up the weaknesses and misdeeds of their past life. The Prophet (peace be on him) is asked to comfort such persons and to tell them that God does not punish those who sincerely repent their sins and mend their ways.

38. 'And thus' refers to the whole of the foregoing discussion, beginning with verse 37: 'And they say: Why has no miraculous sign been sent down to him?' The purpose of this remark is to stress that the persistence of some people in their denial of the Truth and in their disbelief, in spite of a host of unmistakably clear signs and arguments, was sufficient to prove beyond doubt that they were merely a bunch of criminals. If they persisted in error and transgression it was neither through any lack of strong arguments in support of the Truth nor, conversely, because of strong arguments in support of falsehood. The reason was rather that they had deliberately chosen to fall into error and transgression.

(58) Say: 'If what you demand so hastily were in my power, the matter between me and you would have been long decided. But Allah knows best how to judge the wrong-doers. (59) He has the keys to the realm that lies beyond the reach of human perception; none knows them but He. And He knows what is on the land and in the sea; there is not a leaf which falls that He does not know about and there is not a grain in the darkness of the earth or anything green or dry which has not been recorded in a Clear Book. (60) He recalls your souls by night, and knows what you do by day; and then He raises you back each day in order that the term appointed by Him is fulfilled. Then to Him you will return whereupon He will let you know what you have been doing. ▶

قُل لَّوْ أَنَّ عِندِى مَا تَسْتَعْجِلُونَ بِهِۦ
لَقُضِىَ ٱلْأَمْرُ بَيْنِى وَبَيْنَكُمْ ۗ
وَٱللَّهُ أَعْلَمُ بِٱلظَّٰلِمِينَ ﴿٥٨﴾
۞ وَعِندَهُۥ مَفَاتِحُ ٱلْغَيْبِ لَا يَعْلَمُهَآ
إِلَّا هُوَ ۚ وَيَعْلَمُ مَا فِى ٱلْبَرِّ وَٱلْبَحْرِ ۚ
وَمَا تَسْقُطُ مِن وَرَقَةٍ إِلَّا يَعْلَمُهَا
وَلَا حَبَّةٍ فِى ظُلُمَٰتِ ٱلْأَرْضِ وَلَا رَطْبٍ
وَلَا يَابِسٍ إِلَّا فِى كِتَٰبٍ مُّبِينٍ ﴿٥٩﴾ وَهُوَ
ٱلَّذِى يَتَوَفَّىٰكُم بِٱلَّيْلِ وَيَعْلَمُ
مَا جَرَحْتُم بِٱلنَّهَارِ ثُمَّ يَبْعَثُكُمْ
فِيهِ لِيُقْضَىٰٓ أَجَلٌ مُّسَمًّى ۖ ثُمَّ إِلَيْهِ
مَرْجِعُكُمْ ثُمَّ يُنَبِّئُكُم بِمَا كُنتُمْ
تَعْمَلُونَ ﴿٦٠﴾

---

39. This alludes to God's punishment. The adversaries questioned why it was that they had openly rejected a Prophet sent by God, but had not been struck down by God's wrath? They said that the fact of his appointment by God meant that anyone who either disbelieved or insulted him would, at once, be either plunged into the earth or struck by lightning. And yet, they pointed out, the Messenger of God and his followers faced new sufferings and humiliations whereas those who abused and persecuted him enjoyed prosperity.

(61) And He alone holds sway over His servants and sets guardians over you[40] till death approaches any of you and Our deputed angels take his soul, neglecting no part of their task. (62) Then all are restored to Allah, their true protector. Behold, His is the judgement. He is the swiftest of those who take account.'

(63) Ask them (O Muhammad!): 'Who is it that delivers you from dangers in the deep darknesses of the land and the sea, and to whom do you call in humility and in the secrecy of your hearts? To whom do you pray: "If He will but save us from this distress, we shall most certainly be among the thankful?" (64) Say: "It is Allah alone Who delivers you from this and from every distress, and yet you associate others with Allah in His divinity."[41] ▶

وَهُوَ ٱلْقَاهِرُ فَوْقَ عِبَادِهِۦ ۖ وَيُرْسِلُ
عَلَيْكُمْ حَفَظَةً حَتَّىٰٓ إِذَا جَآءَ أَحَدَكُمُ
ٱلْمَوْتُ تَوَفَّتْهُ رُسُلُنَا وَهُمْ
لَا يُفَرِّطُونَ ﴿٦١﴾ ثُمَّ رُدُّوٓا۟ إِلَى ٱللَّهِ
مَوْلَىٰهُمُ ٱلْحَقِّ ۚ أَلَا لَهُ ٱلْحُكْمُ وَهُوَ
أَسْرَعُ ٱلْحَـٰسِبِينَ ﴿٦٢﴾ قُلْ مَن
يُنَجِّيكُم مِّن ظُلُمَـٰتِ ٱلْبَرِّ وَٱلْبَحْرِ
تَدْعُونَهُۥ تَضَرُّعًا وَخُفْيَةً لَّئِنْ أَنجَىٰنَا
مِنْ هَـٰذِهِۦ لَنَكُونَنَّ مِنَ ٱلشَّـٰكِرِينَ ﴿٦٣﴾
قُلِ ٱللَّهُ يُنَجِّيكُم مِّنْهَا وَمِن كُلِّ كَرْبٍ
ثُمَّ أَنتُمْ تُشْرِكُونَ ﴿٦٤﴾

---

40. The angels who keep watch and maintain a record of everything, i.e. all their movements, deeds and so on.

41. That God alone possesses all power and authority, and has full control over the things which cause either benefit or harm to men, and that He alone holds the reins of their destiny are facts to which there is ample testimony in man's own being. For instance, whenever man is faced with a really hard time, and when the resources upon which he normally falls back seem to fail him, he instinctively turns to God. In spite of such a clear sign, people set up partners to God without any shred of evidence that anyone other than God has any share in His power and authority.

(65) Say: "It is He Who has the power to send forth chastisement upon you from above you, or from beneath your feet, or split you into hostile groups and make some of you taste each others' violence. Behold, how We set forth Our signs in diverse forms, so that maybe they will understand the Truth".[42] (66) Your people have denied it even though it is the Truth. Say: "I am not a guardian over you.[43] (67) Every tiding has its appointed time; you yourselves will soon know (the end)."

قُلْ هُوَ ٱلْقَادِرُ عَلَىٰٓ أَن يَبْعَثَ عَلَيْكُمْ عَذَابًا
مِّن فَوْقِكُمْ أَوْ مِن تَحْتِ أَرْجُلِكُمْ أَوْ
يَلْبِسَكُمْ شِيَعًا وَيُذِيقَ بَعْضَكُم بَأْسَ بَعْضٍ ۗ
ٱنظُرْ كَيْفَ نُصَرِّفُ ٱلْءَايَٰتِ لَعَلَّهُمْ
يَفْقَهُونَ ﴿٦٥﴾ وَكَذَّبَ بِهِۦ قَوْمُكَ
وَهُوَ ٱلْحَقُّ ۚ قُل لَّسْتُ عَلَيْكُم بِوَكِيلٍ ﴿٦٦﴾
لِّكُلِّ نَبَإٍ مُّسْتَقَرٌّ ۚ وَسَوْفَ تَعْلَمُونَ ﴿٦٧﴾

The anomaly is that even though they are nourished by resources that God alone has created, they acknowledge others than Him to be their lords. Even though they have been delivered from danger and distress by His grace and mercy, they consider others than God to be their protectors and helpers. Even though they were born slaves of God, it is to others that they devote their worship. Even though it is God alone Who relieves their distress and to Whom they cry in adversity for deliverance, no sooner are they out of immediate danger than they extol others as their rescuers, and it is to them rather than to the One True God that they pay homage and make offerings.

42. God's punishment can strike in an instant. This is the warning to those who, supposing such punishment to be remote, were growing bolder in their hostility towards the Truth. They could be destroyed in a moment by a hurricane. Just a few earthquake tremors could raze villages and cities to the ground. Likewise, a few sparks of hostility could ultimately wreak such havoc among tribes, nations and countries that bloodshed and lawlessness plague them for years on end. Hence if they are spared punishments for a while that should not drug them to heedlessness and lead them to live in total disregard of distinctions between right and wrong. They should rather be grateful that God had given them respite and by means of a number of signs He was making it possible for them to recognize the Truth and follow it.

(68) When you see those who are engaged in blasphemy against Our signs, turn away from them until they begin to talk of other things; and should Satan ever cause you to forget,[44] then do not remain, after recollection, in the company of those wrong-doing people. (69) For those who are God-fearing are by no means accountable for the others except that it is their duty to admonish them; maybe then, they will shun evil.[45] (70) Leave alone those who have made a sport and a pastime of their religion and whom the life of the world has beguiled. But continue to admonish them (with the Qur'ān) lest a man should be caught for what he has himself earned for there shall neither be any protector nor intercessor apart from Allah; and though he may offer any conceivable ransom it shall not be accepted from him, for such people have been caught for the deeds that they have themselves earned. Boiling water to drink and a painful chastisement to suffer for their unbelief is what awaits them.

وَإِذَا رَأَيْتَ ٱلَّذِينَ يَخُوضُونَ فِىٓ ءَايَٰتِنَا
فَأَعْرِضْ عَنْهُمْ حَتَّىٰ يَخُوضُوا۟ فِى حَدِيثٍ
غَيْرِهِۦ ۚ وَإِمَّا يُنسِيَنَّكَ ٱلشَّيْطَٰنُ فَلَا تَقْعُدْ
بَعْدَ ٱلذِّكْرَىٰ مَعَ ٱلْقَوْمِ ٱلظَّٰلِمِينَ ﴿٦٨﴾
وَمَا عَلَى ٱلَّذِينَ يَتَّقُونَ مِنْ حِسَابِهِم
مِّن شَىْءٍ وَلَٰكِن ذِكْرَىٰ لَعَلَّهُمْ
يَتَّقُونَ ﴿٦٩﴾ وَذَرِ ٱلَّذِينَ ٱتَّخَذُوا۟
دِينَهُمْ لَعِبًا وَلَهْوًا وَغَرَّتْهُمُ ٱلْحَيَوٰةُ
ٱلدُّنْيَا ۚ وَذَكِّرْ بِهِۦٓ أَن تُبْسَلَ نَفْسٌۢ
بِمَا كَسَبَتْ لَيْسَ لَهَا مِن دُونِ ٱللَّهِ
وَلِىٌّ وَلَا شَفِيعٌ وَإِن تَعْدِلْ كُلَّ
عَدْلٍ لَّا يُؤْخَذْ مِنْهَآ ۗ أُو۟لَٰٓئِكَ ٱلَّذِينَ
أُبْسِلُوا۟ بِمَا كَسَبُوا۟ ۖ لَهُمْ شَرَابٌ مِّنْ
حَمِيمٍ وَعَذَابٌ أَلِيمٌۢ بِمَا كَانُوا۟
يَكْفُرُونَ ﴿٧٠﴾

---

43. A Prophet is neither required to compel people to see what they are not prepared to see nor to force into their hearts what they fail to comprehend. It is not a Prophet's task to chastise people for failing to see

(71) Ask them (O Muḥammad!): 'Shall we invoke, apart from Allah, something that can neither benefit nor harm us, and thus be turned back on our heels after Allah has guided us? Like the one whom the evil ones have lured into bewilderment in the earth, even though he has friends who call him to true guidance saying: "Come to us." Say: "Surely Allah's guidance is the only true guidance, and we have been commanded to submit ourselves to the Lord of the entire universe,

قُلْ أَنَدْعُواْ مِن دُونِ ٱللَّهِ مَا لَا يَنفَعُنَا
وَلَا يَضُرُّنَا وَنُرَدُّ عَلَىٰٓ أَعْقَابِنَا بَعْدَ إِذْ
هَدَىٰنَا ٱللَّهُ كَٱلَّذِى ٱسْتَهْوَتْهُ ٱلشَّيَٰطِينُ
فِى ٱلْأَرْضِ حَيْرَانَ لَهُۥٓ أَصْحَٰبٌ يَدْعُونَهُۥٓ
إِلَى ٱلْهُدَى ٱئْتِنَا ۗ قُلْ إِنَّ هُدَى ٱللَّهِ
هُوَ ٱلْهُدَىٰ ۖ وَأُمِرْنَا لِنُسْلِمَ لِرَبِّ
ٱلْعَٰلَمِينَ ﴿٧١﴾

---

and comprehend the Truth. His task is merely to proclaim Truth as distinct from falsehood. If people fail thereafter to accept it, they will be overwhelmed by the very misfortunes against which that Prophet had warned.

44. In case the Muslims fail to remember this directive and mistakenly continue to remain in the company of those who were indulging in making fun of their faith, they should withdraw from such company as soon as they remember this directive.

45. Those who avoid disobedience to God will not be held responsible for the errors of those who disobey. This being the case, the former have no justification for taking it upon themselves to persuade the latter to obedience or to consider themselves obliged to answer all their questions, however absurd and flimsy, until the Truth is forced down their throats. Their duty is merely to admonish and place the Truth before those whom they find stumbling about in error. If there is no response to this call except remonstration and obstinate argument they are under no obligation to waste their time and energy on them. They should rather devote their time and energy to instructing and admonishing those who have an urge to seek out the Truth.

(72) and to establish Prayer, and to have fear of Him. It is to Him that all of you shall be gathered. (73) And He it is Who has created the heavens and the earth in truth;[46] and the very day He will say: "Be!" (resurrection) there will be. His word is the Truth and His will be the dominion[47] on the day when the Trumpet is blown.[48] He knows all that lies beyond the reach of human perception as well as all that is visible to man;[49] He is the All-Wise, the All-Aware.'

وَأَنْ أَقِيمُوا الصَّلَوٰةَ وَاتَّقُوهُ وَهُوَ
الَّذِي إِلَيْهِ تُحْشَرُونَ ﴿٧٢﴾ وَهُوَ
الَّذِي خَلَقَ السَّمَوَٰتِ
وَالْأَرْضَ بِالْحَقِّ وَيَوْمَ يَقُولُ كُن
فَيَكُونُ قَوْلُهُ الْحَقُّ وَلَهُ الْمُلْكُ
يَوْمَ يُنفَخُ فِي الصُّورِ عَالِمُ الْغَيْبِ
وَالشَّهَدَةِ وَهُوَ الْحَكِيمُ الْخَبِيرُ
﴿٧٣﴾

46. It has been asserted again and again in the Qur'ān that God created the heavens and the earth 'in truth'. This covers a wide range of meanings:

First, that the heavens and the earth have not been created just for the fun of it. This existence is not a theatrical play. This world is not a child's toy with which to amuse oneself as long as one wishes before crushing it to bits and throwing it away. Creation is rather an act of great seriousness. A great objective motivates it, and a wise purpose underlies it. Hence, after the lapse of a certain stage it is necessary for the Creator to take full account of the work that has been done and to use those results as the basis for the next stage. This is stated at various places in the Qur'ān in the following manner:

> Our Lord, You did not create this in vain (*Sūrah Āl 'Imrān* 3: 191).
>
> And We did not create the heavens and the earth and whatever lies in between them playfully (*Sūrah al-Anbiyā'* 21: 16).
>
> And did you think that We created you out of play and that you will not be brought back to Us? (*Sūrah al-Mu'minūn* 23: 115).

Second, it means that God has created this entire system of the universe on solid foundations of truth. The whole of the universe is based on justice, wisdom and truth. Hence, there is no scope in the system for falsehood to take root and prosper. The phenomenon of the prosperity of falsehood which we observe, is to be ascribed to the will of God, Who grants the followers of falsehood the opportunity, if they so wish, to expend their efforts in promoting unrighteousness, injustice and untruth. In the end, however, the earth will throw up all the seeds of untruth that have been sown, and in the final reckoning every follower of falsehood will see that the efforts he devoted to cultivating and watering this pernicious tree have all gone to waste.

Third, it means that God has founded the universe on the basis of right, and it is on the ground of being its Creator that He governs it. His command in the universe is supreme since He alone has the right to govern it, the universe being nothing but His creation. If anyone else's commands seem to be carried out in this world, this should not cause any misunderstanding. For in reality the will of no one prevails, and cannot prevail in the universe, for no one has any right to enforce his will.

47. This does not mean that the present dominion is not His. The purpose of this statement is rather to stress that when the veil which keeps things covered during the present phase of existence is lifted and the Truth becomes fully manifest, it will become quite clear that all those who seemed or were considered to possess power and authority are absolutely powerless, and that the true dominion belongs to the One True God Who created the universe.

48. In what manner the Trumpet will be blown is difficult for us to grasp. What we know through the Qur'ān is that on the Day of Judgement the Trumpet will be blown on God's command, whereupon all will die. Then after an indefinite period of time – a period that is known to God alone – the second Trumpet will be blown, whereupon all people of all epochs will be resurrected and will find themselves on the Plane of the Congregation. Thus, when the first Trumpet is blown the entire order of the universe will be disrupted, while on the blowing of the second Trumpet a fresh order will be established, in a new form and with a new set of laws governing it.

49. *Ghayb* signifies all that is hidden from, and is beyond the ken of man's knowledge. *Shahādah*, as opposed to *ghayb*, signifies that which is manifest and thus can be known to man.

(74) And recall when Abraham said to his father, Azar:* 'Do you take idols for gods?[50] I see you and your people in obvious error.' (75) And thus We showed Abraham the kingdom of the heavens and the earth,[51] so that he might become one of those who have sure faith.[52] ▶

۞ وَإِذْ قَالَ إِبْرَٰهِيمُ لِأَبِيهِ ءَازَرَ أَتَتَّخِذُ
أَصْنَامًا ءَالِهَةً إِنِّىٓ أَرَىٰكَ وَقَوْمَكَ فِى
ضَلَٰلٍ مُّبِينٍ ﴿٧٤﴾ وَكَذَٰلِكَ نُرِىٓ إِبْرَٰهِيمَ
مَلَكُوتَ ٱلسَّمَٰوَٰتِ وَٱلْأَرْضِ وَلِيَكُونَ
مِنَ ٱلْمُوقِنِينَ ﴿٧٥﴾

50. The incident relating to Abraham (peace be on him) is adduced in order to confirm and reinforce the view that just as Muḥammad (peace be on him) and his Companions – thanks to the guidance vouchsafed by God – had denounced polytheism and had turned away from all false gods, bowing their heads in obedience to the One True Lord of the universe, so had been done by Abraham in his time. In the same way as ignorant people were then opposing the Prophet Muḥammad (peace be on him) and those who believed in him, Abraham, too, had been opposed in his day by the people among whom he lived. Furthermore, the answer Abraham gave to his people in the past can also be given by Muḥammad (peace be on him) and his followers, for he was on the same path as Noah, Abraham and the other Prophets who had descended from Abraham. Those who had refused to follow the Prophet (peace be on him) should therefore take note that they had deviated from the way of the Prophets and were lost in error.

At this point it should also be noted that Abraham was generally acknowledged by the Arabs to be their patriarch and their original religious leader. The Quraysh, in particular, were proud of their devotion to Abraham, of being his progeny and of being servants to the shrine built by him. Hence, the mention of Abraham's doctrine of monotheism, of his denunciation of polytheism and his remonstration with his polytheistic people, amounted to demolishing the very basis on which the Quraysh had prided themselves. It also amounted to destroying the confidence of the people of Arabia in their polytheistic religion. This also proved to them that the Muslims stood in the shoes of Abraham himself, whereas their own position was that of an ignorant nation which had remonstrated with Abraham out of ignorance and folly.

51. The adversaries are told that they can observe God's signs in the phenomena of the universe, just as Abraham could. The difference is that

*'Tehra' of the Bible, variously spelt as Zerah and Therach in the Talmud and Athar by Eusebius – Ed.

they see nothing, as if they were blind, whereas Abraham saw with open eyes. The sun, moon and stars which rise and set before their eyes day after day and night after night witness them as misguided at their setting as at their rising. Yet the same signs were observed by the perceptive Abraham, and the physical phenomena helped him arrive at the Truth.

52. To obtain a full understanding of this section, as well as of those verses which mention the dispute between Abraham and his people, it is necessary to cast a glance at the religious and cultural condition of the latter. Thanks to recent archaeological discoveries, not only has the city where Abraham is said to have been born been located, but a good deal of information is also available about the condition of the people of that area during the Abrahamic period. We reproduce below a summary of the conclusions which Sir Leonard Wooley arrived at as a result of the researches embodied in his work, *Abraham* (London, 1935).

It is estimated that around 2100 B.C., which is now generally accepted by scholars as the time of the advent of Abraham, the population of the city of Ur was at least two hundred and fifty thousand, maybe even five hundred thousand. The city was a large industrial and commercial metropolis. Merchandise was brought to Ur from places as far away as Palmir and Nilgiri in one direction, and in the other it had developed trade relations with Anatolia. The state, of which this city was the capital, extended a little beyond the boundaries of modern Iraq in the north, and exceeded its present borders further to the west. The great majority of the population were traders and craftsmen. The inscriptions of that period, which have been discovered in the course of archaeological research, make it clear that those people had a purely materialistic outlook on life. Their greatest concern was to earn the maximum amount of wealth and enjoy the highest degree of comfort and luxury. Interest was rampant among them and their devotion to money-making seemed all-absorbing. They looked at one another with suspicion and often resorted to litigation. In their prayers to their gods, too, they generally asked for longer life, prosperity and greater commercial success, rather than for spiritual growth, God's pardon and reward in the Hereafter.

The population comprised three classes of people: (1) *amelu*, the priests, the government and military officers; (2) *mushkinu*, the craftsmen and farmers; and (3) the slaves.

The people of the first class mentioned, i.e. *amelu*, enjoyed special privileges. In both criminal and civil matters, their rights were greater than those of the others, and their lives and property were deemed to be of higher value.

It was in such a city and in such a society that Abraham first saw the light of day. Whatever information we possess with regard to him and his family through the Talmud shows that he belonged to the *amelu* class and that his father was the highest functionary of the state. (See also *Towards Understanding the Qur'ān,* vol. I, *Sūrah* 2, n. 290.)

In the inscriptions of Ur there are references to about five thousand deities. Each city had its own deity. Each city had a chief deity which it considered its chief protector and, therefore, that deity was considered worthy of greater reverence than all the others. The chief deity of Ur was Nannar (the moon god), and it is for this reason that the city later became known as Kamarina.* The other major city was Larsa, which replaced Ur as the capital of the kingdom. Its chief deity was Shamash (the sun god). Under these major deities there was a myriad of minor deities which had generally been chosen from among the heavenly bodies – stars and planets. People considered them responsible for granting their innumerable minor prayers. Idols had been carved in the image of these celestial and terrestrial gods and goddesses and were made objects of ritual worship.

The idol of Nannar had been placed in a magnificent building on the top of the highest hill. Close to it was the temple of Nin-Gal, the wife of Nannar. The temple of Nannar resembled a royal palace. Every night a female worshipper went to its bedroom, adorned as a bride. A great number of women had been consecrated in the name of this deity and their position was virtually that of religious prostitutes. The woman who would sacrifice her virginity for the sake of her 'god' was held in great esteem. For a woman to give herself to some unrelated person 'for the sake of God' was considered a means to salvation. Needless to say, it was generally the priests who made most use of this institution.

Nannar was not merely a deity, but the biggest landlord, the biggest trader, the biggest industrialist and the most powerful ruler. Many orchards, buildings and huge estates had been consecrated to his temple. In addition to this, cereals, milk, gold, cloth, etc., were brought as offerings to the temple by peasants, landlords and merchants, and there was a large staff in the temple to receive the offerings. Many a factory had been established on behalf of the temple. Large-scale trading was also carried out on its behalf. All these activities were conducted by the priests in the name of the deity. Moreover, the country's main court was also located in the temple. The priests functioned as judges and their judgements were equated with those of God. The authority of the royal family was derived from Nannar. The concept was that Nannar was the true sovereign and that the ruler of the country governed merely on his behalf. Because of this relationship, the king himself was raised to the rank of a deity and was worshipped.

The founder of the dynasty which ruled over Ur at the time of Abraham was Ur-Nammu. In 2300 B.C. he had established an extensive kingdom, stretching from Susa in the east to Lebanon in the west. Hence the dynasty acquired the name 'Nammu', which became Nimrud in Arabic. After the emigration of Abraham, both the ruling dynasty and the nation of Ur were subjected to a succession of disasters. Firstly, the Elamites sacked Ur and captured Nimrud along with the idols of Nannar. Later on, an Elamite

---

**Qamar* is the Arabic word for 'moon' – Ed.

(76) Then, when the night outspread over him, he beheld a star, and said: 'This is my Lord.' But when it went down, he said: 'I do not love the things that go down.' (77) Then, when he beheld the moon rising, he said: 'This is my Lord!' But when it went down, he said: 'Were that my Lord did not guide me, I surely would have become among the people who have gone astray.' ▶

فَلَمَّا جَنَّ عَلَيْهِ ٱلَّيْلُ رَءَا كَوْكَبًا قَالَ
هَٰذَا رَبِّى فَلَمَّآ أَفَلَ قَالَ لَآ أُحِبُّ
ٱلْءَافِلِينَ ﴿٧٦﴾ فَلَمَّا رَءَا ٱلْقَمَرَ
بَازِغًا قَالَ هَٰذَا رَبِّى فَلَمَّآ أَفَلَ قَالَ
لَئِن لَّمْ يَهْدِنِى رَبِّى لَأَكُونَنَّ مِنَ
ٱلْقَوْمِ ٱلضَّآلِّينَ ﴿٧٧﴾

---

state was established in Larsa which governed Ur as well. Later still, Babylon prospered under a dynasty of Arabian origin and both Larsa and Ur came under its hegemony. These disasters shook the people of Ur's faith in Nannar, for he had failed to protect them.

It is difficult to say much, with certainty, about the extent of the subsequent impact of the teachings of Abraham on these people. The laws which were codified by the Babylonian King Hammurabi in 1910 B.C. show the impress of the prophetic influence, whether direct or indirect. An inscription of this code was discovered in 1902 by a French archaeologist and its English translation by C. H. W. John was published in 1903 under the title *The Oldest Code of Law*. Many articles of this code, both fundamental principles and substantive laws, bear some resemblance to the Mosaic Law.

If the conclusions of these archaeological researchers are correct, it becomes quite evident that polytheism did not consist merely of a set of religious beliefs and polytheistic rites, it rather provided the foundation on which the entire order of economic, cultural, political and social life rested. Likewise, the monotheistic mission which was undertaken by Abraham was not merely directed against the practice of idol-worship. It had far wider implications, so much so that it affected the position of the royal family both as rulers and deities. It also affected the social, economic and political status and interests of the priestly class, and the aristocracy in general, ~~and~~ in fact the entire fabric of the social life of the kingdom. To accept the teaching of Abraham meant that the entire edifice of the existing society should be pulled down and raised anew on the basis of belief in the One God. Hence, as soon as Abraham launched his mission, ordinary people as well as the privileged classes, ordinary devotees as well as Nimrud, rose at once to oppose and suppress it.

(78) Then when he beheld the sun rising, he said: 'This is my Lord. This is the greatest of all.' Then, when it went down, he said: 'O my people! Most certainly I am quit of those whom you associate with Allah in His divinity.[53] (79) Behold, I have turned my face in exclusive devotion to the One Who originated the heavens and the earth, and I am certainly not one of those who associate others with Allah in His divinity.' ▶

فَلَمَّا رَءَا ٱلشَّمْسَ بَازِغَةً قَالَ هَٰذَا
رَبِّى هَٰذَآ أَكْبَرُ ۖ فَلَمَّآ أَفَلَتْ قَالَ
يَٰقَوْمِ إِنِّى بَرِىٓءٌ مِّمَّا تُشْرِكُونَ ﴿٧٨﴾
إِنِّى وَجَّهْتُ وَجْهِىَ لِلَّذِى فَطَرَ
ٱلسَّمَٰوَٰتِ وَٱلْأَرْضَ حَنِيفًا ۖ
وَمَآ أَنَا۠ مِنَ ٱلْمُشْرِكِينَ ﴿٧٩﴾

---

53. Here some light is thrown on the mental experience through which Abraham passed in the beginning and which led him to an understanding of the Truth before prophethood was bestowed on him. This experience shows how a right-thinking and sound-hearted man, who had opened his eyes in a purely polytheistic environment and had received no instruction in monotheism, was ultimately led to discover the Truth by careful observation of, and serious reflection on the phenomena of the universe. The account of the conditions prevailing among the people of Abraham shows that when he began to think seriously the scene was dominated by the worship of the heavenly bodies – the moon, the sun and the stars. It was natural, therefore, that when Abraham began his quest for the Truth, he should have been faced with the question: Is it possible that any of these – the sun, the moon and the stars – is God? He concentrated his reflection on this central question and by observing that all the gods of his nation were bound by a rigid law under which they moved about like slaves, he concluded that those so-called gods were not possessed of even a shadow of the power of the One True Lord, Who alone had created them all and had yoked them to serve His will.

The Qur'ānic passage describing Abraham's reactions on observing first a star, then the moon, and finally the sun, has puzzled some readers because the words seem to suggest that Abraham had never before witnessed these common phenomena. This misconception has made the whole narration such a riddle for some scholars that they could only solve it by inventing the strange anecdote that Abraham was born and grew to maturity in a cave and was thus deprived of the opportunity to observe the heavenly bodies. What is said, however, is so plain that one need not fall back on any such incident in order to comprehend it. It is well known, for instance, that when Newton saw an apple fall from a tree in his orchard this incident instantly raised in his mind the question: Why do things always fall to the ground? As a result of his reflection on this question he arrived at his theory of gravity. On reading this incident one might wonder if Newton had never before seen anything fall to the ground! Obviously, he must have seen things fall. For what reason, then, should the falling of an apple cause in his mind a reaction quite different from those caused by hundreds of earlier observations of similar things falling? The answer is that a reflecting mind does not react uniformly to similar observations. A man may observe something over and over again without this observation creating any stir in his mind, but then there comes a moment when suddenly the same observation agitates his mind and his mental faculty begins to work in a different direction. It may also happen that while a man's mind is wrestling with a problem, he encounters something which is otherwise quite ordinary but which suddenly seems to provide the key. Something to this effect happened with Abraham. Certainly, he was as familiar as anyone else with nightfall and the ensuing daybreak. The sun, the moon and the stars had all risen before his eyes in the past and had then disappeared from sight. But on one particular day his observation of a star was to stimulate his thinking in a certain direction and to lead him in the end to perceive the truth of God's Oneness. It is possible that Abraham's mind was already engrossed in reflecting on whether, and if so to what extent, the beliefs which served as the foundation of the entire life-system of his people embodied the Truth, when he spotted a star which provided him with the initial key to the solution of the problem. It is also possible that the observation of a particular star first set him thinking about the problem.

Another question that arises is whether Abraham's statements about the star, the moon and the sun show that he lapsed into polytheism temporarily. The answer must be that, while a seeker after the Truth may pause on the way to his goal, what really matters is his direction and the end-point of his journey rather than the intermediary stages. These stages are inevitable for every seeker of the Truth. A man stops at them to inquire and question rather than to pronounce his final judgement. During these stages of the quest a man may seem to express the opinion: 'That is so', but what he is really doing is asking himself the question: 'Is it really so?' When serious investigation leads to a negative answer, he proceeds further and continues the quest. Hence, it would be wrong to think of such a seeker having temporarily fallen victim to polytheism and unbelief whenever he paused at an intermediary stage for critical reflection.

(80) His people remonstrated with him whereupon Abraham said: 'Do you remonstrate with me concerning Allah Who has guided me to the right way? I do not fear those whom you associate with Allah in His divinity. Only that which my Lord wills, indeed that alone will come by. My Lord embraces all things within His knowledge. Will you not take heed?[54] (81) Why should I fear those whom you have associated (with Allah in His divinity) when you do not fear associating others with Allah in His divinity – something for which He has sent down to you no authority. Then, which of the two parties has better title to security? Tell us, if you have any knowledge! (82) Those who believe and did not tarnish their faith with wrong-doing for them there is security, and it is they who have been guided to the right way.'[55]

وَحَآجَّهُۥ قَوْمُهُۥ ۚ قَالَ أَتُحَٰٓجُّوٓنِّى فِى ٱللَّهِ
وَقَدْ هَدَىٰنِ ۚ وَلَآ أَخَافُ مَا تُشْرِكُونَ بِهِۦٓ
إِلَّآ أَن يَشَآءَ رَبِّى شَيْـًٔا ۗ وَسِعَ رَبِّى
كُلَّ شَىْءٍ عِلْمًا ۗ أَفَلَا تَتَذَكَّرُونَ
﴿٨٠﴾ وَكَيْفَ أَخَافُ مَآ أَشْرَكْتُمْ
وَلَا تَخَافُونَ أَنَّكُمْ أَشْرَكْتُم بِٱللَّهِ
مَا لَمْ يُنَزِّلْ بِهِۦ عَلَيْكُمْ سُلْطَٰنًا ۚ
فَأَىُّ ٱلْفَرِيقَيْنِ أَحَقُّ بِٱلْأَمْنِ ۖ إِن كُنتُمْ
تَعْلَمُونَ ﴿٨١﴾ ٱلَّذِينَ ءَامَنُوا۟ وَلَمْ
يَلْبِسُوٓا۟ إِيمَٰنَهُم بِظُلْمٍ أُو۟لَٰٓئِكَ لَهُمُ
ٱلْأَمْنُ وَهُم مُّهْتَدُونَ ﴿٨٢﴾

---

54. The word used here is *tadhakkur*, which conveys the sense that somebody who had been either heedless or negligent of something suddenly wakes up to its true meaning. The purpose of Abraham's statement was to recall them to their senses by reminding them that their true Lord was not uninformed about their deeds, for His knowledge encompasses everything.

55. This entire section shows that those people did not deny the existence of God as the creator of the heavens and earth. Their real guilt was that

(83) That was Our argument which We gave to Abraham against his people. We raise in ranks whom We will. Truly your Lord is All-Wise, All-Knowing.

(84) And We bestowed upon Abraham (offspring) Isḥāq (Isaac) and Ya'qūb (Jacob) and each of them did We guide to the right way as We had earlier guided Noah to the right way; and (of his descendants We guided) Dā'ūd (David) and Sulaymān (Solomon), Ayyūb (Job), Yūsuf (Joseph), Musá (Moses) and Hārūn (Aaron). Thus do We reward those who do good.

وَتِلْكَ حُجَّتُنَآ ءَاتَيْنَٰهَآ إِبْرَٰهِيمَ عَلَىٰ
قَوْمِهِۦ نَرْفَعُ دَرَجَٰتٍ مَّن نَّشَآءُ إِنَّ
رَبَّكَ حَكِيمٌ عَلِيمٌ ﴿٨٣﴾ وَوَهَبْنَا
لَهُۥٓ إِسْحَٰقَ وَيَعْقُوبَ كُلًّا
هَدَيْنَا وَنُوحًا هَدَيْنَا مِن قَبْلُ
وَمِن ذُرِّيَّتِهِۦ دَاوُۥدَ وَسُلَيْمَٰنَ
وَأَيُّوبَ وَيُوسُفَ وَمُوسَىٰ وَهَٰرُونَ
وَكَذَٰلِكَ نَجْزِى ٱلْمُحْسِنِينَ ﴿٨٤﴾

---

they associated others in His attributes and His rights over man. In the first place, Abraham himself clearly states that they associated others with God as His partners. In the second place, the way in which Abraham mentions God in addressing these people is suitable only for a people who did not deny the existence of God. We must, therefore, regard as incorrect the opinion of those Qur'ānic commentators who try to explain this verse on the assumption that the people of Abraham either denied or were unaware of the existence of God, and considered their own deities to be the exclusive possessors of godhead.

The expression 'and did not tarnish their faith with wrong-doing' led some Companions to the misapprehension that perhaps this 'wrong-doing' signified 'disobedience'. But the Prophet (peace be on him) has made it clear that this wrong-doing signifies *shirk* (associating others with God in His divinity). The verse means, therefore, that they alone are fully secure and rightly-guided who believe in God and do not mix their faith with any polytheistic belief and practice.

It is interesting to learn that this incident, which is the starting-point of Abraham's prophetic career, has found no place in the Bible. It is mentioned only in the Talmud. The Talmudic version, however, is different from the Qur'ānic version in two ways. First, in the Talmudic version Abraham's quest for the Truth begins with the sun and then proceeds by

(85) (And of his descendants We guided) Zakarīyā (Zachariah), Yaḥyá (John), Isá (Jesus) and Ilyās (Elias): each one of them was of the righteous. (86) (And of his descendants We guided) Ismā'īl (Ishmael), al-Yasa' (Elisha), Yūnus (Jonah), and Lūṭ (Lot). And each one of them We favoured over all mankind. (87) And likewise We elected for Our cause and guided on to a straight way some of their forefathers and their offspring and their brethren. (88) That is Allah's guidance wherewith He guides those of His servants whom He wills. But if they ever associated others with Allah in His divinity, then all that they had done would have gone to waste.[56] (89) Those are the ones to whom We gave the Book, and judgement and prophethood.[57] And if they refuse to believe in it now, We will bestow this favour on a people who do believe in it.[58] ▶

وَزَكَرِيَّا وَيَحْيَىٰ وَعِيسَىٰ وَإِلْيَاسَ كُلٌّ
مِّنَ الصَّالِحِينَ ﴿٨٥﴾ وَإِسْمَاعِيلَ
وَالْيَسَعَ وَيُونُسَ وَلُوطًا وَكُلًّا
فَضَّلْنَا عَلَى الْعَالَمِينَ ﴿٨٦﴾ وَمِنْ
آبَائِهِمْ وَذُرِّيَّاتِهِمْ وَإِخْوَانِهِمْ وَاجْتَبَيْنَاهُمْ
وَهَدَيْنَاهُمْ إِلَىٰ صِرَاطٍ مُّسْتَقِيمٍ ﴿٨٧﴾
ذَٰلِكَ هُدَى اللَّهِ يَهْدِي بِهِ مَن يَشَاءُ
مِنْ عِبَادِهِ وَلَوْ أَشْرَكُوا لَحَبِطَ عَنْهُم
مَّا كَانُوا يَعْمَلُونَ ﴿٨٨﴾ أُولَٰئِكَ الَّذِينَ
آتَيْنَاهُمُ الْكِتَابَ وَالْحُكْمَ وَالنُّبُوَّةَ
فَإِن يَكْفُرْ بِهَا هَٰؤُلَاءِ فَقَدْ وَكَّلْنَا بِهَا
قَوْمًا لَّيْسُوا بِهَا بِكَافِرِينَ ﴿٨٩﴾

---

way of the stars to his discovery of the One True God. Second, it states that Abraham not only held the sun to be his Lord but even worshipped it, and that the same happened in connection with the moon.

56. Had those people also ascribed partners to God like the people of Arabia, they would not have achieved the positions they had attained. Some might perhaps have earned places in the rogues' gallery of history

(90) (O Muḥammad!) Those are the ones Allah guided to the right way. Follow, then, their way, and say: 'I ask of you no reward (for carrying on this mission); it is merely an admonition to all mankind.'

(91) They did not form any proper estimate of Allah when they said: 'Allah has not revealed anything to any man.'[59] Ask them: 'The Book which Moses brought as a light and guidance for men and which you keep in bits and scraps, some of which you disclose while the rest you conceal, even though through it you were taught that which neither you nor your forefathers knew – who was it who revealed it?'[60] Say: 'Allah!' – and then leave them to sport with their argumentation. ▶

أُوْلَٰٓئِكَ ٱلَّذِينَ هَدَى ٱللَّهُۖ فَبِهُدَىٰهُمُ
ٱقۡتَدِهۡۗ قُل لَّآ أَسۡـَٔلُكُمۡ عَلَيۡهِ أَجۡرًاۖ
إِنۡ هُوَ إِلَّا ذِكۡرَىٰ لِلۡعَٰلَمِينَ ٩٠
وَمَا قَدَرُواْ ٱللَّهَ حَقَّ قَدۡرِهِۦٓ إِذۡ قَالُواْ مَآ أَنزَلَ
ٱللَّهُ عَلَىٰ بَشَرٖ مِّن شَيۡءٖۗ قُلۡ مَنۡ أَنزَلَ
ٱلۡكِتَٰبَ ٱلَّذِي جَآءَ بِهِۦ مُوسَىٰ نُورٗا
وَهُدٗى لِّلنَّاسِۖ تَجۡعَلُونَهُۥ قَرَاطِيسَ
تُبۡدُونَهَا وَتُخۡفُونَ كَثِيرٗاۖ وَعُلِّمۡتُم مَّا لَمۡ
تَعۡلَمُوٓاْ أَنتُمۡ وَلَآ ءَابَآؤُكُمۡۖ قُلِ ٱللَّهُۖ ثُمَّ
ذَرۡهُمۡ فِي خَوۡضِهِمۡ يَلۡعَبُونَ ٩١

as either ruthless conquerors or monuments to greed. But had they not shunned polytheism and adhered to their exclusive and unadulterated devotion to God, they would certainly neither have had the honour of becoming the source of light and guidance to others nor of assuming the leadership of the pious and the God-fearing.

57. Here the Prophets are mentioned as having been endowed with three things: first, the revealed guidance embodied in the Book; second, *ḥukm*, i.e. the correct understanding of the revealed guidance, the ability to apply its principles to the practical affairs of life, the God-given capacity to arrive at right opinions regarding human problems; and third, prophethood, the office by virtue of which they are enabled to lead human beings in the light of the guidance vouchsafed to them.

58. God does not care if the unbelievers and polytheists choose to reject the guidance which has come down from Him, for He had already raised a sizeable group of men of faith to truly appreciate its worth.

59. In the light of the foregoing discussion and commentary, it is quite evident that this statement comes from the Jews. Since the Prophet (peace be on him) had asserted that he was a Prophet and that a Book had been revealed to him, the unbelieving Quraysh and other polytheists of Arabia naturally used to approach the Jews and the Christians – who believed in the Prophets and in the Scriptures – and tried to solicit a candid answer from them as to whether God's words had indeed been revealed to Muḥammad (peace be on him). Whatever answer they gave was then disseminated on all sides by the active opponents of the Prophet (peace be on him) in order to create revulsion against Islam. This is the reason for mentioning, and then refuting, this statement by the Jews, which had been used by the opposition as an argument against Islam.

One might wonder how a Jew, who believes in the Torah as a revealed Book of God, could say that God had revealed nothing to anyone. At times blind obstinacy and bigotry cause people to resort to arguments which strike at the roots of their own belief. These people were bent upon denying the prophethood of Muḥammad (peace be on him), and this fanaticism had come to dominate them so much that they went so far as to deny the very institution of prophethood.

To say that people have not formed any proper estimate of God means that they have erred grossly in assessing His wisdom and power. Whoever says that God did not reveal knowledge of Reality and the code for man's guidance has fallen into one of two errors. Either he considers it impossible for man to become the recipient of God's revelation, and this constitutes a gross misjudgement of God's power, or he thinks that even though God has equipped man with intelligence and with the power to act as he chooses, He has nevertheless made no arrangement for his guidance, but has left him in this world altogether unguided and thus conferred upon him the right to behave in any way he likes. This is obviously a misjudgement of God's wisdom.

60. The revelation of the Torah to Moses (peace be on him) is adduced by way of evidence since the Jews, to whom this response is addressed, believed that it had been revealed. It is obvious that their recognition of the Torah as the Book revealed to Moses negated their standpoint that God had never revealed anything to any human being. Their belief in the Torah at least proved that revelation to man is possible, and had actually taken place.

(92) (Like that Book) this too is a Book which We have revealed; full of blessing, confirming what was revealed before it so that you might warn the people of the Mother of Cities (Makka) and those around it. Those who believe in the Hereafter believe in it, and are ever-mindful of their Prayers.[61] (93) Who can be more unjust than he who places a lie on Allah and who says: 'Revelation has come to me' when in fact nothing was revealed to him, and who says: 'I will produce the like of what Allah has revealed?' If you could but see the wrong-doers in the agonies of death, and the angels stretching out their hands (saying): 'Yield up your souls! Today you will be recompensed with the chastisement of humiliation for the lie you spoke concerning Allah, and for you waxing proud against His signs.' ▶

وَهَٰذَا كِتَٰبٌ أَنزَلْنَٰهُ مُبَارَكٌ مُّصَدِّقُ
ٱلَّذِى بَيْنَ يَدَيْهِ وَلِتُنذِرَ أُمَّ ٱلْقُرَىٰ وَمَنْ
حَوْلَهَا وَٱلَّذِينَ يُؤْمِنُونَ بِٱلْءَاخِرَةِ
يُؤْمِنُونَ بِهِۦ وَهُمْ عَلَىٰ صَلَاتِهِمْ
يُحَافِظُونَ ﴿٩٢﴾ وَمَنْ أَظْلَمُ مِمَّنِ ٱفْتَرَىٰ
عَلَى ٱللَّهِ كَذِبًا أَوْ قَالَ أُوحِىَ إِلَىَّ وَلَمْ
يُوحَ إِلَيْهِ شَىْءٌ وَمَن قَالَ سَأُنزِلُ مِثْلَ مَآ
أَنزَلَ ٱللَّهُ وَلَوْ تَرَىٰٓ إِذِ ٱلظَّٰلِمُونَ فِى
غَمَرَٰتِ ٱلْمَوْتِ وَٱلْمَلَٰٓئِكَةُ بَاسِطُوٓا۟
أَيْدِيهِمْ أَخْرِجُوٓا۟ أَنفُسَكُمُ ٱلْيَوْمَ
تُجْزَوْنَ عَذَابَ ٱلْهُونِ بِمَا كُنتُمْ
تَقُولُونَ عَلَى ٱللَّهِ غَيْرَ ٱلْحَقِّ وَكُنتُمْ عَنْ
ءَايَٰتِهِۦ تَسْتَكْبِرُونَ ﴿٩٣﴾

61. The point argued above was that God's word can be, and in the past has been, revealed to human beings. The next point is that the message of Muḥammad (peace be on him) is indeed the revealed word of God. In order to establish this, four things are adduced as evidence:

First, that this Book is overflowing with God's grace and beneficence. In other words, it contains the best possible principles for the well-being and salvation of mankind. It lays down the true doctrines of belief. It urges man to righteous conduct and inspires him to moral excellence. It contains guidance as to how one may live a life of purity. And above all, it is free from any trace of the ignorance, egocentricity, narrow-mindedness, iniquity, obscenity and other corruptions with which the Jews and the

(94) (And Allah will say): 'Now you have come to Us all alone even as We had created you in the first instance, and you have left behind all that We had bestowed upon you in the world. We do not see with you your intercessors whom you imagined to have a share with Allah in your affairs. You have now been cut off from one another and all those whom you imagined (to be Allah's associates in your affairs) have failed you.'

(95) Truly it is Allah Who causes the grain[62] and the fruit-kernel to sprout. He brings forth the living from the dead and brings forth the dead from the living.[63] Such is Allah. So whither are you tending in error? ▶

وَلَقَدْ جِئْتُمُونَا فُرَٰدَىٰ كَمَا خَلَقْنَٰكُمْ
أَوَّلَ مَرَّةٍ وَتَرَكْتُم مَّا خَوَّلْنَٰكُمْ وَرَآءَ
ظُهُورِكُمْ ۖ وَمَا نَرَىٰ مَعَكُمْ
شُفَعَآءَكُمُ ٱلَّذِينَ زَعَمْتُمْ أَنَّهُمْ فِيكُمْ
شُرَكَٰٓؤُا۟ ۚ لَقَد تَّقَطَّعَ بَيْنَكُمْ وَضَلَّ
عَنكُم مَّا كُنتُمْ تَزْعُمُونَ ﴿٩٤﴾
۞ إِنَّ ٱللَّهَ فَالِقُ ٱلْحَبِّ وَٱلنَّوَىٰ ۖ
يُخْرِجُ ٱلْحَىَّ مِنَ ٱلْمَيِّتِ وَمُخْرِجُ ٱلْمَيِّتِ
مِنَ ٱلْحَىِّ ۚ ذَٰلِكُمُ ٱللَّهُ ۖ فَأَنَّىٰ تُؤْفَكُونَ ﴿٩٥﴾

Christians had overlaid their revealed Scriptures. Second, this Book does not propound any guidance which is essentially divergent from that previously revealed; rather it confirms and supports it. Third, the purpose of the revelation of this Book is the same as that of the revelation of Scriptures in the past, viz., to shake people out of their heedlessness and warn them of the evil consequences of their corruption. Fourth, that the call of this Book did not attract those who merely worshipped worldly advantages and were slaves of their animal desires. On the contrary, it attracted those whose vision goes beyond the narrow limits of worldly life. Moreover, the revolution wrought in the lives of people under the influence of this Book has rendered them conspicuously distinct from others in respect of piety and godliness.

A Book with such characteristics and with such a wholesome impact on human beings can only be from God.

(96) It is He Who causes the dawn to split forth, and has ordained the night for repose, and the sun and the moon for reckoning time. All this is determined by Allah the Almighty, the All-Knowing. (97) It is He Who has made for you the stars that you may follow the right direction in the darkness of the land and the sea. We have indeed spelled out signs for the people who have knowledge.[64] (98) It is He Who created you out of a single being,[65] and appointed for each of you a time-limit and a resting place. We have indeed spelled out Our signs for those who can understand.[66] ▶

فَالِقُ ٱلْإِصْبَاحِ وَجَعَلَ ٱلَّيْلَ سَكَنًا
وَٱلشَّمْسَ وَٱلْقَمَرَ حُسْبَانًا ذَٰلِكَ تَقْدِيرُ
ٱلْعَزِيزِ ٱلْعَلِيمِ ﴿٩٦﴾ وَهُوَ ٱلَّذِى جَعَلَ
لَكُمُ ٱلنُّجُومَ لِتَهْتَدُوا۟ بِهَا فِى ظُلُمَٰتِ
ٱلْبَرِّ وَٱلْبَحْرِ قَدْ فَصَّلْنَا ٱلْءَايَٰتِ لِقَوْمٍ
يَعْلَمُونَ ﴿٩٧﴾ وَهُوَ ٱلَّذِىٓ أَنشَأَكُم
مِّن نَّفْسٍ وَٰحِدَةٍ فَمُسْتَقَرٌّ وَمُسْتَوْدَعٌ
قَدْ فَصَّلْنَا ٱلْءَايَٰتِ لِقَوْمٍ يَفْقَهُونَ
﴿٩٨﴾

62. The one who causes the seed-grain to split open under the surface of the earth and then makes it grow and appear on the surface as a plant is no other than God.

63. To 'bring forth the living from the dead' means creating living beings out of dead matter. Likewise, 'to bring out the dead from the living' means to remove the lifeless elements from a living organism.

64. By 'signs' are meant all that support the proposition that there is only one God, that is, no one has either the attributes of God or any share in His authority or can rightfully claim any of the rights which belong exclusively to Him. But the ignorant cannot benefit from these signs, which are scattered all around, in order to arrive at an understanding of the Truth. Only those who observe the phenomena of the universe in a careful and systematic manner, and do so with a correct perspective, can truly benefit from these signs.

65. This means that God caused the human race to originate from one human being.

(99) And it is He Who has sent down water from the heavens, and thereby We have brought vegetation of every kind, and out of this We have brought forth green foliage and then from it close-packed ears of corn, and out of the palm-tree – from the sheath of it – thick-clustered dates, hanging down with heaviness, and gardens of vines, and the olive tree, and the pomegranate – all resembling one another and yet so different. Behold their fruit when they bear fruit and ripen! Surely, in all this there are signs for those who believe. (100) And yet, some people have come to associate the *jinn* with Allah in His divinity,[67] even though it is He Who created them; and in ignorance they impute to Him sons and daughters.[68] He is Holy and Exalted far above that which they attribute to Him. ►

وَهُوَ ٱلَّذِىٓ أَنزَلَ مِنَ ٱلسَّمَآءِ مَآءً
فَأَخْرَجْنَا بِهِۦ نَبَاتَ كُلِّ شَىْءٍ فَأَخْرَجْنَا
مِنْهُ خَضِرًا نُّخْرِجُ مِنْهُ حَبًّا
مُّتَرَاكِبًا وَمِنَ ٱلنَّخْلِ مِن طَلْعِهَا
قِنْوَانٌ دَانِيَةٌ وَجَنَّٰتٍ مِّنْ أَعْنَابٍ
وَٱلزَّيْتُونَ وَٱلرُّمَّانَ مُشْتَبِهًا وَغَيْرَ
مُتَشَٰبِهٍ ٱنظُرُوٓا۟ إِلَىٰ ثَمَرِهِۦٓ إِذَآ أَثْمَرَ
وَيَنْعِهِۦٓ إِنَّ فِى ذَٰلِكُمْ لَءَايَٰتٍ لِّقَوْمٍ
يُؤْمِنُونَ ﴿٩٩﴾ وَجَعَلُوا۟ لِلَّهِ شُرَكَآءَ
ٱلْجِنَّ وَخَلَقَهُمْ وَخَرَقُوا۟ لَهُۥ بَنِينَ
وَبَنَٰتٍۭ بِغَيْرِ عِلْمٍ سُبْحَٰنَهُۥ
وَتَعَٰلَىٰ عَمَّا يَصِفُونَ ﴿١٠٠﴾

---

66. If one were to observe carefully the creation of the human species, its division into male and female, the proliferation of the human race by procreation, the passing of life through its several stages in the womb of the mother from conception to childbirth, one would perceive innumerable signs to help one grasp the truth mentioned above. But only those who make proper use of their intellect can be led by means of these signs to an understanding of Reality. Those who live like animals, who are concerned merely with the satisfaction of their lusts and desires, can perceive nothing significant in these phenomena.

(101) He is the Originator of the heavens and the earth. How can He have a son when He has had no mate? And He has created everything and He has full knowledge of all things. (102) Such is Allah, your Lord. There is no god but He – the Creator of all things. Serve Him alone – for it is He Who is the guardian of everything. (103) No visual perception can encompass Him, even though He encompasses all visual perception. He is the All-Subtle, the All-Aware.

(104) The lights of clear perception have now come to you from your Lord. Then, he who chooses to see clearly, does so for his own good; and he who chooses to remain blind, does so to his own harm. I am not your keeper.[69]

بَدِيعُ ٱلسَّمَٰوَٰتِ وَٱلْأَرْضِ أَنَّىٰ يَكُونُ
لَهُۥ وَلَدٌ وَلَمْ تَكُن لَّهُۥ صَٰحِبَةٌ وَخَلَقَ كُلَّ
شَيْءٍ وَهُوَ بِكُلِّ شَيْءٍ عَلِيمٌ ﴿١٠١﴾
ذَٰلِكُمُ ٱللَّهُ رَبُّكُمْ لَآ إِلَٰهَ إِلَّا هُوَ
خَٰلِقُ كُلِّ شَيْءٍ فَٱعْبُدُوهُ
وَهُوَ عَلَىٰ كُلِّ شَيْءٍ وَكِيلٌ ﴿١٠٢﴾
لَّا تُدْرِكُهُ ٱلْأَبْصَٰرُ وَهُوَ يُدْرِكُ
ٱلْأَبْصَٰرَ وَهُوَ ٱللَّطِيفُ ٱلْخَبِيرُ ﴿١٠٣﴾
قَدْ جَآءَكُم بَصَآئِرُ مِن رَّبِّكُمْ فَمَنْ أَبْصَرَ
فَلِنَفْسِهِۦ وَمَنْ عَمِىَ فَعَلَيْهَا وَمَآ أَنَا۠
عَلَيْكُم بِحَفِيظٍ ﴿١٠٤﴾

---

67. Because of man's imaginativeness and superstitious disposition, he has often held other invisible beings to be associated with God in His governance of the universe and in making and marring man's destiny. For example, the deity of rain, and the deity of vegetation, the god of wealth and the god of health, and so on. Such beliefs are found among all the polytheistic nations of the world.

68. The ignorant Arabs considered angels to be the daughters of God. In the same way, other polytheistic nations wove a network of blood-relationships with God, producing thereby a whole crop of gods and goddesses descended from the Creator.

69. Even though this statement is from God, it is expressed through the mouth of the Prophet (peace be on him). We observe that in the Qur'ān

(105) Thus do We make Our signs clear in diverse ways that they might say: 'You have learned this (from somebody)'; and 'We do this in order that We make the Truth clear to the people of knowledge.'[70] (106) (O Muḥammad!) Follow the revelation which has come to you from your Lord, other than Whom there is no god, and turn away from those who associate others with Allah in His divinity.

وَكَذَٰلِكَ نُصَرِّفُ ٱلْـَٔايَٰتِ وَلِيَقُولُوا۟
دَرَسْتَ وَلِنُبَيِّنَهُۥ لِقَوْمٍ يَعْلَمُونَ ﴿١٠٥﴾
ٱتَّبِعْ مَآ أُوحِىَ إِلَيْكَ مِن رَّبِّكَ ۖ لَآ إِلَٰهَ
إِلَّا هُوَ ۖ وَأَعْرِضْ عَنِ ٱلْمُشْرِكِينَ ﴿١٠٦﴾

---

the speaker frequently changes – sometimes it is God Who is speaking, sometimes it is the angel who carries the revelation, and sometimes a group of angels; on some occasions it is the Prophet (peace be on him) who is speaking, while on others it is the men of faith. Likewise, those addressed by the Qur'ān also change – sometimes it is the Prophet (peace be on him); sometimes it is the men of faith; sometimes it is the People of the Book; sometimes it is the unbelievers and the polytheists; sometimes it is the Quraysh; sometimes it is the Arabs; and sometimes, mankind as a whole. Regardless of these changes, however, the content of the message always remains the same – it consists of God's guidance to mankind.

The statement 'I am not your keeper' signifies that the task of the Prophet is confined to carrying the light of true guidance to others, it is then up to them either to use it to perceive Reality for themselves or to keep their eyes closed. The Prophet (peace be on him) is not asked to compel those who deliberately kept their eyes shut to open them, forcing them to see what they did not wish to see.

70. The same has been said earlier, viz. that genuine seekers after the Truth arrive at it even when it is couched in parables about such apparently trivial things as flies and gnats (see *Sūrah al-Baqarah* 2: 24). As for those who have been seized by a biased negativism, they are prone to ask, sarcastically: What have these trivial things to do with the Book of God? The same idea is expressed here in a slightly different form. The import of the statement is that the Book of God has become a touchstone, which helps mark off the true from the false.

These include the sort of people who, once they have come to know the teachings of the Book of God, try in earnest to reflect on its substance and

(107) Had Allah so willed they would not have associated others with Him in His divinity; and We have not appointed you a watcher over them, and you are not their guardian.[71] (108) Do not revile those whom they invoke other than Allah, because they will revile Allah in ignorance out of spite.[72] For We have indeed made the deeds of every people seem fair to them.[73] Then, their return is to their Lord and He will inform them of what they have done.

وَلَوْ شَآءَ ٱللَّهُ مَآ أَشْرَكُوا۟ ۗ وَمَا جَعَلْنَٰكَ
عَلَيْهِمْ حَفِيظًا ۖ وَمَآ أَنتَ عَلَيْهِم بِوَكِيلٍ
١٠٧ وَلَا تَسُبُّوا۟ ٱلَّذِينَ يَدْعُونَ مِن
دُونِ ٱللَّهِ فَيَسُبُّوا۟ ٱللَّهَ عَدْوًۢا بِغَيْرِ عِلْمٍ ۗ
كَذَٰلِكَ زَيَّنَّا لِكُلِّ أُمَّةٍ عَمَلَهُمْ ثُمَّ إِلَىٰ
رَبِّهِم مَّرْجِعُهُمْ فَيُنَبِّئُهُم بِمَا كَانُوا۟
يَعْمَلُونَ ١٠٨

seek to benefit from the wisdom and admonition it contains. Another group reacts quite differently. When they hear or read the Book, their minds are not attracted by the substance of its message. Rather, their curiosity is aroused and they begin probing as to where this Prophet, who had no formal education, derived the teachings which the Book contains. And since a negative prejudice has already seized their hearts, they find it reasonable to conceive of any possibility except the possibility that the Qur'ān is a revelation from God. Such people proclaim their opinion with such strong conviction that one might feel inclined to believe that they had indeed discovered the real 'source' of the Book by means of scientific investigation.

71. It is emphasized that the Prophet (peace be on him) is only required to preach the Truth and try to call people to embrace it. His responsibility ends at that for he is, after all, not their warden. His task is to present this guidance and spare no effort in elucidating the Truth. Anyone who still rejects it does so on his own responsibility. It is not part of the Prophet's task to compel anybody to follow the Truth, and he will not be held accountable for not having been able to bring an individual out of the fold of falsehood. Hence he should not overstrain his mind by his desire to make the blind see, or compel those bent on keeping their eyes shut, to observe. For, had it been an objective of God's universal plan not to allow anyone to remain devoted to falsehood, He need not have sent Prophets for that purpose. Could He not have turned all human beings, instantly,

into devotees of the Truth by His mere will? Quite obviously God did not intend to do so. The entire basis of the Divine plan is that men should have free-will and be allowed to choose between the Truth and falsehood; that the Truth should be explained to them in order that they be tested with regard to their choice between truth and falsehood. The right attitude, therefore, is for them to follow the Straight Way which has been illuminated by the light bequeathed to them and to keep on calling others towards it. They should naturally value very highly all those who respond to the message of the Truth. Such persons should not be forsaken or neglected, however humble their station in the world. As for those who wilfully reject the message of God, one need not pursue them too far. They should rather be left alone to proceed towards their doom since they themselves wish so, and are insistent on doing so.

72. The Prophet (peace be on him) and his followers are admonished not to allow their proselytizing zeal to dominate them so that their polemics and controversial religious discussions either lead them to be offensive to the beliefs of non-Muslims or to abuse their religious leaders and deities. Far from bringing people closer to the Truth, such an attitude is likely to alienate them from it further.

73. Here we should bear in mind, as we have pointed out earlier, that God declares those things which take place as a result of the operation of the laws of nature to be His own acts, for it is He Who has made those laws. Whatever results from the operation of those laws, therefore, results from His command. Whenever God states that a certain act was His, the same might be described by humans as occurring in the natural course of things.

(109) They swear by Allah with their most solemn oaths that if a sign[74] comes to them, they will certainly believe in it. Say: 'Signs are in Allah's power alone.'[75] What will make you realize that even if those signs were to come, they would still not believe?[76] (110) We are turning their hearts and eyes away from the Truth even as they did not believe in the first instance[77] – and We leave them in their insurgence to stumble blindly. (111) Even if We had sent angels down to them and the dead had spoken to them, and even if We had assembled before them all the things, face to face, they would still not believe unless it be Allah's will that they believe.[78] Most of them behave in utter ignorance.

وَأَقْسَمُوا۟ بِٱللَّهِ جَهْدَ أَيْمَـٰنِهِمْ لَئِن
جَآءَتْهُمْ ءَايَةٌ لَّيُؤْمِنُنَّ بِهَا ۚ قُلْ إِنَّمَا
ٱلْـَٔايَـٰتُ عِندَ ٱللَّهِ ۖ وَمَا يُشْعِرُكُمْ أَنَّهَآ
إِذَا جَآءَتْ لَا يُؤْمِنُونَ ﴿١٠٩﴾ وَنُقَلِّبُ
أَفْـِٔدَتَهُمْ وَأَبْصَـٰرَهُمْ كَمَا لَمْ يُؤْمِنُوا۟
بِهِۦٓ أَوَّلَ مَرَّةٍ وَنَذَرُهُمْ فِى طُغْيَـٰنِهِمْ
يَعْمَهُونَ ﴿١١٠﴾ ۞ وَلَوْ أَنَّنَا نَزَّلْنَآ إِلَيْهِمُ
ٱلْمَلَـٰٓئِكَةَ وَكَلَّمَهُمُ ٱلْمَوْتَىٰ وَحَشَرْنَا
عَلَيْهِمْ كُلَّ شَىْءٍ قُبُلًا مَّا كَانُوا۟ لِيُؤْمِنُوٓا۟
إِلَّآ أَن يَشَآءَ ٱللَّهُ وَلَـٰكِنَّ أَكْثَرَهُمْ
يَجْهَلُونَ ﴿١١١﴾

74. 'Sign' in this context signifies a tangible miracle which is so impressive that it leaves people with no alternative but to believe in the veracity of the Prophet (peace be on him) and the truth of his claim to have been appointed by God.

75. The Prophet (peace be on him) denies his ability to perform miracles.* That power lies with God alone. If God wants a miracle to take place, He has the power; if He does not want miracles to take place, none will.

76. These words are addressed to the Muslims. Driven by the restless yearning to see people embrace Islam – a yearning which they sometimes

*And so indeed does every Prophet of God – Ed.

(112) And so it is that against every Prophet We have set up the evil ones from among men and *jinn*, some of them inspire others with specious speech only by way of delusion.[79] Had it been your Lord's will, they would not have done it.[80] Leave them alone to fabricate what they will. (113) So that the hearts of those who do not believe in the Life to Come might incline towards this attractive delusion, and that they may be well pleased with it and might acquire the evils that they are bent on acquiring.

وَكَذَٰلِكَ جَعَلْنَا لِكُلِّ نَبِيٍّ عَدُوًّا
شَيَٰطِينَ ٱلْإِنسِ وَٱلْجِنِّ يُوحِى
بَعْضُهُمْ إِلَىٰ بَعْضٍ زُخْرُفَ ٱلْقَوْلِ
غُرُورًا وَلَوْ شَآءَ رَبُّكَ مَا فَعَلُوهُ فَذَرْهُمْ
وَمَا يَفْتَرُونَ ﴿١١٢﴾ وَلِتَصْغَىٰٓ إِلَيْهِ
أَفْـِٔدَةُ ٱلَّذِينَ لَا يُؤْمِنُونَ بِٱلْـَٔاخِرَةِ
وَلِيَرْضَوْهُ وَلِيَقْتَرِفُوا۟ مَا هُم
مُّقْتَرِفُونَ ﴿١١٣﴾

expressed in words – they wished some miracle to happen which might lead their erring brethren to the true faith. In response to this wish and longing they are told that their embracing the true faith does not depend upon their observing any miraculous sign.

77. This shows that they still suffer from the same mentality which had made them reject the call of the Prophet (peace be on him) at the outset. Their outlook has undergone no change. The same mental confusion, the same opacity of vision which had kept them from developing sound understanding and a correct perspective still warps their understanding and clouds their vision.

78. The people under discussion are so perverse that they do not prefer to embrace the Truth in preference to falsehood by rightly exercising their choice and volition. The only way that is left for them to become lovers of the Truth is, therefore, that by His overpowering will God should render them truth-loving not by their choice and volition, but by metamorphizing their very nature. Such a course, however, goes against the wisdom which underlies the creation of man. Hence it is futile to expect God to intervene in the matter and to force those people to believe by the exercise of His will.

79. The Prophet (peace be on him) is told that he should not be unnerved even if the evil ones among both mankind and the *jinn* stood united against

him and opposed him with all their might. For this was not the first time that such a thing had happened. Whenever a Prophet came and tried to lead people to the Truth, all the satanic forces joined hands to defeat his mission.

'Specious talk' signifies all the trickery and manoeuvring to which the enemy resorts, all his efforts aimed at sowing doubts about Islam and undermining people's faith in it, so as to arouse them against both the Prophet (peace be on him) and his message. Taken as a whole, these are characterized as 'delusion', for the weapons used in their crusade by the opponents of the Truth have the effect of deluding others as well as themselves, no matter how beneficial and successful those weapons may appear to be.

80. Furthermore, we should always bear in mind that, according to the Qur'ān, there is a tremendous difference between 'God's will' and 'God's good pleasure'. The failure to differentiate between the two often gives rise to serious misconceptions. If a certain thing takes place in accord with the universal will of God, and thus by His sanction, that does not necessarily mean that God is pleased with it. Nothing at all takes place in the world unless God permits it to take place, unless He makes it a part of His scheme, and unless He makes it possible for that event to take place by creating its necessary conditions. The act of stealing on the part of a thief, the act of homicide on the part of a murderer, the wrong and corruption of the wrong-doer and the corrupt, the unbelief of the unbeliever and the polytheism of the polytheist – none of these are possible without the will of God. Likewise, the faith of the believer and the piety of the pious are inconceivable without the will of God. In short, both these require the will of God. But whereas the things in the first category do not please Him, those in the second do.

Even though the will of God is oriented to ultimate good, the course of the realization of that good is paved with conflict between the forces of light and darkness, of good and evil, of what is sound and pure on the one hand and what is corrupt and defiled on the other. With larger interests in view, God has endowed man with the disposition of obedience as well as of disobedience. He has created in man Abrahamic and Mosaic as well as Nimrodic and Pharaonic potentialities. Both the pure, unadulterated human nature and the satanic urges are ingrained in man's being and have been provided with the opportunity to work themselves out by coming into conflict with each other. He has granted those species of His creatures who are possessed of authority (viz. man and *jinn*) the freedom to choose between good and evil. Whosoever chooses to act righteously has been given the power to do so, and the same is the case with him who chooses to be evil. People of both categories are in a position to use material resources within the framework of the broader considerations underlying God's governance of His universe. God will be pleased, however, only with those who are working for good. God likes His creatures to exercise their freedom of choice properly and commit themselves to good of their own volition.

(114) Shall I look upon anyone apart from Allah for judgement when it is He Who has revealed to you the Book in detail?[81] And those whom We gave the Book (before you) know that this (Book) has been revealed in truth by your Lord. Do not, then, be among the doubters.[82] (115) The Word of your Lord is perfect in truthfulness and justice; no one can change His words. He is the All-Hearing, the All-Knowing.

أَفَغَيْرَ ٱللَّهِ أَبْتَغِى حَكَمًا وَهُوَ ٱلَّذِىٓ
أَنزَلَ إِلَيْكُمُ ٱلْكِتَٰبَ مُفَصَّلًا ۚ
وَٱلَّذِينَ ءَاتَيْنَٰهُمُ ٱلْكِتَٰبَ يَعْلَمُونَ
أَنَّهُۥ مُنَزَّلٌ مِّن رَّبِّكَ بِٱلْحَقِّ ۖ فَلَا تَكُونَنَّ
مِنَ ٱلْمُمْتَرِينَ ﴿١١٤﴾ وَتَمَّتْ كَلِمَتُ
رَبِّكَ صِدْقًا وَعَدْلًا ۚ لَّا مُبَدِّلَ
لِكَلِمَٰتِهِۦ ۚ وَهُوَ ٱلسَّمِيعُ ٱلْعَلِيمُ ﴿١١٥﴾

Unlike the angels, who carry out God's commands without resistance from any quarter, the task entrusted to men is to strive to establish the way of life sanctioned by God in the face of opposition and hostility from evil-doers and rebels against Him. In the framework of His universal will, God allows even those who have chosen the path of rebellion to strive for the realization of their goals, even as He grants the believers every opportunity to strive along the path of obedience and service to God. Despite this granting of freedom and choice to all there is no doubt that God is pleased with, and guides, directs, supports and strengthens the believers alone because their overall direction is to His liking. Nevertheless, they should not expect that by His supernatural intervention God will either force those who are disinclined to believe into believing or that He will forcibly remove the satanic forces – among both men and *jinn* – who are resolved to spare neither their mental and physical energy nor their material resources to impede the triumph of the Truth. Those determined to strive in the cause of the Truth, and of virtue and righteousness are told that they must prove their earnest devotion by waging a fierce struggle against the devotees of falsehood. For had God wanted to use miracles to obliterate falsehood and usher in the reign of the Truth, He would not have required human beings to accomplish the task. He could have simply seen to it that no evil one remained in the world, leaving no possibility for polytheism and unbelief to exist.

81. The implied speaker in this sentence is the Prophet (peace be on him) and the words are addressed to the Muslims. The purpose of the sentence is to impress upon the Muslims that God has elucidated the

(116) (O Muḥammad!) If you obey the majority of those who live on earth, they will lead you away from Allah's path. They only follow idle fancies, indulging in conjecture.[83] (117) And your Lord knows well who stray from His path, and also those who are rightly-guided.

وَإِن تُطِعْ أَكْثَرَ مَن فِي ٱلْأَرْضِ
يُضِلُّوكَ عَن سَبِيلِ ٱللَّهِ ۚ إِن يَتَّبِعُونَ
إِلَّا ٱلظَّنَّ وَإِنْ هُمْ إِلَّا يَخْرُصُونَ ﴿١١٦﴾
إِنَّ رَبَّكَ هُوَ أَعْلَمُ مَن يَضِلُّ عَن
سَبِيلِهِۦ ۖ وَهُوَ أَعْلَمُ بِٱلْمُهْتَدِينَ ﴿١١٧﴾

---

relevant truths, and has also proclaimed that in their endeavour to make the Truth prevail they will have to follow the path of striving and struggle. The devotees of the Truth should, therefore, resort to those means which human beings normally employ for the successful achievement of their objectives rather than wait for any supernatural intervention that would enable them to achieve their mission without struggle and sacrifice. Moreover, since God Himself had chosen that human effort rather than supernatural intervention should lead to the prevalence of the Truth, who had the power to change this basic fact and bring about the victory of the Truth without any resort to human effort and sacrifice.

82. This is no mere concoction designed to explain away the current problems. All those versed in the Scriptures, and possessing true understanding of the mission of the Prophets (peace be on them all), will confirm that everything in the Qur'ān is perfectly true and in fact constitutes that eternal truth which cannot suffer any change or modification.

83. One need not follow the way of life of the majority, for the majority tend to follow their conjectures and fancies rather than sound knowledge. Their beliefs, their ideas and concepts, their philosophies of life, the guiding principles of their conduct, their laws – all these are founded on conjecture. On the contrary, the way of life which pleases God, was revealed by Him and hence is based on true knowledge rather than conjecture. Instead of trying to discover the way of life of the majority, a seeker after truth should, therefore, persevere in the way prescribed by God, even if he finds himself to be a solitary traveller.

(118) If you believe in the signs of Allah, eat (the flesh) of that over which Allah's name has been pronounced.[84] (119) And how is it that you do not eat of that over which Allah's name has been pronounced even though He has clearly spelled out to you what He has forbidden you unless you are constrained to it?[85] Many indeed say misleading things without knowledge, driven merely by their lowly desires. But your Lord knows well the transgressors. (120) Abstain from sin, be it either open or secret. Indeed those who commit sins shall surely be requited for all they have done. ▶

فَكُلُوا۟ مِمَّا ذُكِرَ ٱسْمُ ٱللَّهِ عَلَيْهِ إِن كُنتُم
بِـَٔايَـٰتِهِۦ مُؤْمِنِينَ ﴿١١٨﴾ وَمَا لَكُمْ أَلَّا
تَأْكُلُوا۟ مِمَّا ذُكِرَ ٱسْمُ ٱللَّهِ عَلَيْهِ
وَقَدْ فَصَّلَ لَكُم مَّا حَرَّمَ عَلَيْكُمْ إِلَّا
مَا ٱضْطُرِرْتُمْ إِلَيْهِ ۗ وَإِنَّ كَثِيرًا لَّيُضِلُّونَ
بِأَهْوَآئِهِم بِغَيْرِ عِلْمٍ ۗ إِنَّ رَبَّكَ هُوَ
أَعْلَمُ بِٱلْمُعْتَدِينَ ﴿١١٩﴾ وَذَرُوا۟ ظَـٰهِرَ
ٱلْإِثْمِ وَبَاطِنَهُۥٓ ۚ إِنَّ ٱلَّذِينَ يَكْسِبُونَ
ٱلْإِثْمَ سَيُجْزَوْنَ بِمَا كَانُوا۟ يَقْتَرِفُونَ ﴿١٢٠﴾

---

84. Many nations have imposed on themselves superfluous religious taboos, which include a variety of dietary restrictions. On the one hand, they have declared lawful many of the things which God has forbidden. On the other, there are many things which God has made lawful but which some people have forbidden to themselves. Some people have even gone so far as to consider eating animals slaughtered in the name of God as unlawful, while those slaughtered with no mention of God's name may be eaten. God repudiates this and urges the Muslims – if they really believe in Him and obey His injunctions – to smash the superstitious and prejudiced notions contrived by human beings in disregard of God's revealed guidance, and to recognize as unlawful all that God has declared to be unlawful, and as lawful all that God has declared to be lawful.

85. See *Sūrah al-Naḥl* 16: 115. We may observe in passing that this allusion indirectly establishes that *Sūrah al-Naḥl* was revealed before the present *sūrah*.

(121) Do not eat of (the animal) over which the name of Allah has not been pronounced (at the time of its slaughtering), for that is a transgression. And behold, the evil ones do inspire doubts and objections into the hearts of their friends so that they dispute with you;[86] but if you obey them, you will surely yourselves turn into those who associate others with Allah in His divinity.[87]

وَلَا تَأْكُلُوا مِمَّا لَمْ يُذْكَرِ اسْمُ اللَّهِ
عَلَيْهِ وَإِنَّهُ لَفِسْقٌ ۗ وَإِنَّ الشَّيَاطِينَ
لَيُوحُونَ إِلَىٰ أَوْلِيَائِهِمْ لِيُجَادِلُوكُمْ ۖ
وَإِنْ أَطَعْتُمُوهُمْ إِنَّكُمْ لَمُشْرِكُونَ ﴿١٢١﴾

86. It has been reported in a tradition transmitted by 'Abd Allāh b. 'Abbās that the Jewish religious scholars used to prompt the ignorant people of Arabia to address many enquiries to the Prophet (peace be on him) so as to discredit him. One of the questions they taught them to ask was: 'Why is it that an animal killed by (the act of) God should be deemed prohibited, while one killed by us is considered lawful?' This is a common example of the warped mentality of the People of the Book. They strained their minds to contrive such questions so as to create doubts in people's minds and to provide them with intellectual weapons in their fight against the Truth.

87. To acknowledge the overlordship of God, yet to follow at the same time the orders and ways of those who have turned away from Him, amounts to associating others with God in His divinity. True belief in the unity of God consists in orienting one's entire life to the obedience and service of God. Those who believe that any other being besides God is to be acknowledged in principle as having an independent claim on man's unreserved obedience should know that such acknowledgement amounts to associating others with God in His divinity at the level of belief. On the other hand, if they actually do obey those who, in sheer disregard of God's guidance and injunctions, arrogate to themselves the right to declare according to their whims certain things to be lawful and others to be unlawful, and to bid and forbid people as they please, this amounts to associating others with God in His divinity at the level of action.

(122) He who was dead and whom We raised to life,[88] and We set a light for him to walk among men – is he like the one steeped in darkness out of which he does not come out?[89] Thus have their own doings been made to seem fair to the unbelievers.[90]
(123) Thus We have appointed the leaders of the wicked ones in every land to weave their plots; but in truth they plot only to their own harm, without even realizing it.

أَوَمَن كَانَ مَيْتًا فَأَحْيَيْنَٰهُ وَجَعَلْنَا
لَهُۥ نُورًا يَمْشِى بِهِۦ فِى ٱلنَّاسِ كَمَن
مَّثَلُهُۥ فِى ٱلظُّلُمَٰتِ لَيْسَ بِخَارِجٍ مِّنْهَا ۚ
كَذَٰلِكَ زُيِّنَ لِلْكَٰفِرِينَ مَا كَانُوا۟
يَعْمَلُونَ ﴿١٢٢﴾ وَكَذَٰلِكَ جَعَلْنَا
فِى كُلِّ قَرْيَةٍ أَكَٰبِرَ مُجْرِمِيهَا
لِيَمْكُرُوا۟ فِيهَا ۖ وَمَا يَمْكُرُونَ
إِلَّا بِأَنفُسِهِمْ وَمَا يَشْعُرُونَ ﴿١٢٣﴾

---

88. 'Death' signifies here the state of ignorance and lack of consciousness, whereas 'life' denotes the state of knowledge and true cognition, the state of awareness of Reality. He who cannot distinguish between right and wrong and does not know the Straight Way for human life, may be alive on the biological plane, but his essential humanity is not. He may be a living animal but is certainly not a living human being. A living human being is one who can distinguish right from wrong, good from evil, honesty from dishonesty.

89. The question is: 'How can they expect one who has been able to attain genuine consciousness of his true human nature and who, by virtue of his knowledge of the Truth, can clearly discern the Straight Way among the numerous crooked ways, to live like those who lack true consciousness and go on stumbling in the darkness of ignorance and folly?'

90. The law of God with regard to those to whom light is presented but who wilfully refuse to accept it, preferring to follow their crooked paths even after they have been invited to follow the Straight Way, is that in the course of time such people begin to cherish darkness, and to enjoy groping their way in the dark, stumbling and falling as they proceed. They tend to mistake cacti for orchids, thorns for roses. They find pleasure in every act of evil and corruption. They look forward to renewed experiences of corruption, hoping that where they were previously unsuccessful they will now find success.

(124) Whenever there comes to them a sign from Allah, they say: 'We will not believe until we are given what was given to the Messengers of Allah.'[91] Allah knows best where to place His message. Soon shall these wicked ones meet with humiliation and severe chastisement from Allah for all their evil plotting.

(125) Thus, (it is a fact that) whomsoever Allah wills to guide, He opens his breast for Islam;[92*] and whomsoever He wills to let go astray, He causes his breast to become strait and constricted, as if he were climbing towards the heaven. Thus Allah lays the abomination (of flight from and hatred of Islam) on those who do not believe (126) even though this way is the straight way of your Lord, and We have distinguished its signs to those who heed to admonition. (127) Theirs shall be an abode of peace[93] with their Lord – their Protector – in recompense for all they have done.

وَإِذَا جَآءَتْهُمْ ءَايَةٌ قَالُوا۟ لَن نُّؤْمِنَ
حَتَّىٰ نُؤْتَىٰ مِثْلَ مَآ أُوتِىَ رُسُلُ ٱللَّهِ ۘ ٱللَّهُ
أَعْلَمُ حَيْثُ يَجْعَلُ رِسَالَتَهُۥ ۗ
سَيُصِيبُ ٱلَّذِينَ أَجْرَمُوا۟ صَغَارٌ
عِندَ ٱللَّهِ وَعَذَابٌ شَدِيدٌۢ بِمَا كَانُوا۟
يَمْكُرُونَ ﴿١٢٤﴾ فَمَن يُرِدِ ٱللَّهُ أَن يَهْدِيَهُۥ
يَشْرَحْ صَدْرَهُۥ لِلْإِسْلَـٰمِ ۖ وَمَن يُرِدْ
أَن يُضِلَّهُۥ يَجْعَلْ صَدْرَهُۥ ضَيِّقًا
حَرَجًا كَأَنَّمَا يَصَّعَّدُ فِى ٱلسَّمَآءِ ۚ
كَذَٰلِكَ يَجْعَلُ ٱللَّهُ ٱلرِّجْسَ عَلَى
ٱلَّذِينَ لَا يُؤْمِنُونَ ﴿١٢٥﴾ وَهَـٰذَا
صِرَٰطُ رَبِّكَ مُسْتَقِيمًا ۗ قَدْ فَصَّلْنَا
ٱلْـَٔايَـٰتِ لِقَوْمٍ يَذَّكَّرُونَ ﴿١٢٦﴾ ۞ لَهُمْ
دَارُ ٱلسَّلَـٰمِ عِندَ رَبِّهِمْ ۖ وَهُوَ وَلِيُّهُم
بِمَا كَانُوا۟ يَعْمَلُونَ ﴿١٢٧﴾

91. This shows that they were unwilling to believe in the statement of the Prophets that an angel of God came to each of them and delivered the message of God. They would believe, they said, only if the angel approached them directly and intimated God's message to them.

*That is, self-surrender to Allah – Ed.

(128) And on the Day when He shall muster them all together, He will say (to the *jinn*):[94] 'O assembly of the *jinn*, you have seduced a good many of mankind.' And their companions from among the humans will say: 'Our Lord! We did indeed benefit from one another[95] and now have reached the term which You had set for us.' Thereupon Allah will say: 'The Fire is now your abode, and therein you shall abide.' Only those whom Allah wills shall escape the Fire. Surely your Lord is All-Wise, All-Knowing.[96]

وَيَوْمَ يَحْشُرُهُمْ جَمِيعًا يَٰمَعْشَرَ ٱلْجِنِّ
قَدِ ٱسْتَكْثَرْتُم مِّنَ ٱلْإِنسِ ۖ وَقَالَ
أَوْلِيَآؤُهُم مِّنَ ٱلْإِنسِ رَبَّنَا ٱسْتَمْتَعَ
بَعْضُنَا بِبَعْضٍ وَبَلَغْنَآ أَجَلَنَا ٱلَّذِىٓ
أَجَّلْتَ لَنَا ۚ قَالَ ٱلنَّارُ مَثْوَىٰكُمْ خَٰلِدِينَ
فِيهَآ إِلَّا مَا شَآءَ ٱللَّهُ ۗ إِنَّ رَبَّكَ حَكِيمٌ
عَلِيمٌ ﴿١٢٨﴾

---

92. 'To open someone's breast to Islam' means to make him feel fully convinced of the truth of Islam and to remove all his doubts, hesitations and reluctance.

93. The righteous will enjoy 'the Abode of Peace' since there he will be safe from every misfortune and evil.

94. The term *jinn* here refers to the evil ones among the *jinn*.

95. This means that they had derived unfair benefit from one another and had served their selfish ends by mutual deception.

96. Even though God has the right to punish whoever He wishes and to forgive whoever He wishes, His punishing and forgiving will be neither arbitrary nor whimsical. It will rather be founded on absolute knowledge and wisdom. God will forgive those whom He knows not to be responsible for their guilt, and thus not liable to punishment according to His wisdom and justice.

(129) In this manner We shall make the wrong-doers friends of each other (in the Hereafter) because they earned (evil together in the world).[97] (130) (Then Allah will also ask them): 'O assembly of *jinn* and men! Did there not come to you Messengers from among yourselves, relating to you My signs, and warning you of the encounter of this your Day (of Judgement)?' They will say: 'Yes, we bear witness against ourselves.'[98] They have been deluded by the life of this world, and they will bear witness against themselves that they had disbelieved.[99] (131) (They will be made to bear this witness to show that) it is not the way of your Lord to destroy cities unjustly while their people were unaware of the Truth.[100]

وَكَذَٰلِكَ نُوَلِّي بَعْضَ ٱلظَّٰلِمِينَ بَعْضًۢا
بِمَا كَانُوا۟ يَكْسِبُونَ ﴿١٢٩﴾ يَٰمَعْشَرَ
ٱلْجِنِّ وَٱلْإِنسِ أَلَمْ يَأْتِكُمْ رُسُلٌ
مِّنكُمْ يَقُصُّونَ عَلَيْكُمْ ءَايَٰتِى
وَيُنذِرُونَكُمْ لِقَآءَ يَوْمِكُمْ هَٰذَا
قَالُوا۟ شَهِدْنَا عَلَىٰٓ أَنفُسِنَا وَغَرَّتْهُمُ
ٱلْحَيَوٰةُ ٱلدُّنْيَا وَشَهِدُوا۟ عَلَىٰٓ أَنفُسِهِمْ
أَنَّهُمْ كَانُوا۟ كَٰفِرِينَ ﴿١٣٠﴾ ذَٰلِكَ
أَن لَّمْ يَكُن رَّبُّكَ مُهْلِكَ ٱلْقُرَىٰ
بِظُلْمٍ وَأَهْلُهَا غَٰفِلُونَ ﴿١٣١﴾

---

97. Just as the wrong-doers had been accomplices in sin and evil during their earthly life, they would remain companions in the After-life as well and share its punishment.

98. The wrong-doers would confess that even though the Prophets had come, in succession, in order to inform them of the Truth, it was their own fault that they did not respond to their call.

99. They were deniers of, and disbelievers in, rather than ignorant of the Truth. They acknowledged that the Truth had been conveyed to them and that they had refused to accept it.

100. God does not want His creatures to have any valid reason to complain that He had left them ignorant of the Right Way, and then convicted them of error. God has forestalled any such grievance by sending

(132) Everyone is assigned a degree according to his deed. Your Lord is not heedless of what they do. (133) Your Lord is Self-Sufficient, full of compassion.[101] If He wills, He can put you away and cause whomever He wills to succeed you just as He has produced you from the seed of another people. (134) Surely what you have been promised shall come to pass;[102] and you do not have the power to frustrate (Allah). (135) Say (O Muhammad!): 'O people! Work in your place; and I too am at work.[103] Soon you will know in whose favour the ultimate decision will be. Surely the wrong-doers will not prosper.'

وَلِكُلٍّ دَرَجَٰتٌ مِّمَّا عَمِلُوا۟ ۚ وَمَا
رَبُّكَ بِغَٰفِلٍ عَمَّا يَعْمَلُونَ ﴿١٣٢﴾
وَرَبُّكَ ٱلْغَنِىُّ ذُو ٱلرَّحْمَةِ ۚ إِن يَشَأْ
يُذْهِبْكُمْ وَيَسْتَخْلِفْ مِنۢ
بَعْدِكُم مَّا يَشَآءُ كَمَآ أَنشَأَكُم
مِّن ذُرِّيَّةِ قَوْمٍ ءَاخَرِينَ ﴿١٣٣﴾
إِنَّ مَا تُوعَدُونَ لَءَاتٍ ۖ وَمَآ
أَنتُم بِمُعْجِزِينَ ﴿١٣٤﴾ قُلْ يَٰقَوْمِ
ٱعْمَلُوا۟ عَلَىٰ مَكَانَتِكُمْ إِنِّى عَامِلٌ ۖ
فَسَوْفَ تَعْلَمُونَ مَن تَكُونُ لَهُۥ
عَٰقِبَةُ ٱلدَّارِ ۗ إِنَّهُۥ لَا يُفْلِحُ ٱلظَّٰلِمُونَ
﴿١٣٥﴾

Prophets and revealing Holy Books to warn both *jinn* and human beings. If people continue to falter in spite of God's arrangements for their guidance, they themselves are to blame for the punishment they will receive, and they have no justification for blaming their misfortune on God.

101. The Qur'ānic statement: 'Your Lord is Self-Sufficient' signifies that God is in need of nothing from anyone, that none of His interests will be jeopardized by disobedience to Him, and that no benefit will accrue to Him from obedience. Even if all human beings became disobedient, God's dominion will not shrink. Nor will His dominion expand if everybody were to become obedient and serve and worship Him as they ought to. God is dependent neither upon their show of veneration nor upon their offerings. He lavishes His limitless treasures on human beings and seeks nothing in return.

The other statement, namely that 'Your Lord is full of compassion', has been made here to emphasize two things. First, that when God urges human beings to follow the Right Way, and asks them not to do anything in conflict with Ultimate Reality, He does not do so because their good behaviour

(136) They[104] assign to Allah a portion out of the produce and cattle that He has created, saying out of their fancy: 'This is for Allah' – so they deem – 'and this is for the associates (of Allah) whom we have contrived.'[105] Then, the portion assigned to the beings whom they have set up as associates (of Allah) does not reach Allah, but the portion assigned to Allah reaches the beings they set up as associates (of Allah)![106] Indeed evil is what they decide!

وَجَعَلُوا لِلَّهِ مِمَّا ذَرَأَ مِنَ الْحَرْثِ
وَالْأَنْعَامِ نَصِيبًا فَقَالُوا هَٰذَا
لِلَّهِ بِزَعْمِهِمْ وَهَٰذَا لِشُرَكَائِنَا ۖ فَمَا
كَانَ لِشُرَكَائِهِمْ فَلَا يَصِلُ
إِلَى اللَّهِ ۖ وَمَا كَانَ لِلَّهِ فَهُوَ
يَصِلُ إِلَىٰ شُرَكَائِهِمْ ۗ
سَاءَ مَا يَحْكُمُونَ ﴿١٣٦﴾

---

benefits Him or their misconduct harms Him. He does so because good conduct is beneficial to man himself, as evil conduct is harmful to him. Hence it is out of sheer benevolence that God urges man to develop righteous conduct, for it will raise him to great heights, and He urges him to avoid evil conduct because it will lead to his own degradation. Second, that God is not unduly stern in judging man. He gets no pleasure from punishing people. He is not on the look-out for slight lapses for which to convict and persecute people. God is highly compassionate towards all His creatures and governs with utmost mercy and benevolence, and the same characterizes His dealings with human beings as well. Hence, He constantly forgives the sins of people. Many disobey, indulge in sins, commit crimes, disregard God's commands, even though they are nourished by the sustenance He provides. God, nevertheless, continually treats them with forbearance and forgives them. Again and again, He grants them respite in order that they may take heed, understand things properly and reform themselves. Had He been excessively stern, He could even have obliterated them instantly and raised up another people. He could have put an end to humanity and brought into being an altogether different species of creation.

102. This refers to the Resurrection, when human beings of every epoch will be raised anew and made to stand before God for final judgement.

103. If people prefer to ignore the Prophet's admonition and do not recant their misconduct, they are at liberty to follow their chosen path,

but they should let the Prophet (peace be on him) follow his. The ultimate results of their conduct will, in due time, become evident to all – to the Prophet (peace be on him) as well as to his opponents.

104. There now follows an elucidation of the 'ignorance' which those people insistently clung to, and which they were not prepared to forsake. They are also told about that major 'wrong' which, if not abandoned, will bar their way to salvation.

105. They themselves acknowledged that the earth belongs to God, and that it is He Who causes the vegetation to grow. They also affirmed that God is the creator of the animals which were yoked to their service. They believed, however, that the grace of God for them was the outcome of the blessing and benediction of the angels, *jinn*, heavenly stars, spirits of their pious ancestors and so on, who cared for their well-being and were their patrons. They therefore used to make a two-fold division of their harvest and livestock offerings. One part was devoted to God in recognition of their gratitude to Him for having granted them farms and animals, while the rest was devoted to the household gods of either their family or tribes in order to ensure their continuing grace and benediction.

First, God censures them for this iniquity and asks them – since all those animals were created and had been granted to them by God alone – what justification there is for making offerings to others. Is it not sheer ingratitude to ascribe the acts of benevolence and grace of the true Benefactor to the intercession of others, and to associate them with God in thanksgiving? Second, they are censured indirectly for assigning quite an arbitrary share in their offerings to God, as if they themselves were the law-maker who could ascribe shares to God and others as they wished. To God alone belong all the bounties He has given man, and only His Law should therefore determine what part of those bounties should be offered to Him in thanksgiving and how the remaining should be spent. Hence even if they spend something in the way of Allah, for the poor and the deprived, but according to their own will, that does not deserve to be accepted by Him.

106. This is subtle sarcasm at the trickery to which the polytheists resorted while dividing the offerings between God and the partners whom they had set up with Him. By one device and another they increased the share of the false deities, which only showed that their heart lay with those sham partners of God rather than with Him.

It is instructive to recall those tricks. If, while they were apportioning God's share of cereals and fruits, anything belonging to His share fell out of its place, it used to be added to the portion earmarked for the share of God's partners. On the contrary, if any part of the partners' share fell out or got mixed up with the portion earmarked for God, they were most careful to return it to where it belonged. Whenever they were criticized

(137) And, likewise, the beings supposed to have a share in Allah's divinity have made the slaying of their offspring seem lawful to many of those who associate others with Allah in His divinity[107] so that they may ruin them[108] and confound them regarding their faith.[109] If Allah had so willed, they would not have done that. Leave them alone to persist in their fabrication.[110]

وَكَذَٰلِكَ زَيَّنَ لِكَثِيرٍ مِّنَ ٱلْمُشْرِكِينَ قَتْلَ أَوْلَٰدِهِمْ شُرَكَآؤُهُمْ لِيُرْدُوهُمْ وَلِيَلْبِسُوا۟ عَلَيْهِمْ دِينَهُمْ ۖ وَلَوْ شَآءَ ٱللَّهُ مَا فَعَلُوهُ ۖ فَذَرْهُمْ وَمَا يَفْتَرُونَ ﴿١٣٧﴾

for this, they had a number of interesting apologies to offer. They said, for instance, that being the Creator, God is Self-Sufficient and hence He does not care if His portion is in some way reduced. As for the 'partners', they were not after all self-sufficient and would therefore take them to task for the slightest diminution in their share.

In order to grasp what lay at the root of these superstitions, it is essential to know that the portion which these ignorant people earmarked for God was devoted to helping the indigent, the poor, travellers, orphans and so on. On the other hand, the portion earmarked for offerings to the 'partners' actually went either directly to the coffers of the priestly class or was offered at the shrines and thus ultimately reached the priests and caretakers of those shrines. Over the course of centuries these selfish religious leaders had impressed upon those simple-minded people that there was no harm in God's share being reduced, but that of God's dear ones, far from being diminished, should be increased.

107. The word 'partners' is now used in a different sense. In this verse the word 'partners' denotes those human beings and devils who had legitimized infanticide and even represented it as a commendable act.

The reason for calling such people 'partners' is that just as God alone deserves to be worshipped, so He alone has the right to make laws for His creatures and to determine the limits of what is lawful and what is unlawful. Also, just as consecrating acts of devotion to anyone other than God amounts to setting up partners with Him, so to follow man-made laws in the belief that human beings have the right to be their own law-makers amounts to acknowledging others as partners of God. Both these acts amount to setting up partners with Him, irrespective of whether or not man applies the word 'God' to those before whom he makes ritual offerings, or to those whose laws he considers to be essentially right and binding for men.

It is pertinent to recall that three forms of infanticide were practised among the Arabs, and the Qur'ān alludes to each:

(1) Girls were put to death either to forestall the intrusion of a son-in-law, to prevent them from falling into the hands of enemies in the event of an outbreak of tribal feuding or to stop them from becoming a source of disgrace for any other reason.

(2) Both male and female children were killed if parents thought they would not be able to support them and that they would thus become an unendurable burden.

(3) Children of both sexes were placed as sacrificial offerings on the altars of the deities in order to gratify them.

108. The use of the word 'ruin' in this verse is significant. It denotes, in the first place, the moral ruination of a people. A man whose callousness and cruelty reach the point where he begins to kill his offspring with his own hands not only becomes bereft of the essence of humanity, but has sunk even lower than the animals. Moreover, this signifies the ruin of a people and of the human race. This is because infanticide necessarily leads to loss of population which is detrimental to the interests of mankind and also of each nation, since it prevents those who could have carried the legacy of a nation from either being born or puts an end to their lives after they are born. This rule also signifies the ultimate ruin, i.e. in the Hereafter. For indeed anyone who treats innocent children with such high-handedness, who cold-bloodedly slaughters the essence of his humanity, who acts so sordidly towards the human species as such, and even towards his own people, deserves severe punishment from God.

109. In the *Jāhilīyah*, the Age of Ignorance, the Arabs both identified themselves with Abraham and Ishmael and were quite convinced that they were indeed followers of Abraham and Ishmael. They therefore considered their religion to be one that had been prescribed by God. The fact, however, was that over the course of centuries a number of innovations had overgrown the religion preached by Abraham and Ishmael. These innovations, which had been introduced by their religious leaders, the tribal chiefs and the elders of noted families, had become hallowed with the passage of time, and were considered an integral part of their original religion. No authentic traces of this original religion, however, existed in the Arab traditions, nor in written sources nor in historical records as such. Hence, when innovations made their inroads into their religious life, they failed to perceive both the innovations and the innovators. This rendered the entire religious tradition of the Arabs unauthentic in the sight of the people of Arabia themselves. They could not assert with conviction which elements were part of the original God-given religion, and which were mere innovations.

(138) They say: 'These animals and these crops are sacrosanct: none may eat of them save those whom we will' – imposing interdictions of their own contriving.[111] And they declare that it is forbidden to burden the backs of certain cattle, and these are the cattle over which they do not pronounce the name of Allah.[112] All these are false fabrications against Allah,[113] and He will soon requite them for all that they fabricate.

وَقَالُوا۟ هَٰذِهِۦٓ أَنْعَٰمٌ وَحَرْثٌ حِجْرٌ
لَّا يَطْعَمُهَآ إِلَّا مَن نَّشَآءُ بِزَعْمِهِمْ
وَأَنْعَٰمٌ حُرِّمَتْ ظُهُورُهَا وَأَنْعَٰمٌ
لَّا يَذْكُرُونَ ٱسْمَ ٱللَّهِ عَلَيْهَا ٱفْتِرَآءً
عَلَيْهِ ۚ سَيَجْزِيهِم بِمَا كَانُوا۟
يَفْتَرُونَ ١٣٨

110. Had God not so willed, they could never have kept to their false ways. But God willed that everybody should be allowed to pursue his own choice. Hence, if people do not believe in spite of the Prophet's admonition, and persist in their false ways, they must be allowed to do as they please. One need not hound such people and pester them into accepting the Truth.

111. There was a practice among the people of Arabia whereby they used to consecrate certain animals and farms to certain shrines, and at offerings at certain altars. These consecrated offerings could not be used by everybody. An elaborate code laid down what kind of offering could be used by what kind of people. God not only judges such practices to be polytheistic, but also censures them as man-made innovations. God was the master of all that they had consecrated as offerings to the deities. He had neither encumbered human beings with the need to make any of those offerings and consecrations nor imposed those restrictions on what they might consume. These were the wilful inventions of headstrong and rebellious people who attributed to themselves the authority to make laws as they pleased.

112. Traditions indicate that there were certain ritual offerings, and that on certain occasions animals were consecrated for sacrifice at which it was deemed unlawful to pronounce the name of God. It was also prohibited to ride such animals during the Pilgrimage, since at that time the pilgrim pronounced the name of God when he recited the formula: *Labbayk Allāhumma Labbayk*. Every care was taken not to pronounce the name of God at the time of milking, mounting, slaughtering and eating of such animals.

(139) And they say: 'What is within the bellies of such-and-such cattle is exclusively for our males and is forbidden to our females; but if it be born dead, they all may share in it.'[114] He will soon requite them for all that they (falsely) attribute to Allah. He is All-Wise, All-Knowing.

(140) Those who slayed their children in folly, without knowledge, and forbade the sustenance that Allah has provided them, falsely ascribing that to Allah, are utter losers; they have gone astray, and are certainly not among those guided to the right way.[115]

وَقَالُوا۟ مَا فِى بُطُونِ هَـٰذِهِ ٱلْأَنْعَـٰمِ
خَالِصَةٌ لِّذُكُورِنَا وَمُحَرَّمٌ عَلَىٰٓ
أَزْوَٰجِنَا ۖ وَإِن يَكُن مَّيْتَةً فَهُمْ
فِيهِ شُرَكَآءُ ۚ سَيَجْزِيهِمْ
وَصْفَهُمْ ۚ إِنَّهُۥ حَكِيمٌ عَلِيمٌ ﴿١٣٩﴾
قَدْ خَسِرَ ٱلَّذِينَ قَتَلُوٓا۟ أَوْلَـٰدَهُمْ
سَفَهًۢا بِغَيْرِ عِلْمٍ وَحَرَّمُوا۟ مَا رَزَقَهُمُ
ٱللَّهُ ٱفْتِرَآءً عَلَى ٱللَّهِ ۚ قَدْ ضَلُّوا۟ وَمَا
كَانُوا۟ مُهْتَدِينَ ﴿١٤٠﴾

---

113. Even though those rules had not been laid down by God, people followed them under the false impression that they had been prescribed by Him. They could not adduce any injunction from God in support of such a belief, and all that they could claim was that it was an integral part of their ancestors' way of life.

114. One of the provisions of this self-contrived religious code of the Arabs was that the flesh of the young, born of the animals consecrated as offerings to the deities, might be eaten by males but not by females. Persons of both sexes were allowed to eat its flesh if it had died either a natural death or was dead at birth.

115. It is put to them plainly that even though such practices had been introduced by their forefathers, religious guides and outstanding leaders, the fact remained that those practices were inherently unsound. That those practices had come down from their ancestors and venerated elders did not necessarily legitimize them. These callous people had introduced such inhuman customs as infanticide, and, without any justification whatsoever, had prohibited to the creatures of God food and drink which He had created. They had also introduced many innovations themselves, making

(141) It is He Who has brought into being gardens[116] – the trellised and untrellised – and the palm trees, and crops, all varying in taste, and the olive and pomegranates, all resembling one another and yet so different. Eat of their fruits when they come to fruition and pay His due on the day of harvesting. And do not exceed the proper limits, for He does not love those who exceed the proper limits. (142) And of the cattle (He has reared) some for burden, and some whose flesh you eat and whose skins and hair you use to spread the ground.[117] Eat of the sustenance Allah has provided you and do not follow in the footsteps of Satan, for surely he is your open enemy.[118] ▶

۞ وَهُوَ ٱلَّذِىٓ أَنشَأَ جَنَّٰتٍ
مَّعْرُوشَٰتٍ وَغَيْرَ مَعْرُوشَٰتٍ
وَٱلنَّخْلَ وَٱلزَّرْعَ مُخْتَلِفًا أُكُلُهُۥ
وَٱلزَّيْتُونَ وَٱلرُّمَّانَ مُتَشَٰبِهًا
وَغَيْرَ مُتَشَٰبِهٍ ۚ كُلُوا۟ مِن ثَمَرِهِۦٓ
إِذَآ أَثْمَرَ وَءَاتُوا۟ حَقَّهُۥ يَوْمَ
حَصَادِهِۦ ۖ وَلَا تُسْرِفُوٓا۟ ۚ إِنَّهُۥ لَا
يُحِبُّ ٱلْمُسْرِفِينَ ﴿١٤١﴾ وَمِنَ
ٱلْأَنْعَٰمِ حَمُولَةً وَفَرْشًا ۚ كُلُوا۟
مِمَّا رَزَقَكُمُ ٱللَّهُ وَلَا تَتَّبِعُوا۟ خُطُوَٰتِ
ٱلشَّيْطَٰنِ ۚ إِنَّهُۥ لَكُمْ عَدُوٌّ مُّبِينٌ ﴿١٤٢﴾

---

them part of their religion and ascribing them to God. How could such people be considered either to have attained salvation or to be rightly-guided? Even though venerated by them as their ancestors, they were nevertheless misguided and were destined to see the evil consequences of their misdeeds.

116. The Arabic expression جَنَّٰتٍ مَّعْرُوشَٰتٍ وَغَيْرَ مَعْرُوشَٰتٍ signifies two kinds of gardens: first, those consisting of trellised plants and, second, those consisting of trees which stand on their own.

117. The word فَرْش (which means 'to spread, to pave, to cover the ground, floor or path') has been used in the context of cattle either (1) because they are relatively short, and in moving about seem to be touching the ground, (2) because when they are slaughtered, they have to be laid on the ground, or (3) because their skins and hair are used for furnishing purposes.

(143) These are eight couples, two of sheep, two of goats. Now ask them: 'Is it either the two males that Allah has forbidden or the two females, or what the wombs of the two females may contain? Tell me about this on the basis of sure knowledge, if you speak the truth.'[119] (144) And likewise, of camels there are two, and of oxen there are two. Ask them: 'Is it either the two males that He has forbidden or the two females, or that which the wombs of the two females may contain?[120] Or were you present when Allah enjoined this commandment upon you?' Who, then, would be more unjust than he who fabricates a lie against Allah that he might lead people astray without knowledge. Surely Allah never guides such a wrong-doing folk.

ثَمَٰنِيَةَ أَزْوَٰجٍ مِّنَ ٱلضَّأْنِ ٱثْنَيْنِ
وَمِنَ ٱلْمَعْزِ ٱثْنَيْنِ قُلْ
ءَآلذَّكَرَيْنِ حَرَّمَ أَمِ ٱلْأُنثَيَيْنِ أَمَّا
ٱشْتَمَلَتْ عَلَيْهِ أَرْحَامُ ٱلْأُنثَيَيْنِ
نَبِّـُٔونِى بِعِلْمٍ إِن كُنتُمْ صَٰدِقِينَ
﴿١٤٣﴾ وَمِنَ ٱلْإِبِلِ ٱثْنَيْنِ وَمِنَ ٱلْبَقَرِ
ٱثْنَيْنِ قُلْ ءَآلذَّكَرَيْنِ حَرَّمَ أَمِ
ٱلْأُنثَيَيْنِ أَمَّا ٱشْتَمَلَتْ عَلَيْهِ أَرْحَامُ
ٱلْأُنثَيَيْنِ أَمْ كُنتُمْ شُهَدَآءَ
إِذْ وَصَّىٰكُمُ ٱللَّهُ بِهَٰذَا فَمَنْ
أَظْلَمُ مِمَّنِ ٱفْتَرَىٰ عَلَى ٱللَّهِ كَذِبًا
لِّيُضِلَّ ٱلنَّاسَ بِغَيْرِ عِلْمٍ إِنَّ ٱللَّهَ لَا
يَهْدِى ٱلْقَوْمَ ٱلظَّٰلِمِينَ ﴿١٤٤﴾

---

118. It becomes clear from the context that God wants to emphasize three things. First, that the orchards, fields and cattle are all bounties of God. No one else has made any contribution to them and hence no one is entitled to any share in the thanks that man ought to give Him in return for these bounties. Second, since all those things are bounties of God, one ought to follow the laws of God alone while making use of them. No one else has the right to regulate their use. To acknowledge oneself bound by customs and practices laid down by others than God, and to make offerings out of a feeling of gratitude for beneficence to someone other than God constitute acts of rebellion and amount to following Satan. Third, as God has created all these things for the fulfilment of man's needs, they should not be unnecessarily suspended from use or be regarded as prohibited. All

(145) Tell them (O Muḥammad!): 'I do not find in what has been revealed to me anything forbidden for anyone who wants to eat unless it is carrion, outpoured blood and the flesh of swine, all of which is unclean; or that which is profane having been slaughtered in a name other than that of Allah.[121] But whosoever is constrained to it by necessity – neither desiring to disobey nor exceeding the limit of necessity – your Lord is surely All-Forgiving, All-Compassionate. ▶

قُل لَّآ أَجِدُ فِي مَآ أُوحِيَ إِلَيَّ مُحَرَّمًا عَلَىٰ
طَاعِمٍ يَطۡعَمُهُۥٓ إِلَّآ أَن يَكُونَ
مَيۡتَةً أَوۡ دَمٗا مَّسۡفُوحًا أَوۡ لَحۡمَ
خِنزِيرٖ فَإِنَّهُۥ رِجۡسٌ أَوۡ فِسۡقًا أُهِلَّ
لِغَيۡرِ ٱللَّهِ بِهِۦۚ فَمَنِ ٱضۡطُرَّ غَيۡرَ بَاغٖ
وَلَا عَادٖ فَإِنَّ رَبَّكَ غَفُورٞ رَّحِيمٞ ١٤٥

restrictions on the use of the means of sustenance and other bounties of God based on conjecture or superstition, are not to His liking at all.

119. That is, they should come forward with arguments based on sound, reliable knowledge, rather than with arguments which have no authority except that of ancestral tradition, conjecture or superstition.

120. Questions as to whether the male offspring is lawful and the female is unlawful are presented in some detail to show how unreasonable their superstitions are. That the male offspring of an animal should be considered lawful for eating while the female be prohibited, or vice versa; and that an animal should itself be considered lawful, but not its offspring, is so manifestly unreasonable that common sense simply refuses to accept it, and no intelligent man can ever conceive such absurdities to have been sanctioned by God. Just as the superstitions in vogue among the Arabs were absurd, as the Qur'ān stresses, likewise many other nations of the world follow even now irrational dietary restrictions, and believe that food and drink become polluted merely by the touch of some other people.

121. See for this *Sūrah al-Baqarah* 2: 173, *Sūrah al-Mā'idah* 5: 3 and *Sūrah al-Naḥl* 16: 115.

The slight difference between this verse and *Sūrah al-Baqarah* 2: 173 is that whereas the latter mentions 'blood' as prohibited, the present verse qualifies it with 'outpoured', i.e. the blood which has flowed as a result of either injuring or slaughtering an animal. This, in fact, constitutes an

(146) And to those who had Judaized We have forbidden all beasts with claws, and the fat of oxen and sheep except the fat which is either on their backs or their entrails, or that which sticks to the bones. Thus did We requite them for their rebellion.[122] Surely We state the Truth. ▶

وَعَلَى ٱلَّذِينَ هَادُوا۟ حَرَّمْنَا كُلَّ
ذِى ظُفُرٍ ۖ وَمِنَ ٱلْبَقَرِ وَٱلْغَنَمِ
حَرَّمْنَا عَلَيْهِمْ شُحُومَهُمَآ إِلَّا مَا
حَمَلَتْ ظُهُورُهُمَآ أَوِ ٱلْحَوَايَآ أَوْ مَا
ٱخْتَلَطَ بِعَظْمٍ ۚ ذَٰلِكَ جَزَيْنَٰهُم بِبَغْيِهِمْ ۖ
وَإِنَّا لَصَٰدِقُونَ ﴿١٤٦﴾

elucidation of the former injunction rather than the revelation of a different one. Likewise, *Sūrah al-Mā'idah* 5: 3 mentions the prohibition of certain other categories – animals strangled or killed by blows, those which have died from either falling or goring, and those devoured by a beast of prey, in addition to the four classes mentioned here. This is not an independent, divergent injunction; it is rather an explanation signifying that the animals thus killed fall into the category of 'carrion'.

There is a group of Muslim jurists who believe that prohibition is confined to these four classes of animal food, and that the eating of everything else is lawful. This was also the view of 'Abd Allāh b. 'Abbās and 'Ā'ishah. Several traditions, however, indicate that the Prophet (peace be on him) either told people not to eat certain things or expressed his disapproval at their eating them, for example, domesticated donkeys, beasts with canine teeth and birds with claws. It is for this reason that the majority of jurists do not consider prohibition confined to these four classes but extend it to several others. These jurists disagree, however, on which of those things are unlawful and which are lawful. Abū Ḥanīfah, Mālik and Shāfi'ī, for example, consider domesticated donkeys to be unlawful. Others argue that the Prophet (peace be on him) forbade them on a special occasion and because of a special reason. To cite another example, the Ḥanafī jurists hold wild beasts, birds of prey and animals which feed on carrion to be absolutely unlawful, whereas Mālik and Awzā'ī hold birds of prey to be lawful. Layth considers the cat to be lawful. In the same way, Shāfi'ī considers prohibition to be confined only to those beasts which actually attack man, such as lion, wolf, tiger and so on. In the opinion of another jurist, 'Ikrimah, both crow and badger are lawful. Likewise, whereas the Ḥanafī jurists declare all crawling creatures to be prohibited, Ibn Abī Laylá, Mālik and Awzā'ī hold the snake to be lawful.

Upon reflection of these divergent opinions and the arguments adduced in support of them, it becomes clear that categorical prohibition embraces only those four classes mentioned in the Qur'ān. As for other types of animal food, regarding which the jurists have expressed a negative view, they seem to carry varying degrees of religious disapprobation. The things whose disapprobation is established by statements of the Prophet (peace be on him) transmitted to us through sound traditions, are relatively close to 'prohibition'. As for things regarding which there is disagreement among jurists, their religious disapprobation becomes doubtful.

Temperamental dislike, however, is quite a different matter. The Law of God does not force anyone to eat everything which is not prohibited. At the same time, the Law does not entitle anybody to exalt his personal likes and dislikes into a criterion of what is lawful and unlawful. No one is justified in reproaching others for consuming lawful things which offend his tastes.

122. This is discussed at three places in the Qur'ān. *Sūrah Āl 'Imrān* 3: 93 states: 'All food was lawful to the Children of Israel except what Israel made unlawful to themselves before the revelation of the Torah. Tell them: "Bring the Torah and recite any passage of it if you are truthful".' *Sūrah al-Nisā'* 4: 160 mentions that because of the misdeeds of the Children of Israel: 'We forbade them many clean things which had earlier been made lawful to them.' And now the present verse says that because of the transgression of the Jews, God forbade unto them 'all beasts with claws; and the fat of oxen and the sheep except the fat which is either on their backs or their entrails or that which sticks to the bones'. If these three verses are taken together, it becomes clear that the differences between Islamic law and Jewish law with regard to what is lawful and what is unlawful in animal foods stem from two considerations. First, that several centuries before the revelation of the Torah, Isrā'īl (Jacob, peace be on him) had given up the use of certain things, which his descendants also abstained from consuming. The result was that Jewish jurists considered them to be absolutely unlawful and recorded their prohibition in the Torah. They included the camel, the hare and the rock-badger, the prohibition of which is mentioned in the fragments of the Torah embodied in the Bible. (See Leviticus 11: 4; Deuteronomy 14: 7.) But the Qur'ān challenges the Jews to come forward with the Torah itself and show where any of those things had been declared unlawful. Their inability to do so shows that those interdictions must have been later interpolations into the Torah.

Second, when the Jews rebelled against the Law revealed by God and set themselves up as their own law-givers, they made several things unlawful for themselves, and as a punishment God allowed them to remain a prey to that misunderstanding. These include birds with claws such as the ostrich, seagull and water-hen, and also the fat of oxen and sheep. In the Bible prohibitions of these kinds have been interpolated among the injunctions of the Torah. (See Leviticus 3: 17; 7: 22–3; 11: 16–18; Deuteronomy 14: 14–16.) But *Sūrah al-Nisā'* 4: 160 shows that those things had not been made unlawful by the Torah itself. They had rather been prohibited after the time of Jesus, and history bears witness to the fact that the present Jewish law was given a definitive formulation by the Jewish jurist, Yehudah, towards the end of the second century of the Christian calendar.

(147) Then if they give you the lie, say: 'Your Lord is of unbounded mercy; but His punishment shall not be averted from the guilty folk.'[123]

(148) Those who associate others with Allah in His divinity will now surely say: 'Had Allah willed, neither we nor our forefathers would have associated others with Allah in His divinity, nor would we have declared anything (which Allah did not forbid) as forbidden.'[124] Even so those who had lived before them gave the lie (to the Truth) until they tasted Our chastisement. Tell them: 'Have you any sure knowledge that you can produce before us? In fact you are only following idle fancies, merely conjecturing.'

فَإِن كَذَّبُوكَ فَقُل رَّبُّكُمْ ذُو
رَحْمَةٍ وَٰسِعَةٍ وَلَا يُرَدُّ بَأْسُهُۥ عَنِ
ٱلْقَوْمِ ٱلْمُجْرِمِينَ ﴿١٤٧﴾ سَيَقُولُ
ٱلَّذِينَ أَشْرَكُوا۟ لَوْ شَآءَ ٱللَّهُ مَآ
أَشْرَكْنَا وَلَآ ءَابَآؤُنَا وَلَا حَرَّمْنَا
مِن شَىْءٍ كَذَٰلِكَ كَذَّبَ ٱلَّذِينَ
مِن قَبْلِهِمْ حَتَّىٰ ذَاقُوا۟ بَأْسَنَا قُلْ هَلْ
عِندَكُم مِّنْ عِلْمٍ فَتُخْرِجُوهُ لَنَآ إِن
تَتَّبِعُونَ إِلَّا ٱلظَّنَّ وَإِنْ أَنتُمْ إِلَّا
تَخْرُصُونَ ﴿١٤٨﴾

It might be asked in view of what has been mentioned above, why the expression 'We forbade for them' is employed in *Sūrah al-Nisā'* 4: 160. The answer is that declaration through a Prophet or a heavenly Book is not God's only way of prohibiting. Another way is to allow fraudulent law-makers and sham jurists to gain predominating influence upon God's rebels. These in turn deprive them of many good, clean things of life by making them believe that they are prohibited. The first kind of prohibition is an act of His mercy, whereas the second kind is in the nature of a curse and punishment from God.

123. If they could still give up their disobedience and return to the true service of God, they would find Him ready to embrace them with His mercy. But if they persisted, they should remember that no one could save them from His wrath.

(149) Then say to them: '(As against your argument) Allah's is the conclusive argument. Surely, had He willed, He would have guided you all to the Truth.'[125]

قُلْ فَلِلَّهِ ٱلْحُجَّةُ ٱلْبَٰلِغَةُ ۖ فَلَوْ شَآءَ
لَهَدَىٰكُمْ أَجْمَعِينَ ﴿١٤٩﴾

---

124. Their apology for their crimes and misdeeds would be that which has always been advanced by criminals and wrong-doers – an apology based on the assumption of absolute determinism. They would plead that when they associated others with God in His divinity, or unwarrantedly regarded certain things as prohibited, they did so because those acts had been willed for them by God. Had He not so willed, they would not have been able to do what they did. Hence, since they were doing everything according to the will of God, everything was proper. If anyone was to blame, it was God and not they. They were under compulsion to do what they did, for the ability to do otherwise lay beyond their power.

125. This provides a complete refutation of their apology. In order to appreciate it fully, careful analysis is required. In the first place they are told that citing God's will to justify one's errors and misdeeds, and making it a pretext for refusing to accept true guidance was the practice of the evil-doers before them. But they should remember that this had led to their ruin and they themselves were witnesses to the evil consequences of deviation from the Truth.

Furthermore, it is being clarified that the plea of the unbelievers that the only reason for their error was that God had not willed that they be guided to the Truth, is based on fancy and conjecture rather than on sound knowledge. They refer to God's will without understanding the relationship between God's will and man's action. They entertain the misconception that if a man commits theft under the will of God, that does not mean that he will not be reckoned a criminal. For the fact is that whichever path a man chooses, be it that of gratitude or ingratitude to God, of guidance or error, obedience or disobedience, God will open that path for him, and thereafter God will permit and enable him within the framework of His universal scheme, and to the extent that He deems fit – to do whatever he chooses to do whether it is right or wrong.

If their forefathers had been enabled by God's will to associate others with Him in His divinity and prohibit clean things, that did not mean that they were not answerable for their misdeeds. On the contrary, everyone will be held responsible for choosing false ways, for having a false intent, and for having striven for false ends.

The crucial point is succinctly made at the end in the words: 'Then say to them, (As against your argument) Allah's is the conclusive argument.

(150) Say to them: 'Call your witnesses to testify that Allah forbade such-and-such.' Then if they do testify, neither testify with them[126] nor follow the desires of those who have given the lie to Our signs and who do not believe in the Hereafter and set up equals with their Lord.

(151) Say to them (O Muḥammad!): 'Come, let me recite what your Lord has laid down to you:[127] ►

قُلْ هَلُمَّ شُهَدَاءَكُمُ الَّذِينَ يَشْهَدُونَ
أَنَّ اللَّهَ حَرَّمَ هَٰذَا فَإِن شَهِدُوا فَلَا
تَشْهَدْ مَعَهُمْ وَلَا تَتَّبِعْ أَهْوَاءَ
الَّذِينَ كَذَّبُوا بِآيَاتِنَا وَالَّذِينَ
لَا يُؤْمِنُونَ بِالْآخِرَةِ وَهُم بِرَبِّهِمْ
يَعْدِلُونَ ﴿١٥٠﴾ قُلْ تَعَالَوْا
أَتْلُ مَا حَرَّمَ رَبُّكُمْ عَلَيْكُمْ

Surely, had He willed, He would have guided you all to the Truth.' The argument which they put forward, viz. 'If Allah had willed, neither we nor our forefathers could have associated others with Allah in His divinity', does not embody the whole truth. The whole truth is that 'had He willed, He would have guided you all to the Truth'. In other words, they were not prepared to take the Straight Way of their own choice and volition. As it was not God's intent to create them with inherent right guidance like the angels, they would be allowed to persist in the error they had chosen for themselves.

126. A person who is conscious that he should testify only to that which he knows, can never testify that the taboos regarding food and other customs prevalent in their society had been enjoined by God. But if some people are brazen enough to feel no compunction in bearing false witness, then at least the believers should not become their partners in lying. The real purpose in asking them to testify honestly whether their customs and practices had in fact been sanctioned by God, is to stimulate those with some sense of honesty to reflect on the character of their customs and practices. Perhaps when they realize that there is no evidence of those prohibitions having been prescribed by God, some of them may decide to get rid of them.

127. The restrictions which had shackled their lives were not those imposed by God. The really worthwhile restrictions are those prescribed by God in order to regulate human life. These have always served as the essential basis of all God-given codes (cf. Exodus, chapter 20).

(i) that you associate nothing with Him;[128]
(ii) and do good to your parents;[129]
(iii) and do not slay your children out of fear of poverty. We provide you and will likewise provide them with sustenance;
(iv) and do not even draw near to things shameful[130] – be they open or secret;
(v) and do not slay the soul sanctified by Allah except in just cause;[131] this He has enjoined upon you so that you may understand;

أَلَّا تُشْرِكُوا بِهِۦ شَيْـًٔا ۖ وَبِالْوَٰلِدَيْنِ
إِحْسَٰنًا ۖ وَلَا تَقْتُلُوٓا أَوْلَٰدَكُم
مِّنْ إِمْلَٰقٍ ۖ نَّحْنُ نَرْزُقُكُمْ
وَإِيَّاهُمْ ۖ وَلَا تَقْرَبُوا الْفَوَٰحِشَ
مَا ظَهَرَ مِنْهَا وَمَا بَطَنَ ۖ
وَلَا تَقْتُلُوا النَّفْسَ الَّتِى حَرَّمَ اللَّهُ
إِلَّا بِالْحَقِّ ۚ ذَٰلِكُمْ وَصَّىٰكُم بِهِۦ لَعَلَّكُمْ
تَعْقِلُونَ ﴿١٥١﴾

128. The first principle is that they should associate none with God in His divinity: neither in His essence, nor in His attributes, nor in His powers and authority, nor in the rights He has against His creatures.

To associate someone with God in His divinity is to declare that the former shares the essence of God's divinity. Instances of associating others in God's essence are the Christian doctrine of the Trinity, the belief of the pagan Arabs that angels are daughters of God, and the belief of other polytheists in the divine character of their self-styled gods and goddesses and, in some cases, of their royalty. Likewise, a person associates others in the attributes of God when he considers someone other than God to be invested with those attributes which belong exclusively to God. One becomes guilty of this kind of polytheism if one believes somebody either to know all the mysteries of the Unseen or to be all-seeing and all-hearing or to be free of all defects and weaknesses and thus infallible. Again, a person associates others in the authority of God when he recognizes someone to be possessed of authority which belongs to God alone by virtue of His godhead; for example, the power to either benefit or harm people in a supernatural manner, to fulfil the needs of people and rescue them from distress, to protect and shield them, to hear their prayers, to make or mar their fate. A person is guilty of the same when he recognizes someone as possessing the rightful authority to determine what is lawful and what is unlawful, and to make laws for the regulation of human life. Such authority belongs to God alone, and recognizing anyone other than God as possessing it is tantamount to associating others with God in His authority.

Moreover, to associate others with God in His divine rights means that one recognizes someone beside God as legitimately deserving that which may be asked of man by God alone, viz. bowing and prostrating, standing in awe and reverence with folded hands, devotional greeting and kissing the earth, slaughtering animals and making any other offerings in thanksgiving for his grace and benevolence and in acknowledgement of his overlordship, vowing offerings in his name, calling him to rescue one from one's affliction and misfortune, and all the other forms of worship, adoration and reverence which are exclusively for God. In the same way, no one has the right to be loved to the exclusion of all other attachments, or to be held in such awe that one always fears his wrath and dreads the violation of his command, both openly and in secret. Likewise, it is God – and God alone – Who has the right to be obeyed unconditionally, and Whose guidance should be considered the only criterion of right and wrong. In the same way, man should not commit himself to obey any authority which is either independent of obedience to God or whose command lacks the sanction of God.

If someone accords any of these rights to anyone other than God, he is guilty of associating others with God in His divinity. His guilt is the same whether or not he calls such beings divine.

129. Accordingly, good treatment of one's parents includes showing them respect and reverence, obeying them, trying to keep them pleased, and serving them. The Qur'ān always mentions this right of the parents immediately after mentioning the duty one owes to God alone. This makes it quite clear that the rights of parents have precedence over those of other human beings.

130. The word *fawāḥish* applies to all those acts whose abominable character is self-evident. In the Qur'ān all extra-marital sexual relationships, sodomy, nudity, false accusations of unchastity, and taking as one's wife a woman who had been married to one's father, are specifically reckoned as 'shameful deeds' (*fawāḥish*). In *Ḥadīth*, theft, taking intoxicating drinks and begging have been characterized as *fawāḥish*, as have many other brazenly indecent acts. Man is required to abstain from them both openly and in secret.

131. This means that human life, which has been declared inviolable by God, can only be destroyed for just cause. As for what is meant by 'just cause', we ought to remember that three cases are embodied in the Qur'ān whereas two additional cases have been stated by the Prophet (peace be on him). The cases mentioned by the Qur'ān are the following:

(152) (vi) and do not even draw near to the property of the orphan in his minority except in the best manner;[132] (vii) and give full measures and weight with justice; We do not burden anyone beyond his capacity;[133] (viii) When you speak, be just, even though it concern a near of kin; (ix) and fulfil the covenant of Allah.[134] That is what He has enjoined upon you so that you may take heed.

وَلَا تَقْرَبُوا مَالَ الْيَتِيمِ إِلَّا بِالَّتِي هِيَ
أَحْسَنُ حَتَّىٰ يَبْلُغَ أَشُدَّهُۥ وَأَوْفُوا
الْكَيْلَ وَالْمِيزَانَ بِالْقِسْطِ
لَا نُكَلِّفُ نَفْسًا إِلَّا وُسْعَهَا وَإِذَا
قُلْتُمْ فَاعْدِلُوا وَلَوْ كَانَ ذَا قُرْبَىٰ
وَبِعَهْدِ اللَّهِ أَوْفُوا ذَٰلِكُمْ
وَصَّاكُم بِهِۦ لَعَلَّكُمْ تَذَكَّرُونَ ﴿١٥٢﴾

---

(1) That a man is convicted of deliberate homicide and thus the claim of retaliation is established against him.

(2) That someone resists the establishment of the true faith so that fighting against him might become necessary.

(3) That someone is guilty of spreading disorder in the Domain of Islam and strives to overthrow the Islamic order of government.

The two cases mentioned in the *Ḥadīth* are:

(1) That a person commits illegitimate sexual intercourse even after marriage.

(2) That a Muslim is guilty of apostasy and rebellion against the Muslim body-politic.

Except for these five reasons, slaying a human being is not permissible, regardless of whether he is a believer, a protected non-Muslim (*dhimmī*) or an ordinary unbeliever.

132. That is, one's handling of the property of orphans should be based on maximum selflessness, sincerity and well-wishing for the orphans; it should be of a kind which lends itself to no reproach, either from God or man.

(153) (x) This is My way – that which is straight: follow it, then, and do not follow other paths lest they scatter you from His path.[135] This is what He has enjoined upon you, so that you may beware.'	وَأَنَّ هَٰذَا صِرَٰطِى مُسْتَقِيمًا فَٱتَّبِعُوهُ وَلَا تَتَّبِعُوا۟ ٱلسُّبُلَ فَتَفَرَّقَ بِكُمْ عَن سَبِيلِهِۦ ۚ ذَٰلِكُمْ وَصَّىٰكُم بِهِۦ لَعَلَّكُمْ تَتَّقُونَ ﴿١٥٣﴾

133. Even though this is a full-fledged postulate of the law of God, it is mentioned here in order to stress that one who tries to remain fair and just to the utmost of his ability, in giving weight and measure and in his dealings with people, will be acquitted of responsibility for error. If any mistakes in weight or measure occur out of oversight, and thus involuntarily, he will not be punished.

134. 'Covenant of Allah' signifies, in the first place, the commitment to God, as well as to human beings, to which man binds himself in His name. It also signifies that covenant between man and God, as well as between one human being and another which automatically takes place the moment a person is born onto God's earth and into human society.

The first two covenants mentioned are voluntary and deliberate whereas the last one is natural. The last one is no less binding than the first two, even though man does not make it of his own volition. For when man enjoys his own existence, makes use of his physical and mental energy, benefits from the means of sustenance and natural resources – in other words, when he benefits from the world created by God and avails himself of the opportunities provided for him by the operation of natural laws – he incurs certain obligations towards God. In the same way, when one derives nourishment and sustenance from the blood of one's mother while in her womb, when one opens one's eyes in a family which is supported by the toil of one's father, when one benefits from the various institutions of human society, one is placed in varying degrees of obligation towards those individuals and institutions. This covenant between man and God and between man and society is inscribed, not on a piece of paper, but on every fibre of man's being. Man has not entered into this covenant consciously and deliberately, yet the whole of his being owes itself to it.

Sūrah al-Baqarah 2: 27 alludes to this covenant when it says that it is the transgressors 'who break the covenant of Allah after its firm binding, and cut asunder what Allah has commanded to be joined, and spread mischief on earth'. It is also mentioned in *Sūrah al-A'rāf* 7: 172 in the following words: 'And recall when your Lord took the children of Adam from their loins and made them testify as to themselves saying, "Am I not your Lord?" (to which) they answered, "Yes, we do bear witness thereto."'

(154) Then We gave to Moses the Book, completing the benediction of Allah upon the one who acts righteously, spelling out everything clearly, a guidance and a mercy; so that they may believe in their meeting with their Lord.[136] (155) And likewise We revealed this (Book) – a blessed one. Follow it, then, and become God-fearing; you may be shown mercy. (156) (You may no longer) say now that the Book was revealed only to two groups of people before us[137] and that we had indeed been unaware of what they read. ▶

ثُمَّ ءَاتَيْنَا مُوسَى ٱلْكِتَٰبَ تَمَامًا عَلَى
ٱلَّذِىٓ أَحْسَنَ وَتَفْصِيلًا لِّكُلِّ
شَىْءٍ وَهُدًى وَرَحْمَةً لَّعَلَّهُم بِلِقَآءِ
رَبِّهِمْ يُؤْمِنُونَ ﴿١٥٤﴾ وَهَٰذَا كِتَٰبٌ
أَنزَلْنَٰهُ مُبَارَكٌ فَٱتَّبِعُوهُ وَٱتَّقُوا۟
لَعَلَّكُمْ تُرْحَمُونَ ﴿١٥٥﴾ أَن تَقُولُوٓا۟ إِنَّمَآ
أُنزِلَ ٱلْكِتَٰبُ عَلَىٰ طَآئِفَتَيْنِ مِن
قَبْلِنَا وَإِن كُنَّا عَن دِرَاسَتِهِمْ
لَغَٰفِلِينَ ﴿١٥٦﴾

135. It is an essential corollary of the natural covenant mentioned above that man should follow the way prescribed by his Lord; any deflection from the orders of God, or serving anyone other than Him, constitutes a primary breach of that covenant. Once this breach has been committed every single article of the covenant is likely to be violated one after the other. Moreover, it should also be remembered that man cannot acquit himself of the highly delicate, extensive and complex set of responsibilities entailed by this covenant unless he accepts the guidance of God and tries to follow the way prescribed by Him.

Non-acceptance of God's guidance necessarily produces two grave and damaging consequences. First, by following any other way, one is inevitably led away from the true path and is thus deprived of the opportunity to approach God and please Him. Second, as soon as man deviates from the Straight Way prescribed by God, he encounters a whole labyrinth of highways and byways, causing the entire human species to fall a prey to total bewilderment and perplexity, and which shatters all dreams of a steady advance towards maturity and betterment. The words 'follow not other paths for they will scatter you away from His path' hint at this damage. (See *Sūrah al-Mā'idah* 5, n. 35 above.)

(157) Nor may you claim that: 'Had the Book been revealed to us, we would have been better guided than they.' Surely clear evidence has come to you from your Lord, which is both a guidance and a mercy. Who, then, is more unjust than he who gave the lie to the signs of Allah and turned away from them?[138] And We shall soon requite those who turn away from Our signs with a severe chastisement for having turned away. ►

أَوْ تَقُولُوا۟ لَوْ أَنَّآ أُنزِلَ عَلَيْنَا ٱلْكِتَٰبُ
لَكُنَّآ أَهْدَىٰ مِنْهُمْ ۚ فَقَدْ جَآءَكُم
بَيِّنَةٌ مِّن رَّبِّكُمْ وَهُدًى وَرَحْمَةٌ ۚ
فَمَنْ أَظْلَمُ مِمَّن كَذَّبَ بِـَٔايَٰتِ ٱللَّهِ
وَصَدَفَ عَنْهَا ۗ سَنَجْزِى ٱلَّذِينَ
يَصْدِفُونَ عَنْ ءَايَٰتِنَا سُوٓءَ ٱلْعَذَابِ
بِمَا كَانُوا۟ يَصْدِفُونَ ﴿١٥٧﴾

---

136. To believe in 'meeting with the Lord' signifies the conviction that one is answerable to God, and which leads one to adopt responsible behaviour in life.

The statement made here could mean two things. It might mean that the teachings of the heavenly Book vouchsafed to Moses could itself create a sense of responsibility among the Israelites. Alternatively, it might mean that when ordinary people observe the wonderful way of life prescribed by God, and note the beneficial effects of its merciful dispensation in the lives of righteous people, they will come to realize that belief in the After-life is, in all respects, a better basis for human life than its denial. In this way, their observation and study might turn them from rejection to true faith.

137. The allusion is to the Jews and the Christians.

138. 'Signs of Allah' include the teachings embodied in the Qur'ān. They are also manifest in the noble life of the Prophet (peace be on him), and the pure lives of those who believed in him. They also include the natural phenomena to which the Qur'ān refers in support of its message.

(158) What! Do they wait either for the angels to appear before them or for your Lord to come unto them or for some clear signs of your Lord[139] to appear before them? When some clear signs of your Lord will appear, believing will be of no avail to anyone who did not believe before, or who earned no good deeds through his faith.[140] Say: 'Wait on; we too are waiting.'

(159) Surely you have nothing to do with those who have made divisions in their religion and become factions.[141] Their matter is with Allah and He will indeed tell them (in time) what they have been doing. (160) Whoever will come to Allah with a good deed shall have ten times as much, and whoever will come to Allah with an evil deed, shall be requited with no more than the like of it. They shall not be wronged.

هَلْ يَنظُرُونَ إِلَّآ أَن تَأْتِيَهُمُ ٱلْمَلَٰٓئِكَةُ
أَوْ يَأْتِىَ رَبُّكَ أَوْ يَأْتِىَ بَعْضُ ءَايَٰتِ
رَبِّكَ ۗ يَوْمَ يَأْتِى بَعْضُ ءَايَٰتِ رَبِّكَ لَا يَنفَعُ
نَفْسًا إِيمَٰنُهَا لَمْ تَكُنْ ءَامَنَتْ مِن قَبْلُ
أَوْ كَسَبَتْ فِىٓ إِيمَٰنِهَا خَيْرًا ۗ قُلِ ٱنتَظِرُوٓا۟
إِنَّا مُنتَظِرُونَ ﴿١٥٨﴾ إِنَّ ٱلَّذِينَ فَرَّقُوا۟
دِينَهُمْ وَكَانُوا۟ شِيَعًا لَّسْتَ مِنْهُمْ فِى
شَىْءٍ ۚ إِنَّمَآ أَمْرُهُمْ إِلَى ٱللَّهِ ثُمَّ يُنَبِّئُهُم
بِمَا كَانُوا۟ يَفْعَلُونَ ﴿١٥٩﴾ مَن جَآءَ بِٱلْحَسَنَةِ
فَلَهُۥ عَشْرُ أَمْثَالِهَا ۖ وَمَن جَآءَ بِٱلسَّيِّئَةِ
فَلَا يُجْزَىٰٓ إِلَّا مِثْلَهَا وَهُمْ لَا يُظْلَمُونَ
﴿١٦٠﴾

139. That is, either tokens of the approach of the Day of Reckoning or God's scourge or any other sign that will uncover the Truth, after which there will be no reason left for testing man.

140. Those tokens will be so clear that after their appearance it will neither avail the unbeliever to repent of his unbelief nor the disobedient to forsake his disobedience. For faith and obedience have meaning and value only as long as the Truth remains hidden, as long as the tenure of life granted to people does not seem to have approached its end and the

(161) Say: 'As for me, my Lord has guided me on to a straight way, a right religion, the way of Abraham[142] who adopted it in exclusive devotion to Allah, and he was not of those who associated others with Allah in His divinity.' (162) Say: 'Surely my Prayer, all my acts of worship,[143] and my living and my dying are for Allah alone, the Lord of the whole universe. (163) He has no associate. Thus have I been bidden, and I am the foremost of those who submit themselves (to Allah).'*

قُلْ إِنَّنِى هَدَىٰنِى رَبِّىٓ إِلَىٰ صِرَٰطٍ
مُّسْتَقِيمٍ دِينًا قِيَمًا مِّلَّةَ إِبْرَٰهِيمَ حَنِيفًا ۚ
وَمَا كَانَ مِنَ ٱلْمُشْرِكِينَ ﴿١٦١﴾ قُلْ إِنَّ
صَلَاتِى وَنُسُكِى وَمَحْيَاىَ وَمَمَاتِى لِلَّهِ
رَبِّ ٱلْعَٰلَمِينَ ﴿١٦٢﴾ لَا شَرِيكَ لَهُۥ ۖ وَبِذَٰلِكَ
أُمِرْتُ وَأَنَا۠ أَوَّلُ ٱلْمُسْلِمِينَ ﴿١٦٣﴾

---

world with all its vanities continues to delude man that, as there may neither be God nor After-life, one should eat, drink and enjoy oneself as best one can.

141. This is addressed to the Prophet (peace be on him) and through him to all followers of the true faith. The import of this statement is that true faith has always consisted, and still consists, in recognizing the One True God as one's God and Lord; in associating none with God in His divinity – neither in respect of His essence, nor of His attributes, nor of His claims upon His creatures; in believing in the Hereafter and hence considering oneself answerable before God; and in living according to those principles and values which have been communicated by God to mankind through His Prophets and Books. This was the religion entrusted to man at the beginning of human life. The religions which emerged later stemmed from the perverted ingenuity of man, from his baser lusts, and from an exaggerated sense of devotion to venerable personalities. Such factors corrupted the original religion and overlaid it with harmful innovations. Hence, people modified and distorted the original beliefs by mixing them with products of their conjecture and philosophical thinking. More and more innovations were added to the original laws of the true religion. Putting aside the Law of God, men set themselves up as their own

*That is, of those who are Muslims – Ed.

(164) Say: 'Shall I seek someone other than Allah as Lord when He is the Lord of everything?'[144] Everyone will bear the consequence of what he does, and no one shall bear the burden of another.[145] Thereafter, your return will be to your Lord, whereupon He will let you know what you disagreed about.

قُلْ أَغَيْرَ ٱللَّهِ أَبْغِى رَبًّا وَهُوَ رَبُّ كُلِّ شَىْءٍ ۚ
وَلَا تَكْسِبُ كُلُّ نَفْسٍ إِلَّا عَلَيْهَا ۚ
وَلَا تَزِرُ وَازِرَةٌ وِزْرَ أُخْرَىٰ ۚ ثُمَّ إِلَىٰ رَبِّكُم
مَّرْجِعُكُمْ فَيُنَبِّئُكُم بِمَا كُنتُمْ فِيهِ
تَخْتَلِفُونَ ﴿١٦٤﴾

---

law-makers, indulged in hair-splitting elaborations, and exaggerated the importance of disagreements in minor legal problems. They showed excessive veneration for some Prophets of God and some standard-bearers of the true religion, and directed their rancour and hatred against the others. Thus there emerged innumerable religions and sects, the birth of each leading to the fragmentation of humanity into an ever-increasing number of mutually hostile groups. Anyone who decides to follow the true religion must therefore cut himself off from all factions and chart an independent course.

142. The 'Way of Abraham' is one further indication of the way of true religion which one is required to follow. This way could also have been designated as the way of Moses or of Jesus. But since their names have become falsely associated with Judaism and Christianity respectively, it was necessary to call it the 'Way of Abraham'. Moreover, Abraham was acknowledged by both the Jews and the Christians as rightly-guided and both knew, of course, that he lived long before either Judaism or Christianity was born. In the same way, the polytheists of Arabia also considered Abraham to be rightly-guided. Despite their ignorance, they at least acknowledged that that righteous man, who had founded the Ka'bah, was a worshipper of God exclusively and no idolator.

143. The Arabic word *nusuk* used here signifies ritual sacrifice as well as other forms of devotion and worship.

144. Since God is the Lord of the entire universe, how could anyone else be His lord? Since the entire universe is yoked to obedience to God, and man is an integral part of the universe, how can he reasonably look for another lord in that area of his life in which he uses his own volition and judgement? Is it appropriate for him to move in diametrical opposition to the entire universe?

(165) For He it is Who has appointed you vicegerent over the earth, and has exalted some of you over others in rank that He may try you in what He has bestowed upon you.[146] Indeed your Lord is swift in retribution, and He is certainly All-Forgiving, All-Compassionate.

وَهُوَ ٱلَّذِى جَعَلَكُمْ خَلَٰٓئِفَ
ٱلْأَرْضِ وَرَفَعَ بَعْضَكُمْ فَوْقَ بَعْضٍ
دَرَجَٰتٍ لِّيَبْلُوَكُمْ فِى مَآ ءَاتَىٰكُمْ ۗ
إِنَّ رَبَّكَ سَرِيعُ ٱلْعِقَابِ وَإِنَّهُۥ لَغَفُورٌ
رَّحِيمٌۢ ﴿١٦٥﴾

---

145. Every person is responsible for whatever he does; and no one is responsible for the deeds of others.

146. This statement embodies three important truths: First, that human beings as such are vicegerents of God on earth, so that God has entrusted them with many things and endowed them with the power to use them. Second, it is God Himself Who has created differences of rank among His vicegerents. The trust placed in some is more than that of others. Some men have been granted control of more resources than others. Some are more gifted in respect of their abilities. Likewise, some human beings have been placed under the trust of others. Third, all this is indeed designed to test man. The entire life of man is, in fact, a vast examination wherein man is being tested about the trust he has received from God: how sensitive he is to that trust, to what extent he lives up to it, and to what extent he proves to be competent with it.

What position man will be able to attain in the Next Life depends on the result of this test.

Glossary of Terms

Ahl al-Dhimmah (or *Dhimmīs*) are the non-Muslim subjects of an Islamic state who have been guaranteed protection of their rights – life, property and practise of their religion, etc. – by the Muslims.

Ahl al-Ḥadīth refers to the group of scholars in Islam who pay relatively greater importance to 'traditions' than to other sources of Islamic doctrine such as *qiyās*, and tend to interpret the traditions more literally and rigorously. The term has also come to be used lately for a group of Muslims in the Indo-Pakistan subcontinent who are close to the Ḥanbalī school in theology, and claim to follow no single school on legal matters.

Ahl al-Kitāb, literally 'People of the Book', refers to the followers of Divine Revelation before the advent of the Prophet Muḥammad (peace be on him).

Al-An'ām, literally 'the cattle', is the title of *Sūrah* 6 of the Qur'ān.

Anṣār means 'the Helpers'. In Islamic parlance the word refers to the Muslims of Madina who helped the Muhajirūn of Makka in the process of the latter's settling down in the new environment.

Bahīmah (plural *bahā'im*) signifies every quadruped animal (of which the beasts of prey are excluded). *Bahīmah* thus refers to goats, sheep, and cows.

Dār al-Ḥarb (Domain of War) refers to the territory under the hegemony of unbelievers, which is on terms of active or potential belligerency with the Domain of Islam, and presumably hostile to the Muslims living in its domain.

Dār al-Kufr (Domain of Unbelief) refers to the territory under the hegemony of the unbelievers.

Dhabḥ means to split or pierce, to cut the throat of any creature. *Dhabḥ* is the process of killing required by Islam for legitimizing the consumption of the flesh of animals.

Dhimmī (see *Ahl al-Dhimmah*).

Dīn: the core meaning of *dīn* is obedience. As a Qur'ānic technical term, *dīn* refers to the way of life and the system of conduct based on recognizing God as one's sovereign and committing oneself to obey Him. According to Islam true *dīn* consists of living in total submission to God, and the way to do so is to accept as binding the guidance communicated through the Prophets.

Farḍ bi al-Kifāyah signifies a collective duty of the Muslim community so that if some people carry it out no Muslim is considered blameworthy; but if no one carries it out all incur a collective guilt.

Fawāḥish applies to all those acts whose abominable character is self-evident. In the Qur'ān all extra-marital sexual relationships, sodomy, nudity, false accusation of unchastity, and taking as one's wife a woman who had been married to one's father, are specifically reckoned as shameful deeds. In *Ḥadīth*, theft, taking intoxicating drinks and begging have been characterized as *fawāḥish* as have many other brazenly evil and indecent acts.

Fī sabīl Allāh (in the way of Allah) is a frequently used expression in the Qur'ān which emphasizes that good acts should be done exclusively to please God. Generally the expression has been used in the Qur'ān in connection with striving or spending for charitable purposes.

Fisq: transgression; consists of disobedience to the command of God.

Ḥadīth: the word *ḥadīth* literally means communication or narration. In the Islamic context it has come to denote the record of what the Prophet (peace be on him) said, did, or tacitly approved. According to some scholars, the word *ḥadīth* also covers reports about the sayings and deeds, etc. of the Companions of the Prophet in addition to the Prophet himself. The whole body of traditions is termed *Ḥadīth* and its science *'Ilm al-Ḥadīth*.

Ḥajj (Major Pilgrimage) is one of the five pillars of Islam, a duty one must perform during one's life-time if one has the financial resources for it. It resembles '*Umrah* (q.v.) in some respects, but differs from it insofar as it can be performed during certain specified dates of Dhu al-Ḥijjah alone. In addition to *ṭawāf* and *sa'y* (which are also required for '*Umrah*), there are a few other requirements but especially one's 'standing' (*wuqūf*) in 'Arafāt during the day-time on 9th of Dhu al-Ḥijjah. For details of the rules of *Ḥajj*, see the books of *Fiqh*.

Ḥijābah refers to the function of keeping the key of the Ka'bah, which has traditionally been considered a matter of great honour in Arabia.

Hijrah signifies migration from a land where a Muslim is unable to live according to the precepts of his faith to a land where it is possible to do so. The *hijrah par excellence* for Muslims is the *hijrah* of the Prophet (peace be on him) which not only provided him and his followers refuge from persecution, but also an opportunity to build a society and state according to the ideals of Islam.

Hubal, the chief of the minor deities, was an image of a man, and was said to have been originally brought to Arabia from Syria.

'Iddah denotes the waiting period that a woman is required to observe as a consequence of the nullification of her marriage with her husband or because of the husband's death.

Iḥrām refers to the state in which the Pilgrim is held to be from the time he performs certain prescribed rituals making his entry into the state of *Iḥrām* (literally 'prohibiting'). *Iḥrām* is so called in view of the numerous prohibitions that ought to be observed (e.g. abstention from all sex acts, from the use of perfume, from hunting or killing animals, cutting the beard or shaving the head, cutting the nails, plucking blades of grass or cutting green trees).

Ijmā' refers to the consensus of eminent scholars (*mujtahidūn*) of Islam in a given age. *Ijmā'* comes next to the Qur'ān and the *Sunnah* as a source of Islamic doctrines.

Imām signifies the leader, and in its highest form, refers to the head of the Islamic state. It is also used with reference to the founders of the different systems of theology and law in Islam.

'Ishā' (Night) Prayer signifies the prescribed Prayer which is performed after the night has well set in.

'Izzah denotes a position which is at once exalted and secure. In other words, the term signifies 'inviolable honour and glory'.

Jāhilīyah denotes all those world-views and ways of life which are based on rejection or disregard of heavenly guidance communicated to mankind through the Prophets and Messengers of God; the attitude of treating human life – either wholly or partly – as independent of the directives of God.

Janābah is the state of major ritual impurity which is caused by menses, coitus, child-birth or *pollutis nocturna*. In the state of *janābah* one may not perform the Prayers.

Jibt signifies a thing devoid of any true basis and bereft of usefulness. In Islamic terminology the various forms of sorcery, divination and soothsaying, in short all superstitions, are called *jibt*.

Jihād literally means 'to strive' or 'to exert to the utmost'. In Islamic parlance it signifies all forms of striving, including armed struggle, aimed at making the Word of God prevail.

Jinn are an independent species of creation about which little is known except that unlike man, who was created out of earth, the *jinn* were created out of fire. But like man, a Divine Message has also been addressed to them and they too have been endowed with the capacity, again like man, to choose between good and evil, between obedience or disobedience to God.

Kaffārah means atonement, expiation.

Kāfir signifies one who denies or rejects the truth, i.e. who disbelieves in the message of the Prophets. Since the advent of Muḥammad (peace be on him), anyone who rejects his Message is a *kāfir*.

Kalālah, according to some scholars, refers to those who die leaving neither issue nor father nor grandfather. According to others it refers to those who die without issue (regardless of whether they are succeeded by father or grandfather).

Khamr literally means 'wine', and has been prohibited by Islam. This prohibition covers everything that acts as an agent of intoxication.

Khul' signifies a woman's securing the annulment of her marriage through the payment of some compensation to her husband. For details see *Towards Understanding the Qur'ān*, vol. I, *Sūrah* 2, n. 252.

Kirpān is a special kind of large dagger which is kept by the Sikhs for religious reasons.

Al-Lāt was the chief idol of the Thaqīf tribe in al-Ṭā'if, and among the most famous idols in pre-Islamic Arabia.

Liwā' means banner, flag, standard. In pre-Islamic Makka, it was an honoured function assigned to one of the clans of Quraysh to carry it which indicated its position of leadership in the battle.

Mahr (bridal-due) signifies the amount of payment that is settled between the spouses at the time of marriage, and which the husband is required to make to his bride. *Mahr* symbolizes the financial responsibility that a husband undertakes towards his wife by virtue of entering into the contract of marriage.

Al-Manāt was the chief idol worshipped by the Khuzā'ah and Hudhayl tribes.

Ma'rūf refers to the conduct which is accepted as good and fair by human beings in general.

Muḥṣanāt means 'protected women'. It has been used in the Qur'ān in two different meanings. First, it has been used in the sense of 'married women', that is, those who enjoy the protection of their husbands. Second, it has been used in the sense of those who enjoy the protection of families as opposed to slave-girls.

Nafl Prayer is a voluntary prayer, an act of supererogatory devotion.

Nasab means family, lineage, descent.

Naṣārá is the name given to the followers of the Christian faith both in the Qur'ān and *Ḥadīth*.

Nubūwah means prophethood.

Nuṣub signify all places consecrated for offerings to others than the One True God, regardless of whether they are images of stone or something else.

Nusuk signify ritual sacrifice as well as other forms of devotion and worship.

Qaṣr, which literally means 'to shorten', is technically used to signify the Islamic rule that during one's journey it is permissible, and indeed preferable, to pray only two *rak'ahs* in those obligatory Prayers in which a person is required to pray four *rak'ahs*.

Qawwām or *qayyim* is a person responsible for administering or supervising the affairs of either an individual or an organization, for protecting and safeguarding them and taking care of their needs.

Qiblah signifies the direction to which all Muslims are required to turn when offering their prescribed Prayers, namely towards the Ka'bah.

Rifādah was the function of providing food to the Pilgrims and like *ḥijābah* (q.v.) and *siqāyah* (q.v.), it was considered an important and honoured function in Arabia during the *Jāhilīyah* period.

Ṣalāt al-Khawf means Prayer in the state of insecurity. For its procedure see *Sūrah al-Nisā'* 4: 102.

Sha'ā'ir Allāh refer to all those rites which, in opposition to polytheism and outright disbelief and atheism, are the characteristic symbols of exclusive devotion to God.

Shahīd in Islamic parlance means martyr.

Shākir means he who acknowledges benefaction. This is the sense of the word when it is used with reference to man. When used in connection with God (see, for instance, *Sūrah al-Nisā'* 4: 147) it denotes appreciation on God's part of man's service.

Sharī'ah signifies the entire Islamic way of life, especially the Law of Islam.

Shirk consists of associating anyone or anything with the Creator either in His being, or attributes, or in the exclusive rights (such as worship) that He has against His creatures.

Shukr means thankfulness. In Islam, it is a basic religious value. Man owes thanks to God for almost an infinite number of things. He owes thanks to God for all that he possesses – his life as well as all that makes his life pleasant, enjoyable and wholesome. And above all, man owes thanks to God for making available the guidance which can enable him to find his way to his salvation and felicity.

Siqāyah signifies the function of providing water to the Pilgrims in the Pilgrimage season. *Siqāyah*, like *ḥijābah* (q.v.), was an office of great honour.

Sukr signifies the state of intoxication.

Sunnah Prayers are prayers which are considered recommended in view of the fact that the Prophet (peace be on him) either performed them often and/or made statements about their meritorious character.

Ṭāghūt literally denotes the one who exceeds his legitimate limits. In Qur'ānic terminology it refers to the creature who exceeds the limits of his creatureliness and arrogates to himself godhead and lordship. In the negative scale of values, the first stage of man's error is *fisq* (i.e. disobeying God without necessarily denying that one should obey Him). The second stage is that of *kufr* (i.e. rejection of the very idea that one ought to obey God). The last stage is that man not only rebels against God but also imposes his rebellious will on others. All those who reach this stage are *ṭāghūt*.

Ṭalāq means repudiation of marriage.

Tashahhud, literally 'testimony', is a declaration of the Muslim faith towards the end of the Prayers, immediately after the recitation of *Taḥīyah*, while sitting with the first finger of the right hand extended as a witness to the unity of God.

Tawbah basically denotes 'to come back; to turn towards someone'. *Tawbah* on the part of man signifies that he has given up his disobedience and has returned to submission and obedience to God. The same word used in respect of God means that He has mercifully turned to His repentant servant so that the latter has once more become an object of His compassionate attention.

Tayammum literally means 'to intend to do a thing'. As an Islamic legal term, it refers to wiping one's hands and face with clean earth as a substitution for ablution when water cannot be obtained.

Ulū al-amr include all those entrusted with directing Muslims in matters of common concern.

Ummī signifies the 'unlettered'. It is also used to refer to those who do not possess Divine revelation.

'Umrah (Minor Pilgrimage) is an Islamic rite and consists of Pilgrimage to the Ka'bah. It consists essentially of *Iḥrām* (q.v.), *ṭawāf* (i.e. circumambulation) around the Ka'bah (seven times), and *sa'y* (i.e. running) between Ṣafā and Marwah (seven times). It is called minor *ḥajj* since it need not be performed at a particular time of the year and its performance requires fewer rituals than the *Ḥajj* proper.

Al-'Uzzá has been identified with Venus, but it was worshipped under the form of an acacia tree, and was the deity of the Ghaṭfān tribe.

Waḥy refers to Revelation which consists of communicating God's Messages to a Prophet or Messenger of God. The highest form of revelation is the Qur'ān of which even the words are from God.

Walī means guardian.

Witr means 'odd number'. *Witr rak'ahs* are odd numbers of *rak'ahs* such as 1, 3, 5, etc. – usually 1 or 3 – which are said after the last Prayer at night.

Wuḍū' refers to the ablution made before performing the prescribed Prayers. It requires washing (1) the face from the top of the forehead to the chin and as far as each ear; (2) the hands and arms up to the elbow; (3) wiping with wet hands a part of the head; and (4) washing the feet to the ankle.

Zakāh (Purifying Alms) literally means purification, whence it is used to express a portion of property bestowed in alms, as a means of purifying the person concerned and the remainder of his property. It is among the five pillars of Islam and refers to the mandatory amount that a Muslim must pay out of his property. The detailed rules of *zakāh* have been laid down in books of *Fiqh*.

Ẓālim is the wrong-doer, he who exceeds the limits of right, the unjust.

Zinā means illegal sexual intercourse and embraces both fornication and adultery.

Ẓulm literally means placing a thing where it does not belong. Technically, it refers to exceeding the right and hence committing wrong or injustice.

Biographical Notes

'Abd Allāh ibn 'Abbās, d. 68 A.H./687 C.E., a Companion of the Prophet (peace be on him), was the most outstanding scholar of Qur'ānic exegesis in his time.

'Abd Allāh ibn 'Amr ibn al-'Āṣ, d. 65 A.H./684 C.E., was a Companion and son of the conqueror of Egypt who embraced Islam before his father. He was noted for his devotion and learning and prepared one of the first collections of *Ḥadīth*.

'Abd Allāh ibn Jubayr, d. 3 A.H./625 C.E., a Companion of the Prophet (peace be on him), participated in the battles of Badr and Uḥud. In the latter battle, in which he was martyred, he was the commander of the archers.

'Abd Allāh ibn Mas'ūd, d. 32 A.H./653 C.E., one of the most learned Companions of the Prophet (peace be on him), was noted especially for his juristic calibre. He was held by the Iraqi school of law as one of its main authorities.

'Abd Allāh ibn Ubayy ibn Salūl, d. 9 A.H./630 C.E., was the foremost enemy of the Prophet (peace be on him) and the ringleader of the hypocrites in Madina.

'Abd Allāh ibn 'Umar, d. 73 A.H./692 C.E., a famous Companion and son of the second Caliph, was famous for his piety and for transmitting many Traditions from the Prophet (peace be on him).

Abū Bakr, 'Abd Allāh ibn 'Uthmān, d. 13 A.H./634 C.E., was the most trusted Companion of the Prophet (peace be on him) and the first Caliph of Islam. Abū Bakr's wisdom and indomitable will ensured the survival of Islam after the death of the Prophet.

Abū al-Dardā', 'Uwaymir ibn Mālik, d. 32 A.H./652 C.E., was a distinguished Companion who contributed to the collection of the Qur'ān, and was known for his bravery as well as his piety and religious devotion.

Abū Dā'ūd Sulaymān ibn al-Ash'ath, d. 275 A.H./889 C.E., was a famous traditionist whose *Kitāb al-Sunan* is one of the six most authentic collections of *Ḥadīth*.

Abū Ḥanīfah, al-Nu'mān ibn Thābit, d. 150 A.H./767 C.E., was a theologian and jurist who dominated the intellectual life of Iraq in the later part of his life and became the founder of a major school of law in Islam known after his name.

Abū Hurayrah, d. 59 A.H./679 C.E., was a Companion of the Prophet (peace be on him) who transmitted a very large number of Traditions.

Abū Mūsá al-Ash'arī, 'Abd Allāh ibn Qays, d. 44 A.H./665 C.E., was a Companion of the Prophet (peace be on him) who embraced Islam in its early years and migrated with other Muslims to Abyssinia. He was later appointed by the Prophet (peace be on him) as governor over Zabīd and 'Adan (Aden); still later he was appointed as governor of Baṣrah, and subsequently of Kūfah. He also served as an arbitrator in the dispute between 'Alī and Mu'āwiyah.

Abū Ṭālib, 'Abd Manāf ibn 'Abd al-Muṭṭalib, d. 620 C.E., was an uncle of the Prophet (peace be on him) and the father of the fourth Caliph, 'Alī (q.v.). Even though he did not embrace Islam, Abū Ṭālib continued to provide protection to the Prophet (peace be on him) from his enemies.

Abū Yūsuf, Ya'qūb ibn Ibrāhīm, d. 182 A.H./798 C.E., an outstanding jurist, was one of the most prominent disciples of Abū Ḥanīfah (q.v.), and is considered among the founders of the Ḥanafi school of law.

'Adī ibn Ḥātim, d. 68 A.H./687 C.E., was a Companion who took a prominent part in the military expeditions against the apostates during the caliphate of Abū Bakr.

Aḥmad ibn Ḥanbal, d. 241 A.H./855 C.E., was the founder of one of the four Sunnī schools of law in Islam. He valiantly suffered persecution for the sake of his religious conviction.

'Ā'ishah, d. 58 A.H./678 C.E., daughter of Abū Bakr, was a wife of the Prophet (peace be on him). She has transmitted a wealth of Traditions, especially those concerning the Prophet's personal life. She was also regarded highly for her mature and sharp understanding of the teachings of Islam.

Al-Akhnas ibn Sharīq was a Companion who committed apostasy and then returned to Islam. He died in the caliphate of 'Umar.

'Alī ibn abī Ṭālib, d. 40 A.H./661 C.E., was a cousin and also son-in-law of the Prophet (peace be on him) and the fourth Caliph of Islam. He was known for his many qualities, especially piety and juristic acumen.

Al-Ālūsī, Maḥmūd ibn 'Abd Allāh al-Ḥusaynī, d. 1270 A.H./1854 C.E., was a leading commentator of the Qur'ān, litterateur, jurist and Sufi of the nineteenth century. His commentary *Rūḥ al-Ma'ānī* is an encyclopaedic work which continues to command considerable respect.

'Ammār ibn Yāsir, d. 37 A.H./657 C.E., was a Companion of the Prophet (peace be on him) and one of the early converts to Islam. He is the first Muslim to have built a mosque. He was appointed the governor of Kūfah by 'Umar, the second Caliph.

Anas ibn Mālik, d. 93 A.H./712 C.E., was a distinguished Companion who had the honour of serving the Prophet (peace be on him) for many years.

'Aqīl ibn abī Ṭālib, d. 60 A.H./680 C.E., was a cousin and Companion of the Prophet (peace be on him) who was famous for his knowledge of pre-Islamic Arabian tribal battles and genealogy.

'Aṭā' ibn abī Rabāḥ, d. 114 A.H./732 C.E., was a Successor and one of the most prominent jurists of Makka in his time.

Al-Awzā'ī, d. 157 A.H./774 C.E., was the foremost jurist of Syria in the second century of Islam.

Al-Baghawī, 'Abd Allāh ibn Muḥammad abī al-Qāsim, d. 317 A.H./929 C.E., was a scholar of *Ḥadīth*, who authored many voluminous works in *Ḥadīth* and related fields.

Bilāl ibn Rabāḥ, d. 20 A.H./641 C.E., was a very famous Companion of the Prophet (peace be on him) and *mu'adhdhin* (caller to Prayer).

Al-Bukhārī, Muḥammad ibn Ismā'īl, d. 256 A.H./870 C.E., is regarded as the most famous traditionist of Islam, whose work is one of the six most authentic collections of *Ḥadīth*, generally considered by Muslims to be the 'soundest book after the Book of Allah'.

Al-Dārimī, 'Abd Allāh ibn 'Abd al-Raḥmān, d. 255 A.H./869 C.E., was one of the outstanding scholars of *Ḥadīth* whose *Musnad* is highly regarded.

Al-Ḥasan al-Baṣrī, d. 110 A.H./728 C.E., known primarily for his piety, was a major theologian of Baṣrah during the last decades of the first century of *Hijrah*/seventh century C.E.

Al-Ḥasan ibn Zayd ibn al-Ḥasan ibn 'Alī ibn abī Ṭālib, d. 168 A.H./784 C.E., was a member of the family of the Prophet (peace be on him), who was appointed by the Abbasid caliph al-Manṣūr as governor of Madina. He was later dismissed and imprisoned in Baghdad.

Ḥudhayfah ibn al-Yamān, d. 36 A.H./656 C.E., was a Companion of the Prophet (peace be on him) who played an important role in the early Islamic conquests.

Ibn Ḥazm, 'Alī ibn Aḥmad, d. 456 A.H./1064 C.E., was an encyclopaedic Spanish scholar, who was renowned for his works in numerous fields including law and jurisprudence, comparative religion, literature and poetry.

Ibn Kathīr, Ismā'īl ibn 'Umar, d. 774 A.H./1373 C.E., was a famous traditionist, historian and jurist and the author of one of the best-known commentaries on the Qur'ān.

Ibn Mājah, Muḥammad ibn Yazīd, d. 273 A.H./887 C.E., was a famous traditionist whose collection of Traditions (*Kitāb al-Sunan*) is one of the six most authentic collections of *Ḥadīth*.

Ibn Rushd, Muḥammad ibn Aḥmad, d. 520 A.H./1126 C.E., was a renowned Spanish jurist of the Mālikī school of law, and grandfather of the famous Ibn Rushd, the philosopher. Apart from other works, he is known for his brilliant work in the field of comparative Islamic law, *Bidāyat al-Mujtahid*.

Ibn Ṣawriyah was a Jewish scholar of the Qurayẓah tribe in the time of the Prophet (peace be on him) who testified that the Jews knew that his claim to be a Prophet was true.

Ibn Sīrīn, Muḥammad, d. 110 A.H./729 C.E., was a noted second generation scholar of Baṣrah, who was especially prominent as a traditionist.

Ibn 'Umar, 'Abd Allāh, d. 73 A.H./692 C.E., a son of the second Caliph, 'Umar ibn al-Khaṭṭāb, was an outstanding Companion in his own right, and is renowned for his piety and knowledge.

Ibrāhīm al-Nakha'ī, d. 96 A.H./715 C.E., was the most prominent jurist of Kūfah in the second generation of Islam and played a major role in the development of the Iraqi school of law.

'Ikrimah ibn abī Jahl, d. 13 A.H./634 C.E., was a Companion of the Prophet (peace be on him) whose father, Abū Jahl, was one of the staunchest enemies of Islam. After conversion to Islam, 'Ikrimah fought valiantly for the cause of Islam and was martyred in the battle of Yarmuk.

Al-Iṣfahānī, Muḥammad ibn Baḥr abū Muslim, d. 322 A.H./934 C.E., was a famous scholar of *Tafsīr*.

Al-Jaṣṣāṣ, Aḥmad ibn 'Alī, d. 370 A.H./980 C.E., was an eminent jurist of the Ḥanafī school of law in his time. He is celebrated for his Qur'ān-commentary, *Aḥkām al-Qur'ān*, which is an erudite commentary on the Qur'ān from a legal perspective.

Khabbāb ibn al-Arat, d. 37 A.H./657 C.E., a Companion and one of the early converts to Islam, who was mercilessly persecuted by the opponents of Islam in Makka.

Khadījah bint Khuwaylid, d. 620 C.E., was the first woman whom the Prophet (peace be on him) married. She gave birth to several sons and daughters including Fāṭimah, Zaynab, Umm Kulthūm and Ruqayyah.

Al-Layth ibn Sa'd, d. 175 A.H./791 C.E., was a famous scholar of *Ḥadīth* and *Fiqh* and a foremost jurist of Egypt in his time.

Makḥul ibn abī Muslim, d. 112 A.H./730 C.E., was a scholar of *Ḥadīth* and *Fiqh* who, after journeying through different lands, settled in Damascus and was recognized as one of the greatest jurists of Syria in his time.

Mālik ibn Anas, d. 179 A.H./795 C.E., was a famous second Islamic century/eighth century C.E. traditionist and jurist of Madina, and the founder of one of the four Sunnī schools of law in Islam. His *al-Muwaṭṭa'*, a collection of Traditions as well as legal opinions of the jurists of Madina, is one of the earliest extant works of *Ḥadīth* and *Fiqh*.

Mu'ādh ibn Jabal, d. 18 A.H./639 C.E., a Companion, was known for his knowledge of Law; he was among those who undertook the collection of the Qur'ān and was appointed by the Prophet (peace be on him) as a judge in Yaman.

Mu'āwiyah ibn abī Sufyān, d. 60 A.H./680 C.E., was a Companion of the Prophet (peace be on him), became a Caliph after 'Alī ibn abī Ṭālib (q.v.) and was the founder of the Umayyad dynasty.

Mujāhid ibn Jabr, d. 104 A.H./722 C.E., was a Successor and among the foremost Qur'ān-commentators of Makka in his time. His *Tafsīr*, which has been published recently, is one of the earliest extant works of that genre.

Muslim ibn al-Ḥajjāj al-Nīsābūrī, d. 261 A.H./875 C.E., was one of the greatest scholars of *Ḥadīth*, whose work is one of the six most authentic collections of *Ḥadīth* and ranks second in importance only to that of al-Bukhārī.

Al-Nasā'ī, Aḥmad ibn 'Alī, d. 303 A.H./915 C.E., was one of the foremost scholars of *Ḥadīth* whose *Sunan* is considered one of the six most authentic collections of Traditions.

Al-Nawawī, Yaḥyá ibn Sharaf, d. 676 A.H./1277 C.E., a famous scholar of *Ḥadīth* and *Fiqh*, was a man of encyclopaedic knowledge who left behind a large number of works, especially in *Ḥadīth* and *Fiqh*. He is famous for several of his works, but particularly for his commentary on the *Ḥadīth* collection of Muslim.

Nawfal ibn Mu'āwiyah, d. *circa* 60 A.H./680 C.E., was a Companion of the Prophet (peace be on him). Initially, when he was not a Muslim, he took part in several battles against the Muslims. Later he embraced Islam and fought on the side of the Muslims against their enemies.

Qatādah ibn Di'āmah, d. 118 A.H./736 C.E., was an erudite scholar of Baṣrah who was known for his knowledge of Qur'ānic exegesis, *Ḥadīth*, Arabic language and Arabic genealogy.

Al-Qurṭubī, Muḥammad ibn Aḥmad, d. 671 A.H./1273 C.E., was one of the most distinguished commentators of the Qur'ān. His *al-Jāmi' li Aḥkām al-Qur'ān* is not only one of the best commentaries on the legal verses of the Qur'ān but also one of the best *tafsīr* works.

Sa'd ibn al-Rabī', d. 3 A.H./625 C.E., was a Companion of the Prophet (peace be on him) and was martyred in the battle of Uḥud.

Sa'īd ibn Jubayr, d. 95 A.H./714 C.E., was a famous scholar of Kūfah in the generation of Successors.

Sa'īd ibn al-Musayyib, d. 94 A.H./713 C.E., was a foremost scholar and jurist of the generation of Successors (*Tābi'ūn*). One of the seven recognized jurists of Madina, he was known for his knowledge of *Ḥadīth* and *Fiqh* as well as for his piety and devotion.

Sālim, the *mawlá* of Abū Ḥudhayfah, d. 12 A.H./633 C.E., originally a slave of Persian origin, was liberated from slavery by the wife of Abū Ḥudhayfah. Sālim was among the early converts to Islam and ranked among the Companions most noted for their knowledge of the Qur'ān.

Al-Sha'bī, 'Āmir ibn Shuraḥbīl, d. 103 A.H./721 C.E., was one of the famous scholars of *Ḥadīth* in Kūfah in his time.

Al-Shāfi'ī, Muḥammad ibn Idrīs, d. 204 A.H./820 C.E., was the founder of one of the four Sunnī schools of law in Islam.

Al-Shaybānī, Muḥammad ibn al-Ḥasan, d. 189 A.H./804 C.E., was a famous Iraqi jurist and disciple of Abū Ḥanīfah (q.v.) and is reckoned as one of the founders of the Ḥanafī school of law.

Shurayḥ ibn al-Ḥārith al-Kindī, d. 78 A.H./697 C.E., was a famous judge of the first century who worked in that capacity for an unusually long period of time.

Ṣuhayb ibn Sinān, d. 38 A.H./659 C.E., was a prominent Companion of the Prophet (peace be on him).

Al-Ṭabarī, Muḥammad ibn Jarīr, d. 310 A.H./923 C.E., was a distinguished historian, jurist and Qur'ān-commentator. His major extant works include his commentary *Jāmi' al-Bayān fī Tafsīr al-Qur'ān* and his *Annals*, viz. *Ta'rīkh al-Rusul wa al-Mulūk*.

Al-Thawrī, Sufyān ibn Sa'īd, d. 161 A.H./778 C.E., was one of the most outstanding scholars of *Ḥadīth* in the second century of Islam.

Al-Tirmidhī, Muḥammad ibn 'Īsá, d. 279 A.H./892 C.E., was a famous traditionist whose collection of Traditions, *Kitāb al-Sunan*, is considered one of the six most authentic collections of *Ḥadīth*.

Ubayy ibn Ka'b, d. 21 A.H./642 C.E., was a prominent Companion who was knowledgeable about the Scriptures and played a key role in the collection of the Qur'ān.

'Umar ibn al-Khaṭṭāb, d. 23 A.H./644 C.E., was the second Caliph of Islam under whose Caliphate the Islamic state became increasingly organized and its frontiers vastly expanded.

Umm Salamah, Hind bint Suhayl, d. 62 A.H./681 C.E., was one of the wives of the Prophet (peace be on him) who has reported several hundred traditions from him.

'Urwah ibn al-Zubayr, d. 93 A.H./712 C.E., was a jurist of the generation of Successors, and is considered one of the famous group of 'seven jurists of Madina'.

'Uthmān ibn 'Affān, d. 35 A.H./656 C.E., was a son-in-law of the Prophet (peace be on him) and the third Caliph of Islam under whose reign vast areas were conquered and the Qur'ān's present codex was prepared.

The Ẓāhirīs constitute a school of law in Islam which was founded by Dā'ūd ibn Khalaf, d. 207 A.H./884 C.E. The characteristic of the school is that it considers legal injunctions to consist merely of clear statements embodied in the Qur'ān and *Sunnah* and is strongly opposed to *ra'y*, *qiyās*, *istiḥsān*, etc., which are accepted in varying degrees as valid sources of laws by the jurists of other schools of Islamic Law. This school did not attain much popularity among Muslims and hardly exists today though in the fifth Islamic century/tenth century C.E. it found a very brilliant and erudite representative in Ibn Ḥazm, d. 456 A.H./994 C.E., of Spain.

Zufar ibn al-Hudhayl, d. 148 A.H./765 C.E., was a disciple of Abū Ḥanīfah and is considered one of the major figures in the Ḥanafī school of law.

Al-Zuhrī, Muḥammad ibn Muslim ibn Shihāb, d. 124 A.H./721 C.E., was an outstanding early second Islamic century/eighth century C.E. scholar of Madina who left an indelible impression on *Ḥadīth* and *Sīrah*.

Bibliography

The Bible, Authorized Version, Swindon, 1985.

Encyclopaedia Britannica, 14th edition, articles 'Christianity', 'Church History', and 'Jesus Christ'.

The Holy Bible, Revised Standard Edition, New York, 1952.

Ibn al-'Arabī, Abū Bakr, *Aḥkām al-Qur'ān*.

Ibn Kathīr, *Mukhtaṣar Tafsīr Ibn Kathīr*, ed. Muḥammad 'Alī al-Ṣābūnī, 7th edition, 3 vols., Beirut, 1402/1981.

Al-Jazīrī, 'Abd al-Raḥmān, *al-Fiqh 'alá al-Madhāhib al-Arba'ah*, 5 vols., Beirut, Dār Iḥyā' al-Turāth, 1980.

Mawdūdī, Sayyid Abul A'lá, *Ḥuqūq al-Zawjayn*, 16th edition, Lahore, 1976.

———, *Rasā'il wa Masā'il*, 6th edition, 3 vols., Lahore, 1976.

———, *Sunnat kī Ā'inī Haythiyat*, 3rd edition, Lahore, 1975.

———, *Yatīm Pōté kī Wirāthat kā Mas'alah*, Lahore, 1954.

Al-Nawawī, Yaḥyá ibn Sharaf, *Al-Arba'īn*.

Polano H., *The Talmud Selections*, London, Frederick Warne & Co.

Al-Ṣābūnī, Muḥammad 'Alī, *Ṣafwat al-Tafāsīr*, 3 vols., 4th edition, Beirut, 1402/1981.

Al-Ṭabarī, Muḥammad b. Jarīr, *Tafsīr*.

Wooley, Leonard, *Abraham*, London, 1935.

Subject Index

Abominable Acts (*fawāḥish*):
— Expounded, 290, 291.

Abraham (Ibrāhīm):
— He did not associate others with Allah in His divinity, 297.
— God's command to the people to follow his way, 88.
— Meaning of the bestowal of 'a mighty dominion' upon his progeny, 49.
— His struggle against polytheism, 245–53.
— His address to his father, 245, 249.
— Religious and cultural conditions of his people, 246–8, 251–3.
— His sound inference from the 'signs of God', 245, 248.
— The Quraysh's pride in being his progeny, 245.
— The period of his advent, 246.
— His initial reflections in the quest for the Truth, 249–50.
— His disavowal of associating others with Allah in His divinity, 249.
— Those affected by his monotheistic mission, 248.
— Remonstration by his people and his perseverance, 251.
— His arguments with his people, 251.
— His people did not deny the existence of God, 251–3.
— God's bestowal of righteous offspring upon him, 252.
— Fallacious notions of Arabs about his religion, 279.
— Definition of the 'way of Abraham', 297–8.

Adam (Ādam):
— Story of his two sons, 153–4.

The Agonies of Death:
— The condition of the wrong-doers in the state of the agonies of death, 256.

Angels:
— They come to take souls, 73, 239.
— Two possibilities of the public appearance of angels, 218.
— There are angels to watch everyone, 239.
— They do not commit any lapse in the performance of their duties, 239.
— How do they take the souls of wrong-doers?, 256.
— They are born rightly-guided, 289.

Apostasy:
— Do not take religion as an object of casual entertainment, 94.

Āyah, pl. *Āyāt* (sign, signs):
— The meanings of the expression 'signs of God', 222, 295.
— There are plenty of signs for those who use their reason, 229, 230.
— Its rejection incurs the divine chastisement, 48, 187, 233, 256.
— What should be the attitude of a Muslim at a place where the signs of God are being rejected and scoffed at?, 97, 242.
— Those heedless of the signs of God are the ones who reject the Truth, 216.
— Abraham's seeking benefit from the signs of God, 245, 246.
— Only those who use their reason can profit from the signs of God, 258.
— The believers alone can profit from the signs of God, 259.
— Variety in the style of expounding these signs in the Qur'ān, 261.
— Prohibition to follow those who give the lie to the signs of God, 289.

Banū Isrā'īl (see Children of Israel; Israelites).

The Bible:
— Human interpolations in the Divine Word, 113, 114.
— Metaphorical usage of the expression 'father', 118.
— The Biblical account of twelve leaders of the Children of Israel, 142.
— Absence of any reference to Abraham's initial pondering in the Bible, 157.

Books, Revealed:
— The term *'al-Kitāb'* used for all the revealed Books, 168, 169.
— The Qur'ān confirms and protects all the revealed Books, 168, 169.

The Bounds set by God (*Ḥudūd Allāh*):
— Meaning of the statement: 'Do not exceed the bounds of right', 188, 189.

Bridal-due:
— Wife remitting the bridal-due, 8.
— It is not lawful to usurp the bridal-due by putting constraint upon the wife, 19.
— Not to take back the bridal-due, 19.
— It is one of the requisites for *nikāḥ*, 27, 137.

Chastisement/Punishment/Torment, God's:
— The kinds of people who will be subjected to God's chastisement, 18, 39, 110, 180, 241, 272.
— Ransom will not save man from it, 241.
— If people follow the path of belief and gratitude, God will not chastise them, 99, 100, 101.
— Punishment in the world cannot save one from chastisement in the Hereafter, 156.
— Eternal chastisement, 158.
— Chastisement is something to be feared, 220.

— Prosperity for the wrong-doers precedes their punishment, 232.
— The wrong-doers alone are afflicted by chastisement, 233.
— Those who reject the signs of God cannot escape chastisement, 233.
— No Prophet has the authority to cause chastisement, 238.
— Various modes of chastisement in the world, 240.
— Details of the torment in the Hereafter, 241.
— A warning precedes the befalling of divine chastisement in the world, 274.
— The divine chastisement cannot be averted from wrong-doers, 287.
— Whoever rejects the Truth tastes divine chastisement, 287.

Christianity:
— The divergence of opinion among Christians about the incident of crucifixion, 106, 108.
— The doctrine of trinity, 116, 117, 118, 180, 181.
— The doctrine of expiation and its refutation, 117, 118, 119.
— Comments of the Rev. Charles Anderson Scott on the doctrines of the Church, 181–3.
— The Rev. George William Knox's discussion on the doctrines of the Church, 184.
— The development of the doctrine about Jesus' divinity, 184–5.
— The doctrine of Mary's divinity and the Christians taking her as the Mother of God, 205, 206, 207.

Christians:
— The covenant was made with them but they broke it, 146, 147.
— The word *'Naṣārá'* expounded, 147, 148.
— Their claim of being God's children and His beloved ones, 149.
— They were asked to judge by God's Law, 167.
— Their doctrine of trinity is disbelief, 180, 181.
— Their inventing of an imaginary Messiah, 181–5.
— The attitude of the righteous Christians towards Islam and Muslims, 187.
— Jesus invited them to monotheism not trinity, 206.

Covenant:
— The punishment for selling away the covenant, 143.
— The covenants that were made with the Children of Israel, 142.
— The 'Covenant of the Mount' made with the Children of Israel, 103, 104.
— Exhortation for the Muslims to follow their covenant with God, 140.
— Covenant regarding 'we hear and obey', 140.
— The covenant was made with the Christians who broke it, 146, 147, 148.
— Three meanings of the covenant of God, 292, 293.
— 'Natural contract' expounded, 293, 294.
— As a requisite of his natural contract man should follow the right way prescribed by God, 294.

— The unalterable law pertaining to the conflict between the truth and falsehood, 227.
— The divine decree for animals and birds, 230.
— God has the power to stray one in error or to guide one, 230, 231, 253.
— Calamities befalling in the time of Prophets and its rationale, 232.
— In God is vested all authority of judgement, 237.
— Everything green or dry is recorded in the Book, 238.
— Angels set as guardians over everyone, 239.
— There is an appointed time for every happening, 240.
— The functioning of the universe is subservient to the divine determination, 258.
— For each human being there is a time limit and a resting place, 258.
— It is not the divine will to compel one to guidance, 262, 263.
— One's deed is made to appear fair to him, 262, 271, 278.
— Why man's deeds are attributed to God?, 263.
— How God turns one's heart and eyes from the Truth, 264.
— The evil ones from among the *jinn* and human beings as the enemy of Prophets, 265, 266.
— The distinction between God's Will and God's good pleasure, 265, 266, 267.
— God does not will that people should be forcibly restrained from evil and made to believe in something, 280.
— Freedom of choice for men and *jinn* to choose between good and evil, 265, 266, 267.
— The leaders of the wicked being a prey to their own wicked plots, 271.
— God's opening or constricting one's breast, 272, 273.
— Laying of the abomination on those who reject faith, 272.
— The unjust ones who fabricate lies against God fail to receive guidance, 283.
— The evil-doers using the divine will as a pretext for their evil deeds, 287, 288.
— God's rejoinder to the above pretext, 288, 289.

Divorce (*Ṭalāq*):
— It is the last resort, 20.

Doing Good:
— Whenever a man does good, God multiplies it two-fold, 40.
— If one has belief in God and in the Hereafter, he does not make a show of his good deeds, 39.
— To assist everyone in doing good, 130.
— Not to resist the offence is not a good deed, 153, 154.
— Whoever comes to God with a good deed shall have ten times as much, 296.

Duties towards God (*Ḥuqūq Allāh*):
— Man owes them as a result of his natural contract with God, 292, 293.

Duties towards other men (*Ḥuqūq al-Nās*):
— Parents, 38, 290, 291.
— Kinsmen, 38.
— Orphans, 6, 38, 88, 292.
— The needy, 38.

— What forces will the faithful have to encounter?, 158, 159.
— Faith is not a mere verbal affirmation, 161.
— To deviate from the law of God negates faith, 163.
— What type of faithful are desired by God?, 173.
— The faithful's company, 174.
— Friendship with those who mock at religion is against faith, 174.
— What deeds betray one's lack of faith?, 175.
— Faith is not anyone's monopoly, 178.
— Its obvious sign, 185.
— Portrayal of the right emotional state at the time of embracing the faith, 187.
— Discrimination between the lawful and the unlawful is a corollary of faith, 188, 189.
— The faithful are accountable, in the main, for themselves, 200.
— Respite for embracing the faith lasts only as long as the Ultimate Reality is concealed from human perception by the veil of the Unseen, 217, 218, 296.
— What type of people greet the call to the Truth?, 228.
— To embrace faith by free choice is required, 228, 229, 265, 266, 267.
— Faith protects one against fear and grief in the world and in the Hereafter, 233.
— The advice to the Prophet (peace be on him) how to treat the faithful, 236.
— Real security is for the faithful in the world and in the Hereafter, 251.
— Meaning of the statement about tarnishing one's faith with wrong-doing, 251.
— Faith being the key to the perception of the Reality, 259.
— Miracles do not help the unfaithful greet faith, 264.
— What type of people remain deprived of faith?, 264, 265.
— Laying of the abomination on those who do not embrace faith, 272.

Falsehood:
— The whole universe has not been created for falsehood to prosper, 243, 244.

Fasād (Corruption; mischief):
— It amounts to overthrowing the Islamic government, 156, 157.
— God does not love those who spread mischief, 176.

Fāsiq (Transgressor; ungodly; disobedient):
— Those who do not judge by God's Law are transgressors, 167, 168.
— God does not guide transgressors, 202.
— To partake of the slaughter on which God's name has not been pronounced is an act of transgression, 270.

Fasting (*Ṣawm*):
— Fasting as a means of expiation, 69, 70, 190, 193, 194.

— His attributes of reckoning, rewarding and chastising, 130, 135, 146, 148, 160, 193, 196, 239, 275, 299.
— The Creator, Originator, Fashioner, 5, 148, 215, 219, 243, 251, 257, 258, 259, 282.
— His knowledge, 14, 15, 18, 27, 30, 34, 37, 40, 54, 57, 69, 70, 81, 88, 90, 94, 99, 101, 114, 120, 140, 173, 181, 196, 205, 215, 219, 220, 236, 238, 243, 251, 252, 258, 260, 267, 268, 269, 273, 281.
— His forbearance and forgiveness, 15, 17, 18, 25, 28, 42, 45, 55, 73, 81, 83, 85, 91, 101, 134, 149, 156, 160, 180, 196, 197, 236, 284, 299.
— His power, capacity, authority, all-pervasiveness, 31, 48, 83, 93, 106, 114, 148, 150, 159, 160, 206, 220, 229, 237, 238, 239, 240, 243, 258, 260, 275.
— His dominion, sovereignty, Lordship, 45, 127, 171, 206, 243.
— The Helper, Protector, 44, 62, 93, 117, 260.
— His wisdom, 14, 18, 27, 30, 69, 81, 91, 106, 114, 115, 159, 206, 220, 243, 273, 281.
— The All-Seeing, 5, 35, 70, 93, 179, 206.
— The All-Embracing, the Munificent, 91, 173.
— The All-Hearing, 70, 93, 101, 181, 219, 267.
— Lord and Master of all that is in the heavens and the earth, 92, 117, 118, 148, 149, 160, 219.
— He is All-Appreciative, 99.
— He guides some and lets others go astray, 65.
— The Judge, 65, 97.
— He sustains the order of the whole universe, 257, 258, 259.
— He is devoid of all defects and weaknesses, 118, 260.
— He is Self-Sufficient, 92.
— The All-High, the All-Glorious, 36, 260.
— Possessor of all good attributes, the Praiseworthy, 92, 215, 232.
— His promises are bound to fulfilment, 87.
— He gives life and causes death, 215, 228, 257, 273, 275.
— He is just and does not cause wrong, 267.
— He transcends space and is omnipresent, 83.

God, Curse of:
— What kind of people deserve it, 44, 47, 69, 85, 175.
— For their worship of falsehood the Jews incurred the curse of God, 44.
— Who is cursed by God cannot find any helper?, 47.
— The curse by David and Jesus on the Children of Israel for their disbelief, 185.

God, Unity of (*Tawḥīd*):
— Evidence of the unity of God, 231, 232, 233, 239, 240, 258.
— There is no god but He, 260.
— Jesus' call to serve the One True God, 180, 206.
— To make one's faith exclusive to God, 99, 100.
— 'Do not say: (God is a) trinity', 116, 117, 118.
— Allah is the One True God, 117, 180.
— God is the Absolute Ruler, 127, 128.
— In God is vested all authority of declaring things lawful and unlawful, 128, 188, 189.

Ḥudaybīyah:
— Historical context of the revelation of *Sūrah al-Mā'idah*, 123, 124.
— Long-term advantages for the Muslims as a result of the Treaty of Ḥudaybīyah, 125.

Hunting:
— Hunting is forbidden in the state of *Iḥrām*, 193, 194, 195.
— Regulations for hunting, 135, 136, 137.
— What are the hunting animals?, 135, 136.
— Expiation for having hunted in the state of *Iḥrām*, 193, 194.
— Permission to eat the game of the sea, 195.

Hypocrisy:
— It is a sign of the lack of belief in God and the Hereafter, 39.

Hypocrites (*Munafīqun,* sing. *munāfiq*):
— Their psychology, 55, 172.
— Their activities in Madina after the Battle of Uḥud, 2, 3.
— How should they be treated?, 4.
— Their opposition to the reforms introduced by Islam, 30, 31.
— Their avoidance of *jihād*, 53, 54.
— Their mental response to the command for *jihād*, 60, 61.
— Their secret counsels, 62.
— Their subversive activities, 62.
— Muslims censured for having two opinions about the hypocrites, 65.
— They want to afflict the Muslims with their disbelief, 66.
— Not to have friendship with them, 66.
— Attitude towards them during the war, 66, 67, 68.
— To deviate from the Prophet's decision betrays hypocrisy, 85.
— Their taking disbelievers as friends in preference to the Muslims, 96.
— They would be placed with the disbelievers in Hell, 97.
— Their dual policy, 97, 98.
— Their deceit towards God, 98.
— Their indecisiveness, 98.
— They would be in the lowest depth of Hell, 99.
— Their inclination towards the enemies of the Truth such as the Jews and Christians, 172.
— The divine decision about their deeds going to waste, 172.
— Their hypocrisy is eventually exposed, 172.

'Ibādah (God, Worship of; Service to):
— For God alone, 38, 181, 260.
— Service to evil-ones incurs God's curse, 175.
— It is forbidden to worship any other than God, 237.
— Jesus' call was also to serve and obey none other than God, 180, 206.
— Worship is deserved by only the one who has the power to do good and harm, 181.

Unlawful Sexual Intercourse:
— The preliminary punishment for unlawful sexual intercourse, 17, 18, 19.
— Number of witnesses required to bear testimony to the committing of unlawful sexual intercourse, 17.
— To commit unlawful sexual intercourse with whom marriage is prohibited is a criminal offence, 21, 22.
— Punishment for unlawful sexual intercourse committed by a married slave-girl, 28, 29.
— Allusion to the punishment of stoning to death, 29.
Wine:
— Punishment for drinking wine, 192, 193, 194.
Testimony:
— Number of witnesses required to bear testimony to the committing of unlawful sexual intercourse, 17.
— Number of witnesses required for testimony for the bequest, 201.
— The witnesses should be trustworthy, 201.
Judicial Procedure:
— Law about the appointment of the jury by the court, 37, 38.
— The Islamic way of administration of justice, 81, 82.
— The Islamic court authorized to take up or decline the cases of Madinan Jews, 163.
Homicide:
— Sanctity of the life of a believer, 68.
— Expiation for intentional homicide of a believer, 68, 69.
— The rule concerning blood-money, 69.
— A single case of homicide endangers the whole of humanity, 155.
— Five cases in which human life can be destroyed for a just cause and its reasons, 290, 291, 292.
— The law of retaliation in the Torah, 166.
Loans and Mortgages:
— The command to pay the debt before the distribution of inheritance, 12, 14.
Law of Inheritance:
— Religious significance of the law of inheritance, 16, 17.
— The right to inheritance corresponds to one's kinship, 11.
— Inheritance includes all that the deceased has left behind, 11.
— Like men, women are also entitled to their share in inheritance, 11.
— Shares of children, 12, 13.
— Shares of parents, 12, 13.
— Distribution of inheritance, will and debts, 12, 14.
— Husband's share in what the deceased wife leaves behind, 14.
— Wife's share in what the deceased husband leaves behind, 14.
— The prevalent 'death tax' and Islamic Law, 16, 17.
— The Islamic Inheritance Law does not recognize foster-relatives, 35.
— Definition of *kalālah*, 120, 121.
— Distribution of inheritance in various forms of *kalālah*, 16, 120, 121.
— Umar's reservations about *kalālah*, 120, 121.

— Conflict between good and evil in his life, 158, 159.
— Process of the degeneration of nations and societies, 185, 186.
— Perfect standard of evaluation and judgement for man, 197.
— His body is composed of earthly elements, 216.
— He incurs self-ruin by rejecting the Truth, 223.
— His real abode is the Next World, 225.
— The divine system of guidance and deviation for him, 228, 229.
— Its two major categories, 231.
— Affirmation of monotheism ingrained in the human soul, 231, 232.
— The whole human race originated from one human being, 258.
— Lessons of instruction in man's creation and the proliferation of the human race, 259.
— His freedom of choice and volition being a trial for him, 262, 263.
— His clinging to conjectures rather than adherence to knowledge, 268, 269, 270.
— Satan deriving unfair benefit from him, 273.
— His own gain in obedience to God and own loss in disobedience to Him, 275, 276.
— Arrangement for guidance being a divine favour to him, 275, 276.
— Different degrees according to one's deeds in the sight of God, 275, 276.
— Unlike angels, man has not been created with inherent right guidance, 288, 289.
— His natural contract with God, 293.
— His natural obligations towards God, 293.
— Significance of divine guidance for him, 294.
— Fragmentation of humanity into mutually hostile groups, 297, 298.
— Three important truths regarding his life in the world, 299.

Marriage:
— Permission for marrying more wives than one, 6, 7.
— Restrictions on marrying more wives than one, 6, 7, 8.
— With whom marriage is not permitted, 21, 22–5, 26.
— Only in marriage is sexual intercourse lawful, 27.
— Bridal-due as a requisite for marriage, 27, 28, 137.
— Permission to marry women from the People of the Book, 137, 138, 139.

Married Life:
— Command for an equal treatment of wives, 6, 91, 92.
— Restrictions on the number of wives, 6, 7, 8.
— Wife giving up the bridal-due, 8.
— Patience to be exercised in married life, 19, 20.
— Do not treat wives unjustly for misappropriating the bridal-due, 19.
— Divorce should be the last resort, 20.
— Male being the head of the family in Islamic society, 35.
— Female's rebellion, 36.
— Qualities of an ideal wife, 36.
— Limits of obedience to the husband, 36.
— Male has the responsibility to support female, 35.

— Mediation as a means for resolving the dispute between the couple, 37.
— Limits of punishing a rebellious female, 36.
— Resolving the dispute rather than divorce is better for the couple, 90.
— Limits of equal treatment between wives, 91–2.
— They should not behave selfishly to each other, 90.
— Do not keep the other wife in suspense, 91–2.
— (See also Suckling, Divorce, Bridal-due and Marriage.)

Martyrs:
— Who are the martyrs?, 57.

Mary (Maryam):
— The mighty calumny of the Israelites against Mary, 104, 105.
— Meaning of the statement: 'God's command was conveyed unto Mary', 116.
— Meaning of the statement: 'a spirit from God', 116, 117.
— She adhered wholly to truthfulness, 180.
— The Christian doctrine about Mary's divinity, 206, 207.

Masjid al-Ḥarām (The Holy Mosque):
— No one has the right to stop pilgrims from visiting it, 130.

Maskh (distortion, deformation):
— The deformation of the Jews into apes and swine, 175.

The Means to come near to God:
— Its meaning, 158.

Migration (*Hijrah*):
— The command for the generality of Muslims to migrate to the 'House of Islam' in Madina, 3.
— Those avoiding it were guilty of hypocrisy, 65, 66.
— The command regarding the hypocrites who did not migrate to Madina, 66, 67.
— In what conditions is it incumbent on the Muslims living in the 'House of Disbelief' to migrate?, 66, 74.
— Directive for migration from a place in which it is not possible to observe God's Law, 74.
— A misunderstanding regarding the tradition: 'There is no *hijrah* after the conquest of Makka', 74.

Miracles:
— Uniqueness of Jesus' raising up, 106, 108–9.
— Details of Jesus' miracles, 203.
— Miracles are performed by God's command, 203.
— The Prophet (peace be on him) did not have power of his own to perform miracles, 228.
— A healthy society cannot be built on the basis of miracles, 228, 229.
— God has the absolute power to cause miracles, 264.

Moral Teachings:
— Good treatment of parents, 38, 290, 291.
— Good treatment of orphans, 6, 7, 38, 88, 292.
— Betrayal of conscience, 83–4.
— Prohibition of usurping another's property by false means, 31, 32.
— Exhortation to be gracious in dealings, 27.
— Moral excellence essential for the struggle to make the Truth prevail, 4.
— Admonition to shun hypocrisy and to be sincere, 39.
— God loves those who pardon the enemies and overlook their deeds and do good, 143.
— 'Do not take outsiders for intimate friends', 99.
— True believers, when they commit any sin, implore God's forgiveness and do not persist in the sin they had committed, 55, 83.
— Admonition to remain steadfast against falsehood, 81.
— Niggardliness of a well-to-do person is all the more blameworthy, 39.
— Admonition to be honest in looking after the property of orphans, 6.
— Exhortation to be generous at the time of distributing inheritance, 11.
— Prohibition of denying someone his due by one's bequest, 15, 16.
— Exhortation to the couple for leading a happy life, 19.
— Three feasible meanings of 'You shall not kill yourselves', 31, 32.
— One should not covet what God has conferred more abundantly on others out of His grace, 34, 35.
— Not to harm obedient wives, 36.
— Exhortation to set things right mutually, 37.
— Good treatment of parents, relatives, orphans, the needy and neighbours, 38.
— God does not approve of pride, 39.
— God does not love the niggardly and those who bid others to be niggardly, 39.
— Exhortation to be just and honest, 49.
— The believers should always work for a good cause, 64.
— Exhortation to mutual greeting and salutation, 64.
— Not to have any bias in meting out justice, 83, 84.
— Prohibition of secret consultations for undesirable deeds, 83, 84.
— Moral effect of laying the blame at other's door, 84, 85.
— Secret conferrings permissible only for a good cause, 84.
— Admonition to shun selfishness, 90.
— Exhortation to bear a just testimony for the sake of God, 94, 95, 140.
— To become upholders of justice, 94, 95.
— Prohibition of speaking evil, 101.
— To respond to someone's evil by doing him good or, at least, by pardoning him, 101.
— Exhortation to adhere to justice, 140.
— Do not transgress the bounds set by God, 188, 189.
— To repose trust in God, 141.
— Exhortation to do justice in legal cases, 163.
— To vie with one another in good works, 168.
— Avoidance of extravagance hinted at, 188.
— Prohibition of wine, 191, 192, 193, 194.

— The Qur'ān being the revelation from God to the Prophet Muḥammad (peace be on him), 220.
— Meaning of denying the sending down of revelation on a human being, 256, 257.
— Four arguments for the Prophets having received the revelation, 256, 257.
— Satan inspiring his friends, 270.

Rewards:
— Rewards of this world and of the Next World, 93.
— Those who deserve rewards, 84, 99, 112, 118, 141.
— God multiplies the reward of goodness out of His grace, 40, 118.
— A mighty reward for those fighting in the way of God, 58.
— The reward of those who emigrate in the way of God is incumbent on God, 74.
— Great reward for those who believe in all the Messengers without differentiating between them, 102–3.

Ribā (Interest):
— Its prohibition in the Torah, 110, 111.

The Righteous Ones:
— Who are the righteous ones?, 57.

The Right Way (*Sawā' al-sabīl*):
— Expounded, 143, 144, 145.
— The Jews gone astray from the Right Way, 175.
— The People of the Book gone astray from the Right Way, 181, 182.

Ruin:
— Its meaningful usage, 278, 279.

Ṣabr (Perseverance; Steadfastness; Patience):
— It is a necessary condition for the success of those devoted to the Truth, 227.

The Sacred Months:
— Its sanctity, 128.

Sacrificial Offering:
— Animals for sacrificial offering should not be desecrated, 128.
— The sacrificial offering made by the two sons of Adam, 153, 154.

Salvation/True Success:
— Faith coupled with righteousness and *Jihād* are required for attaining salvation, 158, 159.
— To attain salvation it is necessary to shun abominable satanic deeds, 191.
— There is no salvation for wrong-doers, 221, 275.

Satan:
— Man's open and eternal enemy, 282.
— His is the worst company, 39.
— His strategy is weak, 59, 60.
— Meaning of the statement about calling upon Satan, 85, 86.

Superstitions and Evil Practices of the Age of Ignorance:
— Baseless notions about the state of menstruation, 31, 32.
— Share in inheritance for the foster relatives, 35.
— Practice of divination and soothsaying, 46, 47, 132, 133.
— To split the ear of an animal in consecration to some deity under the influence of polytheistic doctrines, 85, 86.
— *Baḥīrah, Sā'ibah, Waṣīlah* and *Ḥām*, 199, 200.
— To regard angels as God's daughters, 260.
— Polytheistic beliefs and making offerings to someone other than God, 276, 277, 278, 281.
— Slaying of offspring, 278, 279, 281, 282.
— Its origin, 278.
— Superstitions and polytheistic notions about the lawfulness and unlawfulness, 280.
— A significant Qur'ānic question in order to analyse the polytheistic superstitions of the Arabs, 284.

Supplication, Prayer:
— The command to make supplication for the bestowal of God's grace, 34.
— Jesus' supplication for sending down the heavenly repast, 204, 205.

Sustenance (*Rizq*):
— The command to use only the clean and lawful sustenance, 188.
— Three important directives about the sustenance from agricultural produce and livestock, 283, 284.
— God provides sustenance to everyone, 290.

Symbols of Devotion to God:
— Expounded, 128, 129.
— Meaning of desecrating them, 128, 129.
— Why should these be held in esteem?, 129.
— *Iḥrām* is one of the symbols of devotion to God, 130.

Tadhakkur (Remembrance):
— Its meaning, 251.

Ṭāghūt (Evil Ones):
— Its meaning, 53.
— To believe in God it is necessary to deny the authority of the evil ones, 53.
— To turn to it in dealings is against faith, 53.
— To fight in its cause amounts to disbelief, 59, 60.

Ṭalāq (see Divorce).

Talmud:
— Talmudic account of Abraham's quest for the Truth, 252, 253.

Taqwá (Piety; Fear of God):
— Significance of piety in the success of Islamic Laws, 5.
— Importance of piety in marital life, 91, 92.

— The People of the Book were likewise instructed in piety, 92.
— To restrain from violating the divine laws, 135.
— God accepts offerings only from the God-fearing, 153.

Tawbah (see Repentance).

Tawḥīd (see God, Unity of).

Tawrāh (see Torah).

Tayammum (symbolic ablution attained through wiping the face and hands with clean earth):
— When was its commandment revealed?, 2.
— How to do it?, 42, 43, 139.
— Its rationale, 43.

Test:
— Tests are inevitable in the cause of the Truth, 266–7.
— Man's life is nothing but a series of tests, 299.
— The 'unseen' should remain as such in order that the test to which man has been put has any meaning, 217–18.
— Man's test in the variations in religious law, 170.
— Test in the struggle between the Truth and falsehood, 228–9.
— As a test prosperity preceding the divine penalty befalling in the world, 232.
— The poor and the indigent preceding in believing as a test for those who wax proud, 236.
— The Qur'ān as a test for its addressees, 261–2.
— Man's test is dependent on his free will and volition, 262–3.
— To believe at the end of the test is of no avail, 296–7.

Testimony:
— Law of testimony, 201.
— The consideration of the character of the witness for the reliability of the testimony, 201.
— The importance of testimony in dealings, 9.
— Four witnesses are required to bear testimony to the committing of unlawful sexual intercourse, 17.
— The command to bear testimony for the sake of God, 94, 95.
— The testimony of God and angels regarding the Qur'ān, 114.
— Number of witnesses for testimony for the will, 201.

Torah (Tawrāh):
— How the People of the Book treat it, 254.
— It prescribed stoning to death as the punishment for unlawful sexual intercourse, 164.
— It was the fountainhead of guidance, 165, 294.
— Those responsible for safeguarding it, 165.
— The Prophets judged by it, 165.
— The Law of retribution, 166.

The Truth:
— The conflict between the Truth and falsehood in human life, 158, 159.
— By rejecting the Truth man incurs self-ruin, 223.
— What kind of persons greet the call to the Truth, 228, 229.
— Meaning of the Qur'ānic statement that the heavens and the earth have been created in truth, 243, 244.

Uḥud, The Battle of:
— The problem of distributing inheritance arising after the Battle of Uḥud, 1.
— The enemy's reaction to the reverses suffered by the Muslims in the Battle of Uḥud, 3, 58.
— The Muslims' reaction to the reverses suffered in the battle, 124.

Ulū al-Amr (those invested with authority):
— Obligation to follow them, 50.
— Real meaning of this term, 50.
— Obedience to them is conditional, 50–1.
— Clarification in *Ḥadīth* about their role, 50, 51, 52.
— Responsibilities of religious scholars, 175.

Unlawful Sexual Intercourse:
— The preliminary directive for its punishment, 17, 18, 19.
— Four witnesses should bear witness to the committing of unlawful sexual intercourse, 17.
— Its punishment for married slave-girls, 28, 29.
— Various degrees of the sinfulness of this crime, 33, 34.

Ur:
— The home town of Abraham, 246.
— The class order of its population, 246.
— Its polytheistic world-view, 247, 248.
— The ruling dynasty in Abraham's period, 247, 248.

Vicegerency (*Khilāfah*):
— Three important truths about man's vicgerency, 299.

Wine:
— The second ruling regarding its gradual prohibition, 40, 41.
— The ruling for its total prohibition, 191, 192, 193, 194.
— It is the handiwork of Satan, 191.
— The detailed rulings of the Prophet (peace be on him) regarding wine, 191, 192, 193, 194.

Wisdom (*Ḥikmah*):
— Bestowed upon the house of Abraham, 48.
— Jesus was taught Wisdom, 203.
— It was bestowed on the Prophet Muḥammad (peace be on him), 84.

General Index

Waṣīlah, 199
Way of Abraham, 298
Wilderness of Paran, 151
Wooley, Sir Leonard, 246
Wuḍū', 194

Yaḥyá (John), 253
Ya'qūb (Jacob), 252
al-Yasa' (Elisha), 253
Yathrib, 210
Yehudah, 286
Yohoyadah, 106
Yūnus (Jonah), 253
Yūsuf (Joseph), 252

Zachariah, 106, 253
Ẓāhirīs, 78
Ẓāhirī School, 77
Zakāh, 60, 189, 198
Zerah, 245
Zufar, 24
al-Zuhrī, 24, 77